Who Was Muhammad?

*An Analysis of the Prophet of Islam
in Light of the Bible and the Quran*

Doug Hardt

TEACH Services, Inc.
P U B L I S H I N G
www.TEACHServices.com • (800) 367-1844

Unless otherwise noted all scripture quotations are taken from the New King James Version®. Copyright © 1982 by Thomas Nelson, Inc. Used by permission. All rights reserved.

Scripture quotations marked NLT are taken from the *Holy Bible, New Living Translation*, copyright © 1996, 2004, 2007 by Tyndale House Foundation. Used by permission of Tyndale House Publishers, Inc., Carol Stream, Illinois 60188. All rights reserved.

Scripture quotations marked NIV are taken from *The Holy Bible, New International Version*®, NIV®. Copyright © 1973, 1978, 1984, 2011 by Biblica, Inc.™ Used by permission. All rights reserved worldwide.

Scripture quotations marked RSV are taken from the Revised Standard Version of the Bible, copyright 1952 [2nd edition, 1971] by the Division of Christian Education of the National Council of the Churches of Christ in the United States of America. Used by permission. All rights reserved.

Unless otherwise noted all quotations from the Quran are taken from *The Holy Quran: Text, Translation and Commentary* by Abdullah Yusuf Ali. Published by Tahrike Tarsile Qur'an, Inc., Publishers and Distributors of the Holy Qur'an, PO Box 731115, Elmhurst, NY 11373-0115, U.S. Edition, 2001.

For information, contact Doug Hardt at doughardt@teachservices.com.

World rights reserved. This book or any portion thereof may not be copied or reproduced in any form or manner whatever, except as provided by law, without the written permission of the publisher, except by a reviewer who may quote brief passages in a review.

The author assumes full responsibility for the accuracy of all facts and quotations as cited in this book. The opinions expressed in this book are the author's personal views and interpretations, and do not necessarily reflect those of the publisher.

This book is provided with the understanding that the publisher is not engaged in giving spiritual, legal, medical, or other professional advice. If authoritative advice is needed, the reader should seek the counsel of a competent professional.

Copyright © 2016 Doug Hardt

Copyright © 2016 TEACH Services, Inc.

ISBN-13: 978-1-4796-0543-9 (Paperback)

ISBN-13: 978-1-4796-0544-6 (ePub)

ISBN-13: 978-1-4796-0545-3 (Mobi)

Library of Congress Control Number: 2015920723

Published by

Table of Contents

Dedication & Acknowledgments 5

Foreword 7

Chapter 1: Who Was Muhammad? 10

Chapter 2: Biblical Roots of Abraham's Religion in the East 18

Chapter 3: The Biblical Perspective on the Seventh Century 25

Chapter 4: Historical Context of the Rise of Islam 29

Chapter 5: The Quran and the Rise of Muhammad 39

Chapter 6: Overview of the Teachings in the Quran 49

Chapter 7: Jesus in the Quran 67

Chapter 8: A Short History of Islam 94

Chapter 9: The Rise of the Ottoman Empire and Revelation 9 114

Chapter 10: The Tests of a Prophet 125

Chapter 11: Was Muhammad a True Prophet? 167

Appendix A: A Concise Concordance to the Teachings of the Quran 193

Appendix B: Son of God:
    "A Word Study in both the Quran and New Testament" 294

Appendix C: A Possible Interpretation of Daniel 11 302

Appendix D 310

Appendix E: Was Muhammad the "Paracletos" of John 14? 312

Endnotes 314

Bibliography 323

Dedication & Acknowledgments

Obviously, I am very grateful to God for the opportunity He gave me to live overseas in Muslim countries. Without that opportunity, I don't think I ever would have even thought about writing such a book. I would like to thank all of the people in the Adventist church system that have worked with me and helped me in my journey to understand Islam better. I have met very sincere believers in the God of Abraham who are Seventh-day Adventists who have educated me and given me insights into Christian-Muslim relations. I am very grateful to my friend Dr. Conrad Vine who was willing to edit my book when I first wrote it. I would especially like to acknowledge Russell Thomas who not only read the book and did a thorough job editing it, but also went through the whole concordance and checked the references to verify their accuracy. His passion for this topic and desire to see it published more widely has inspired me greatly.

Foreword

I have to be clear that this is a book that anyone can read, Christian or Muslim, and gain something. However, this book was written specifically with Seventh-day Adventists in mind. I am a fourth-generation Adventist—I grew up on the campus of Adventist academies where my parents were teachers, and I attended Adventist schools from first grade through my master's degree in theology. Unfortunately, for too long in my life I was a cultural Adventist. But that all changed when I was truly converted during my college years.

Eventually, I became a pastor and later, with my wife, went overseas to serve as a missionary. It was refreshing to live in countries where there were no Adventist institutions and hardly any Adventists.

I began to have thoughts about writing a book like this when I was serving the church in the Middle East and countries of the former Soviet Union where there are a great number of Muslims. It was an eye-opening experience for me to work with Muslims and to get acquainted with their religion.

Like most Adventists, I believed that Islam is a false religion and Muhammad was a false prophet. But the more I studied the Quran and the life of Muhammad the more questions I had. It was sad to me that though Adventists have been working for approximately 100 years in Muslim countries that the church still had not fully wrestled with the foundational issue to Muslims—that is, "Who was Muhammad?"

When researching this topic I found it difficult even to locate information about Muhammad from an Adventist perspective. There is much more information about Muhammad and Islam in evangelical Christian circles. Additionally, the information I did find through the Adventist Muslim Relations office of the world church was sketchy and, I later found out, was itself considered controversial.

A few Adventists believe Muhammad to be a true prophet, a few others believe him to be a reformer, but most believe him to be a Satanically-inspired false prophet. The church does not have a consensus position on him, and I have found very few evidences that the Adventist Church has really truly grappled with this issue. As far as I know, this is the first book in the history of the Adventist Church to systematically discuss the topic of the prophethood of Muhammad.

Since the vast majority of Adventists already believe that Muhammad is a false prophet, one might wonder why a book on the topic is even necessary. If he is a false prophet, we should not fear studying his life, delineating the biblical position, and by comparison showing why we believe him to not be of God.

If God has raised us up as a remnant church to prepare the way for the second coming of Christ, has He not gifted us with the Holy Spirit? One of the jobs of the Holy Spirit is to help us discern between good and evil spirits (1 Cor. 12:10). It begs the question then, "How can we be so sure that he was a false prophet when we have not conducted a thorough study of his ministry and writings?"

For the average Adventist layperson in North America this question is not one that gnaws at him/her daily. However, for Adventist Church workers serving in a Muslim context this question is absolutely essential to carry on an effective work. Such questions as, "Should we use the Quran to begin a Bible study with Muslims?" "Should we call God 'Allah'?" "Can we have Adventist 'Muslims' in contexts where it is impossible to register Christian organizations?" "Should we pray with Muslims in a mosque?" all affect an Adventist's ministry on a daily basis. All of these questions depend on the answer one gives to the question, "Who was Muhammad?"

As I write this book, there are entire world church divisions that can't even begin to formulate a statement on Adventist/Muslim relations because they do not agree about the inspiration of Islam. Therefore, there is no agreement about how Adventists should relate to Muslims. Unfortunately, too many Adventist workers and ministries have already experienced the bitter consequences which division and misunderstanding bring to any organization. Therefore, I have taken it upon myself to get the conversation started.

I understand that this book will be controversial. But, in a sense, that will be good. I can't think of a time when God tried to move His people to a new land or new understanding of Scripture that was not engulfed in controversy. In fact, if the "great controversy" theme that Adventists preach is true (and I believe that it is), there almost certainly will be controversy if we are following God.

My main sources for this book will be the Bible, Spirit of Prophecy, and the Quran. I have used some other sources in the writing of this book, but mainly for historical and critical viewpoints regarding Muhammad and his time. There are many sources I could use by authors who have written *about* the Bible or *about* the Quran, but I believe as an Adventist that we should abide by the Protestant principle that the Bible is its own interpreter. This is especially true in Islam since Muslims believe that the Quran is the direct revelation of Allah to mankind.

In this study I will give direct translations from the Quran. They will be from the Yusuf Ali translation of the Quran unless otherwise noted. Muslims teach that the "true" Quran is only in Arabic and that all translations are just that—translations—they are not *the* Quran. So when it is necessary I will refer to the Arabic and give a transliteration of the Arabic word to help clarify the original meaning of the Quran.

Many of the biblical characters and other names mentioned in the Quran are quite different from the names that we know them by. Examples of this are God, "Allah"; Jesus, "Isa"; Mary, "Maryam"; John the Baptist, "Yahya"; Moses, "Musa"; and Noah, "Nuh." The Bible may also be called the "Injil," the Gospels or New Testament; "Turah," the Torah (Moses' writings); and "Zaboor," the Psalms and other books of the Old Testament. So, for the benefit of my Adventist and Christian readers, in this book I will refer to them by their English biblical names and spelling.

Some Christians have believed that Allah is actually a "different" god (which in Adventist Christian perspective would equal Satan). I deal with this issue later in the book and, therefore, refer to "Allah" as "God" throughout.

Even though this is not a dogmatic theology of Islam, I have taken great pains to allow the Quran to explain itself, just as Protestants do with the Bible. We have all seen what happens when Christians don't follow the hermeneutic of working from the clear to the unclear texts of the Bible and allowing the Bible as a whole to speak on a topic. Hence, we have popular doctrines raging through Christianity that are built around a few texts that have been taken out of context. One can do the same thing with the Quran. If a few controversial texts are taken out of their context and analyzed without the help of other texts in the Quran, one could come to some appalling conclusions.

For this reason I went verse-by-verse through the whole Quran and assembled a simple concordance, ordered by topic, to attempt to show a complete picture of what the Quran teaches on any given topic. The reader may reference the concordance in Appendix A to answer questions on most topics in the Quran.

I hope that this book will serve as a starting point for further discussion and study on this topic. Again, I have not intended this book to be a dogmatic theology of Islam and have not meant this as an ending point in the discussion about the inspiration of Muhammad. Personally, I am just beginning my study of the Quran, and I hope that this book will inspire many more to join me in that journey. As one Christian author stated in the introduction to his book about Christ in the Quran, "the present time is for plowing, not for reaping, for making soundings, not for making maps."[1] I pray that this volume will be enjoyable for you to read, will enlighten you, and will help you as you encounter Muslims around the world.

Chapter 1

WHO WAS MUHAMMAD?

This is a question that has intrigued Christians for the last 1,400 years. It is not hard to believe that the medieval church during the time of Muhammad and his followers, with its two centers in Rome and Constantinople, was not overjoyed to see a new religion forming on the Arabian Peninsula and then rapidly expanding by conquering territories that were once bastions of Christianity. One can understand why Christians saw this as a threat to the existence of Christianity and formed the opinion that the prophet of this new religion was "of the devil." This negative view of Muhammad and the adherents of this new religion culminated in the Crusades of the Middle Ages and has, more or less, remained intact to our day in Christian lands.

Furthermore, in the last few years we have seen, in response to the rise of Islamic extremist terrorism, a renewed disdain among Christians for Muhammad, whom they deem responsible for fostering violent methods to fight the "infidels" in Western countries.

So who was this illiterate Arab orphan who successfully established a worldwide religion? His followers now number more than 1.7 billion, predominantly in the Middle East, North Africa, and South Asia, but with ever increasing adherents in Western countries. In countries such as Germany, France, England, Canada, and America, there are now millions of Muslims living, working, and practicing their religion. Approximately one out of every five people on the planet is a Muslim and holds this man who lived in Saudi Arabia over 1,400 years ago in very high regard as a prophet of God.

Importance of This Question for Adventists

To say that the Seventh-day Adventist Church has not been successful in gaining adherents from among Muslims would be an understatement. Whereas millions of Catholic, Orthodox, and Protestant Christians have heard and believed the three angels' messages and joined the

Adventist Church, only a few hundred Muslims all over the globe have joined its ranks. In fact, if one looks at major Muslim countries such as Turkey, Iran, Saudi Arabia, Kuwait, Morocco, Tunisia, Egypt, Yemen, Bahrain, Oman, Libya, United Arab Emirates, Syria, Jordan, and Qatar (with a combined population more than the United States) and count all the former Muslims in an Adventist Church on Sabbath, one would be fortunate to find a hundred. In many of those countries, not even one would be found! Even though the Adventist Church considers the three angels' messages to be God's last warning to all peoples, languages, nations, and tribes, and have established work in many Muslim countries (in some, for 50–100 years already), it has not been able to convince many Muslims to join its ranks in proclaiming this message.

The cause of this failure could probably be attributed to many reasons, but none could be any greater than the lack of a clear, coherent answer to the question "Who was Muhammad?" Muhammad is revered by all Muslims as being the last prophet of God, bearing a final message for mankind, and creating God's final, true, monotheistic religion. His life is scrupulously studied and imitated by his followers, and he is held in higher esteem than any other religious figures that are depicted in his writings.

So when Christians deal with Muslims, it is only natural that the Muslim wonders what position the Christian holds in regard to Muhammad. Do they hold that he was a true prophet of God? Or was he a great reformer? Or was he a false prophet that Satan raised up to obscure the truths of the Bible and compete with Christianity?

Most Adventists would probably agree with the last opinion and view Muhammad as an antichrist power whom Satan raised up to obscure the gospel. However, probably the most disturbing thing about the position of the vast majority of Adventists, regardless of what they believe, is that they have come to their conclusion without a thorough study of the life of Muhammad and his writings in the Quran and their historical context.

Since working in the Muslim world and studying the Quran and the life of Muhammad, I am surprised when I talk to other Adventists about Islam to discover how ignorant most Adventists are regarding Muhammad and the Quran. It is a rarity to meet an Adventist who actually confesses to owning a Quran and having studied it. Yet most Adventists are convinced that it is not an inspired book.

Do Unto Others…

Christ's teaching from Scripture is, "And just as you want men to do to you, you also do to them likewise" (Luke 6:31). The Adventist Church teaches that it had a post-biblical prophet who helped establish it—just as Muslims claim. Most of the two billion Christians on the planet do not believe Adventists' claim that Ellen White was a prophet, deeming her a false prophet. Even many of the early Adventist members doubted the authenticity of her claim to be a "messenger" of God who was inspired by dreams and visions, and they sometimes actually attributed the visions to Satan or mesmerism[2] (as do some even today). The Adventist Church should be able to empathize with Islam since the vast majority of Christianity rejects both of these alleged prophets.

I know that it is difficult for Adventists even to imagine that Muhammad could *possibly* be an inspired prophet and that the religion of Islam could have any biblical basis for existence. However, as followers of Christ, Christians should follow the Golden Rule, and do unto others as they would want others to do unto them—which means, in short, that an Adventist should not exclude from the realm of possibility the prophethood of Muhammad, just as an Adventist expects other Christians and Muslims not to exclude from the realm of possibility the prophethood of Ellen White without giving the subject careful and prayerful study.

Most Adventist pastors that I have heard responding to people who doubt whether or not Ellen White was from God counsel them to pray, study the Bible, and read a wide variety of her work, especially such books as *The Desire Ages, Steps to Christ, Thoughts from the Mount of Blessing*, etc. Why is this so? The answer is obvious—the pastor wants the new convert, usually a Christian of another denomination, to see the breadth of her writings and get a sense of how much she has in common with the Bible and how she lifts up Christ. They do not expect the new convert to just take them at their word, but rather to put her to the test by spending hours, days, and possibly even months or years reading, praying, and comparing the Bible with the clear, Christ-centered writings of Mrs. White.

But how many Adventists have taken hours, days, months, or even years to study Muhammad and the Quran? Unfortunately, not very many have. This is the main reason that I believe this book is necessary at this time.

"But It's a Well Established Belief in Christianity"

I know some readers are probably thinking, "This is outrageous. Muhammad said that God has no son. Therefore, he is not a true prophet. Every true Christian knows that." Again, we need to apply the Golden Rule. The vast majority of Christians believe that the Bible teaches an everlasting, tortuous hell, that the Ten Commandments were abolished at the cross, and that Sunday is God's holy day. They consider these to be well established beliefs within Christianity. How do Adventists feel about these "well established doctrines" of Christianity? The Adventist Church has spent decades and billions of dollars finding truth by studying the Bible, the context of the passages in question, and the prophecies that foretold these doctrinal changes, analyzing the history and archaeology of the Bible times, and then publishing its findings through literature, the Internet, radio, television, educational institutions, and personal ministries. Thus, we contradict many mainstream beliefs held within Christianity.

"If the majority of Christians believe it, it must be true, right?" You won't hear any Adventist evangelist using that argument when discussing the prophetic gift of the remnant church as personified in Ellen White. Nor will one ever hear any Adventist evangelist use this argument in doing an evangelistic presentation about the state of the dead, the true Sabbath, the sanctuary in heaven, or the validity of the Ten Commandments.

Jesus warned His followers, "Enter by the narrow gate; for wide is the gate and broad is the way that leads to destruction, and there are many who go in by it" (Matt. 7:13). Christ has warned us that we should never use the argument that "lots of people do it (or believe it)" to justify our actions, because Satan is called the "ruler of this world" (John 12:31; 14:30; 16:11) and has deceived a majority of the people who live in it. The Bible actually goes as far as to say that Satan has "deceived the whole world" (Rev. 12:9). So, when approaching the subject of Muhammad, the fact that most Christians believe that he was a false prophet should, if anything, put Adventists on guard. And they should be very diligent in verifying if that actually is the case. The biblical injunction is to "test all things" and "hold fast [to] what is good" (1 Thess. 5:21).

Seriousness of Accusations

This is a very serious matter. By calling someone a false prophet we are saying that this "prophet" was actually inspired by Satan. An Adventist believes there are only two sides in this great controversy playing out on our planet before the universe—God's side and Satan's side. This may sound too simple, but Jesus said it like this, "He who is not with Me is against Me, and he who does not gather with Me scatters abroad" (Matt. 12:30). That is to say, if someone comes to church and claims to have had dreams and visions from the Lord and that they are a prophet, there are only two options for the source of these "inspirations": either they really are a prophet and a fulfillment of Joel 2:28, 29 or they are prophesying and helping the side of Satan in the battle between good and evil.

For this reason the tests by which the Israelites were supposed to judge the prophets, and the corresponding punishment in case they were found to be a false prophet was very clear in the Old Testament. Deuteronomy 13:1–5 states that if a false prophet arose and prophesied things that were not in harmony with the instructions of the living God, that "prophet" was to be put to death. There was no wiggle room for calling him a "lesser" prophet or a "reformer" prophet or a "bit-misguided" prophet. Nobody was to keep him alive and consult him just for information or entertainment—the Lord was explicit in His instructions; the camp of the people of God was to be clean. All who were inspired by God were to minister to His people in order that they might worship Him and Him only. All other false prophets were to be put away in order to keep His people on the right path.

Clifford Goldstein, in his book *Graffiti in the Holy Place*, puts it like this in regards to the prophethood of Ellen White:

> Ellen White made claims about her ministry that leave no room for compromise or ambivalence about those claims. She claimed to have seen things that could have come only from supernatural inspiration. Either her claims are true or she was a lunatic and/or a powerful liar who promulgated her insane ravings or amazing deceptions from the middle of the nineteenth into the second decade of the twentieth century.
>
> What rational options are there for someone who claimed to have seen, in vision, what she claimed to have seen? She claimed to have seen Jesus bring the redeemed into the Holy City. She claimed to have seen people living on other planets and angels protecting God's people. She claimed to have seen, in vision, Jesus in the heavenly sanctuary or what Satan looked like in heaven before he sinned. She claimed to have seen angels visiting Adam and Eve in Eden. She said that she saw the look on Adam's face when he realized that Eve had sinned. She claimed

to have seen Jesus, in vision, and what His face was like after the wilderness fast. She claimed to have seen the resurrection of Jesus from the tomb, as well as an angel release Paul and Silas from prison. She claimed to have seen Satan lead lost multitudes into the final rebellion against God after the second resurrection. She claimed to have seen, in vision, life in the new earth, and on and on….

What does one do with these claims? Those who place her ministry on the level, for instance, of Martin Luther, are living in a logical fantasy world. Either we take her for what she has claimed for herself (which, of course, leaves open a whole group of questions that we, as a church, haven't always answered in the most fortuitous manner), or we have to reject her as liar, a lunatic, or someone inspired by the devil. These are the only logical options.[3]

If the same approach is taken with Muhammad, then there can only be one of two conclusions: either he was inspired by the God of heaven, or he wasn't. He never claimed to be just a consecrated layman or a reformer; he claimed to have dreams and visions from the God of Abraham, Isaac, Ishmael, and Jacob. He claimed to have contact with the angel Gabriel. He claimed to have seen heaven and the glories of paradise. He claimed to have divine insight into the matters of God and the events surrounding his life and the lives of the adherents of Islam. We don't have many options to select from in forming our conclusions after an honest study of his life.

Consequences of Our Study

There are very serious consequences and benefits possible from a study of Muhammad. One of the biggest questions that Adventist Church workers' wrestle with is whether or not to use the Quran in ministry to Muslims. Many sincere Christians fear using a book that is widely considered in Christian circles to be demonically inspired, even though their goal is to bring a Muslim to the Bible. But this complicates a Christian's ministry since Muslims will read the Quran, but fear reading the Bible, a book they view as having been tampered with by Jews and Christians. Therefore, Christians don't talk about the book that Muslims are reading, and instead talk about a book they refuse to read. Needless to say, this creates a chasm in understanding between Muslims and Christians.

Another benefit of our study is that we will be able to talk to Muslims objectively about someone they hold in very high esteem. It is natural that Muslims want to talk about the prophet who helped start their movement, just as Adventists can hardly keep themselves from talking about Ellen White. Most Christians either try to avoid conversations about Muhammad or try to disparage him in hopes that a Muslim will be drawn away from Muhammad to Christ. However, that approach doesn't bring much success. Think about it from their point of view. How would we respond if an adherent of another religion came to an Adventist and disparaged Mrs. White openly as a false prophet?

Regardless of the conclusion you as the reader comes to in regards to the prophethood of Muhammad, you will be able to discuss the teachings of Islam and the life of Muhammad in an informed and respectful manner.

Guilty Until Proven Innocent

One of the biggest problems of studying with Christians about Muhammad is that they have been indoctrinated in how bad he is without ever studying him. He is assumed guilty until proven innocent. While I was writing this book, a terrible shooting occurred in Aurora, Colorado. The crime appeared to have been committed by a man who dressed up in a costume and went into a theater, setting off smoke bombs and firing multiple weapons, killing twelve people and wounding fifty-eight. There were over a hundred witnesses to this horrific act, and he was caught by police on the premises right after the shooting. Everybody assumed he was guilty—he was already the object of much outrage. Not long after, I was in an airport listening to two lawyers discussing the case. One of them made a statement that made it sound like the man was clearly guilty. He then caught himself, apologized, and stated that this man must be presumed innocent.

The theory of presumed innocence states that even when we are almost 100 percent sure that someone committed a crime, they are not pronounced guilty until they have been given the right to get a defense lawyer and have a trial by jury. I have lived in countries where this is not the case. It leaves one in a state of uncertainty. If there is just one accusation against someone, they are assumed guilty even if they haven't committed the crime. Then they must spend an enormous amount of money, time, and energy attempting to prove their innocence.

Muhammad usually does not have this luxury of being presumed innocent, which is prized so dearly in democratic societies of the West. But, for purposes of analyzing him in this book, I will use that principle and assume that Muhammad's account is accurate and that Gabriel did visit him and give him revelations from God. I will suppose that God blessed this new religion so much that for 1,400 years Christianity has not been able to conquer it.

If we accept this presupposition, Muhammad will be in heaven someday. One can only imagine the surprise on most Christians' faces if they were to see Muhammad communing with God upon the sea of glass. This might be difficult for many to imagine, but until a thorough examination is done of his life and teachings, this would be the only fair assumption. Ellen White makes an interesting comment,

> There will be many who will be greatly surprised in the last day. Jesus says, "Many shall come from the east and west, and shall sit down with Abraham, and Isaac, and Jacob, in the kingdom of heaven; but the children of the kingdom shall be cast out into outer darkness; there shall be weeping and gnashing of teeth [Matt. 8:11]."[4]

Are you, the reader, even though with what you know about Muhammad believe he was a false prophet and that therefore Islam is a completely false religion, willing to set that conclusion aside and give the "defense" a fair hearing? Are you ready, without doing that, to give to God a report on the day of judgment as to why you believe the way you do (Rom. 14:12) and therefore how you acted?

Solomon warns us in Proverbs 18:17 that "in a lawsuit the first to speak seems right, until someone comes forward and cross-examines" (NLT). I hope that you will allow me to "cross-examine" the common Christian assumption about Muhammad. Even if he will be found guilty, he deserves a "trial" and a worthy defense (which I will attempt to give him in this book). John Gilchrist, one of Muhammad's major Christian critics, states, "Those Christians who seek to degrade the Prophet of Islam and demonise him in every possible way have never seriously tried to evaluate him in the light of his own generation."[5] Are you willing to do just that?

Christ's Serious Warning

Before moving on, there is one other statement of Christ that should cause the Christian to be very attentive and thorough when examining the source of God's revelations. In Matthew 12 Jesus responded to the accusations of religious leaders of His day that He was doing miracles through power from Satan. He warned that "every sin and blasphemy will be forgiven men, but the blasphemy against the Spirit will not be forgiven men" (verse 31). This is the unpardonable sin, when the believer begins to accuse those who are inspired by God of being inspired by Satan. This means that the believer has called "good" "evil" and "evil" "good." There is then no hope of God's Spirit being able to reach them—they are completely lost (cf. Isa. 5:20)!

I am not trying to make any assertions about Muhammad's prophethood right now; I am only trying to make the point that in Christ's mind it is the most serious sin, one that can't even be forgiven, to say that someone who is inspired of God is inspired of Satan. Therefore, when taking the Old Testament counsel of Isaiah 8:20 and comparing the writings of a "prophet" and checking if they speak according to the "law and the testimony," the believer should come with an open mind, willing to be led and directed by the Almighty, because the stakes are very high. One always needs to be open to the Spirit of God. The Spirit of Prophecy states,

> Whenever the people of God are growing in grace, they will be constantly obtaining a clearer understanding of His word. They will discern new light and beauty in its sacred truths. This has been true in the history of the church in all ages, and thus it will continue to the end. But as real spiritual life declines, it has ever been the tendency to cease to advance in the knowledge of the truth. Men rest satisfied with the light already received from God's word, and discourage any further investigation of the Scriptures. They become conservative and seek to avoid discussion.
>
> The fact that there is no controversy or agitation among God's people, should not be regarded as conclusive evidence that they are holding fast to sound doctrine. There is reason to fear that they may not be clearly discriminating between truth and error. When no new questions are started by investigation of the Scriptures, when no difference of opinion arises which will set men to searching the Bible for themselves, to make sure that they have the truth, there will be many now, as in ancient times, who will hold to tradition, and worship they know not what."[6]

Conclusion

I hope that you, the reader, will not give up on this book but will prayerfully enjoy the journey of exploring the life and writings of one of the most controversial figures in human history. It is a very important study. What one takes from this study will affect how one relates to, what one says to, and what one expects from roughly twenty percent of the earth's population. This is a question regarding which the promise of Psalms 32:8–10 must be claimed: "I will instruct you and teach you in the way that you should go; I will guide you with My eye. Do not be like the horse or like the mule, which have no understanding, which must be harnessed with bit and bridle, else they will not come near you. Many sorrows shall be to the wicked; but he who trusts in the Lord, mercy shall surround him." May mercy surround us as we journey back more than a thousand years into the past to the roots of the religion known as Islam.

Chapter 2

BIBLICAL ROOTS OF ABRAHAM'S RELIGION IN THE EAST

Before digging into the theology of Islam or the life of Muhammad, let us go to the Bible, and back to the original roots of Islam, more than 3,000 years ago to the time of Abraham. It would be logical to try to understand the history of the father of all three major monotheistic religions of the world before analyzing their relationships.

Muhammad claimed to have been in the direct lineage of Ishmael, the eldest son of Abraham, whom Abraham's maidservant, Hagar, bore him. So Muhammad claimed to be a clear follower of the religion of Abraham.

Most Christians haven't studied in much detail the story of Ishmael. This is probably since the rest of the book of Genesis and the rest of the whole Old Testament recount the history of his half-brother, Isaac, and his descendants.

Also, in one passage, according to Paul, Hagar was called the "bondwoman" and represents the "earthly" and "the law," whereas Isaac represents grace and those who are "born of the Spirit" (Gal. 4:24–30). However, the whole Bible should be examined to find any other possible clue to help us understand the context of Islam. So I will start by examining the biblical account of Muhammad's forefathers.

It Wasn't Hagar's Idea

The first thing that should be noticed in the story of Abraham and Hagar is that neither Hagar nor Ishmael asked to be in this drama that they ended up in the middle of. Hagar was just a personal attendant who had probably been given to Sarah during her time in Pharaoh's court in Egypt.[7] As far as one can tell from the account, she never approached Abraham with a request to give him an heir or to be a part of the spiritual fulfillment of God's promise to make him a great nation. She was brought into the story as a result of the lack of faith on the part of the "chosen" woman, Sarah. Hagar had no aspiration to become the competitor of Abraham's first wife, and did not devise any plans through which she might sneak into the inheritance. This was a case of God's first chosen missionaries, Abraham and Sarah, being tested by God and failing the test.

God's displeasure with His chosen couple may explain why, after having appeared to Abraham and Sarah four times in the eleven years leading up to the birth of Ishmael, He waited thirteen years before appearing to Abraham again.[8] God had a purpose for this couple and wanted to fulfill Sarah's deep longing to bear a child, but He was testing them to see if they would retain their faith through adversity. Their lack of faith has had extremely long-term consequences—the results of which can be seen in the volatile politics of the Middle East today, and also in the strife between the religions around the globe that claim Abraham as their spiritual father.

In Genesis 21 Hagar and Ishmael are forced to "flee to the wilderness" where they end up making a new life for themselves away from the camp of Abraham.

In Moses' account of this story, the person who especially bears the brunt of the blame is Sarah. In chapter 16 it is evident that Sarah's faith journey with the Lord was unstable. In verse 2 she accuses the Lord of not allowing her to have children and then concocts a plan for Abraham to have a child with Hagar, her pagan personal attendant. Of course, Hagar began to resent the fact that although she bore a son for Abraham he was considered Sarah's offspring (which could have been expected from any woman, and especially a pagan one).

Then Sarah gets upset with Abraham and blames him! She even blasphemously invokes a judgment of the Lord upon her own husband in verse 5. In verse 6 Abraham basically tells her to do what she wants with her, and Sarah "dealt harshly" with Hagar. The Hebrew in this passage implies that there was some physical abuse involved.[9] So here is Sarah, the mother of the innumerable spiritual descendants that God had promised her, blaming three innocent parties—God, Abraham, and Hagar—for her own sin and then physically abusing her own servant. Later, in chapter 21, Sarah did not want to share the camp with Hagar, even though this was a problem of her own devising, and asked Abraham to send the slave woman and her child away. It is not a flattering picture of Sarah, but it is one that we must take note of as we consider the origin of Hagar, Ishmael, and Islam.

Ishmael's Blessing

The second thing that can be learned from this story is that Ishmael was promised God's blessing. Ishmael was the first unborn child to be named by God in the Bible. His name means "God shall hear." In Genesis 16:10 the Lord told Hagar, "I will multiply your descendants exceedingly, so that they shall not be counted for multitude." In Genesis 17:20 the Lord told Abraham about Ishmael, "I have blessed him, and will make him fruitful, and will multiply him exceedingly. He shall beget twelve princes, and I will make him a great nation."

In Genesis 21 the Lord repeats the promise twice more, promising that Ishmael would become a great nation (verses 13 and 18). Genesis 21:20 tells us very clearly that God was "with" Ishmael as he grew up in the wilderness. God did not abandon Hagar and Ishmael even though Hagar had been raised a pagan in Egypt and neither of them possessed perfect characters (Gen. 16:4; 21:9).

A common theme may be noticed in this story, which is a recurring theme of the Bible—God's overriding, gracious providence in spite of the faults of His people. The Bible is different than other Eastern literature in that it allows its heroes to have faults, and it describes even their gross sins. The Bible is not meant to glorify people but to glorify God for being so gracious and loving to humanity as not to cast them off in His plan of salvation.

Hagar and Ishmael are no different in that regard. There is no doubt that they were also at fault for Sarah's demand that they be exiled to the wilderness in Genesis 21. However, God promised that He would go with them to the wilderness and bless them there in spite of their sin.

In both instances when Hagar had to run from Sarah, there are touching accounts given to us by Moses that describe how the Lord pursued her. In chapter 16 he mentions that the angel of the Lord "found" her (verse 7) on the road to Shur. He comforted her with the fact that she would have a son and that even his name, Ishmael, would remind her that God "heard" her and knew of her afflictions (verse 11). He promised her that he would be independent (he used some interesting Eastern illustrations to describe that in verse 12) and that he would live "in the presence of all his brethren" (verse 12). Hagar was amazed that she had seen a messenger of God and was still alive.

Then again, a little over fourteen years later when she fled from Sarah, Moses depicts her in desperate straits—she has "wandered around the wilderness" and run out of water, put her son under a bush to die, and both of them are weeping in the expectation that their lives have come to an end (Gen. 21:14–16). For some reason, in verse 17, the Bible says that God heard the weeping of Ishmael (and not Hagar) and in answer to his cry the angel of the Lord addressed Hagar. God either miraculously caused a well of water to appear or showed her where there was one in the vicinity, and again He repeated the promises given earlier to Hagar that her boy would be blessed and that he would become a great nation (verses 17–19). Had God wanted Hagar and Ishmael just to fade out of history this would have been His golden opportunity simply to allow that to happen. But God didn't. He was faithful and full of grace toward Hagar and Ishmael and to their descendants.

Why would God bless Hagar with her pagan upbringing and her weakness of character? Genesis 17:4 gives us a clue why God would do this—because He had made a covenant with Abraham. Genesis 21:13 is even clearer, stating, "Yet I will also make a nation of the son of the bondwoman, because he is your seed." Even though Abraham and Sarah had lost faith and taken matters into their own hands, God was faithful to His promise.

God changes the name of Abram to "Abraham" in Genesis 17—just one chapter after the whole story of Hagar. God changed his name (which was very important to Semitic peoples) from "exalted father" to "father of a great number." Now he would be the spiritual father to two nations—composed of the twelve tribes of Jacob and the twelve tribes of Ishmael (Gen. 17:20).

Hagar was blessed because of her association with Abraham in the same way as we believe Abraham was blessed and as we are due to the merits of Christ. Hagar was living "under grace," so to speak. She was blessed because of who Abraham was in his relation to God. We see in the story that Hagar is a great recipient of the abundant mercies of God. (A characteristic of God that we will see reiterated often in the Quran.)

Importance of Wells

Another interesting point in this story is the important role that water and wells play. In chapter 16 when Hagar is running away from Sarah, the angel of the Lord finds her by a spring of water on the road to Shur. In Genesis 21 Hagar was at the verge of death due to the fact that she had no water. It was then that the Lord provided water and, with that, life to these refugees in the desert.

In the very next verse after they find water, the Bible summarizes the life of Ishmael by saying, "So God was with the lad; and he grew and dwelt in the wilderness, and became an archer" (Gen. 21:20). To any person who makes their home in the desert, like Hagar and Ishmael, water is the top priority for survival.

Again, it is worth noting that due to the grace Hagar and Ishmael received they were blessed by the One who would later say to another non-Jewish woman by a well, "Whoever drinks of this water will thirst again, but whoever drinks of the water that I shall give him will never thirst. But the water that I shall give him will become in him a fountain of water springing up into everlasting life" (John 4:13, 14). This is another important detail that should be noted when examining the later history of the descendants of Ishmael, since they not only lived in arid places, but also ended up being separated from the Water of Life that God provided to humanity through Jesus.

A Great Nation

God's promise to Abraham included having his descendants become a "great nation." The first time that God promised this to anybody was to Abraham in Genesis 12:2. Most Christians believe that this is a reference to the followers of the "people of the covenant"—the twelve tribes of Jacob. However, the first two instances in which God stated to Abraham the promise of Genesis 12 are references to Ishmael and his descendants, not to Isaac and his side (Gen. 17:20; 21:18).

Not until Genesis 35 when God was assuring Jacob that it was permissible to go down to Egypt to be with Joseph did he mention Isaac's line as becoming a "great nation" (verses 11, 12).

The word "nation" does not imply just a people group within the Jewish "nation"—they themselves would be a "nation." This language cannot be coincidental. Ishmael's descendants would have their own sovereignty as a people. They would be distinct from Isaac's side. Obviously God intended for them to have peaceful "half-brother" and "cousin" relationships, but the fact is that God did not expect them to live in the camp of the Israelites, just as Americans don't expect Canada to propose its legislative bills to Congress in Washington, DC. They would be peaceful neighbors who would always have their tie to Abraham as a cord that would bind their hearts together.

Circumcision

Another interesting detail of Ishmael's story is that he was circumcised at the age of thirteen along with Abraham after Abraham received an order from God (Gen. 17:23). We know from later in Scripture that circumcision was a sign that God would take human fleshly hearts and make them new, clean creations (Deut. 10:16; 30:6; Jer. 4:4; Rom. 2:29; Phil. 3:3). So along with giving Ishmael sovereignty as a nation, Abraham made him a partaker in the true religion of the God of heaven.

This is probably symbolic of the fact that God's plan was to make the descendants of Ishmael spiritual participants in the plan of salvation. Circumcision played a major role in foreshadowing that divine plan. Ishmael's descendants' religion in their new nation would be the religion of Abraham.

So what was the difference between the intended religions of Ishmael and Isaac? Upon analyzing it, one has to come to the conclusion that there was no difference, except that the covenant God made to send His Son to this world was promised to come through Sarah's offspring and not Hagar's. And Ishmael had to know this.

Ishmael's religious foundation already included the creation account of the world, the stories of the flood, the fall of Adam and Eve and the ensuing plan of salvation through the sacrificial system, the law of God and the Sabbath, the coming of the Messiah, the day of judgment, and the reward of heaven for the righteous. These truths were the same truths as those that were to be propagated through Isaac's descendants. The only difference again was in whom was "chosen" to be the bearer of the Messiah.

Submission

The word used in Genesis 16 to give the solution to Hagar's problems is a fascinating one. One doesn't get a sense of the word play the angel used when it is read in English, but in the Hebrew it is very noticeable. The word "submit" in verse 9 is the same root word, only in a different form, as the word "dealt harshly" in verse 6: the Hebrew word *anah*—Piel imperfect form in verse 6, and Hithpael imperative in verse 9. Since English doesn't have a word-for-word equivalent that can have this dual meaning, the meaning of the angel's command might be best expressed in the word play of "oppress yourself and return to your oppressor."

This would have been a difficult command for someone who had suffered abuse at the hands of a professed believer in the living God. It is interesting to note in the story that she did go back. The angel had asked her to "bear a cross," figuratively speaking, and she agreed to do that. She didn't deserve the harsh treatment (possibly even physical abuse) that she received at the hands of Sarah, yet now God asked her to return to her abusive boss. From the story it can be assumed that she was touched enough by the fact that God had found her and given her a promise that He would bless her and her descendants that she found enough strength to go back to Sarah. But we must note the fact that the spiritual dimension of submission, even in the face of oppression, was the key spiritual component for the Ishmaelite side of Abraham's family.

History

The Bible does not give long descriptions of what became of the twelve tribes of Ishmael, so the history that is known of them is fragmentary. It appears that even though Ishmael was expelled from Abraham's household that he maintained good relations with Isaac's side of his family.[10] The Bible records that one of his daughters was later married to Esau (Gen. 28:9) and that he took part in Abraham's funeral rites (Gen. 25:9). Ellen White indicates that even though he had come under the influence of his idolatrous wives, the early influence of Abraham was not without effect, and Ishmael repented in his old age and will be saved.[11]

It is known that the home of most of the twelve tribes of Ishmael was in the deserts of northern Arabia and eastern Syria. They generally lived a nomadic life as predicted by God in Genesis 16:12. Some of them, such as the Nabateans, came to fame and power later on.[12] Like their ancestor, Ishmael, they were skilled bowmen (Isa. 21:17), and they were also caravan leaders who brought the products of Arabia to Egypt and Mesopotamia (Gen. 37:25). In Judges 8:5, 21–24 the writer uses the word "Ishmaelite" to describe the Midianites. Technically, the Midianites were descendants of Midian, Abraham's son by his third wife, Keturah (Gen. 25:2, 6), but it appears that both Keturah's and Hagar's descendants lived to the east of where Sarah's descendants lived, but by virtue of their geographic proximity, they associated with one another frequently. Therefore, the Bible writers grouped them together as "Ishmaelites," even though in a technical sense, they were different families. However, there is a Jewish tradition among some rabbis that Hagar and Keturah were actually one and the same woman and that Abraham went and got her back as a wife after Sarah's death. The argument comes from the word "Hagar" being related to the concept of "immigrant," which is what the word means, and therefore, some assume Hagar was not a name but a title.[13] In any case, they weren't Sarah's descendants, so the Bible writers treated them alike, as the sons of the "other" women.

With this in mind, if the Midianites are considered to be possible descendants of the Ishmaelites, our understanding of their history can be enlarged. The Bible says that the Midianites had large numbers of camels (Num. 10:29–31; Isa. 60:6; Hab. 3:7), which would make sense if they were engaged in the trading business.

One must also notice that these "sons of the East" appeared in the Bible in a positive light at times and at other times in a negative light. God used the Ishmaelites to transport Joseph to Egypt where He used him to save his family and a large part of the world from famine. Moses, after fleeing Egypt because of his murder of an Egyptian, found refuge in the east with Midianites and later married one himself (Exod. 3:1; Num. 10:29–31).

Some biblical scholars have proposed that some of the oils and spices found in Exodus 30 that were used in the desert sanctuary when the Israelites came out of Egypt could only be procured through their cousins to the east.

When the Israelites dwelt near the Jordan before crossing into western Palestine, the Midianites joined the Moabites in seducing the Israelites into idolatry and licentiousness. As a consequence, Moses waged war against them and killed their five kings and many of their people (Num. 22:4–6; 25:1–18; 31:1–12).

In Joshua 13:21 it is recorded that the Midianite kings had been allies of Sihon, the Amorite king of Heshbon, who had also been defeated by the Israelites under Moses.

Later it was the Midianites, along with the Amalekites and other Eastern tribes, who raided Israel during the time of the judges and oppressed the Israelites for seven years. It was in response to this oppression that God raised up Gideon to overcome them and chase them from Israel's territory (Judges 6–8; Ps. 83:11; Isa. 9:4; 10:26). After this attack there is little mention of the Midianites having much interaction with the Israelites.

The Bible does have interesting perspectives on the "East." The following conclusions can be drawn from the few Bible references to it:

- There was spiritual wisdom in the East. Job was a man of the East. Jethro was spiritually wise enough to be able to instruct the great patriarch, his son-in-law, Moses. Some Midianites made the journey out of Egypt with Moses and the Israelites (Num. 10:29). Though Balaam clung to his love for money, God spoke with him and used him to prophesy about the coming Messiah (Num. 22).[14] Even at the time of Christ we see that "wise men" from the East came and met the Savior with lavish gifts fit for a king (Matt. 2:1). So there was a spiritual connection between the western relatives of Abraham and the eastern. Even the apostle Paul said that he went to "Arabia" for a time after his conversion much as Moses had done over a thousand years before him (Gal. 1:17).

- Of course, the eastern side of Abraham's family was not immune from falling into idol worship. As mentioned above, at times they even fought wars against their Israelite cousins, and God had to destroy many of them. They were, at times, a spiritual stumbling block for the people of God. But, it must be noted when reading the Old Testament story of Isaac's descendants that this was a problem that both sides of the family shared.

That is about the extent of what is known from the Bible about the lineage into which Muhammad was born in 570 CE (Common Era). We will now turn our attention to the biblical perspective on the historical context in which Muhammad was born.

Chapter 3

THE BIBLICAL PERSPECTIVE ON THE SEVENTH CENTURY

Before we examine the historical context in which Muhammad lived and preached, we will examine the biblical prophetic perspective on life in the sixth century as traditionally interpreted from a Seventh-day Adventist's perspective. Then, in the next chapter we will examine what is known about the history of the Arabian Peninsula and Muhammad's appearance.

The first thing that stands out about Muhammad is the era in which he was born—late sixth century (570 CE to be exact). Traditional SDA interpretation of prophecy posits that this was at the beginning of the Bible's most often repeated and probably its most stunning prophecy—the 1260-day (year) prophecy. The Bible's seven references to this time period help one to grasp what the conditions would be like in God's church 500 years after Christ ascended to heaven. I will not try to explain the traditional Adventist understanding of these prophecies. For that, the reader can reference such books as Mervyn Maxwell's *God Cares, Vol. 1 & 2*, (as well as many other books that deal with this topic in depth).

Adventists have traditionally understood these prophecies to mean that the Bible makes a daring prediction that God's own church would turn into an antichrist power that would do the following:

- Try to change God's "laws and times" – Dan. 7:25

- Speak against the Most High – Dan. 7:25

- Oppress the "saints" – Dan. 7:25

- Be so corrupt that the prophecies of Daniel would have to be "sealed" until the end of this period – Dan. 12:7

- Would "trample" on the "holy court" – Rev. 11:2

- Be so corrupt that God's two witnesses would "prophesy" in "sackcloth" – Rev. 11:3

- Would cause the "woman" (true church) to flee to the "wilderness" where she would be taken care of – Rev. 12:6, 14

- Utter proud words and blaspheme God – Rev. 13:5

If one accepts the principle that Joseph explained to Pharaoh in Genesis 41:32 when he told him that God had revealed the vision to him twice because this was a matter that was urgent to God, then it must be said that this 1260-day prophecy is not just urgent, but that it is *hyper-urgent*! No other prophecy in the Bible is mentioned more than twice, let alone repeated seven times like this one. This was an extremely important prophecy if God decided to give it on seven different occasions to Daniel and John. When one thinks about it, it is clear why it would be so.

After Christ left the disciples, they obeyed His command and stayed in Jerusalem, waiting for the Holy Spirit. Once Pentecost occurred, the church got off to a good start. The book of Acts records the missionary endeavors of the first evangelists establishing this new faith in the Messiah who was predicted through the Old Testament Scriptures. God now had a people who would victoriously carry a message of a crucified and risen Savior to the whole world. The apostles believed that God had now established His new people and they would "finish the work."

However, history shows that things didn't turn out exactly the way the apostles envisaged. As Adventists we believe that in the first half of Revelation God gave a prophetic description of the eras that this new people would pass through. He begins in Revelation 2 with the seven churches of Asia Minor. The first and best era—the era of the apostles—Christ depicts as the "church of Ephesus." The church of this time period was described as hard working, persevering, pure, and willing to endure hardships (Rev. 2:1–3). Usually this church is identified as the time period from 31 CE–100 CE.

As time progressed, however, the church's zeal began to wane, and Revelation 2:8–10 describes the church of Smyrna as afflicted and poor, without the accolades that were given to Ephesus. The counsel for Smyrna was—"remain faithful" because they were about to suffer persecution. The Smyrna time period is generally equated with the church from around 100 CE–313 CE. At the end of that period, Christianity became the religion of the Roman Empire with the conversion of the emperor Constantine.

Next comes the church of Pergamum, usually associated by Adventists with the time period from 313 CE–538 CE. This church was told they live where "Satan has his throne." They are commended for not losing their faith and being faithful, but they are reprimanded for holding to teachings that allow for promiscuity and elements of idol worship. Traditionally, it has been viewed that the church's introduction of pagan practices during this time of so-called "prosperity" for the church was the cause of the church losing its biblical foundations.

This leads nearly to the time of Muhammad. According to prophecy, by 538 CE Christianity had lost its grasp on the Bible and had adopted pagan practices. So what can we say about Thyatira—the time period in which Muhammad would have arisen in Revelation 2?

Thyatira is told that they have some deeds of "love and faith" and they have some service and perseverance, but they are severely reprimanded for tolerating "Jezebel, who calls herself a prophetess" (verse 20). She leads God's servants into promiscuity and idol worship—in other words, she builds on the errors that were growing in the church during the Pergamum time period. God warns that He will make those who follow her suffer intensely, "unless they repent of their deeds," and that He will "kill her children with death" (verses 22, 23). He states that then the churches "shall know that I am He who searches the minds and hearts. And I will give to each one of you according to your works" (verse 23). In this period conditions become so bad that in verses 24 and 25 God states that he will "put on you no other burden," and He implores them just to hold on to what they have until He comes—in other words, "just hang on and survive this time period."

Another interesting detail in Revelation 2 is that even though all of these messages are given by the "Son of man" who is described in chapter 1, only in the Thyatira message is it mentioned that this message is from the "Son of God" (verse 18). This is a helpful detail as the time period of Muhammad is analyzed, since the issue of Jesus' "sonship" to God was a huge issue within Christianity at the time.

The seals of Revelation 6, which Adventists have traditionally interpreted as a description of the history of the church after Christ, should also be analyzed. This is the traditional interpretation by the Adventist Church of these seals:

- First seal – white horse (30 CE–100 CE)

- Second seal – red horse (100 CE–313 CE)

- Third seal – black horse (313 CE–538 CE)

- Fourth seal – pale horse (538 CE–1517 CE)

Parallels can be seen between the description of church history in Revelation 6 and the description found in Revelation 2. The church starts out victorious and pure (white horse); goes through persecution from the state (red horse); enters an era of spiritual darkness when church and state unite (black horse); and by the time of Muhammad the church is "pale."

Revelation 6:8 is the only verse that describes the period of the pale horse, but it is a frightening picture to say the least. Death and hell are pictured ravaging over a quarter of the earth with the sword, hunger, and beasts of the earth. These were the natural consequences from the "black horse" period when a "preoccupation with material things"[15] caused spiritual things to be set aside. For the purposes of this discussion, I will not continue interpreting the other seals.

From the perspective of the Bible, Muhammad appeared on the Arabian Peninsula in a time where Christianity was not only "not doing very well," but it was in advanced apostasy and dead. The Bible is clear that the history of Christianity would not be a perfect one in which God's people would progress from one victory to another as they spread the knowledge of a risen, soon-coming Savior. On the contrary, the Bible foretold that a "lawless" power would arise before the Savior's appearing and be manifested, not with the power of God, but with the power of Satan (2 Thess. 2:8–10). It is stunning to think that Satan would be so cunning as to infiltrate the church and take it over to the point that the Bible said that this apostate church would have to be slain by "the breath of His mouth" and the glory of His coming (2 Thess. 2:8). Muhammad came near the beginning of this baleful period when spiritual death and stagnation were rampant in Christianity.

Conclusion

Even though the historical setting into which Muhammad was born and began preaching has not been examined yet, by just examining briefly the prophecies of the Bible, the following conditions in Christianity at the end of the sixth century should be anticipated:

1. The Christian church would be the main antichrist power in the world.

2. The Christian church would be arrogant, even speaking against the Most High God and attempting to change His law.

3. A Christian church would persecute the "saints," the faithful followers of Christ.

4. Bible truth and prophecies would be neglected.

5. Spiritual life amongst Christianity's members would wane, even being characterized by words like "death" and "hell."

6. Idol worship and promiscuity (sexual and spiritual) would be identifying marks of Christianity.

7. Jesus' sonship to God would be an issue.

8. The "woman" (true believers) would be forced to flee into the "wilderness."

With that in mind, we will now turn to historical sources to see if that matches what the Bible foretold.

Chapter 4

Historical Context of the Rise of Islam

The *Oxford History of Islam* begins its article entitled "Islam and Christendom" with the following statement, "The Christian world into which Islam so unexpectedly burst in the seventh century CE had undergone a succession of divisions, controversies, and power struggles such that east and west were at serious odds, and each contained within its regions deep tensions and disagreements." It can be deduced from this brief, introductory sentence of a history book that the Bible had done a good job in predicting the spiritual darkness and death that would permeate the church of that time. The Christian world was not united by the gospel when Muhammad began his ministry—it was deeply divided. In fact, to many observers within Christianity at the time, the rise of Islam appeared to be just another Christian heresy.[16] In this chapter we will look at some of the salient issues that set a backdrop to the rise of Islam and its acceptance by a huge portion of Christianity.

Brief History of the Controversies in the Early Christian Church
By the time of Muhammad, the Christian church had adopted Sunday as its "holy day," introduced the doctrine of the immortality of the soul, and ceased to preach the soon return of a coming Savior since they believed that the church triumphant on earth (in politics, that is) was the fulfillment of the biblical millennium. However, ironically enough, these issues were not "hot topics" in Christianity in the sixth century. The main controversy that then raged in the church was over the nature of Christ. This topic will be examined first.

Differing Theories of the Nature of Christ
Beginning in the Smyrna time period (100 CE–313 CE), the church began to try to explain the Bible in the terms of the world.

The Christian Apologists of the 2nd century were a group of writers who sought to defend the faith against Jewish and Greco-Roman critics. They refuted a variety of scandalous rumors, including allegations of cannibalism and promiscuity. By and large, they sought both to make Christianity intelligible to members of Greco-Roman society and to define the Christian understanding of God, the divinity of Christ, and the resurrection of the body. To accomplish this, the Apologists adopted the philosophical and literary vocabulary of the broader culture to develop a more refined expression of the faith that could appeal to the sophisticated sensibilities of their pagan contemporaries.[17]

Due to this, the preeminent role of the Bible in the church began to subside so that by the third century the people needed to have the Bible explained to them. This brought to prominence theologians like Origen who wrote commentaries.[18] This development gave more influence to the "elite" theologians who could write more eloquently, using Greek philosophical language to appeal to the general public. As Paul stated in 1 Corinthians 8:1, "Knowledge puffs up, but love edifies," and with this new knowledge there seemed to be less and less love in the church and more and more "puffing up," which resulted in the church being divided over various theories.

In order to understand Muhammad and his writings in the Quran, it is necessary to understand what controversies were swirling around in the Christian church at the time. We will concentrate on the controversies in the church of the East, headquartered in Constantinople, since this part of the church had more of a presence and greater influence on the Arabian Peninsula at the time of Muhammad and on the succeeding generations of Islam.

Arianism

Followers of Arius, a priest in Alexandria, taught that Jesus was a created being and that He was not the divine Son of God. According to them, God created the universe through Jesus. By 325 CE the church, under the guidance of the newly converted Roman emperor, Constantine, had to convene a council at Nicaea to combat the Arian teaching. The council established the teaching that is still believed in most Christian churches: that Jesus and the Father are equal. They expressed it, of course, in a Greek word from philosophy—*homoousis* ("of the same substance").

Adoptionism (or Dynamic Monarchianism)

This position held that Christ was a mere man, miraculously conceived, but constituted the Son of God by the infinitely high degree in which he had been filled with divine wisdom and power. This later evolved into the teaching that Christ was not born as the Son of God, but at some time during His life, God "adopted" Him as His Son. This belief continues with many modern Unitarians.

Modalistic Monarchianism (also known as "Patripassianism")

This view "took exception to the 'subordinationism' of some of the Church Fathers and maintained that the names Father and Son were only different designations of the same subject, the one God, who 'with reference to the relations in which He had previously stood to the world is called the Father, but in reference to His appearance in humanity is called the Son.' "[19] About 200 CE Noetus began to preach this theory. When Praxeas brought these views to Rome, Tertullian commented that, "he drove out prophecy and brought in heresy, he put to flight the Comforter and crucified the Father."[20] Much of the orthodox Christian teaching on the *Logos*, the Word or the "Son" of God, was compiled as a defense against this heresy. Modalistic Monarchianism opposed the doctrine of an independent, personal subsistence of the *Logos* and affirmed the sole deity of God the Father, thus representing an extreme monotheistic view.

Even after the Council of Nicaea, Christological controversies did not completely subside. The emperor Constantine himself had Arian leanings, and his son was an outright Arian. In 381 CE at the next ecumenical council, the church proclaimed Catholic Christianity (Western Christianity) as the official religion of the empire, thus eliminating Arianism from the East (since Arius had been a priest in Alexandria, Egypt—one of the centers of the Eastern church).[21] Since the Western church was then coming into prominence, this decision gave rise to political challenges from the church of the East, which colored the controversies over the doctrine of Christ that arose next.

Melchites

This group was popular in the Middle East, especially among royalty. They taught that Jesus was truly God and truly man. They believed that one was not different from the other. It was the human in Him, they taught, who was crucified and killed, but nothing happened to the divine in Him. They also taught that Mary gave birth to both the divine and the human nature of God.

Nestorianism

The next Christological debate was discussed at the Council of Ephesus in 431 CE. Led by Cyril, the patriarch of Alexandria, an extreme Christology as taught by Nestorius, the patriarch of Constantinople was condemned as being heretical. Nestorius taught that the man Jesus is an independent person beside the divine Word and that therefore Mary, the mother of Jesus, may not be properly called the "mother of God" (Greek, *theotokos*, or "God-bearer"). It is difficult to tell what Nestorius actually taught, because it is generally assumed that Cyril, as the patriarch of Alexandria, was looking to belittle his rival at the see of Constantinople, so his decision to condemn his rival was probably as much a political maneuver as a religious one.

What Nestorius actually taught was probably more like a prosopic union. The Greek term *prosōpon* means the external, undivided presentation, or manifestation, of an individual that can be extended by means of other things—e.g., a painter includes his brush within his own *prosōpon*. So the Son of God used manhood for his self-manifestation, and manhood was, therefore, included in his *prosōpon*, so that he was a single object of presentation.[22]

However it came about, Nestorianism, as it was understood at the time by its opponents and eventually by those who adhered to it, so insisted upon the full humanity of Christ's human nature that it was believed to divide Him into two persons, one human and the other divine. Whereas orthodox Christology of the time came to hold that Christ has two natures, divine and human, ineffably united in one person ("*hypostasis*" in the Greek), Nestorianism so stresses their independence as to suggest that they are in effect two persons, or "hypostases," loosely joined by a moral union. Nestorianism envisages the divine Word as having associated with itself at the incarnation a complete, independently existing man.

From the orthodox point of view, Nestorianism therefore denies the reality of the incarnation and represents Christ as a God-inspired man rather than as God-made-man.[23] It was very similar to the Melchites' position with the exception that Mary didn't give birth to the divine element of Christ.[24]

In any case, Cyril's stated formula for resolving this problem was "one nature for the Word Incarnate." This led to the next controversy over the nature of Christ.

Monophysitism

This teaching asserts that Jesus Christ's nature remains altogether divine and not human, even though He has taken on an earthly and human body with its cycle of birth, life, and death. Monophysite doctrine thus asserted that in the person of Jesus Christ there was only one (divine) nature rather than two natures, divine and human.

Pope Leo of Rome led out in protesting this doctrine, which culminated in the Council of Chalcedon in 451 CE. "Chalcedon adopted a decree declaring that Christ was to be 'acknowledged in two natures, without being mixed, transmuted, divided, or separated.' This formulation was directed in part against the Nestorian doctrine—that the two natures in Christ had remained separate and that they were in effect two persons—and in part against the theologically unsophisticated position of the monk Eutyches, who had been condemned in 448 [CE] for teaching that, after the Incarnation, Christ had only one nature and that, therefore, the humanity of the incarnate Christ was not of the same substance as that of other human beings."[25]

During the next 250 years the Byzantine emperors and patriarchs desperately sought to reconcile the monophysites, but all of their attempts failed. Chalcedon's "two natures" continues to be rejected by the Armenian Apostolic Church, Coptic Orthodox Church of Egypt, Ethiopian Orthodox Church, and the Syrian Orthodox Patriarchate of Antioch (Syrian Jacobites).[26]

Jacobites

These were Christians who followed Jacob Baradeus and were mainly located in Egypt. The Jacobites took monophysitism to another level and declared that Jesus Himself is God. According to their belief, God Himself was crucified and the whole universe remained without its Provider and Maintainer for three days while Christ lay in the tomb. Then God rose up and returned to His place. Thus God became originated and the originated became eternal. They believed that it was God who was conceived and carried in Mary's womb.[27]

Collyridians

This Arabian female sect of the fourth century believed that Jesus and His mother were separate deities from God. They especially had an affinity for worshiping Mary. They offered cakes of bread (*collyrida*—hence, the name of the sect) to her as others had done to great mother earth in pagan times. Such Christians as Epiphanus opposed this heresy and attempted to help Christians see that Mary should not be worshiped.[28]

It can be seen from this abbreviated study of the history of the Christian church and its tremendous struggles in understanding the nature of Christ, why Jesus refers to Himself in Revelation 2:18 as the "Son of God" for this Thyatira time period as mentioned in the previous chapter. It was an issue that needed to be dealt with in Christianity. However, that wasn't the only problem in the church.

Mariology

As mentioned in the paragraph above on the Collyridians, there were many problems brewing in the church in regards to Mary. Within a few centuries of the inception of Christianity, Mary came to be venerated among the laity as a blessed lady with the incredible privilege of bearing the Son of God, as evidenced by frescos found depicting her and Jesus in the Roman catacombs. However, this went to an extreme, and she gradually became known as the "mother of God," and apocryphal versions of her life surfaced, along with a preoccupation with her relics.

Even though it was rigorously protested by some (including Nestorius), the Council of Ephesus in 431 CE formally sanctioned the veneration of the virgin as the *Theotokos*, the "Mother of God" (or more accurately the "God-bearer"), and it condoned the creation of icons to the virgin and her Child. In that same year, Cyril, the archbishop of Alexandria, applied to Mary many of the terms fondly ascribed by the pagans in Ephesus to their "great goddess" Artemis/Diana.

Gradually the most beloved features of the ancient female goddesses Astarte, Cybele, Artemis, Diana, and Isis were synthesized in the worship of Mary. In that century the church established the Feast of the Assumption of the Blessed Virgin Mary, commemorating the day she ascended to heaven on August 15, the date of the ancient festivals of Isis and Artemis. Mary eventually came to be considered an intercessor on behalf of humanity before the throne of her Son. She became the patron saint of Constantinople and of the imperial family. Her picture was carried at the head of every great procession and was hung in every church and home in Christendom.[29]

The veneration of Mary is exemplified by the prayer of Lucius:

> (Thou) by thy bounty and grace nourishest all the world, and bearest a great affection to the adversities of the miserable as a loving mother ... Thou art she that puttest away all storms and dangers from men's life by stretching forth thy right hand ... and appeasest the great tempests of fortune ...[30]

Walter Hyde comments on this new phenomenon in Christianity:

It is, then, only natural that some students have seen her influence as "mother of sorrows" and "mother of Horus," in whom the Greeks saw their grief-stricken Demeter searching for her daughter Persepone raped by Pluto, on the Christian concept of Mary. The motif of mother and child appears in many statuettes, which have been found in her ruined shrines on the Seine, Rhine, and Danube, and which the early Christians mistook for the Madonna and Child, and little wonder since it is still difficult to differentiate between the two types.

The epithet "Mother of God" as applied to Mary … became common in the fourth (century) being used by Eusebius, Athanasius, Gregory of Nazianzus in Cappadocia and others, with Gregory saying that "the man who does not believe Mary was the Theotokos has no part in God."[31]

It must be noted that the process of the acceptance of Mary was quicker in the Eastern part of Christianity (the part closer to Muhammad) than in the West. This is witnessed to by the fact that when Pope Agapetus visited Constantinople in 536 CE he was reprimanded by his Eastern counterpart for opposing the veneration of Mary and the placement of icons to the *Theotokos* in Western churches. However, gradually the veneration of Mary became accepted in the West as in the East. In 609 CE (one year before Muhammad allegedly had his first vision), the Roman Pantheon was dedicated to Mary and renamed "*Santa Maria ad Martyres*" ("Holy Mary and the Martyrs"), and one of the oldest churches, *titulus Julii et Calixti*, was re-dedicated as Santa Maria in Travestere. By the end of the century, Pope Sergius I had introduced the earliest Marian feasts into the Roman liturgical calendar. The table was now set for veneration of the *Theotokos* since the theory of the assumption of Mary was widespread, and Christians from both the East and the West could now offer their prayers to another "intercessor" besides the One given to us in the Bible (1 Tim. 2:5).

Dr. Kenneth Oster, a longtime Adventist pastor in Iran, states:

> Pre-Christian Roman cults emerged in the Church with 'Christian' names. Diana, the virgin goddess contributed something to the worship of the Virgin Mary. The Roman Juno, the Greek Hera, the Carthaginian Dea Caelestis, the Egyptian Isis, the Phoenician Astarte, and the Babylonian Mulitta had all been queens of heaven. Egypt had no small part to play in this prostitution of the simple teachings of Christ. The extant figurines of Isis nursing Horus are a striking similarity to familiar representations of the Madonna and Child. Thus it becomes apparent that this heresy of profligate paganism, that of a male god raping a female deity, from which abominable, incestuous union produced a 'son of god' (Matt. 26:54), was conceived in the Canaanite cults of Ras Shamra and Egypt, incubated in Greco-Roman mythology, especially the mystery religions, borne full stature in the apostate Church, and foisted off onto the non-Christian world as truth.[32]

This point really cannot be overemphasized when studying the context of Muhammad. The reader must grasp a sense of what was really happening in Christianity if one wants to understand what Muhammad was speaking about in the Quran. Arabia was not immune to these developments in Christianity. So widespread was this concept of a "Trinity"—a father god, a mother god, and physical biological offspring to make a third, a son god— that the residents of Mecca had placed in their pantheon of gods, the Kabah, a Byzantine icon of Mary and Jesus so that the Christian merchants that made the trek to Mecca would have something to worship along with their hundreds of other deities.[33] An understanding of the widespread apostasy in regards to the Trinity, Mary, and the "Son of God" is absolutely essential before embarking on an examination of the Quran.

Monasticism

Another development within Christianity that would have long-term effects on the rise of Islam was monasticism. By the fifth century this movement was attracting many followers. One of the early founders of a monastic order, Pachomius, founded eleven monasteries in Upper Egypt before his death in 346 CE and had about 7,000 followers. Jerome reports that within a century 50,000 monks participated in the annual convention. Just in the Oxyrhynchus region of Upper Egypt there were an estimated 10,000 monks and 20,000 virgins. These numbers are just representative of the trend that was gaining momentum in the Christian world. Thousands of people migrated to the Syrian Desert and established monasteries with the sole purpose of leading a life of contemplation.[34]

This movement was based on the teachings of Plato of the division of body and spirit. The body, they believed, was a transitory stage of human existence. The spirit was the true expression of the divine and was only temporarily imprisoned in the body of flesh. Origen and Clement had adopted and promoted this dualistic view of reality, which in turn caused many to leave the "evils" of all that is associated with the flesh and withdraw to isolated places to pursue "spiritual perfection." This teaching especially took hold in Eastern Christianity where Muhammad would come in contact with Christians. It especially contrasted with the less philosophical, more practical teachings that he espoused. This was a topic that Muhammad addressed in the Quran.

Lack of Fervor

Another development in Christianity was the remarkable flagging of zeal to take the gospel to the world. Zeal for the gospel was the leitmotif of the apostles and early church, but as can be seen from the above-mentioned points, the church had grown content merely to argue about the correctness of doctrine and split hairs over theological/philosophical terms. By the seventh century there were few bright spots in Christian mission—though Nestorians had taken the gospel as far as India and China, and the Celts had begun taking Christ to the Germanic peoples.[35]

Adventists can find themselves with mixed emotions over these developments; yes, all people groups need to hear about Christ, but as noted above, the Nestorians actually had a very unorthodox view of Christ. And yes, Adventists do want the gospel of Jesus preached in "all the world," but do they want that done by people who will teach that God's law has been abolished, the doctrine that man has an immortal soul, threatening people with an eternal hell, teaching a Sunday day of worship, and other false doctrines?

One situation in the seventh century that all Christians can deplore was the lack of translations of the Bible. As far as scholars can tell, the first Arabic translation of the Bible wasn't completed until 837 CE, and then not widely copied (beyond a few scholarly manuscripts) until first published in 1516 CE![36]

This shows the lack of zeal on the part of Christians to share the gospel with the Arabs. This trend continues in modern times, with only one of twelve Christian workers being sent to Muslim countries even though Muslims total one-fifth of the world's population. It seems that even though the Bible had been translated into some lesser-known cultures' languages—such as Chinese or Syriac, but not Arabic—that some level of prejudice existed toward the Arabs.[37] In any case, it is believed by Christian scholars that neither Muhammad nor any other Arabs at that time had a chance to read a manuscript of the Bible in their native tongue.

Persecution

Even though Christianity had degenerated into arguing over the philosophy of the nature of Christ, embracing the immortality of the soul, rejecting the biblical Sabbath and God's law, and promoting extreme forms of withdrawal from the world, probably the most repugnant of all its characteristics was the use of force to promote its teachings. It is one thing to teach error and yet have the loving, Christian spirit that Jesus tried to instill in His followers ("love your enemies ... do good to those who hate you" [Matt. 5:44]); but, it is an another thing to teach heresy, be proud of it, and kill anyone who doesn't agree with it! Yet, this is exactly what was being practiced by Christians when Muhammad arrived on the scene. This was a clear and complete fulfillment of Revelation 6—darkness and death had encompassed the church.

This development began immediately following a time of severe persecution of Christians by the emperor of the Roman Empire, Diocletian, from 303-313 CE. Within a generation Christianity went from being persecuted to being the persecutor after the acceptance of the religion by the emperor Constantine. When the Council of Nicaea declared the teachings of Arius heretical, Constantine believed that the binding of "orthodoxy" should be enforced to keep the empire united. It was decreed that any belief held against the official teachings of the church was not just an offense against the church, but also the state.

Eusebius, the leading church historian at the time of Constantine, reflected the thinking of the majority of the Christians at the time when he praised Constantine and promoted him as the chosen vessel of God to bring the reign of Christ on the earth. One author, when discussing Eusebius, states:

> Though a man of the church, as propagandist and historian he founded the political philosophy of the Christian state, more indebted to the Roman empire than to the New Testament for evidence to buttress his conclusions. His perspective is thoroughly politicized. His accolade contains 'no wistful regret at the blessings

of persecution, no prophetic fear of imperial control of the Church.' It lies outside his mental framework that protection by the state leads to religious servitude on the part of the church, and persecution of dissenters to religious hypocrisy, even though both of these pitfalls could easily be discerned in his own day.[38]

Christianity had sacrificed its spiritual purity and its commitment to a principle that Christ taught—separation of church and state—for popularity and temporal gain. By the time of emperor Theodosius I (379–395 CE), "heretics" were forbidden to assemble or own property, and even their church properties were being confiscated. Theodosius II (408–450 CE) went even further and decreed that heretics who didn't believe in the Trinity or who taught repeated baptism (Donatists) were worthy of the death penalty.

Widespread persecution did not occur, however, until the reign of Justinian (527–565 CE) when Arians, Montanists, and Sabbatarians were all pursued as enemies of the state. The historian Procopius, a contemporary of Justinian, states that Justinian "engineered an incalculable number of murders. His ambition being to force everybody into one form of Christian belief, he wantonly destroyed everyone who would not conform, and that while keeping up a pretense of piety. *For he did not regard it as murder, so long as those who died did not happen to share his beliefs.*"[39]

This might explain why God considered this as the beginning point of absolute apostasy on the part of the Christian church. As evidenced in the Bible and the account of the creation of Lucifer and his subsequent rebellion and attempt to establish a government on God's newly created planet, we see that God values, above all else, religious freedom. In spite of knowing the untold suffering and death that would occur because of the fall of Lucifer, and consequently of Adam and Eve, God upheld the principle of liberty of conscience. We see in history that whenever an entity, be it a church or a government, decides to deprive human beings of this sacred right, it begins to work against the Most High, and God's blessings can no longer accompany it.

Conclusion

All of the above-mentioned facts, which historians have ably documented, had telling effects on the Arabian Peninsula where Muhammad lived and preached for over two decades. By the time of Muhammad, Arabia had become home to many significant communities of Jews and Christians, particularly in the south. Christians were living in Medinah, Mecca, Khyber, Yemen, and Najran.[40] It is known that after the Council of Ephesus there was much activity on the part of the Nestorians that moved eastward and probably had many converts in Arabia.[41]

It also must be noted that the death of Pope Gregory the Great preceded Muhammad's first vision by only six years. Gregory was the first dominant leader that the Church of Rome had had, hence the name historians give him as the "great." He was the first zealous missionary pope, sending missionaries as far as Britain. So, it can be deduced that had Muhammad not appeared on the scene, the Arabian religious landscape was probably about to change in that it would have become the field of competition between Rome and

Byzantium and with the Christian sects, which were opposed to both the Eastern and Western Christian churches.

To call the condition of Christianity wretched by the end of the sixth century would be an understatement. It already had all of the makings of "Babylon" as the Bible foretold it. If the truth were told, it couldn't really even be considered a monotheistic religion anymore. As far back as the fifth century, true believers noted the spiritual apostasy:

> The sacrifices you [the Christians] change into love feasts, the idols into martyrs, to whom you pray as they do to their idols. You appease the shades of the departed with wine and food. You keep the same holidays as the Gentiles; for example, the calends and the solstices. In your way of living you have made no change. Plainly, you are a mere schism; for the only difference from the original is that you meet separately.[42]

And Muhammad appeared at the time that Christianity was being championed by its greatest proponent, Gregory the Great. By that time it had become a most intimate union of true Christianity with a subterranean, superstitious, and polytheistic Christianity. These doctrines and practices have never been completely uprooted in over 1,500 years to this day.

It is important to note here that God gave humanity the following instructions in Deuteronomy 29:29, "The secret things belong to the LORD our God, but those things which are revealed belong to us and to our children forever, that we may do all the words of this law." These controversies over the substance of Christ that raged through the Christian world for 300 years, and all of the strange polytheistic beliefs regarding the Godhead, were not revealed in Scripture.

Is it any wonder that there was a flagging desire on the part of the church to translate and print the Holy Scriptures in the languages of the world? Had they done that it would have weakened their power. It took Christianity one thousand more years until the Protestant Reformation to begin to return to the Bible for its beliefs and practice. To this day it hasn't recovered completely—the Bible has prophesied that only a remnant will be faithful to God's Word and be saved.

It is with this historical context fresh in our minds that we begin our look at the life and teachings of Muhammad.

Chapter 5

THE QURAN AND THE RISE OF MUHAMMAD

Before looking at the Quran and the teachings of Islam from an Adventist perspective, one must examine the life of Muhammad. There are a multitude of books that explain his life thoroughly, so I will not attempt to duplicate their works. However, it is necessary to have a basic overview of his life and the historical realities that surrounded his ministry in order to understand his teachings as laid out in the Quran. One of the problems in trying to relate the story of Muhammad is that, on one hand, Muslim sources have almost deified him; therefore, they either disregard or minimize the unseemly aspects of his life; while, on the other hand, non-Muslims disregard or minimize his positive aspects. I will try to give as objective a portrayal of his life as possible.

The Kabah and the Religious Milieu of Mecca
Muhammad was born in 570 CE to one of the ruling families of Mecca on the Arabian Peninsula. To Muslims this year is known as the "Year of the Elephant." It was given that name because Abrahah, the king of nearby Abyssinia, sent an overwhelming force to Mecca to destroy the Kabah, the sanctuary Muslims believe to have been built by Abraham and Ishmael and which Abrahah viewed as a rival to his newly constructed temple in Sanaa, Yemen. According to tradition, the elephant that marched at the head of Abrahah's army knelt as it approached Mecca, refusing to go farther. Soon the sky blackened with birds that pelted the army with pebbles, driving them off in disarray.

This was significant to the people of the area because the Kabah (and its 360 gods in the form of idols) was the main tourist attraction of Mecca, and therefore, the economy was greatly dependent upon the pilgrims that came to this sanctuary. Even though the Arabs of the region believed that this structure was on the site where Abraham had built an altar with his son, Ishmael, the vast majority of them had abandoned the monotheistic faith of their forefathers in favor of polytheistic forms of religion. For the most part there was no developed religious belief system, and most worshiped many time-honored gods and goddesses without any particular feeling of devotion or commitment. They believed time to be synonymous with fate or death and that one should make the most of his life while here on earth.

> These sentiments were expressed in eloquent odes recounting deeds of chivalry and generosity, deploring fate, and praising the wise man who drowned his sorrows in the pleasures of wine, women and sentimental verse, but who was sure to leave behind a good name for his tribe to boast of after him.[43]

This devotion to hedonistic pleasure and the accompanying belief that denied an afterlife (Quran 45:24) was a continual source of anguish for Muhammad throughout his lifetime. Once he was called by God to restore an Abrahamic, monotheistic faith in the region, it was his main goal to cleanse the Kabah of the polytheistic gods and again see the Arabs worship the God of Abraham and Ishmael. Without the understanding of the crucial role that the Kabah played in the region and its history, it is impossible to understand the Quran and the events surrounding the life and ministry of Muhammad.

Genealogy

Arabs attached great significance to genealogy and kept track of it scrupulously both before and after the rise of Islam. People of that time and Muslims to this day believe that Muhammad was a direct descendant of Ishmael, and therefore of Abraham. Although questioned by modern historians, even medieval European opponents of Islam accepted this fact.[44] There is no way of verifying if it is true, but in any case, for Muhammad and the succeeding Muslim generations, the belief that they were in the lineage of Abraham and Ishmael played a key role in their understanding of Islam and the revelation of the Quran.

Childhood

Muhammad's parents were members of the powerful Quraysh tribe. This tribe was the ruling tribe of Mecca, and their main duty was to guard the Ka'bah, the traditional site where Abraham came and offered a sacrifice to God with his son Ishmael. Unfortunately, while Muhammad's mother, Aminah, was still pregnant with him, his father passed away. Even though Abd al-Muttalib, his grandfather, was a leader in the Meccan community, his life became increasingly difficult without a father. It was a tradition for Arab children to be sent out into the desert to master the Arabic language and learn the traditional Arab qualities of self-discipline, nobility, and freedom from the roaming Bedouins. It was also believed that this was a good experience spiritually for the children since they would avoid the corruptions that were present in the city. With these thoughts in mind, Aminah sent young Muhammad into the desert for several years to learn the basics of the Arabic language in which he became fluent during his later years of life.

At the age of six, tragedy struck again, and Aminah, his mother, passed away. Since he was now deprived completely of parents, his grandfather, Abd al-Muttalib, assumed the responsibility for his upbringing. However, in just two short years, when Muhammad was eight, Abd al-Muttalib died. At this point Abu Talib, Muhammad's uncle, assumed the role of parent. It is hard to estimate the effect of losing the three closest people to him by the age of eight. It is not difficult with this context to see that the care of orphans played a great role in Muhammad's teachings and overall in the religion of Islam

In spite of all his hardships, it is believed that Muhammad grew up to be a handsome, generous, and well-respected young man. When he was twenty-five years old, Khadijah, a wealthy woman of Mecca for whom he worked, proposed to him. In spite of the fact that she was fifteen years older than he, Muhammad married her, and while she was alive he never took another wife, even though polygamy was accepted and common in Arabia at that time. They had two sons who died when they were very young, and four daughters—Zaynab, Ruqayyah, Umm Kulthum, and Fatimah—who came to play a key role in the history of Islam. Khadijah had had many suitors who wanted to marry her, but she reportedly was attracted to Muhammad's character and his reputation as an honest person.[45]

Only ten years after his marriage to Khadijah, Muhammad was well respected in Mecca and would, from time to time, arbitrate disputes concerning some of the tribes of the region. Part of the respect that he commanded was due to the fact that he was viewed as a deeply spiritual person. He was known to spend large amounts of time in prayer and meditation in the regions surrounding Mecca. One legend recalls how after a big storm destroyed the Kabah the tribes of Mecca were arguing who would have the right to replace the famous black stone that had been in the east corner (probably a meteorite). The tribes got together and agreed that whoever came through a certain gate of Mecca would be the one who would have the privilege of replacing this black stone. It happened to be Muhammad that came through the gate. This made the tribes happy because he was known as al-Amin (the trusted one). It is widely accepted that Muhammad was considered an upstanding, honest person in Mecca before his call to be a prophet.

The Prophetic Call

It was during one of his periods of retreat when he was forty years old, while meditating in a cave called al-Hira in the Mountain of Light (Jabal an-Nur) near Mecca, that Muhammad experienced the presence of the archangel Gabriel and the process of the Quranic revelation began. This occurred in the month of Ramadan in the year 610 CE.

In this encounter Gabriel asked him to "recite" (*iqra in Arabic—the root word is where the word Quran is derived*), and then gave him a strong embrace. "Muhammad told the stranger that he was not a reciter. But the angel repeated his demand and embrace three times, before the verses of the Qur'ān, beginning with 'Recite in the Name of thy Lord who created,' were revealed. Although the command *iqra'* is sometimes translated as 'read,' 'recite' is a more appropriate translation because, according to traditional Islamic sources, the Prophet was *ummī* ('unlettered'), meaning that his soul was unsullied by human knowledge and virginal before it received the divine Word."[46] Some Christian and Muslim commentators have translated *ummi*, as just meaning "illiterate." Other Christian scholars have shown that the term "*an-nabiyyal-ummi*" (the unlettered prophet) is usually used in the Quran in contrast to the "people of the Book." They contend that it doesn't imply that Muhammad was illiterate or unlettered but that he was simply a prophet that was not from the "people of the Book" (Jews or Christians).[47] Even if this last theory is true, it is also possible that Muhammad was not formally educated, and maybe even illiterate.

In any case, Muhammad left the cave believing that he had encountered a demon and that he was now possessed even though he had been told that he was the messenger of God and that the angel was not a demon, but that it was Gabriel. As he was descending the mountain, he saw the angel once again. Terrified, he tried to look away from the angel, but, according to his later account, everywhere he looked he could only see this heavenly messenger. He said that the whole sky was covered by this angel and that the sky had turned green (which is the reason green is still the official color of Islam to this day). Upon arriving home, he allowed himself some time to come to his senses. Then he recounted to Khadijah what had happened to him. Khadijah believed him, but since she didn't have much religious knowledge, she sent for her blind cousin, Waraqah, who had converted to Christianity. When Waraqah heard the account, he believed this to be a similar call as God gave the prophets of the Bible and encouraged Muhammad to follow this prophetic call. Shortly after this episode, Muhammad had a second revelation. According to Islamic tradition, these revelations were either direct sayings from an angel or a vision related directly to his heart, and they were accompanied by bell-like reverberations. They lasted for almost twenty-three years up until Muhammad's death.

Muhammad's ministry

Muhammad first began preaching this message from the God of Abraham inconspicuously to his family and a few close friends. However, three years after the call, God told him to begin preaching openly to the city of Mecca. Some of the early converts to this message of Islam (submission to the one God) were Khadijah, Ali, Zayd ibn al-Harith, and Abu Bakr, who was one of a small group of esteemed members of Meccan society (he also became the first leader of the Islamic community after the death of Muhammad). From this core group, Islam began to expand in ever-wider circles. However, initially, the majority of Meccans, especially the ruling class, rejected these new messages. Abu Lahab, Muhammad's uncle and a prominent leader of Muhammad's tribe, the Quraysh, became one of the greatest opponents of Muhammad. The messages that Muhammad gave about worshipping only one God was very threatening to the Quraysh and the citizens of Mecca. They were the keepers of the Ka'bah and its 360 gods, and the business of pilgrimage of the Arab tribes to come and worship their tribal gods was a lucrative one. In Muhammad and this new religion of Islam, they saw a financial calamity awaiting for the crown jewel city of the Arabian peninsula.

It is interesting to note that the Quraysh considered that "The God" (Allah) was already the Lord of the Kabah since it was known as *al-baitullah*—the house of Allah. But they had other reasons for opposing this new preacher:

From some texts and traditions we should gather that the Meccan objection was not to the glorification of *Allah*, but to the identification of their familiar deity with him whom the Jews called *Rahmān* (the Merciful), a title applied to pagan deities also.[48]

The Quraysh apparently distinguished between Allah and ar-Rahman of the Jews, but the Quran identifies the two as the same Lord of all:

Say: "Call upon Allah, or call upon *Rahman*: by whatever name ye call upon Him, (it is well): for to Him belong the Most Beautiful Names." (17:110)

In some of the earliest surahs, we find the name ar-Rahman being used more often for God instead of the more common name Allah (e.g. Surah 43 where "ar-Rahman" appears seven times and "Allah" on only three occasions). The Arabs of Mecca considered this blasphemy.

While many Christians believe that Muhammad rejected and adamantly opposed Christianity, Christianity didn't play a role in the new religion for many years, as will be seen later in more detail. The main opponent of Islam over the lifetime of Muhammad was the Quraysh ruling tribe in Mecca, and this became the overarching theme of his ministry and the Quranic revelations.

As Muhammad gathered more believers, there started to be more and more persecution of the Muslims in Mecca. Some of the early Muslims were tortured and one was even executed. Muhammad was protected by his family, especially by his powerful uncle, Abu Talib, but he realized that for the safety of many of the new converts they needed to escape from Mecca. So in 615 CE he gave them permission to run away from Mecca to the king of Abyssinia, a Christian, who gave them protection until they could rejoin Muhammad and the rest of the believers in Medinah many years later.

In 619 CE both his wife, Khadijah, and his uncle, Abu Talib, passed away. These tragic events coupled with the continuing persecution in Mecca, and his lack of success in converting his own tribe in Mecca and the neighboring towns to Islam led to soul-searching for the prophet. This led to the infamous "Satanic verses" incident, immortalized in the novel on this topic by Salman Rushdie.

Muhammad greatly desired for his fellow tribesmen to accept his religion, but his efforts seemed to be futile. The Quraysh realized that he was almost despondent and came to him and offered to worship his god for a year if he would worship Al-Lat, Al-'Uzza, and Manat for a year (these were three of the most respected of the some 360 gods worshiped in Mecca at the Kabah). They made this offer at least twice, but each time a Quranic revelation was sent instructing Muhammad not to concede to them (109:1–6, 39:64–66). Muhammad even confided to his closest friends that he wished that God wouldn't have revealed anything "distasteful" to the Quraysh.[49]

According to a tradition he received a "revelation" that Muslims could pray to these three goddesses, but only as intercessors before God.[50] The Quraysh rejoiced in this new revelation, but it was perplexing to all because it seemed to contradict previous revelations. Muhammad was bitterly grieved and his conscience wouldn't allow him to have peace with this new decision; later he claimed that he had given in to Satan, hence the "Satanic verses." God gave him another revelation simultaneously reprimanding him and comforting him with the assurance that every prophet desires to have his people receive his message and is tempted to compromise the message. But He exhorted him to not concede to their demand. The Quraysh were more enraged after Muhammad did an about-face, and they became even more avowed enemies of Muhammad. This made life well nigh impossible for Muhammad and his followers in Mecca.

Around the year 621 God provided a way of escape for the nascent Islamic community. A delegation arrived from the city north of Mecca called Yathrib (the present day city of Medinah) arrived and asked Muhammad to move to Yathrib and become their leader. They had heard of Muhammad and his reputation of being a spiritual and just man and they asked him to come and mediate between the two main Jewish tribes of the city that were constantly quarreling – the 'Aws and the Khazraj. The Muslims believed this to be providential and agreed to move to Yathrib during the pilgrimage season of 622 CE. Muhammad sent his followers there in small groups so as not to attract the attention of the Quraysh.

On September 25, 622 CE, Muhammad completed what is now called the Hijrah (which means "migration" in Arabic) when he arrived in Yathrib. The city became known as Medina (which means "city" in Arabic, to denote that this was the "city of the prophet"). Muhammad was almost caught during the journey, but according to Islamic tradition he was miraculously spared being killed by the Quraysh. This was such a significant event for Islam that it has become the starting point for the Islamic calendar.[51]

The Medina Period

Life in Medina proved to be a challenge for Muhammad from the very beginning. On one hand, Muhammad's most trusted followers were the Muslims from Mecca who had emigrated with him (*al-muhajirun*), and on the other hand he had the Jewish tribes of Yathrib (who were the majority of the population) and the other Arab families. Muhammad had hoped that everyone, including the Jews, would convert to Islam. It is believed that all of the Arabs of Yathrib eventually did accept Islam; however, only a few Jews ever became Muslims. This new group of converts came to be known as "the helpers" (*al-ansar*). Muhammad's main challenge was to unite this newly formed Islamic community with the contentious Jewish tribes.

During the second year of the Hijrah, Muhammad crafted the Constitution of Medina, which defined the relations between these groups. In the document each group agreed that loyalty to tribe and clan was superseded by loyalty to the new Medinan community (the "*ummah*"). This meant that each group was equal before the law and would protect each other in case one group was attacked by its enemies. This was a radical concept for the tribal culture that had existed for centuries on the Arabian Peninsula.

Muhammad became the judge and main interpreter of the constitution. All cases from the varied groups had to come to him to be settled. For the most part, the society functioned fairly well, but as time passed and the Islamic community continued to grow and the coalition was tested in battles with the Quraysh, tensions between the Jewish tribes and Muslims grew. Some of the harshest texts in the Quran are dedicated to delineating the problems between these factions.

Up to this point, Muhammad and the Muslim community had been passively suffering at the hands of the Quraysh. A revelation of the Quran while Muhammad was in Mecca stated:

> As for them [Quraysh], they are but plotting a scheme, and I am planning a scheme. Therefore grant a delay to the unbelievers: give respite to them gently (for awhile). (86:15–17)

The Muslims believed in God and had, therefore, not put up any military resistance to the Quraysh. However, the text stated that God was planning and that this respite was only temporary. Upon arriving in Medinah, Muhammad received another revelation:

> To those against whom war is made, permission is given (to fight), because they are wronged;—and verily, God is Most Powerful for their aid;—(they are) those who have been expelled from their homes in defiance of right, (for no cause) except that they say, "Lord is God". Did not God check one set of people by means of another, there would surely have been pulled down monasteries, churches, synagogues, and mosques, in which the name of God is commemorated in abundant measure. God will certainly aid those who aid His (cause);—for verily God is Full of Strength, Exalted in Might ... (22:39, 40)

> Fight them on until there is no more tumult or oppression, and there prevail justice and faith in God altogether and everywhere. (8:39)

Muslims believed these revelations to mean that the time of respite had ended and now God was going to deliver the pagan oppressors into their hands and that the Arabian Peninsula would not be a safe place for this nascent religion until they had conquered paganism there. During this time Muslim warriors from Medinah began to attempt to intercept Quraysh caravans from Mecca going to or coming from Syria. Fighting a traditional military battle with the Quraysh didn't seem feasible at the moment to Muhammad but the raids provided much needed financial help for the new emigrants to Medinah.

For the first eleven months in Medinah, Muhammad sent out bands of warriors (only those of the emigrants), but due to misinformation of the whereabouts of the Quraysh or poor planning on the part of the Muslims, they didn't have any success. Muhammad himself led a couple of raids, but again they were unsuccessful. The Quraysh realized that they were in danger of being attacked by their enemies as they traveled to the north, but they didn't suspect being raided on their southern trade routes.[52]

This led to a significant raid in Muslim history at Nakhla. Muhammad sent his cousin

Abd Allah ibn Jahsh with eight other emigrants to scout the Quraysh southern trade caravans and determine the level of security accompanying them. Muhammad had not commanded them to fight, and it was Rajab, one of the four sacred months of the Arabic year, when there was no fighting allowed. However, the Muslims saw that there were many enemies of Islam in the small Quraysh caravan, so they attacked them, killing some and taking others prisoners. They transported the prisoners and the plunder back to Medinah. At first Muhammad reprimanded them for fighting during the sacred month since it was an Arab tradition that no tribes could fight during the four holy months of the year when pilgrimages to Mecca were done. But then a revelation came from God:

> They ask thee concerning fighting in the *prohibited month*. Say: "Fighting therein is a grave (offense); but graver is it in the sight of God to prevent access to the path of God, to deny Him, to prevent access to the Sacred Mosque and drive out its members." Tumult and oppression are worse than slaughter. Nor will they cease fighting you until they turn you back from your faith if they can. (2:217)

Muhammad and the Muslims then forgave Abd Allah and his fellow warriors. Due to this revelation they came to believe that this would be a battle with the Quraysh until the finish—either the Quraysh would conquer Islam or Islam would conquer the Quraysh. This led to the first major battle between the two parties.

In 624 CE Muhammad led a band of warriors to overtake an especially rich Quraysh caravan led by Abu Sufyan (one of the main enemies of Islam) returning to Mecca from Syria. Abu Sufyan found out about the devices of the Muslims and called for an army from Mecca to come to his aid. A 1,000 soldier strong army was assembled by the Quraysh and marched to meet him. They met a small force of 313 Muslims at a place called Badr.

Although on the face of it this battle might appear as an insignificant blip on the radar screen of history, it is probably one of the most momentous battles fought in history. Had this small band of Muslims been exterminated by the much larger and stronger Quraysh army, it is hard to estimate how the history of the world would have been changed. The Muslims inflicted heavy casualties on the Quraysh while only nine of the Muslims were killed. The Muslims believed that the battle was won with the direct intervention of God and that the angels had fought with them. To this day it is considered to be the most significant battle in Islamic history.

The Quraysh felt keenly the loss of their northern trade routes and after another caravan from Mecca to Iraq was ambushed by the Muslims, they began to prepare to deal a final blow to their enemies in Medinah.

The Quraysh were upset that the Muslims had defeated them and could now interrupt their lucrative trade on northern routes near Medina. In 624–625 CE, after the Muslims raided yet another of the Quraysh's caravans, they sent out an army of over 3,000 men to deal a final blow to this new religious group. They met and fought the Muslims, led by Muhammad, at a place called Uhud. Again, as before at Badr, the Muslims initially overcame the Quraysh even though they were far outnumbered. However, during the battle

Muhammad commanded the Muslim warriors to guard the left flank from one of the Quraysh's fiercest warriors, Khalid Ibn al Walid; the soldiers, upon seeing that the Muslim army was winning, left their posts and Khalid was able to encircle the Muslim army with his horsemen and inflict serious casualties. Instead of being a decisive victory for the Muslims, they ended up fighting to basically a draw with the Quraysh with both sides suffering heavy casualties. The Jews of Medina had allegedly plotted with the Quraysh during the battle, and they rejoiced that Muhammad and the Muslims had not been victorious. This resulted in Muhammad expelling one of the Jewish tribes, the Banu Nadir, to the north of Medina in Khaybar.

With their relationship with Muhammad soured, the Jews encouraged the Quraysh to overtake the Muslims in Medina once and for all in 626–627 CE. This time the Quraysh marched on Medina with an enormous army of 10,000 men. It appeared that this might be the end of the nascent Islamic community. However, the first Persian convert to Islam was familiar with the tactic of digging trenches around a city to protect it. He suggested that the Muslims do this for Medina, and they agreed to try it. When the Quraysh arrived and laid siege to Medina, they were unable to cross the trench without being killed by the Muslim archers. After attempting this for a few weeks, a cold wind began to blow, and the Quraysh army dispersed to Mecca disheartened that they were not able to deliver a deathblow to Muhammad and the Muslims. This battle became known as the Battle of the Trench.

Relations soured even further with the Jews of Medina once he discovered that the Jewish tribe, Qurayzah, had been complicit with the Quraysh during the Battle of the Trench. Muhammad, after consulting with one of the Qurayzah's allies, ordered that the men of the Qurayzah be put to death for treachery. This was a tragic episode that had repercussions for years to come between the Muslim community and the "People of the Book" (Jews and Christians). After this event Muslims had a difficult time making alliances with non-Muslim groups. It appeared to many that the Constitution of Medina had not worked.

By 628 the Muslim community had become solidly established in Medina so Muhammad and the Muslims decided to make the ʿumrah ("lesser pilgrimage") to the Kaʿbah in Mecca. The Quraysh met his large entourage outside of Mecca and forbade them to enter. Muhammad insisted that this was a peaceful religious ritual, but the Quraysh balked at allowing the Muslims to enter the city that they had kicked them out of. However, a compromise was reached between the two parties where a ten-year truce was signed between the Quraysh and Muslims (with the condition that neither side would attack each other's caravans), and the Muslims were allowed to perform the ʿumrah the following year. Many of the Muslims viewed this compromise as a grave mistake on the part of Muhammad.

In the years 628–630 CE the Islamic community began to prosper. More and more Arab tribes converted to Islam, and Medina became a thriving city now that the tensions between themselves and the Jews had dissipated. During these years they conquered different parts of the Arabian Peninsula. Muhammad even sent letters to the rulers of Abyssinia, Byzantium, and Persia inviting them to accept Islam. This was the time when Muhammad instituted the "jizyah" tax on the "People of the Book" (Jews and Christians) in exchange for them living freely in Islamic territory.

By 629 CE the Quraysh had broken their pact with the Muslims, which enabled Muhammad in 630 CE to march on Mecca. By this time he had amassed an army of 10,000 Muslims (many of the Quraysh's best military and political leaders had converted to Islam), and Mecca had no chance to withstand him. The Quraysh leaders pleaded for amnesty, which he agreed to give. Muhammad, even though he and the Muslims had suffered exile from Mecca for over eight years, commanded the army not to take revenge and shed blood upon entering the city. The soldiers complied, and there was no bloodshed on that day. Muhammad and the Muslims overtook the Ka'bah in the center of the city where they instituted the practice of public prayer. Mecca had finally become Muslim.

During the next two years the whole Arabian Peninsula either accepted Islam or had been conquered and agreed to live peacefully under Islamic rule. For the first time in the history of Arabia the Arabs were now united primarily under the banner of a religion and not under tribal alliances. This closed the "age of ignorance" (*jahiliyyah*) as Muslims refer to the pre-Islamic epoch. This was the beginning of a Muslim empire that would be one of the greatest empires the world has ever seen. However, Muhammad didn't live long to see this new age. He suddenly fell ill in the spring of 632 CE and died on June 8 of that year.

Now we are ready to turn our attention to the Quran and the teachings of Muhammad.

Chapter 6

OVERVIEW OF THE TEACHINGS IN THE QURAN

Most Christians concentrate largely on Muhammad's teachings about Jesus and don't study the breadth of his teaching, taking that into consideration too when examining his life and prophethood. However, one must look objectively at what he wrote in its entirety and not condemn or accept him based upon anecdotal evidence. Since the texts in the Quran that mention Christ are relatively far and few between, one should look at the bulk of his teaching before getting to those texts.

If one were to sit down and just read the Quran from cover to cover (which I would recommend to anyone interested in speaking to Muslims about their faith), this is a brief summary of the major teachings within its pages. A full listing by topic is found in Appendix A of this book.

When analyzing the main teachings, one needs to keep in mind a few facts about the Quran:

- The Quran has 114 chapters. Muslims do not call them "chapters"—they refer to them as "suras." Verses are referred to as "ayahs"—which is a term that originally meant a sign from God to reveal His wisdom.[53] For the purpose of this book I will refer to the chapters as "suras," but will simply use the word "verse" for the Arabic word "ayah."

- The Quran was not compiled in any chronological order. It is simply ordered by the length of the suras. The only exception to this is the first sura, which is the most recited sura of all, and was placed as the first one. Otherwise the second sura is the longest and the 114th is the shortest. This is an important fact to remember when reading the Quran because each sura was composed during a different time period of Muhammad's ministry. So one can't read the Quran like one reads the Bible and see a chronological sequence of events and thoughts. God, in the Quran, states that it was revealed gradually to the Arabs so that people might accept it (25:32–34), but when the Quran was collected there was no attempt to structure it chronologically.

- The name of each sura is derived from a name or a quality from within the sura itself. Muslims believe that Muhammad named each sura, perhaps by the command of God.

- Muhammad did not actually "write" the Quran (this commonly held Muslim tradition has been challenged by Western scholars—but for our purposes we will look at the Sunni tradition of how it was compiled). Since he was uneducated (and in some traditions, illiterate), the Quran was only recited by him, not written down. When he received his revelations from God, he would then recite them to his followers, many of whom would attempt to memorize every word that he said in each sura. Some wrote down parts on whatever they could find, including even bodies of believers, camel bones, or palm fronds.

- After Muhammad passed away, Abu Bakr, Muhammad's successor as the leader of the Muslims, commissioned Zayd ibn Thabit, who had written down parts of the revelations of Muhammad, to compile a collection of all suras that had been revealed. He did so, and the completed text was then passed on to Umar, Abu Bakr's successor, who gave the copy to his daughter Hafsah. However, during Uthman's reign, the successor to Umar, a quarrel broke out among some Muslim soldiers as to the meaning of some of the texts (they had some copies of the original text), so Uthman re-commissioned Zayd ibn Thabit to come up with a definitive text of the Quran, which he did with the help of three natives of Mecca. A copy was kept in Medinah and copies were sent to Damascus, Kufa, Yemen, and possibly Basra. Other copies with alternate readings were destroyed, and this has been the authoritative text of the Quran ever since.[54]

With this background in mind we will now turn to the teachings of the Quran.

Bible/People of the Book (Christians and Jews)

What does the Quran teach about the Bible and Christianity? The Quran deals extensively with this topic. In Sura 2:4 God says that the Quran was revealed for believers who believe in the Quran *and* in the revelation "before thy [Muhammad's] time." So, according to the Quran itself, the Quran is not for anyone who doesn't believe in the Bible.

In Sura 53:36 the Quran says that one who hardens his heart and turns his back on religion is not acquainted with the "books of Moses." Sura 11:110 states that God gave the "books of Moses" to humanity but differences arose among the Jews in interpretation of it.

The Quran explicitly tells Muslims that when Christians and Jews try to persuade them to follow their religion (he considered many of them idol worshippers) they are to say,

> We believe in God and the revelation given to us and to Abraham, Ismail, Isaac, Jacob and the Tribes and that given to Moses and Jesus, and that given to (all) Prophets from their Lord: we make no difference between one and another of them: and we bow to God (in Islam). (2:136)

Some Muslims argue that this text proves that no one should make any difference between Jesus and the prophets, but the context actually gives more credence to the understanding that their revelations are all of God, and that one shouldn't try to distinguish which prophet's message is more important than others.

In Sura 2:177 the Quran defines "righteousness" in part as believing in "the Book and the Messengers." The Quran acknowledges that God chose Adam, Noah, Abraham, Ishmael, Isaac, Jacob, Moses, David, Solomon, Job, Ezekiel, Aaron, Elijah, Elisha, Zechariah, John, Joseph, Jonah, Lot, and Jesus to reveal His will to mankind and tells of their faithfulness to God (3:33, 84; 4:163–166; 6:83–86; 17:55; 19:50–60; 21:78–86). The Quran is clear—Muhammad viewed himself as a *continuation of the revelations of the God of the Bible*. Nowhere in the Quran can one find an injunction not to study the Bible; on the contrary, Muhammad stated that all the prophets and messengers were from God and should be revered.

So one might be thinking, "Why would God need to inspire another prophet after the Bible?" Most Christians are uncomfortable admitting that there might have been any prophets since the close of the first century. However, an Adventist believes that God saw fit to call another prophet to set up a movement that would usher in the second coming of Jesus. So our church doesn't adhere to the opinion that God would not call a prophet under any circumstances after the time of the apostles. Thus, the Quran must explain itself and justify its existence in the line of the prophets:

> To thee We sent the Scripture in truth, confirming the Scripture that came before it, and guarding it in safety… (5:48)

The Quran repeats itself many times—this was a revelation of God that would protect the earlier revelations (Bible) and help the Arabs understand it.

> This Quran is not such as can be produced by other than God; on the contrary, it is a confirmation of (revelations) that went before it, and a fuller explanation of the Book—wherein there is no doubt-from the Lord of the Worlds. (10:37)

From the Quranic texts, the main reason God gave Muhammad dreams was the lack of biblical knowledge in Arabic (13:37; 26:192–206; 41:3, 44; 43:3; 54:17, 22, 32, 40).

> And before this, was the Book of Moses as a guide and a mercy: and this Book confirms (it) in the Arabic tongue… (46:12)

> But we had not given them books which they could study, nor sent apostles to them before thee as warners. (34:44)

The Quran implies that it was due to the lack of zeal among the people of the Book and the lack of Bibles translated into Arabic that Muhammad was sent to them. Muhammad reports that God told him even the following:

> Had we revealed it to any of the non-Arabs, and had he [Muhammad] recited it to them, they would not have believed in it. (26:198, 199)

In fact, according to the Quran, God told Muhammad: "Nothing is said to thee that was not said to the apostles before thee…" (41:43). According to these texts Muhammad cannot be charged with introducing "new revelation" that would replace the Bible or a new religion that was meant to supplant Christianity. He believed that these revelations would make it possible for many to be led from the darkness of their pagan religion to the light and salvation of the one true God (10:57; 14:1; 26:1–10; 27:1–5; 42:51–53). This is what Muhammad stated to the Christians who came to try to prove to him that Christianity was superior to Islam:

> Will ye dispute with us about God, seeing that He is our Lord and your Lord; that we are responsible for our doings and ye for yours; and that we are sincere (in our faith) in Him? (2:139)

The Quran goes on to make this quite surprising statement:

> So if they dispute with thee, say, 'I have submitted my whole self to God and so have those who follow me'. And say to the People of the Book, 'Do you (also) submit yourselves?' If they do, they are in right guidance… (3:20)

This obviously is a rebuke to both modern Christians and Muslims who believe that Muhammad wanted to abolish or supersede Christianity. Muhammad said that if Christians "submit" themselves to God they are in "right guidance."

Muhammad approved of sincere Christians who were not just "political" Christians or proud heretics. While Muhammad does criticize Jews and Christians, his main criticisms are reserved for the pagans of Mecca and some of the Jews amongst whom he lived in Medinah. His warmest affections were reserved for the Christians of his day:

> Strongest among men in enmity to the believers wilt thou find the Jews and the pagans; and nearest among them in love to the believers wilt thou find those who say, 'We are Christians': because amongst these are men devoted to learning

and men who have renounced the world and they are not arrogant. And when they listen to the revelation received by the apostle, thou wilt see their eyes overflowing with tears, for they recognize the truth: they pray: 'Our Lord! We believe; write us down among the witnesses. What cause can we have not to believe in God and the truth which has come to us, seeing that we long for our Lord to admit us to the company of the righteous?' And for this their prayer hath God rewarded them with gardens, with rivers flowing underneath, - their eternal home. (5:82–85)

It is clear from the above passages that Muhammad wasn't attempting to undermine or supersede Christianity. His purpose, as he understood it from the revelations of the Quran, was to lead his people (the Arabs) from the darkness of paganism into the light of the salvation of the God of Abraham. As we just read, he states very clearly that there are some in Christianity who are true believers and will inherit eternal life. But he also states that there are some who are apostate, and he warns people not to listen to them (3:100; 4:51–55).

One passage will serve as an example that speaks very clearly in the Quran. It is a passage written when people had approached Muhammad asking him when the "final hour" or day of judgment would arrive. God instructed him with the following:

Say: 'I have no power over any good or harm to myself except as God willeth. If I had knowledge of the unseen, I should have multiplied all good, and no evil should have touched me: I am but a warner, and a bringer of glad tidings to those who have faith. (7:188)

According to the Quran, Muhammad was to warn those who were polytheists and didn't worship the true God but bring "glad tidings" to those who already had faith, that is, those who believed in the God of the Bible. This is foundational for the remainder of this study, so it is worth repeating before going on—the Quran teaches the following about the Bible and people of the Book:

- The prophets of the Bible are authentic

- The Quran was sent to protect the Bible

- Nothing "new" was revealed to Muhammad that wasn't already in the Bible

- The Quran was revealed in Arabic for the Arabs due to the fact that Scripture was not written in Arabic

- The people of the Book were divided and not teaching the revelation of God

- Christianity is a valid religion if Christians are humble and submit themselves to God to learn of His revelations (in contrast to arguing over the superiority of their religion)

- Muhammad was sent to warn of the day of judgment to unbelievers and to encourage believers

Most of the accusations that are now put forth to dispute the authority of Muhammad's revelations are not new; he had to deal with many of these accusations during his lifetime. Many of his contemporaries believed that the Quran was a forgery. Muhammad declared forthrightly that the Quranic messages revealed to him were in no way a forgery but a direct revelation from the God of the Bible (11:13, 14; 25:1–9; 27:6; 28:85; 55:2).

Others claimed that the Quran was revealed to him by demons. Muhammad responded by stating unequivocally that the Quran was not revealed by demons because in no way would it be beneficial for them to reveal these messages (26:208–220), although, according to Islamic legend, as mentioned in chapter 5, Muhammad himself at first was afraid that he was visited by demons the first time Gabriel approached him. With the encouragement of his Christian relative, however, he became convinced that this was a revelation from the God of Abraham, Ishmael (his direct ancestor), Isaac, and Jacob, and that this was a revelation to lead the "righteous" on God's straight path (10:108, 109; 13:1; 17:9, 10; 38:29; 39:1, 2; 43:43–45).

Muslims to this day acknowledge that Muhammad believed the "original" Bible to be an authentic revelation of God's will to mankind. However, due to a few texts in the Quran in which Muhammad says that there are many among the people of the Book who "distort" the Bible to try to obstruct people from the true path (3:78, 98–101; 11:15–24), Muslims believe that Christian and Jewish translators and scribes have distorted the words of the original translation in such a way as to confirm their erroneous conceptions of God. Therefore, a huge number of Muslims resist studying the Bible (much as most Christians will not study the Jehovah Witnesses' Bible translation). However, this was not always so in the Muslim world. This development will be examined in chapter 8.

In summary, from the Quran it is evident that Muhammad believed himself to be in the line of biblical prophets witnessing to the One God of the universe, the Creator of heaven and earth, the Revealer of the Bible, the Sender of Jesus, and the Master of the day of judgment. This is critical in our study of this topic, because according to the Quran a Bible-believing Christian should be the best judge of the authenticity of Muhammad's message. In Sura 10:94 God told Muhammad: "If thou were in doubt as to what We have revealed unto thee [Muhammad], then ask those who have been reading the Book from before thee."

Therefore, our hermeneutic could already be delineated as the following:

- The Quran should be allowed to interpret itself when possible.

- If it is not possible to make an accurate judgment based on the text of the Quran, the Bible should be referenced.

- If there are two or more explanations of a certain text, the one that agrees with the Bible should be accepted.

Because of Muhammad's claims, if it is found that the Quran deviates from Scripture, it will be easy to pronounce him a false prophet.

The Characteristics of God

Many Christians believe that the God of the Quran is not the same god as the God of the Bible; however, Muhammad states otherwise—he believed that the God of the Jews and Christians is the same God of Quranic revelation (2:139). These are the characteristics of God in the Quran:

- The one and only eternal God—there is no other (2:163, 177, 255; 3:2, 18, 62; 4:87; 112:4)

- God is full of grace, most forgiving (1:1; 3:89, 155; 5:74, 98, 101; 6:12, 54; 9:117, 118; 10:107; 16:47; 17:44, 66–70; 34:1, 2; 41:43; 48:14; 49:5; 60:4–7; 67:2; 85:14)

- The Lord of the world, Almighty (1:2; 2:20, 29, 106; 3:109, 165, 189)

- Master of the day of judgment (1:4; 2:85, 177)

- The straight way (1:6; 2:142, 186, 257; 3:101)

- The Creator of everything (2:21, 117, 255; 3:6; 4:1)

- The Lord of life and resurrection (2:28, 112, 212, 258, 259)

- All-knowing (2:29, 215; 3:5, 29, 121, 153, 154, 180; 4:39, 63)

- Forgiving of our sins (2:28, 187, 268, 284, 286)

- Close to His followers (2:186)

- An answerer of prayer (2:186, 214; 3:122, 159–161)

- The only Source of truth (3:60)

- Always just—doubles good deeds with His grace (4:40)

- The God of Christians and Jews (2:139)

The Quran records God's creation of Adam and Eve, the sending of a flood during the time of Noah, the call of Abraham, and God's dealings with such people as Lot, Isaac, Ishmael, Jacob, Joseph, Moses, Aaron, David, Solomon, Jonah, Elijah, Elisha, and John the

Baptist. For the most part, the accounts of the Quran correspond with the biblical accounts (with a few additional details not recorded in the Bible), and all of these heroes of the faith are extolled for their belief in and faithfulness to God.

As is evident from this representative selection of texts from the Quran, a Bible-believing Christian can agree with Muhammad as to his teaching about God. But some readers may be wondering, "Isn't the God of the Quran a strict, cruel god who enjoys punishing humanity?"

Judgment, Second Coming, and Hell

With the leitmotif of the day of judgment being so prominent in the Quran, this teaching of the Quran, along with the teachings about the second coming of God and hell, since they are closely related, will now be examined.

The Quran states that all are to live with the thought in mind that everyone will meet their Lord, God, to whom they belong, when He comes with clouds of angels (2:46, 156, 210; 4:59; 7:172–174).

The wicked are also raised at the day of resurrection (2:174; 17:45–52; 19:65–70). At some point after He comes, the wicked (those who resisted God) will be punished by fire (2:24, 39, 165; 3:10–12, 131, 151, 185; 4:14, 55, 56; 5:86; 8:14, 36; 13:18; 16:29; 18:102–108; 22:18–22); these include those who haven't kept His covenant (3:187; 4:37; 16:95).

The earth will be changed into a "different earth" and the mountains will be swept away at that day (14:48; 27:88) and that day will come and fulfill what was written "in the Psalms, after the Message (given to Moses): 'My servants, the righteous, shall inherit the earth'" and the heavens will be rolled up like a scroll (21:104, 105).

The "hour" of the day of judgment is known only to God and will come unexpectedly (7:187). The righteous will be elevated on the day of judgment (2:212; 20:104–112; 27:87–90; 29:50–65; 30:41–45). God, who has recorded every good deed, takes this into account on the day of judgment (21:94; 22:66–68; 38:27, 28).

Those who have been given more signs (privileges) will be judged more harshly by God (2:211; 7:1–10). According to the Quran, God does not bring judgment for "one wrong" if a community is likely to repent (11:117), and He does not pour out His wrath until He sends a messenger to warn a community (17:15–17; 28:59).

The day of judgment will be very fair for everyone—everyone will bear his own guilt (21:47; 29:12, 13). The wicked will blame false teachers at this point and wish that they had accepted the "right path" (28:63–67). The demons and the wicked will be in hell together; and this number constitutes "many" (11:119; 7:175–181).

It is not clear in the Quran just how God forgives sins, although there are interesting texts about intercession on the day of judgment. Muhammad raises the question of who will be the intercessor for humanity on the day of judgment (4:109; 10:27; 30:13; 40:18; 73:48). He doesn't directly answer this question in the Quran, but he does state that the wicked will have no helper or intercessor except God (6:51, 70). Multiple times he points to God as the almighty creator of the world and the only one able to intercede for man at the judgment (32:4; 39:44; 45:19) and that only "one" who receives permission from God can intercede (19:87; 20:109; 34:23). It is not stated who that "one" is, but it is clear that nobody except for God's designated intercessor, including angels (53:26), can intercede for a person on the day of judgment.

One of the main purposes of the day of judgment will be to decide who is "right" between the religions (10:93, 94; 22:16–18; 39:31, 46). From the previous discussion in chapter 4 of the state of Christianity, it would be easy to see why Muhammad and other believers looked forward to a time when God would put to rest all of the theological controversies.

Contemporary Christians and Muslims would probably expect Muhammad to proclaim the day of judgment as a resounding condemnation of Christians (and Jews, along with all other religions) and complete exoneration of Islam. However, Muhammad isn't quite so categorical. As mentioned previously he even goes so far as to state that if a Jew or a Christian ("people of the Book") submits to God and what He has revealed to them, then that person's religion is "right" (3:20). He told the Arabs that if they submitted their will to God in Islam it is the right religion (3:19, 83–85; 39:12; 61:9). In any case, Muhammad looked forward to the day of judgment to do away with all theological misunderstandings.

Great Controversy Theme

The theme that Adventists have come to call the "great controversy" is also prominent in the Quran. The story of the creation of the world in six days and the subsequent creation of Adam and Eve are related, and then it is stated that Satan (known as "Iblis" in the Quran) came and deceived them into sinning. Satan caused them to lose their garden home and their happiness, and he is called an avowed enemy of humanity (2:36, 168, 208; 12:5; 17:53; 24:21; 35:5–7; 43:62).

Muhammad states that the reason for Satan's rebellion was that he was proud and when God commanded the angels to "worship" (serve) Adam, he refused (2:34; 7:15; 15:26–44; 17:61–65; 18:50; 20:116–127; 38:74). According to the Quran, Satan has now become the leader of the wicked (16:63) and is trying to "dupe" humanity with his false promises (4:120; 14:22). He tries to frighten humanity (3:175), whispers into the hearts of mankind (114:4, 5), and destroys the messages of the prophets and introduces schisms in religious groups (22:52–57).

When someone doesn't serve God, the One God, they are in actuality serving Satan (4:116–120; 19:65; 28:88). Satan was created from fire (in contrast to Adam being created from "clay") and was given respite until the "dead will be raised" (38:71–86). Satan's ultimate fate will be in the fire of hell where he will be forever (18:50–54).

The Ten Commandments

The Quran states that the Ten Commandments had been given to Moses as a "criterion" for distinguishing between right and wrong and that they would be a security for the peace of those who "fear the Day of Judgment" (2:53, 87, 93, 248; 3:3; 21:48–50). Interestingly, special attention is given to the fourth commandment in the Quran:

And remember We took your covenant and we raised you (the towering height) of Mount (Sinai): saying: 'Hold firmly to what We have given you and bring (ever) to remembrance what is therein: perchance ye may fear God. But ye turned back thereafter: had it not been for the grace and mercy of God to you, ye had surely been among the lost. And well ye knew those amongst you who transgressed in the matter of the Sabbath: We said to them: 'Be ye apes despised and rejected.' So We made it an example to their own time and to their posterity and a lesson to those who fear God. (2:63–66)

There is another story in the seventh sura confirming this passage:

Ask them concerning the town standing close by the sea. Behold! they transgressed in the matter of the Sabbath. For on the day of their Sabbath their fish did come to them, openly holding up their heads, but on the day they had no Sabbath, they came not. Thus did We make a trial of them, for they were given to transgression. When some of them said: 'Why do ye preach to a people whom God will destroy or visit with a terrible punishment?' said the preachers: 'to discharge our duty to your Lord and perchance they may fear Him. When they disregarded the warnings that had been given them, We rescued those who forbade evil; but We visited the wrong-doers with a grievous punishment, because they were given to transgression. When in their insolence they transgressed (all) prohibitions, We said to them: 'Be ye apes despised and rejected.' (7:163–166)

In both accounts those who didn't observe Sabbath were considered to be sinning and were told by God, "Be ye apes and be despised." What is interesting is that God stated that this admonition and punishment would serve as an example to their generation, succeeding generations and to all who fear God (2:65). This is an especially startling statement when one considers the simultaneous movements that have raged in the world starting in the 1840s: the movement toward renewed Sabbath keeping on one hand, and on the other the evolution of man from apes.

It is clear from these texts that at the time of this revelation to Muhammad God still considered the Sabbath commandment to be binding, which would mean that in contrast to the majority of Christians in his day, Muhammad did not believe that the Ten Commandments (and specifically the fourth commandment) were only for the Jews. On the contrary, the Quran posits that Sabbath and the law, which were given as a covenant with mankind, would continue to be binding and should be observed by all who fear God, in succeeding generations after him.

Sin

Muhammad believed that the Quran was revealed to warn unbelievers to repent of their unbelief and evil (10:1, 2; 11:1–5; 12:2; 17:105–111; 18:2; 31:1–8; 32:2; 36:1–11; 38:1). Therefore, God defines what sin is throughout the revelations to Muhammad.

First of all, Muhammad notes that the hearts of mankind tend to stray from God (3:8, 13:1) and everyone has sinned and needs to ask for forgiveness from God (3:16–30). Only with God's help can we determine good from evil (5:100). And God will only condemn a person at the day of judgment if one "ceases not … sinning" (6:49).

Muhammad states that God had even sent suffering upon nations to turn them from evil, but that Satan makes sin "alluring" to the human race (6:42–45). Muhammad counsels Muslims to avoid sin—secret or open—because God will repay them for their deeds (6:120). The Quran's view of evil is that all good is from God and that evil is from our own souls (4:79)

According to the Quran there are four things that are absolutely forbidden by God (7:33):

- Shameful deeds, whether open or secret

- Sins against reason and truth

- Assigning of "partners" to God that are not granted authority by God

- Saying things that you have no knowledge of

Other qualities of the wicked are:

- Hindering people from entering the path of God (7:45)

- Pride and mocking God's judgments when He delays them (11:8–10)

- Ingratitude to our Creator (23:77–82; 27:73; 36:77–83)

- Unstable, like waves of sea, tossed in a tempest (24:40)

- Denial that there will be a judgment or resurrection (25:10–19; 27:67–70; 34:3–5)

- Follow their own lust, divide religion into sects, and change it (30:28–32)

- Deny revelations of God (34:31)

- Deaf and blind to God (47:23)

- After rejecting light their hearts are hardened (71:6–14)

- Mind that is "maddened" and strays from truth (54:47)

- Desire rewards only in this life (53:29, 30)

- Fretful and impatient when evil comes—arrogant when times are good (70:19–21)

- Defraud brothers (83:1–4)

- Violent, and their love for wealth makes them greedy (100:1–11; 102:1–4; 104:2)

However, the greatest sin that one can do according to the Quran is to invent falsehood about God (61:7; 62:5). Muhammad viewed himself as being sent specifically to the Arabs to lead them from the sins of their paganism to sanctification, which comes through the worship of the one true God—the god of Abraham, Ishmael, and his direct descendants (13:37; 26:192–206; 41:3, 44; 43:3; 54:17, 22, 32, 40). Sura 2:151 states:

> A similar (favour have ye already received) in that we have sent among you an apostle of your own, rehearsing to you our signs, and sanctifying you, and instructing you in Scripture and Wisdom, and in new knowledge.

The vast majority of descriptions of the wicked were directly aimed at the polytheistic Quraysh tribe of Mecca that was so vehemently trying to impede the progress of this new religion, which they supposed threatened their source of income.

Grace/Forgiveness

Probably due to the radical elements in Islam, most Christians associate the God of the Quran with a severe, unforgiving, works-oriented God. However, if one picks up an English language Quran and looks at the beginning of each sura, they will find the words, "In the name of God, Most Gracious, Most Merciful." The foundation of Muhammad's message was to return to this god who is the "most" gracious and merciful and will accept any forlorn sinner. According to the Quran, mankind was without life, but God gave us life by forgiving us (2:28, 187, 268, 284, 286).

> God knoweth what ye used to do secretly among yourselves; but He turned to you and forgave you … (2:187)

> God is kind to those who serve Him and will forgive their sins and evil (3:30, 31, 89, 136; 4:110; 9:104; 13:6; 22:50; 23:116–118; 42:19; 46:31).

> O our people, hearken to the one who invites (you) to God, and believe in Him: He will forgive you your faults, and deliver you from a penalty grievous. (46:31)

God gives an interesting picture in the Quran of the sinner coming to the day of judgment:

> On the Day when every soul will be confronted with all the good it has done, and all the evil it has done, it will wish there were a great distance between it and

its evil. But God cautions you (to remember) Himself. And God is full of kindness to those who serve Him. (3:30)

Sura 6:16 is even more direct in its rejection of works-oriented salvation:

> On that day [Day of Judgment], if the penalty is averted from any, it is due to God's mercy.

As mentioned in the section on sin, Muhammad viewed the heart as hopelessly corrupt and acknowledged that it tends to stray from God. He then states that only by mercy can we overcome this evil tendency.

> 'Our Lord', (they say), 'Let not our hearts deviate now after Thou hast guided us, but grant us mercy from Thine own Presence; for thou art the Grantor of bounties without measure.' (3:8)

Only God can give this grace, forgive our sins, and make our conduct right (3:135, 193; 14:10; 33:71; 39:53; 40:2; 42:25). Sura 3:103 states: "And hold fast, all together, by the rope which God (stretches out to you), and be not divided among yourselves; and remember with gratitude God's favour on you; for ye were enemies and He joined your hearts in love, so that by His grace, ye became brethren."

In the Quran grace is what gives the believer strength. Sura 3:107 elaborates, "But those whose faces will be (lit with) white—they will be in (the light of) God's mercy; therein to dwell (forever)."

With God's grace one can stay out of the "clutches of Satan" (4:83). God never changes His blessing of grace unless people change what's in their souls, i.e. they quit asking for it and turn away from Him (8:53, 54). However, the Quran states that to those who receive His grace and continue in it, sin will become hateful (49:7). Unfortunately, Muhammad states, even though God is most full of grace, most people on the planet remain ungrateful for His mercy (27:73; 33:73).

The image of a cruel tyrant God who saves people based on their deeds is a foreign one to the Quran. The God of the Quran is abounding in grace; it is just not clear *how* He forgives sin. However, just as there is tension in the Bible between righteousness by faith, and the good deeds God has created us to do, so there is in the Quran.

Righteousness/Good Deeds

According to the Quran, God is the straight way, and He guides and protects the sincere in the straight way (1:6; 2:142, 186, 257; 3:101; 10:25; 24:46; 28:56). God desires for His believers in this straight way to do deeds of righteousness, and the Quran states that it is important to learn these deeds (since they don't come naturally due to our sinful hearts that stray from God). Sura 2:21 beckons believers with the words, "O ye people! Adore your Guardian-Lord, who created you and those that came before you, that ye may have the chance to learn righteousness."

A very interesting passage in Sura 7 draws an analogy from the story of Adam and Eve,

> O ye children of Adam! We have bestowed raiment upon you to cover your shame, as well as to be an adornment to you. But the raiment of righteousness, - that is the best. Such are among the signs of God, that they may receive admonition. O ye children of Adam! Let not Satan seduce you, in the same manner as he got your parents out of the garden, stripping them of their raiment, to expose their shame ... (26, 27)

In this passage, as noted in the previous section on "sin," righteousness is granted by God and taken away by Satan when we fall into sin. It is not something "earned" or "deserved" in the Quran, but it is a garment, which Muhammad warns not to lose since it is granted only by God.

So what does this garment consist of? The Quran attempts to delineate what it is that God wants to clothe us with:

- Do not only study Scripture, but practice true godliness (2:44; 3:17; 14:23–27; 16:95–99)

- Have a lowly spirit when seeking God (2:45; 7:55; 23:2)

- Be charitable to wayfarers, kindred, and God (2:43, 110, 177, 195, 254; 3:17; 8:1–3; 16:90; 22:35; 30:37–40; 51:19; 73:20)

- Not to seek after pleasures of this world (2:86; 3:14; 17:18–22)

- Have faith and work righteousness—repent, pray, and do good (2:82, 112, 160; 3:89; 4:17, 18; 10:9, 26; 23:54–60; 28:67, 83; 73:20; 84:25; 103:3)

- Think about God (2:206)

- Persevere through trials (2:155, 177, 214; 3:141, 142; 47:31)

- Be near to God—surrender completely to Him (3:14, 102; 73:8)

- Prayer restrains us from evil deeds, so we need regular prayer (29:45; 73:1–6; 76:24)

- Be patient and self-controlled (3:17; 17:53; 41:35; 74:7; 103:3)

- Fight for justice (4:135)

- Gain knowledge and wisdom (5:101–104; 40:67)

- Build character on purity—this is rock and not sand (9:107–109)

- Fulfill the covenant one makes with God (13:18–27)

- Don't murder or commit adultery; treat parents and orphans properly (17:23–40; 23:1–11)

- Praise to God should be on our lips at all times; our hearts should tremble at His word (30:17–19; 39:23)

- Be faithful friends (33:6)

- Be generous and give of our possessions to the cause of God (47:36–38; 57:10–20)

- Don't judge others—allow God to judge at the day of judgment (73:11–14)

- Shun all worldly gain and keep "garments" unstained (74:1–6)

- Don't drink alcohol or gamble (2:219)

- Eat what is lawful and good—not unclean meat, blood, or swine (2:168–176, 3:93; 5:88)

- Should not boast about tomorrow—say "Insha Allah" or "If God wills" (18:23–26)

This summary only touches the surface of all that God expects from believers in the Quran. There are whole sections similar to those in Deuteronomy on laws for divorce, inheritance issues, penalty for murder, adultery, loans, marriage, treaties, slaves, wars, and many other daily, practical issues that confronted the believers who followed Muhammad on the Arabian Peninsula (2:177–283; 4:2–36; 5:105–108; 9:1–20; 93:9–11; 107:2—see Appendix A for full listing).

State of the Dead/Heaven

In the Quran, death is the destiny of all (3:185; 21:35; 29:57). Muhammad was absolutely clear that no one is eternal: "We granted not to any man before thee eternal life (here): if then thou shouldst die, would they live permanently? Every soul shall have a taste of death" (21:34, 35).

At death all return unto "God, their Protector" (6:61, 62). Most Muslims believe, as do most Christians, that the soul goes to heaven and is in essence a living being immediately after death. But as the Bible refutes this theory, so does the Quran.

> Nor are alike those that are living and those that are dead. God can make any that He wills to hear; but thou canst not make those to hear who are (buried) in graves. (35:22)

At death we all return to dust (50:3). There is an interesting text that states that for all who will be awakened at the day of judgment it will have been as "one evening," implying that the righteous have been sleeping and awaken to meet their God (79:46).

In the Quran, the day of judgment is the day of entrance for the wicked to hell and for the righteous to heaven (82:15; 88:23). Belief in a life after death is a central theme in the Quran (2:4; 6:27–30, 32; 13:35; 57:20–24). There are hundreds of texts promising the righteous a special garden that is fed by rivers, which certainly would have appealed to a people acclimatized to living in the barren, desertlike conditions of Arabia. The rivers of paradise are made of milk, wine (certainly juice, since the Quran states that God forbids alcoholic beverages), and honey, and there is an abundance of fruit there (47:15).

God will take away all sicknesses from the righteous as they enter paradise (48:5) and believing families will all live together there (52:21). God has prepared mansions for the righteous there (39:20).

The righteous will be dressed in rich garments and fine clothes and have big, beautiful eyes. Interestingly, in this passage Muhammad states that those in paradise will not taste death, except for the first death (44:51–58). From this passage it appears that those who had believed in God and the day of judgment had repented and prayed but did not escape the death of the body on this earth. But rather they will be saved for eternity or given immortality at the resurrection.

Some of the most interesting texts in the Quran about paradise are the ones in regards to the "companions" that God will grant the righteous. It states that they will have "beautiful, big, and lustrous eyes" (44:54), and they will be chaste and "restraining their glances" whom no man or Jinn has ever touched (55:56) and they will be of "equal age" to the righteous (78:33). It appears that Muhammad was promising men whose spouses would not be among the righteous that God would give them a "companion" when they enter heaven, since Muhammad states that believing families would thoroughly enjoy paradise together in a text directly following one that talks about the reward of the "companions" (52:20, 21).

Contrary to popular belief, the Quran makes no mention of the righteous receiving seventy virgins—this appears to be a later Islamic tradition derived from the Hadith.

According to the Quran, this life is just vanity in comparison with the eternal life that we will experience with God (29:64–68). God will bring paradise close to the believers (50:30–35), and it seems as if paradise will be on this earth, since the Quran states that this earth will be brought "to life" after its death (57:17).

According to the Quran, the righteous will thoroughly enjoy bliss and will recline on thrones (52:17–20). The Quran gives encouragement to those who submit their wills to God and promises a reward of spending eternity with the "Most Gracious, Most Merciful."

Holy Spirit

The Quran also deals with one of the most difficult concepts in the Bible—the Holy Spirit. Anyone who has tried to describe the third "person" of the godhead from the Bible to a new believer will understand the difficulties present in trying to describe a "person" or "being" with a "mind" but who is omnipresent and a spirit. It is a difficult enough topic in the Bible, and it is even more so in the Quran since it deals with this topic very little. But there are some interesting references.

In Sura 78:38 it says: "The Day that the Spirit and the angels will stand forth in ranks, none shall speak except any who is permitted by (God) Most Gracious."

In the Arabic it is not just "a spirit"—the definite article is present which makes it "the Spirit." So, according to the Quran there is "the" Spirit and He is present at the day of judgment. According to the Quran, on that day He will be silent.

So what is the Holy Spirit's role in the Quran? Sura 40:15 states: "By His [God's] command doth He send the Spirit (of inspiration) to any of His servants He pleases, that it may warn (men) of the Day of Mutual Meeting."

One of the main works in the Quran is the work of warning humans about impending judgment. It states that God sends His Spirit to whom He pleases of His servants to aid in this job in preparing people to meet their God ("Day of Mutual Meeting").

Elsewhere, in Sura 2:87 and 253 "the Holy Spirit" was sent to strengthen Jesus. In Sura 58:22 it states: "For such He has written Faith in their hearts, and strengthened them with a spirit from Himself."

A couple things will be noticed in this text. The Spirit described here comes from God—God is the sender of this Spirit. Also, the Spirit is given in relation to strengthening true believers who will inherit heaven (if one reads on in the text) in the context of writing "faith in their hearts." So, not only did God strengthen Jesus with this Spirit, but He also strengthens us as believers.

Suras 97:4 and 70:4 also list the "angels and the Spirit" as being sent by God either to unbelievers or believers to do His errands. It is clear from the Quran that the Spirit is a specific entity that is given specific tasks by God.

Muhammad claimed that it was the Holy Spirit that inspired him with the Quran (16:101, 102; 17:85–88). Even though most modern Muslims deny the Christian doctrine of the Trinity, just as in the Bible, there are multiple references to God and His Spirit. In the next chapter we will also look at what the Quran has to say about Jesus and His relation to God.

Other Topics

A whole book could be written about the theology of the Quran, so I will not be able to go into detail about all the rest of its teachings. But themes that occur often in the Quran include the importance of prayer, believing in angels, God as Creator of the world in six days, importance of treating women fairly, and the importance of fighting for the cause of God (*jihad*).

Muhammad included stories from the Bible in many different suras—stories of Adam and Eve, Noah, Job, Abraham, Isaac, Ishmael, Joseph, Moses and the Exodus, Elijah, David,

Solomon, and John the Baptist. He doesn't recount the stories in detail like the Bible does, but uses them more as examples in his preaching and mainly for rebuking the unbelief of the Quraysh tribe of Mecca, or in some cases, the Jews and Christians ("people of the Book") living on the Arabian Peninsula. There are some differences in the stories, which will be discussed in a later chapter.

Now we will turn our attention to the topic that most Christians love to discuss—Jesus in the Quran.

Chapter 7

JESUS IN THE QURAN

Once when I was attending a seminar on Muslim relations, I became acquainted with a man from the Middle East who had grown up Muslim but had converted to Adventism when he moved to the United States. I asked him one time, "How did you become attracted to Christ as your Savior?" I will never forget his answer—"through the Quran." I was shocked. Up until this point, I had been preaching that Muhammad was a messenger of Satan who was a false prophet and had created a false religion. I couldn't understand how someone could be attracted to my Savior through the Quran—things didn't add up.

So, I began to probe more. "How did you obtain a desire for knowing about Christ through the Quran?" I asked.

"Well," he replied, "I remember hearing the Quran read to me in my childhood and thinking that Jesus was very unique to the Quran. From that time I had always wanted to learn more about Jesus." He then went on to tell me about his long journey of coming to America, beginning to study the Bible, of eventually getting married to an Adventist lady, and finally being baptized into the Adventist Church.

His journey had not been an easy one due to the chasm that exists between Islam and Christianity, between the Quran and the Bible, and the hostilities that exist on both sides. It was a new concept for me to think about—someone being attracted to Christ from the pages of the Quran. Since then I have learned of various Christian missionaries who introduce Muslims to Christ through Muhammad's teachings about Him. This is what has prompted me to study the Quran and compile a list of its teachings (Appendix A) and write this book. And it is interesting that as I read the Quran cover to cover—I was astounded to learn that my friend was right—Jesus (*Isa*—in Arabic) is the most outstanding figure of the Quran.

However, in order to understand the Quran's portrayal of Christ, one must understand the chronology of the Quran. As was seen in chapter 5, Muhammad's ministry began in

610 CE and continued until his death in 632 CE. Quranic scholars have divided his ministry into four periods:

- First Meccan (610–614)—the beginning of his sermons
- Second Meccan (615–621)—after his followers left for Abyssinia
- Third Meccan (622)—after his return from Taib
- Medinah (622–630)—after his followers migrated to Medinah[55]

This chapter will examine the chronological picture Muhammad paints of Jesus in the Quran.

First Meccan Period (610–615)

Forty-eight of the one hundred and fourteen suras were from this period. These suras exalt the One God above all other gods and give many eschatological warnings about the day of judgment and encouragement to the righteous about the day of resurrection. But in all of these suras, Jesus is not mentioned one time. That is to say that for the first four years of Muhammad's ministry and in about 40 percent of the suras of the Quran not one word is mentioned about Jesus. Even though Jesus is not mentioned in any of these suras, there are two passages worth examining from this period:

> Woe to the makers of the pit (of fire). Fire supplied (abundantly) with fuel: Behold! They sat over against the (fire). And they witnessed (all) that they were doing against the Believers. And they ill-treated them for no other reason than that they believed in God Exalted in Power worthy of all Praise! Him to Whom belongs the dominion of the heavens and the earth! And God is Witness to all things. (Sura 85:4–9)

According to Islamic tradition, Muhammad was referring to an event that occurred in Yemen in the last half of the sixth century when a local ruler, Zu-Nawas (meaning "man with curly hair"), converted to Judaism and began to persecute Christians. He attacked a Christian settlement in Najran, and upon realizing that it would be difficult to take it by force, he promised that if all the inhabitants surrendered he would allow them to confess whatever religion they wanted. However, once his goal was obtained, he changed his mind and his army looted the city, dug huge pits, and lit all dissenters on fire. Arab historians documented the death of thousands of Christians in those pits who died for not recanting their faith.[56] Notice that during this time period the only mention of anything relating to Jesus was a reference to Christians. And that reference was a positive one, even praising them for faithfulness to God.

Say: He is God, The One and Only; God, the Eternal, Absolute; He begetteth not, nor is He begotten; And there is none like unto Him. (Sura 112:1–4)

This is one of the most popular texts of Muslims to refute the Christian doctrine of Christ being the "only begotten" Son of God. However, as previously mentioned, Muhammad at this point of his ministry is not focused at all on a doctrine of Jesus. Rather he is warning the Quraysh tribe of Mecca to repent of the worship of their 360 gods and urging them to return to worshiping the only true God of Abraham. So, it would seem out of place for him to be making any kind of statement in regards to the personhood or divinity of Jesus. Muslim historians acknowledge that this sura was most likely a reply to the Quraysh when they asked for the attributes of the god of Muhammad. Muslim historians themselves write that this was a direct rebuke to their polytheistic belief that their gods were "sons and daughters" of the Most High God.[57]

Even if he was rebuking Christians in this text, it could be for the theory of "begetting"—as in having intimate relations with a woman. This concept will be examined later when analyzing the texts about God having no "son."

Second Meccan Period (615–621)

There are twenty-one suras relating to this period. Muhammad's sermons turned into poetry. There is less of the eschatological "doomsday"-type prophecy and more prose tending to point his followers to the God of the universe who has created all things in the heavens and on earth for the enjoyment of His creation. Also in this period, Muhammad begins to mention history more and take examples from the past, showing how God acted in the continuum of human existence. Moses is the most-mentioned figure in this period.[58]

During this period Muhammad reached the tenth anniversary of his preaching in Mecca (620 CE). However, he was not having much success. As examined in chapter 5, in 615 CE a group of his followers had been forced to leave Mecca and journey to Abyssinia where they were protected from the attacks of the Quraysh by a Christian king. Muhammad had remained in Mecca, protected mainly by his powerful uncle, Abu Talib. He persisted in calling the Quraysh to give up their idolatry and to worship the God of Abraham.

In 619 CE Abu Talib and Muhammad's beloved wife, Khadijah, passed away. This was a time of soul-searching for the prophet. His steadfast preaching to his beloved tribe and hometown were not being rewarded with the success he had longed for. Muslim legend tells of how he decided to journey sixty miles to the southeast of Mecca to a town named Taib. There he hoped to find more success in winning converts to Islam than in the wealthy, hardened city of Mecca. The inhabitants of Taib, however, did not accept the message either and attempted to stone him to death; he only won one convert there.[59] Things didn't appear very bright to Muhammad, and one certainly would never have guessed at that time that he would one day be recognized as the prophet of the world's second largest religion. During this period, Muhammad mentioned Jesus in four separate suras.

Sura 19

This whole sura is named "Maryam" after the mother of Jesus. The first part of the sura (1–15) recalls the story of Zechariah and John the Baptist. The story is related of how Zechariah was too old to have children and he cried out to the Lord to give him a child that would "represent the posterity of Jacob … (and) one with whom thou art well pleased!" (6). The Lord gave him "good news" of a son and told him that he should name him "Yahya"—a name that signified that God "conferred distinction" upon him (7). John the Baptist was told to "take hold of the Book with might" (12) and the Quran states that God gave him wisdom, and peace was upon him on "the day that he was born, the day that he dies, and the day that he will be raised to life (again)" (15).

Directly after the story of John the Baptist, comes the story of Mary. According to Muslim tradition, this is the passage that the Muslim emigrants recited to the Abyssinian king when the Quraysh tribe sent a delegation to him asking him to compel the followers of Muhammad to return to Mecca. Being a Christian, the king asked them to recite something from their "book" (Quran), proving the authenticity of their belief. They proceeded to recite to him portions of this sura. He was convinced that they were fellow believers and warded off the attempts of the Quraysh to deport them back to Mecca.[60]

> Relate in the Book (the story of) Mary, when she withdrew from her family to a place in the East. She placed a screen (to screen herself) from them; then We sent to her our angel, and he appeared before her as a man in all respects. She said: 'I seek refuge from thee to (God) Most Gracious: (come not near) if thou doest fear God.' He said, 'Nay, I am only a messenger from the Lord, (to announce) to thee the gift of a holy son. She said: 'How shall I have a son, seeing that no man has touched me, and I am not unchaste?' He said: 'so (it will be) thy Lord saith, "That is easy for me: and (We wish) to appoint him as a sign unto men and a mercy from us." It is a matter (so) decreed. (16–21)

This account is very similar to the biblical account: an angel appears to Mary, who is a virgin and promises the birth of a "holy" son that would be a "sign" and a "mercy" to humanity. So what is meant by the word "holy"?

Al-Fahr Al-Rahzi, a Muslim commentator, gives three potential meanings for this word:

- Untainted by sin

- A plant that cleans itself

- Cleanliness

As he points out, many Muslim commentators on this text agree that in this context the word "holy" means "untainted by sin" or "sinless."[61] He also goes on to comment about verse 21 and the words, "to appoint him as a sign unto men and a mercy from us" when he says, "We will make His birth a sign to humanity, in that He was born without a father; and the words 'a mercy from us' means that humanity will receive a blessing through this sign, because it will be a significant pointer to His truth and it will help people trust in His words."[62]

The next few verses of Sura 19 have created quite a bit of confusion among Christian commentators and given them an argument against the prophethood of Muhammad. Verses 23–27 describe Mary being in the pains of childbirth and crying out to the Lord under a palm tree and asking Him to let her die. But a voice answers her from under the palm tree and assures her by saying "cool (thine) eye"—that is, "comfort yourself and be glad."[63] While this account is foreign to us as Christians now, it is similar to the account in the twentieth chapter of the apocryphal gospel of Pseudo-Matthew.[64] In the apocryphal account Joseph and Mary were escaping to Egypt when they came to rest under a palm tree. The young boy Jesus commanded a palm tree to bend over and feed His parents, and he caused a well to spring up from under the tree.

While these stories seem far-fetched to modern Christians, it was probably a common way of recalling the childhood of Jesus at that time. However, since knowledge of the religious milieu of the Arabian Peninsula at that time is very limited, one can only infer from the references in the Quran. This will be a recurring theme in dealing with this topic, and in a later chapter Muhammad's practice of borrowing from contemporary literature of his day will be examined.

Sura 19:27–33 continues by telling how Mary approached "her people" with the baby Jesus in her arms. They began to reprimand her for her "unchaste" behavior and remind her that she is a descendant of Aaron and imply that she should have known better than to bear a child out of wedlock. Then she points to baby Jesus, and they ask her how they can talk to one who is a child in the cradle. Jesus replies:

> I am indeed a servant of God: He hath given me Revelation and made me a prophet; and He hath made me blessed wheresoever I be, and hath enjoined on me prayer and charity as long as I live. He hath made me kind to my mother, and not overbearing or miserable; so peace is on me the day I was born, the day that I die, and the day that I shall be raised up to life (again). (30–33)

Both Christians and Muslims bring this text forward to confirm their own views—and each to prove that the other's teaching about Jesus is false. However, one needs to take a step back and analyze what Muhammad is saying.

First of all, this story seems too "fairy tale"-like for most Christians—hearing a story about Jesus speaking in the cradle. But one shouldn't get caught up in the surrealism of the story. After all, Adventists explain the biblical parable of the rich man and Lazarus in Luke 16 as a parable that has a deeper, symbolic meaning than the surface details of the parable. If we did not, we would have to believe in the immortality of the soul and hell as existing right now.

Secondly, there is no certainty that the words "babe" and "cradle" in this passage have a literal meaning. In the English language when a man of forty years age marries a twenty-year-old woman, it can be said of him that he is "robbing the cradle." Obviously, nobody would accuse him of actually marrying a "baby." Therefore, this Quranic usage of "cradle" could also be metaphorical.

In chapter 6 it was noted that Muhammad stated that he revealed in the Quran nothing that wasn't in the Bible. Moreover, he encouraged Christians, Jews, and Muslims alike to study the Scriptures from before him. In the Bible account of Jesus' life, it tells us that by the time Jesus was twelve He could confound the Pharisees with His religious knowledge. So is it possible that Jesus could have said some precocious things as a child up until this time? One can only speculate, since the Bible records no details of his conversations before the age of twelve.

What is Muhammad trying to say here? We will keep reading with verse 34:"Such (was) Jesus the son of Mary: (it is) a statement of truth, about which they (vainly) dispute."

Muhammad is actually trying to bring clarity to the differing beliefs about the birth of Jesus. In verse 37 he adds, "the sects differ among themselves." In other words, there were many different ideas about the birth of Christ circulating among the listeners of Muhammad, and he is trying to straighten them out. And from his other statements in the Quran, he viewed himself as being in line with the Gospels of the Bible. Verse 35 also helps one realize what theory he was combating: "It is not befitting to (the majesty of) God that he should beget a son. Glory be to Him! When He determines a matter, He only says to it, 'Be,' and it is."

How was Jesus born according to this passage? He was created by the command of God to "Be." Who was His father? There is only one conclusion—God. But wait a minute, you might be thinking, Muhammad just contradicted John 3:16 by saying—"It is not befitting to God that he should beget a son." One needs to look closer at this passage. If one doesn't fixate on the medium of the far-fetched (for us) story, this is what Muhammad believed about Jesus:

1. He was the "son of Mary" (34). This was very odd for an Eastern author to call a boy "the son of his mother." It was usual, and is the usual practice to this day in Eastern cultures to refer to a man as the son of his father. There are instances in Arabic history of men being called the "son of …" their mothers, but it is very rare and probably honorific in nature.[65] However, Muhammad's admission that Jesus had no earthly father is telling in this passage, as we see in his recounting of the relatives contempt for the "wayward" Mary.

2. Although it sounds strange to modern Christians—Jesus could talk as a "babe"! This is very unusual even in the Quran. Nobody else is recorded as having spoken as a baby. In Eastern culture children were described as speaking "in the cradle" in order to signify that they were extraordinary children.

3. He was a "servant" and "prophet" of God. (30) Although Muslims point to this text to say that Jesus was "nothing but" a servant or prophet of God, these are not

foreign concepts to our biblical understanding of Jesus (Deut. 18:15; Isa. 52:13; Phil. 2:7).

4. Jesus was "blessed" and "peace" was upon Him for His whole life. He led a life of "prayer and charity," and he was kind to His mother, and not overbearing and miserable. Jesus would also be resurrected.

The word used here in the Quran in Arabic that is translated "beget" is "*yattaxhidha*," which means literally "take to himself" or "acquire." In relation to children, this word is usually translated "adopt." Muhammad could be stating here that it is not befitting that God would "adopt" or "take to himself" a son. This is a recurring theme in other Quranic passages (10:69; 25:2; 19:93, 94; 4:169). The Quran is very strongly against any teaching of Adoptionism that we know was taught among Christians of that time.

And surprising as it might be for most Christians, Muhammad's position is much more biblical than the Adoptionists—Jesus is the son of Mary because God was His Father from conception—God didn't "adopt" a good man to be His son, or allow the divine *Logos* to become closely associated with a human Jesus as the Nestorians were asserting.

In the rest of the passage until verse 40, Muhammad then calls people to believe in the one true God who shows the "straight way," warns of impending judgment, and warns the unbelievers and those that are in "error" (38) that a day is coming when all matters will "be determined" (39). This is a recurring theme in the Quran.

Sura 43

This is a parable about the second coming of Jesus that was addressed to the pagan Arabs whom Muhammad was still calling to repentance in Mecca.

> When (Jesus) the son of Mary is held up as an example, behold thy people raise a clamor thereat (in ridicule)! And they say, 'Are our gods best, or he?' This they set forth to thee, only by way of disputation: yea, they are a contentious people. He was no more than a servant: We granted our favor to him, and we made him an example to the children of Israel. (43:57–59)

First of all, Jesus is again referred to as the son of Mary in non-traditional style among Arabs. Secondly, the pagan worshippers of Mecca were asking whose god was better—theirs or Jesus. Thirdly, Muhammad points out that these people were not "truth-seekers"; they came with the spirit of the ruling class of the Jews during the time of Jesus Himself—they wanted to argue about this topic, presumably with the intent of proving the superiority of their gods.

However, one issue must be dealt with that is present in this text that will arise again in other suras. God states that Jesus was "no more" than a servant. Muslims now believe that if one ascribes to Jesus any other title more than a "servant," "apostle," or "prophet," such as "Son of God," you are committing blasphemy (or as they call it—*shirk*).

Unfortunately, many times, due to this presupposition, Quranic translators insert the word "only" even though it does not appear in the original Arabic. This modifies the text so that it fits with their belief system.

But in this case, the words "no more than a servant" do appear in the original (*ila 'abd*), so this phrase must be analyzed in its context. Did Muhammad really intend to teach that Jesus was only a servant and not a god?

The Bible also states that Jesus was a servant. The apostle Paul states the following about Him:

> Your attitude should be the same as that of Christ Jesus: Who, being in very nature God, did not consider equality with God something to be grasped, but made himself nothing, taking the very nature of a servant, being made in human likeness. And being found in appearance as a man, he humbled himself and became obedient to death—even death on a cross! Therefore God exalted him to the highest place and gave him the name that is above every name, that at the name of Jesus every knee should bow, in heaven and on earth and under the earth, and every tongue confess that Jesus Christ is Lord, to the glory of God the Father. (Phil. 2:5–11, NIV)

So what does Paul's text have in common with Muhammad's?

1. They are both discussing the superiority of gods. The context of the verse is that the pagan Arabs were trying to compare their gods to Jesus and were asking "which god" was better (and as pointed out earlier, their motives were only to 'prove' the superiority of their gods, not to come to a knowledge of the truth). If Muhammad had believed that Jesus was not "a god," this would have been a perfect time to tell the Arabs, "You are all wrong—your gods aren't gods and Jesus isn't a god, only Allah is god." But, conspicuously enough, he doesn't state that, but merely states that Jesus was "only a servant." Paul's writings also show that to the pagans of his time, to whose gods were ascribed superhuman qualities, the message of a simple Jewish carpenter who was executed in the manner of a vile criminal and proclaimed to be the one true God was "foolishness" (1 Cor. 1:23). This was against all their sensibilities of what would be appropriate for a god. One can assume that is what was meant when Paul in the passage above says that Jesus made Himself "nothing." Both Paul and Muhammad here downplay what Jesus was while on this earth ("nothing" and "only a servant").

2. Both Paul and Muhammad, after downplaying what He was here on this earth, say that God specifically "granted favor" and "exalted" Jesus. Again, it must be noted that if Muhammad had had a view that Jesus was an impostor (since He Himself claimed to be the Messiah), this would have been a perfect time to agree with a "contentious people" who were ready to mock the fact that Jesus was supposedly

a god by telling them that God would condemn Jesus someday for making such blasphemous claims. However, he doesn't, and he actually states just the opposite—that God granted favor to Jesus, which was obviously not an answer that the contentious Arab pagans wanted to hear.

3. Both Paul and Muhammad in these passages hold up Jesus as an example worthy to emulate. Muhammad states that He was an "example" to the children of Israel, and Paul exhorts believers of Christ to have the "same attitude" of Jesus.

Sura 43 continues:

> And (Jesus) shall be a Sign (for the coming of) the Hour (of Judgment): Therefore, have no doubt about the (hour), but follow ye Me; this is the Straight Way. Let not the evil one hinder you: for he is to you an enemy avowed. When Jesus came with clear signs, he said, 'Now have I come to you with wisdom, and in order to make clear to you some of the (points) on which ye dispute; therefore, fear God and obey me. For God, He is my Lord and your Lord: so worship ye Him: this is a straight way. (61–64)

Many Muslims acknowledge that this passage refers to the second coming of Jesus in the last days, which directly precedes the judgment.[66] Obeying Jesus here is shown to be the "Straight Way." Jesus is juxtaposed with Satan, and Muhammad is clear that one should choose to be on Jesus' side, because Satan is an "avowed enemy." Jesus was endowed with wisdom and was sent to clear up disputes that were raging amongst believers and unify them. He called people to obey Him—a unique reverence toward Him that is commanded in this passage.

Of course, some Muslim commentators see the statement, "For God, He is my Lord and your Lord: so worship ye Him," as an admission that Jesus was a man like us and was trying to get people to understand the belief which Islam proclaims now—that there is only one God (and Jesus not being Him). However, these words are very similar to Jesus' statement in John 20:17 about having not yet returned to "my Father and your Father, to my God and your God" (NIV).

Sura 21:91

The next reference to Jesus during the second Meccan period is a single verse found in Sura 21: "And (remember) her who guarded her chastity: we breathed into her of Our Spirit, and We made her and her son a Sign for all peoples" (91).

Muhammad here reminds his followers that Mary was a virgin and that she and Jesus were "signs" for all peoples of the world. The context of this verse is that Muhammad is recalling the stories of Bible heroes such as David, Job, Solomon, Noah, Ezekiel, and Zechariah and telling them to be careful not to reject God's messengers—they are "signs" for the people of the world to learn from. Again Jesus is considered one of these signs, and the story that is told in the Bible of Jesus' miraculous birth is referenced, which story is very similar to the biblical account (Luke 1:34–38).

The only other reference to Jesus in this second Meccan period is also a very short one and is very similar to the above-mentioned verse in the 21st chapter. It is found in Sura 23:50 and again states that Jesus ("the son of Mary") and His mother were a sign for mankind, that they were given "shelter on high ground," and were "furnished with springs." He doesn't elaborate in the text how this was accomplished, but again Jesus, the Quran says, is a "sign" to mankind, and He is viewed in a very positive light.

Third Meccan Period (622)

This was the period after Muhammad returned to Mecca from Taib without success and with foreboding clouds of persecution hanging over him in his hometown. He was preaching to the other Arabs who would come to the market in Mecca and was gaining more of a reputation as a wise, prophetic man of God among the neighbors of Mecca than amongst his peers.

Muhammad gave twenty-one suras during this period, which became more poetic and narrative in nature. The events recorded and the ideas presented become more consistent, and the rhythm of the suras is more even. The sura that many Muslims consider the most beautiful was given in this period—Sura 12 about Joseph.[67]

There are only two short passages during this period in which Jesus is mentioned. Because of the interesting context surrounding the passage in Sura 42, it will be examined first and in greater depth.

Sura 42:13

Here Muhammad mentions Christ in a list of other people God has "inspired":

> The same religion has He established for you as that which He enjoined on Noah—and that which We have sent by inspiration to thee—and the which we enjoined on Abraham, Moses and Jesus: namely, that ye should remain steadfast in religion, and make no divisions therein: to those who worship other things than God, hard is the (way) to which thou callest them. God chooses to Himself those whom He pleases, and guides to Himself those who turn (to Him).

Again, Jesus is mentioned in a very positive light, but more interesting is the context in which He was mentioned. Sura 42 begins with God telling Muhammad that He had inspired him and had sent down to him a Quran in Arabic. God tells him that he is to warn "the mother of cities" (Mecca). In verse 8 he states that if God "had so willed" He could save everybody and make them one people, but that He doesn't do this because He doesn't allow the "wrongdoers" into heaven. Then in verse 10 Muhammad states that in "whatever decision they differ" the decision is with God. He goes on in verse 12 to state that the "keys of heaven and earth" are with Him. It is in this context that He makes the statement about the religion that was given by God in the verse we just read—and He mentions Jesus in the list of the inspired. He then continues in verse 14, reprimanding the Christians:

And they became divided only after knowledge reached them, - through selfish envy as between themselves. Had it not been for a Word that went forth before from thy Lord, (tending) to a Term appointed, the matter would have been settled between them. But truly those who have inherited the Book after them are in suspicious (disquieting) doubt concerning it.

From this passage the conclusion can be drawn that as of 622 CE one of Muhammad's main contentions with Christianity at this time was their unbelief in the Bible. He says that "knowledge had reached them," but due to "selfish envy" they were now divided up into sects and were not following the Bible.

Also interesting in this passage is that this is a direct statement to Christians and not Jews, even though there were many Jews living on the Arabian Peninsula at the time. How does one know this? He lists Jesus in the list of the righteous, which would have been a rebuke to any Jew that would have heard or read this sura.

Another interesting detail about verse 14 is that he mentions that there is a "term appointed" for the Christians to come to belief in the Bible and repent. Did Muhammad know about the 1260-day prophecy given by the prophets Daniel and John for the Christian church of his time? One can't know for sure, but it is an interesting detail considering the prominence of this biblical prophecy in relation to Muhammad's era of Christianity. The next verse of Sura 42 (15) confirms this understanding of the text:

Now then, for that (reason), call (them to the Faith), and stand steadfast as thou art commanded, nor follow thou their vain desires; but say: 'I believe in the Book which God has sent down; and I am commanded to judge justly between you. God is our Lord and your Lord: For us (is the responsibility for) our deeds, and for you for your deeds. There is no contention between us and you. God will bring us together and to Him is (our) final goal.

Muhammad prefaces this instruction to his followers to give a beautiful appeal to Christians of their time by saying, "now then, for that reason"—for what reason? Christians were appointed a time to come to faith in the Bible and come to unity of belief by a sincere turning from self and sin and returning to God and His Word. This was Muhammad's view of Christianity in 622 CE. He goes on to say that there should be "no contention" between Christians and Muslims—that they both serve the same God and are both responsible to Him for their lives and works, and that both are groups of sojourners upon the path that was laid down by Abraham, Moses, and Jesus.

Sura 6:85

This is a short mention of Jesus again in a list of the "righteous." He is mentioned along here with Isaac, Jacob, Noah, David, Solomon, Job, Joseph, Moses, Aaron, Zechariah, John the Baptist (or Elijah), Ishmael, Elisha, Jonah, and Lot. They are all said to be in the "straight way" (87), and which also includes those to whom were entrusted "the Book." God states that if a people reject those listed, then He will find a new people who will accept them (89). Again, it must be noted that as of 622 CE Muhammad considers true religion as being one that includes both Jesus and the Bible.

Medinah Period (622-630)

This is the period after Muhammad had been called to make the *hijra* (emigration) and escape for his life from Mecca to Medinah. His efforts were now being crowned with more success and the tone of his ministry was shifting from an admonitory to a didactic and judicial tone. There are twenty-four suras from this time period and they are longer, more monotonous, filled with laws and rules, and more prosaic than earlier ones. However, many of them are filled with complex rhythms and literary value. Many of them are directed to Jews—among whom the Muslims were living at the time in Medinah. Very few of them are directed at Christians, but the ones that are tend to be friendly in nature.[68]

Sura 2

This is the oldest of the Medinah suras and the longest in the Quran. Starting in verse 40, Muhammad tells the story of the children of Israel and their shortcomings. In verse 87 God states:

> We gave Moses the Book and followed him up with a succession of Apostles; We gave Jesus the son of Mary clear (signs) and strengthened him with the holy spirit. Is it that whenever there comes to you an Apostle with what ye yourselves desire not, ye are puffed up with pride? Some ye called impostors, and others ye slay!

Some Muslim commentators state that those who were "slain" at the hands of the Jews were Zechariah and John the Baptist.[69] However, that is not stated directly and seems unlikely since God is condemning the Jews for calling some prophets "impostors" and slaying others and the two mentioned in this text were Moses—whose main problem with the Israelites was being called an impostor—and Jesus—who was slain at the prompting of the Jewish leadership of His time also under the pretext of being an impostor. In any case, Muhammad records that Jesus was a sign, was the son of Mary, and was strengthened by a "holy spirit."

Further along in the second sura there is an interesting passage in which God states: "Whoever is an enemy to God and His angels and apostles, to Gabriel and Michael,- Lo! God is an enemy to those who reject faith" (98).

It isn't known whom Muhammad believed Michael to be—the main angel in heaven (as most Christians do now) or Jesus (as Adventists believe; Jude 9; Dan. 10:13, 21; 12:1; Rev. 12:7). However, it is an interesting detail that the Quran claims that all enemies of Michael are enemies of God.

Later on in verse 130 Muhammad begins to chastise all those who turn away from the religion of Abraham. In verse 135 he tells his followers that if a Christian or a Jew approaches them and appeals to them to join their religion their reply should be, "Nay! (I would rather) the religion of Abraham the True ("hanif"—in Arabic), and he joined not gods with God."

Then he states in 136:

> Say ye: 'We believe in God, and the revelation given to us, and to Abraham, Ismail, Isaac, Jacob, and the Tribes, and that given to Moses and Jesus and that given to (all) Prophets from their Lord: We make no difference between one and another of them: And we bow to God (in Islam).'

Again Muhammad is committed to the revelations that were given to Abraham's posterity: the Jewish prophets including Jesus. And he says that they make "no difference" between them. Many commentators say that this proves that Muhammad made "no difference" between Jesus and the other prophets, but it appears that he is actually referring to the books of the Bible as the "revelations" and states that there are no differences between the importance of the revelations since they are all important to God (otherwise He wouldn't have sent them). One can come to that conclusion firmly once we examine the next passage:

> Those apostles we endowed with gifts, some above others: to one of them God spoke: others He raised to degrees (of honor); to Jesus the son of Mary we gave clear (Signs), and strengthened him with the holy spirit. If God had so willed succeeding generations would not have fought among each other, after Clear (Signs) had come to them, but they (chose) to wrangle, some believing and others rejecting. If God had so willed, they would not have fought each other; but God fulfilleth His plan. (253)

This is an interesting passage because it directly refutes that there are "no differences" between those sent by God. And it is doubly interesting in that the only "sent" one mentioned in this passage is Jesus with another reference of being a sign (a "clear" one) and also being strengthened by the "holy spirit."

This passage has convicted many Muslim commentators to admit that there is a difference between Jesus and other prophets, even though they don't believe in His divinity. Al-Baidavi, an Islamic commentator, comments on this text, "God gave Him a special commission and made His miracles the basis of superiority among other apostles (prophets). He had clear signs and great miracles that superseded in number those of others (prophets)."[70]

Another interesting side note here that can be made about this passage is that it appears that the purpose of the "clear signs" (Jesus Himself) was to unite all believers in the God of Abraham, but as Muhammad points out, some didn't believe and some began to fight amongst each other. But even in all of this, God gave "religious freedom" and didn't force them to get along. Yet He continued to fulfill His "plan."

Sura 3

The next mention of Jesus comes in Sura 3, known as the "Family of Imran." This sura was given immediately after the battle of Badr. The context of this passage is that Muhammad is proving the authority of the Bible and the fact that his followers believe in it. In verse 20 he again tells Muslims that if Christians or Jews doubt in their sincerity, that Muslims should inquire of them if they in fact submit themselves to God. He then states that if they do, they are "in right guidance." He goes on to tell of those whom God has chosen in the past—Adam, Noah, Abraham, and Imran (33).

According to the Quran, Imran and his wife (her name is not mentioned) dedicated their soon-to-be-born child to the Lord in hopes that it would be a male. However, even though there seemed to be initial disappointment that a female was born, they resigned themselves to the fact that God knew best and prayed that she (they named her Mary) would be protected from the evil one (36).

Mary was then "assigned" to Zechariah to somehow be under his care. Muhammad recalls how Zechariah prayed for a son who was pure and somehow useful for God's kingdom. In verse 39 it states:

> While he was standing in prayer in the chamber, the angels called unto him: 'God doth give thee glad tidings of Yahya, witnessing the truth of a Word from God, and (be besides) noble, chaste, and a Prophet, - of the (goodly) company of the righteous.

What is significant about this passage is that even Muslim scholars acknowledge that the "Word from God" here is referring to Jesus and that John the Baptist (Yahya—as he is known in the Quran) was the one that "witnessed" about Jesus and prepared the way for Him.[71] Some commentators are of the opinion that this account is similar to the "Gospel of James," which will be examined later.[72]

Muhammad continues in verse 42 and tells of the angels informing Mary about the birth of a miraculous child and exhorting her to be faithful unto God. Verse 45 states:

> Behold! The angels said: 'O Mary! God giveth thee glad tiding of a Word from Him: his name will be Christ Jesus, the son of Mary, held in honour in this world and the Hereafter and of (the company of) those nearest to God.'

This text is especially significant because it is known to be a Medinah sura and the majority of those who were living there were Jews. In this verse Muhammad unequivocally states that Jesus was the "Christ" (in Arabic—*Masih*). This would have left no doubt in any Jewish mind that Muhammad believed Jesus to be the Messiah foretold in the Old Testament, whom the Jews living around him were rejecting.

The Quran again calls Jesus the "Word" and states that Jesus will be held in "high honor" here in this world, and in heaven, and by those who are "near to God." This text, when seen in the chronological sequence of suras, is especially poignant, giving us insight into Muhammad's conception of Jesus. He continues in the next verses to relate the following about Jesus:

- He will speak in childhood and maturity (46)

- He is "righteous" (46)

- He was born miraculously—God said "be" and it was! Similar to Adam (47, 59)

- God taught Him the book, wisdom, the law, and the gospel (48)

- He was an apostle to the Israelites (49)

- He could make an inanimate object come alive (like a clay bird) (49)

- He could heal the blind, lepers, and raise the dead to life (49)

- He could declare what people were eating, and what they stored in their houses (49)

- He was to attest to the law that had come before Him (50)

- He came to make lawful some things that had been unlawful (50)

- He came to show a "straight way" (51)

- He chose "helpers" (disciples) who were Muslims (52)

This is the most positive account of Jesus that we have examined so far in the Quran. And Muhammad doesn't stop there:

> Behold! God said: 'O Jesus! I will take thee and raise thee to Myself and clear thee (of the falsehoods) of those who blaspheme; I will make those who follow thee superior to those who reject faith, to the Day of the Resurrection; then shall ye all return unto me, and I will judge between you of the matters wherein ye dispute. (55)

Muhammad's unambiguous position here is that Jesus was "raised" and that He was taken to be with God.

One must note that in the translation above Yusuf Ali (like all Muslim commentators and translators of the Quran) says that God told Jesus that He would "take" Him, but that is not what is written in the original Arabic—the original states that God told Jesus "I will make you die" (Arabic—"*mutawaffika*"). Muslims have interpreted a passage (which will be examined later in this chapter) to mean that Jesus was not crucified. Therefore, Muslims for over a millennium have criticized Christians for believing in the crucifixion of Jesus supposedly because the Quran says that He wasn't crucified, and at no time died, before God took Him to Himself. However, the Quran (at least in the original Arabic) is unequivocal that God's plan for Jesus was to put Him to death. This topic will be covered later in the chapter when examining Sura 4.

Also, God directly states that those who "follow" Jesus will be made superior to those who don't. It is surprising to most Christians when reading the Quran to realize that Muhammad believed in Jesus as the Messiah whom God was sending to die. God will make followers of Jesus superior to others who reject faith. Again, it must be noted that Muhammad's position in this account is very similar to the biblical account. In verses 64–68 we can see why he was relating this to his believers. He tells them:

> Say: 'O People of the Book! Come to common terms as between us and you; that we worship none but God; that we associate no partners with Him; That we erect not, from among ourselves lords and patrons other than God. If then they turn back, say ye: 'Bear witness that we (at least) are Muslims (bowing to God's will). Ye People of the book! Why dispute ye about Abraham, when the Law and Gospel were not revealed till after him? Have ye no understanding? Ah! Ye are those who fell to disputing (even) in matters of which ye had some knowledge! But why dispute ye in matters of which ye have no knowledge? It is God Who knows and ye know not! Abraham was not a Jew nor yet a Christian; But he was true in Faith, and bowed his will to God's (which is Islam), and he joined not gods with God. Without doubt, among men, the nearest of kin to Abraham, are those who follow him, as are also this Apostle and those who believe: And God is the Protector of those who have faith.'

It becomes clear in this passage that the context of this whole sura is an argument about Abraham, and since Muhammad was living in Medinah when this sura was given, it would only be logical that this was an argument with some of the Jews who composed the majority of the city.

His main point is that it does not matter what one calls oneself, but rather, if one submits his will to God. And if one wanted to be known as a follower of Abraham, one should not just call himself a descendant of Abraham but do what Abraham did. This was also a theme that Jesus touched upon in His ministry when the "children of Abraham" were seeking to kill Him (John 8:31–41). Again, in this passage Muhammad calls the "people of the Book" (Jews and maybe some Christians in Medinah) back to "the Book" and a belief in the Messiah and the special ministry of Jesus.

Sura 4

The next mention of Christ comes in the next sura, Nisaa or "The Women." This is what is written about the crucifixion of Jesus:

> That they said (in boast), 'We killed Christ Jesus the son of Mary, the Apostle of God'; but they killed him not, nor crucified him, but so it was made to appear to them, and those who differ therein are full of doubts, with no (certain) knowledge, but only a conjecture to follow, for of a surety they killed him not. (157)

Most Muslims teach that this text is saying that somebody else was crucified in place of Jesus, such as Judas; and Christians have used this text to prove that the Quran is not inspired. As was just studied in Sura 3:55, Muhammad was clear that God sent Jesus to die on this earth.

When seen in its context, this passage does not appear nearly so controversial. The context of this passage is that God is blaming the Jews for asking for signs to believe in the inspiration of Muhammad (153), for transgressing the covenant that was made with them on Sinai, and in particular, a lack of Sabbath observance (154). God is also blaming the Jews for rejecting His messengers (155) and uttering false accusations against Mary (156). This is a rebuke to the Jews that were living in Medinah. Oddly, in the above passage the Jews who are claiming that they killed Jesus refer to Him as "Masih" or the "Messiah." Hence the translator, Yusuf Ali, put in parentheses "in boast" because it appears that this is a haughty affront to those who believed in Jesus as the Messiah—how can you kill the "Messiah," the chosen of God?

So what does it mean that they didn't "kill" or "crucify" Jesus? The answer is in the next verses:

> Nay, God raised him up unto Himself; and God is exalted in Power, Wise; and there is none of the People of the Book but must believe in him before his death; And on the Day of Judgment He will be a witness against them. (158, 159)

The Quran's line of reasoning is the same as the Bible portrays it—the Jews believed that they had killed Jesus and that He was dead. However, the Sunday morning following the crucifixion, this was not correct—He was risen! Jesus also made it clear that nobody could "kill" Him—He was giving up His life voluntarily (John 10:17, 18). After all, it would be sacrilegious to believe that a created being could kill its Creator without the express consent of the Creator. In Sura 3:55 the Quran states that God told Jesus that He "will make you die." The Quran is clear that no human being could put Jesus to death and/or make Him stay in the grave. According to the Quran, Jesus had to die and had to arise and be taken to God Himself.

The Quran gives an exalted status to Jesus by stating that on the day of judgment that Jesus will be a witness against the Jews who asked for signs, disobeyed the covenant from Sinai, rejected His messengers and in the end participated in the "execution" of the Messiah.

Commentators are not in agreement about what the "and there is none of the People of the Book but must believe in him before his death" statement means. Most Muslim commentators don't believe that Jesus died, so this presents a conundrum for them. It would appear from the context and the overall presentation of Jesus in the Quran, that Muhammad was teaching that all "People of the Book" (and in this case, specifically Jews) should come to believe in Jesus as the Messiah before "they" die. This would have been a very poignant rebuke to the Jews living with him in Medinah, which may have contributed to their desire to betray him in the Muslim battles with the Quraysh tribe from Mecca during this time.

The next mention of Jesus comes later in the sura in verse 171:

> O People of the Book! Commit no excess in your religion: nor say of God aught but the truth. Christ Jesus the son of Mary was (no more than) an apostle of God, and His Word, which He bestowed on Mary, and a Spirit proceeding from Him: so believe in God and His apostles. Say not "Trinity": desist: It will be better for you: For God is One God: Glory be to Him: (Far exalted is He) above having a son. To Him belong all things in the heavens and on the earth. And enough is God as a disposer of affairs.

There are a few interesting things in this text:

1. As mentioned briefly before, many translators of the Quran add the words "no more than" or "only" when referring to titles of Jesus in order to minimize the role of Jesus—and this is one of those instances. Fortunately, Yusuf Ali, the translator of the Quran that I usually use, has the intellectual probity to put in parentheses the words that he adds that are not actually there in the original Arabic—which he did in this verse. So, if one analyzes the context and what the actual text is saying, it becomes clear that it is incongruous to say that Jesus was "no more than" God's apostle. Muhammad is addressing "People of the Book" (Jews and Christians—and as already mentioned he was surrounded predominately by Jews in Medinah). In the exact sentence in which Muhammad is allegedly downplaying the status of Jesus, he refers to Him as the "Messiah." To a Jew or a Christian, this title would make it obvious what Muhammad meant. The Jews would have accused him of being a Christian and the Christians would have thought he was "one of them."

2. Muhammad is actually praising Jesus here as the Word of God, an apostle of God, and as a "Spirit proceeding from Him." He calls people to believe in God and His apostles—which includes Jesus. Again, Muhammad could be considered a "believer in Jesus."

3. Muhammad, according to Muslim commentators, here calls on all believers not to believe in the "Trinity." Since this is such a controversial topic between Muslims and Christians, one needs to delve deeper into this issue. Just as in the Bible, the word "trinity" is never used in the Quran. In this text, the Arabic reads, "Do not say 'three.'" This makes things much clearer in the text, because directly after that he goes on to

say that, "God is One God." Ibn Ishaq, an early biographer of Muhammad, helps one to understand the context of this passage. According to him, Christians of the Byzantine rite declared of Christ, "he is the third person of the Trinity, which is the doctrine of Christianity ... They argue that he is the third of three in what God says: We have done, We have commanded, We have created and We have decreed, and they say, 'If he were one he would have said, "I have done, I have created, and so on," but He is He and Jesus and Mary.' Concerning all these assertions the Quran came down."[73] It appears that the Egyptian gods—Osirus (father), Isis (mother), and Horus (son)—had been replaced in Christianity with God the Father, Mary, and Jesus. As noted in chapter 4, Mary was venerated as the *Theotokos* (mother of God) in Christianity and especially in the eastern Christianity that was nearest to Medinah. Since Deuteronomy 6:4 is acknowledged by mainstream Jews and Christians alike as setting their religions apart in the world as monotheistic religions, one must assume that Muhammad was combating some sect that had, in his words, taken truth to an "excess" and added something that wasn't true—in this case, a perversion of what is now called the doctrine of the Trinity. It may amaze the Christian who hasn't studied the Quran, but many Christian scholars are now coming to the awareness that the Quran actually defends an orthodox position on the topic of the Trinity.[74] God the Father is God in the Quran, Jesus is the Messiah, and the Holy Spirit is the "strengthening and inspiring" aspect of the Godhead.

The next verse (172) continues: "Christ disdaineth not to serve and worship God, nor do the angels, those nearest (to God): those who disdain His worship and are arrogant—He will gather them all together unto Himself to (answer)."

Here is another clue as to what "excesses" some Christians of that time were going to—saying that Jesus didn't worship God and that Christians should worship only Jesus. This obviously is not a biblical doctrine since Jesus referred to God as His God and our God (John 20:17), and nowhere gave a command that Christians now should worship only Him. Muhammad concurs with this. Muhammad directly refers to Jesus as "Messiah" here, which would explicitly put him in the camp of being a "Christian."

Sura 5

Sura 5 refers to Jesus quite extensively. We will begin with verse 17:

In blasphemy indeed are those that say that God is Christ the son of Mary. Say: 'Who then hath the least power against God, if His will were to destroy Christ the son of Mary, his mother, and all—every one that is on the earth? For to God belongeth the dominion of the heavens and the earth, and all that is in between. He createth what He pleaseth. For God hath power over all things.'

Again, this appears to most Christians and Muslims as an outright attack on the divinity of Jesus. However, since in previous passages Muhammad forthrightly calls Jesus the

Messiah to Jews and Christians alike, it would seem incongruous for him to call Him otherwise here.

So one needs to look for other explanations that would agree with the Bible and with other texts of the Quran. One explanation might be that he wasn't aware what the term "Messiah" meant, but that would seem almost infeasible considering he lived among Jews in Medinah when this sura was given. Another, more feasible, explanation is found when analyzing the context of this verse. Ibn Isaak states that this verse was given as a response to the Christians from Nadjran in order to correct the differences of belief in their sects.[75] One of the heresies then being taught by Christians was the theory that God the Father and Jesus were just different designations of the same subject ("Modalistic Monarchianism"—as covered in chapter 4), which would in fact also make many Bible texts inconsistent and almost absurd (i.e. John 3:16, "For God so loved the world that He gave His only begotten Son," or Jesus crying on the cross "My God, my God, why have You forsaken me?"). If the text in the Quran were to be stated as such, "In blasphemy indeed are those that say that God the Father is Christ the son of Mary," it would appear that Muhammad was actually defending a very biblical position. He consistently claimed he was called to uphold previous revelations of God.

His next argument about who would have power against God if His will were "to destroy Christ" would also make sense in this explanation; in other words, "who was offering up Christ on the cross if that was God the Father?" Muhammad actually seems to be touching on one of the deep spiritual truths of the plan of salvation, that Jesus, in becoming the Messiah (which he again calls him in this verse), did give up being "God" in the sense that he became the "Son of man" (as the Bible writers and even He called Himself). And He relinquished some of the privileges that His Father still retained as God of the universe. In any case, the plan of salvation becomes jumbled if one were to subscribe to Modalistic Monarchianism, and the Quran appears to debunk that theory as being inconsistent with previous revelations from God.

The next mention of Jesus in Sura 5 is found in verses 46–49 where God states that Jesus was sent to "confirm" the law that was before Him and that He was sent the "gospel." Then he admonishes the "people of the gospel" (Christians) that they should judge by "what God hath revealed" to them. He also states that God could have made "a single people" but His plan was to test them in what He gave to them as revelation. Again, Muhammad has nothing but good to say about Jesus, and exhorts Christians to be more faithful to their Scriptures.

The next mention of Jesus comes a little later in verses 72–75:

> There will for the wrong-doers be no one to help. They do blaspheme who say: 'God is Christ the son of Mary.' But said Christ: 'O Children of Israel! Worship God, my Lord and your Lord.' Whoever joins other gods with God, - God will forbid him the Garden, and the Fire will be his abode. There will for the wrong-doers be no one of help. They do blaspheme who say: God is one of three in a Trinity: for there is no god except One God. If they desist not from their word (of blasphemy),

verily a grievous penalty will befall the blasphemers among them. Why turn they not to God and seek His forgiveness? For God is Oft-forgiving, Most Merciful. Christ the son of Mary was no more than an apostle; many were the apostles that passed away before him. His mother was a woman of truth. They had both to eat their (daily) food. See how God doth make His Signs clear to them; yet see in what ways they are deluded away from the truth!

Once again, most Christian and Muslim commentators see this text as a clear text that Muhammad did not believe in the divinity of Jesus. However, one must take notice of a few things in the text:

1. Twice in this passage Muhammad refers to Jesus as the Messiah. As mentioned before, it is highly unlikely that he didn't understand the ramifications of this term since he was living at that time surrounded by Jews.

2. It appears that he was dealing with multiple heresies in this passage. This verse is very similar to the one just preceding it in the chapter wherein "God" is not "Christ, the son of Mary." As before, it appears by his argumentation that this is a rebuke to Modalistic Monarchianism when he states that Jesus Himself called on the Jews to worship God, "My Lord and your Lord" (72). This would be an absurd statement if they were both the same "person" and "subject." The Bible states that "God was reconciling the world to himself in Christ" (2 Cor. 5:19, NIV); so one can see what theological problems would exist if the equation was applied—"God = Christ," something that the Bible writers never did.

3. Muhammad states that there is no "Trinity" and that God is not "one of three" gods—a statement that Christians can agree with, if he is referring to the "gods" of God the Father, Mary, and Jesus. And this does appear to be the case when he states directly after the above-mentioned passage that Mary was a "woman of truth" and that she and Jesus "ate their food" (75). It could be inferred from this that there were those who had "joined other gods with God" (72) and stated that both Jesus and Mary were gods and had the same characteristics of Jehovah. Apparently in this case that meant not having any need to eat earthly food. This was considered blasphemy to Muhammad, as it would to a Bible-believing Christian.

The next mention of Jesus comes in verses 110–116. We will look first at 110–111:

"Then will God say: 'O Jesus the son of Mary! Recount My favour to thee and to thy mother. Behold! I strengthened thee with the holy Spirit, so that thou didst speak to the people in childhood and maturity. Behold! I taught thee the Book and the Wisdom, the Law and the Gospel. And behold! Thou makest out of clay, as it were, the figure of a bird, by my leave, and thou breathest into it, and it becometh a bird by my leave, and thou healest those born blind, and the lepers, by my leave. And behold! I did restrain the children of Israel from (violence to) thee when thou didst show them the Clear Signs, and the unbelievers among them said: "This is nothing but evident magic." And behold! I inspired the disciples to have faith in Me and Mine Apostle: They said, "We have faith and do thou bear witness that we bow to God as Muslims".'"

These are recurring themes about Jesus in the Quran: being favored of God, strengthened with the Holy Spirit, speaking in childhood and maturity, being taught the Bible and gospel, being able to bring animate and inanimate objects to life as a Creator (this is another illustration of Muhammad using apocryphal Christian accounts about Jesus), and being protected by God during His ministry. It is interesting to note that in the Quran the disciples of Jesus are described as Muslims, not because they accepted that as a name for their new religion, but because they were submissive to the will of God and accepted what He sent as a revelation.

Muhammad continues in the next four verses to tell of how the disciples asked for a sign of food and how God made a miraculous meal for them. Some commentators think that this is the Last Supper and others think that it could be a reference to the feeding of the 5,000 recorded in the Bible.

Then come the last verses that reference Jesus in Sura 5:

"And behold! God will say: 'O Jesus the son of Mary! Didst thou say unto men, worship me and my mother as gods in derogation of God?' He will say, "Glory to Thee! Never could I say what I had no right (to say). Had I said such a thing, Thou wouldst indeed have known it. Thou knowest what is in my heart, though I know not what is in Thine. For Thou Knowest in full all that is hidden." (116)

This is a clear text in helping us understand Muhammad's context where he was living. It is apparent that there were those who were ascribing to Mary and Jesus that which belongs only to God the Father, as was seen before in this sura, that they were not really "human" and had no need of eating.

The statement here does raise some Christians' eyebrows where Jesus states that He doesn't know what is in God's heart, although God knows what is in His. However, Jesus' own statement also raises the eyebrows of many believers for He said, "I can of Myself do nothing" (John 5:30). Again, He said that "My Father only" knows the hour and the day of His second coming (Matt. 24:36). We must admit as Christians that based on the Bible, knowledge of the relationship within the Godhead is still, for the most part, a mystery to mankind, and there are precious few details of how each interacts with the others.

Sura 9:30, 31

This is one of the most complex texts in the Quran that mentions Jesus. First, the concept of the word "son" in Arabic must be analyzed and how Muhammad used it (the reader may reference appendix B for a more in-depth word study done by an Adventist scholar, Edwin Dysinger).

Unlike English, there are two words in Arabic that signify what English speakers call a "son." The first is *walad*, which denotes "offspring"; the other word is *ibn*, which can mean being a son through a relationship of love or adoption.[76] The Quran is categorically against God having a *walad* for this would put the God of Abraham, the Creator of the universe, on a level with the previous Arabic gods who had intimate physical relations in order to procreate. The God of the Quran can speak things into existence. Any association of the word *walad* with Jesus is rejected as heresy and denounced in the Quran.

Usually the term *ibn* is associated with Jesus in the Quran, and He is known as the *ibn* of Mary. This is similar to the usage of the two Greek words for "son" in the New Testament.[77] Sura 9 is the only place where Jesus is referenced as an *ibn* of God.

> The Jews call 'Uzair a son of God and the Christians call Christ the Son of God. That is a saying from their mouth; (in this) they but imitate what the unbelievers of old used to say. God's curse be on them: how they are deluded away from the Truth! They take their priests and their anchorites to be their lords in derogation of God, and (they take as their Lord) Christ the son of Mary; yet they were commanded to worship but One God: There is no god but He. Praise and glory to Him. (Far is He) from having the partners they associate (with Him). (30, 31)

Most Muslim commentators agree that 'Uzair is the biblical Ezra.[78] This verse is interpreted by many Christians and Muslims to roundly denounce the theory of the divinity of Christ. One of the main reasons is that the word used here is *ibn* for being the "Son of God." Upon deeper analysis of the text, the following must be noted:

1. A key phrase in understanding this text is "they but imitate what the unbelievers of old used to say." Whatever he had against the Jews and Christians of his time, it reminded Muhammad of the pagan Arabs who occupied the Arabian Peninsula before him. Due to their claims about Ezra and Jesus, he issued this warning because they were continuing their pagan ways. Thus many commentators believe that even though Muhammad uses the word *ibn* here, that the false Christians and Jews still implied that if the Messiah was the *ibn* of God that that entailed having a sexual encounter with a woman.[79]

2. Others suggest that this meant saint-worship since priests and "anchorites" (monks) are mentioned here as being as "lords in derogation of God."[80] In any case, Muhammad viewed this as a return to paganism.

3. The translator Yusuf Ali is honest enough to put the words that he added which are not in the Arabic original, and one notices that the words *"they take as their Lord"* were added when referencing Christians' blasphemy in taking Christ the son of Mary as their Lord. This makes it appear that by claiming Christ as Lord that the Christian is ascribing "partners" to God and thereby committing blasphemy.

> However, the text needs to be read without the words in parentheses: "They take their priests and their anchorites to be their lords in derogation of God and Christ the son of Mary."

It reads a lot differently if one doesn't add any words! In other words, in the original it appears Muhammad is actually reprimanding Jews for taking their priests as "lords" instead of God and Christians for taking their monks ("anchorites") as "lords" instead of Christ, the son of Mary. Oddly enough, it appears that instead of saying that it is a blasphemy to worship Jesus, he is exhorting the Christians to return to Him. It would seem this would be a much better translation of the text for the following reasons:

- This would fit the pattern of the texts that have been examined so far about the "exalted" status of Jesus, and the fact that Muhammad is so profuse with his praise of Jesus throughout the Quran.

- This would also fit what is known about Judaism and Christianity of that time—they had taken the Word of God out of the hands of the people and were adding whatever they wanted to their theology.

- The fact that Muhammad is condemning the Jews and Christians for insinuating that God had had a sexual relationship with a woman would also fit the last line of verse 31 where Muhammad talks about not "associating partners" with God.

Additionally, the passage states that the Messiah is the "son of Mary," which is an obvious reference to Jesus, and that he would have been considered a "Christian" by the Jews in Medina of his day for stating this. Again, he is clear that he is against the pagan concept of the procreation of the gods sneaking into Judaism and Christianity of his time, and he is reprimanding the Jews and Christians in Arabia for taking humans as their guides instead of God and Jesus.

Sura 57:27

The next mention of Jesus is found in this very interesting passage:

> Then in their wake [Noah, Abraham and other prophets], we followed them up with (others of) our apostles; we sent after them Jesus the son of Mary, and bestowed on him the Gospel: and we ordained in the hearts of those who followed him compassion and mercy. But the Monasticism which they invented for themselves, We did not prescribe for them: (We commanded) only the seeking for the good pleasure of God; but that they did not foster as they should have done. Yet We bestowed, on those among them who believed, their (due) reward, but many of them are rebellious transgressors.

This is a very telling verse in that it reveals that Muhammad didn't condone the monasticism that was becoming so prevalent in Christianity. He once again states that Jesus was given "the gospel" and declares that His true followers were granted "compassion and mercy" in their hearts and a "reward" was bestowed upon them. Muhammad believed that true Christianity was not found in separating oneself from society to a life of monastic solitude, but was found in pleasing God by being filled with compassion and mercy for the suffering people who surround all of us. He then rebukes the Christians of his day by declaring that "many of them are rebellious transgressors." This view would be consistent with Adventist prophetic interpretation of that time period of Christianity.

Sura 33:7

This is a short mention of Jesus in a list along with Noah, Abraham, and Moses as people that God "took ... a solemn covenant." This is a fairly inconsequential mention of Jesus since Adventists believe that Jesus (along with the others mentioned) made solemn vows to God to be faithful as His witnesses and apostles.

Summary

The main texts that deal directly with Jesus have been examined in this chapter in their chronological order. There are a few more that deal with Mary and His birth—please reference Appendix A for a complete list. It seems that it would be difficult for an Adventist to criticize Muhammad's position on Christ if he really was combating the heresies about Jesus circulating in Christianity at that time.

Even Muslim historians admit that Muhammad had a deep veneration for Jesus and Mary. The oldest historian of Mecca, Azraqi (d. 858 CE), tells the story of how when Muhammad returned triumphantly to Mecca in 630 CE he commanded that all idols be removed from the Kaba and that all of the paintings of prophets and angels must be washed off. However, Muhammad walked to the column nearest the front door and laid his hands on a picture of Mary with baby Jesus on her knee and said, "Wash out all except what is below my hands."[81]

From the Quran one can state the following about the position of Muhammad toward Christ:

- Jesus is the Messiah

- Christians and Jews are reprimanded for not taking Him as their Lord

- Jesus was born at the direct command of God as Adam was

- Jesus had no earthly father, was born miraculously

- Jesus was not adopted

- Jesus and "God" are separate beings, not the same

- Stating that Jesus was born due to intimate relations of God with a woman is heresy

- Mary was "chaste" and was falsely accused by the Jews of her time

- Jesus was Mary's child

- Jesus was a "sign," "prophet," "servant," "spirit of God," and a "Word from God"

- Jesus was able to do miracles, including healing the sick and raising the dead

- Jesus is a sign for the day of judgment

- Jesus and His followers will be blessed by God in this life and the life to come

- Jesus was given the "gospel"

- God sent Jesus to die

- God raised Jesus, even though the Jews believed that He was dead

This isn't exactly the type of list that most Christians would expect to find about Jesus in the Quran. No one can accuse Muhammad of having a negative view of Jesus after reading all of the texts in the Quran concerning Him.

Muhammad did reprimand Christians, but his overall attitude toward them was more positive than toward the Jews. We can summarize his relationship to Christians as:

- Christians were in "right guidance" if they submitted their wills to God

- Monasticism was not of God

- He reproved them for apparent heresies found in Modalistic Monarchianism, Adoptionism, Nestorianism, and in the movement of the Collyridians

- He reproved them for arguing among themselves and trying to prove their superiority

- He reproved the priests/monks for being corrupt and "misappropriating" wealth

- He reproved Christians for taking their monks ("anchorites") as "lords" instead of Christ, the son of Mary

- He challenged them to study and live by the Bible

Geoffrey Parrinder, a Christian scholar, summarizes the Quran's position on Jesus nicely in his book *Jesus in the Qur'an*:

> The Quran gives a greater number of honorable titles to Jesus than to any other figure of the past. He is a 'sign', a 'mercy', a 'witness' and an 'example'. He is called by his proper name Jesus, by the titles Messiah (Christ) and Son of Mary, and by the names Messenger, Prophet, Servant, Word and Spirit of God. The Qur'an gives two accounts of the annunciation and birth of Jesus, and refers to His teachings and healings, and his death and exaltation. Three chapters or suras of the Qur'an are named after references to Jesus (3, 5 and 19); he is mentioned in fifteen suras and ninety-three verses. Jesus is always spoken of in the Qur'an with reverence; there is no breath of criticism, for he is the Christ of God.[82]

One might be thinking, "How can that be? Why are Muslims so hostile to the idea of Jesus being considered the Messiah now? And why are Christians so sure that the Quran denies the divinity of Christ?"

This will be the topic of study for the next chapter.

Chapter 8

A SHORT HISTORY OF ISLAM

Before Muhammad died after a short illness in 632 CE, he had established Islam in Arabia and had sent one expedition to Syria. At this time Islam was far from being a major "player" on the world scene. However, by 711 CE, less than a century after the death of Muhammad, Islam was the religion of one of the largest empires in the world, stretching from the borders of France through North Africa and the Middle East into Central Asia and India. This is one of the most phenomenal stories of growth of an empire or the spread of a religion in the history of the world.

The Christian perception that Muhammad and his new, violent religion spawned a monolithic, rapacious empire is too simplistic. Without understanding the nuances of the history of the years following Muhammad's life, and how Islam related to Christianity, one can understand neither the present condition of Islam, nor the actual legacy of Muhammad. So, it merits taking a chapter to examine the development of Islam.

Formative Years of Growth
At the time of Muhammad's death, no provision had been made for the next leader of this nascent religion. Muhammad had established a monocracy in Medinah where his civil authority was inextricably tied to his prophetic office. The Quran had admonished Muslims to obey God and His messenger, Muhammad, and those who possess authority or command (in Arabic—*amr*—from which the word for those who led expeditions was derived—*amir*). With the prophet's death came the controversy of who would rule Islam, or in other words, who is the *amir* that should be obeyed in Islam. As Muhammad lay dead and unburied, the elders of Medinah were already meeting to decide who would take his place; when the Muslims of Mecca heard this, they rushed to join the meeting. With tribal loyalties dividing the group, it was finally decided that someone from Muhammad's

Meccan tribe, the Quraysh, should replace him.

The majority gave their allegiance to Abu Bakr who was a respected member of the tribe and father-in-law of the prophet. Many of the Hashimites (Muhammad's clan within the Quraysh tribe) favored Ali who was the son-in-law of Muhammad and the first convert to Islam after Muhammad's wife, Khadijah.

Since Abu Bakr was not elected by the Quranic principle of consultation (42:38), nor was he elected by the traditional Arabic tribal representative council, this opened the door for conflicts between Muslims that still exist to this day. This also played a significant role in the brief caliphate (rulership) of Abu Bakr (632–634 CE). Much of his two and a half year reign was spent fighting wars with factions of Islam that didn't want to pay tribute (*zakat*) now that Muhammad was gone and also defending himself from pretenders to his title.

These wars were known as the wars of apostasy (*riddah*). While they seemed to be wars of survival for Islam, they actually laid a foundation for future conquest by uniting the previously nomadic, independent tribes of Arabia and preparing them for battle.[83]

Abu Bakr and the elders of Islam at that time defined what would become the accepted role of the caliph—the chief leader (*amir*) of the Islamic community (*ummah*) and also the chief religious leader (*imam*) of Muslims. This became the model that Islam followed for the next few centuries.

Before his death Abu Bakr appointed as his successor Omar who had stood by him through his brief reign. Omar ruled for ten years (634–644 CE) and was the first administrator of an ever-expanding Muslim rule. He was the first to establish state registers to record and handle foreign correspondence and treaties, and the first to efficiently distribute vast revenues in gifts and stipends to a growing Muslim population and army.

During this time Syria, Palestine (including Jerusalem), Egypt, modern-day Iraq, and Persia were incorporated into the Islamic state. These provinces soon became centers of Islamic learning and culture. Then one day a disgruntled Persian slave fatally stabbed Omar during morning prayers at the main mosque in Medinah.

Before Omar died he had established a committee of six men to elect a new caliph from among themselves. Two candidates emerged: Ali (who had been passed over twice) and Othman, a rich scion of the influential Umayyad clan of the Quraysh. After much heated debate, Othman was elected, which promptly ushered in an era of political strife and religious debate in an increasingly troubled Muslim state.[84]

Othman ruled for twelve years (644–656 CE). It was during his time that the Muslim navy subdued Cyprus, brought Carthage under tribute, and attacked Rhodes. The Berbers of North Africa were "converted," and Afghanistan was made a Muslim province. The Muslim coffers were overflowing from tributes they received in Damascus, Jerusalem, Alexandria and Ctesiphon.

Othman was a pious and generous man as well as being a close friend of Muhammad and twice his son-in-law. However, he was too biased toward his Umayyad clan and became a malleable tool in their hands, which they used to their advantage whenever possible. His nepotism and abuse of authority was against Quranic principles of justice and fairness as well as Arabic custom, and this led to the first sedition (*fitnah*) in the Muslim community.

The people complained bitterly about one of Othman's unscrupulous relatives whom he had appointed as the governor of Egypt. When Othman failed to act decisively, a mob of angry Egyptians (and locals) laid siege on his house in Medinah for forty days and eventually broke in and killed him. His bloodstained shirt was then carried to Damascus where the governor there, Muawiyah, also a close Umayyad relative of Othman, demanded revenge for this cold-blooded killing. Muawiyah accused the close friends of Muhammad in Medinah, especially Ali, of being accomplices in the murder.

Fearing that this situation might deteriorate even further, the men of Medinah elected Ali as the fourth caliph. Muawiyah insisted that Ali punish Othman's murderers, which he refused to do. This led to the division between Ali's supporters (*Shia*) and the supporters of Othman (now known as *Sunnis*).

Ali had no easy road ahead of him as the caliph. Not long after his election two well-regarded friends of Muhammad, Talhah and al-Zubayr, persuaded Aisha, Muhammad's young widow (who had long held a grudge against Ali) to join them in leading a revolt against him. Ali's forces met them in what is now southern Iraq (near Basra) and the battle raged around Aisha's camel, hence it became known as the "Battle of the Camel."

Ali's opponents were defeated; Talhah and al-Zubayr were both killed. Aisha was sternly reprimanded and sent back to Medinah. This was the first bloody battle of Muslim against Muslim.[85]

Ali moved the capital of the *ummah* (community) from Medinah to Kufah, a town in southern Iraq where he had much support. He was a man of high ideals, and he attempted to remove those unscrupulous officials who had been placed in office as a result of Othman's nepotism. Muawiyah, who had been in office for many years and was a close relative of Othman (of the Ummayad clan) refused to abdicate his position. This led to the next Muslim battle at Siffin (southern Iraq) in 657 CE.

There were two months of skirmishes and negotiations, but finally a decisive battle was fought. Although Muawiyah's forces were more disciplined and highly trained (due to the fact that Damascus was a cosmopolitan and modern city) than Ali's forces of mainly nomadic soldiers, Ali's forces were about to conquer them. One of the friends of the prophet who supported Muawiyah, Amr, convinced Muawiyah to hold up leaves of the Quran on the tips of their spears and call on God to judge between their two forces. Ali, believing this to be a ploy to avoid defeat, refused to quit fighting.

However, a large group within his forces believed that the bloodshed between Muslims must stop and peace should be negotiated. Ali finally acquiesced, and two negotiators were chosen to arbitrate—Amr (a staunch supporter of Muawiyah) and Abu Musa (who it turned out was not a staunch supporter of Ali). They agreed to remove both Ali and Muawiyah and allow the Muslims to elect a new caliph.

However, after seeing that Abu Musa had agreed to annul Ali's caliphate, Amr revoked the agreement and proclaimed Muawiyah as the new caliph. Ali's men who had pressed for arbitration realized their mistake now and considered their proposal and Ali's acquiescence to their suggestion as a sin (*kufr*—act of unbelief). They urged Ali to "repent" and fight against the usurper of his authority, Muawiyah.

Ali declined their offer of support, as he didn't believe that it had been a sin, which caused them to leave Ali and his camp. They became known as "Kharijites" (*khawarij*—"seceders" or "dissenters") and continued to play a significant role in the development of Islamic history.

At this time there was a growing movement that, based upon the arguments given for the election of Abu Bakr, stated that caliphs could only come from the Quraysh tribe. The Kharijites rejected this theory altogether and insisted that any pious Muslim could be caliph even if it was an "Abyssinian slave with a mutilated nose."[86]

They further argued that any Muslim who committed a grave sin was an unbeliever whose blood could be shed and whose property (including wife and children) could be treated as war booty. They accepted Abu Bakr and Omar as righteous caliphs but rejected Othman and Ali as infidels and also declared Muawiyah and Amr to be unbelievers. Having thus condemned all Muslim institutions of the time, they began to indiscriminately kill or pillage all those who didn't agree with them.

Interestingly enough, the Kharijites were very pious men who could stay up all night long in prayer and recitation of the Quran and strictly adhered to the tenets of their faith. Ali repeatedly invited them "back to the fold," but they believed that this would be a sin and refused these invitations. They actually began to fight Ali's forces, and he finally struck them a decisive blow when he defeated them at the battle of al-Nahrawan.

The Kharijites then became an underground movement and, oddly enough, this increased their thirst for martyrdom. They vowed to kill Ali, Muawiyah, and Amr. The two men who were charged with the task of killing Muawiyah and Amr failed and were themselves executed. However, on January 27, 661 CE, a Kharijite assassin struck Ali on the head with a poisoned sword as he was leading morning prayers. He died two days later.

Ali's supporters quickly proclaimed Ali's son, Hasan, as caliph after him. Hasan realized that Muawiyah was no match for him militarily and he agreed to a peace treaty with Muawiyah. This set the stage for the Umayyad dynasty, which would rule Islam for the next century. It was founded by Muawiyah and his followers in Damascus.

Umayyad Caliphate (661–750 CE)

Muawiyah was a shrewd diplomat, and he succeeded in establishing peace and prosperity that lasted throughout his twenty-year reign (661–680). He moved the capital of the Islamic empire to Damascus from Kufah. This fact had telling changes on the realities of the new Islamic caliphate. Medinah and Kufah had had a simple, nomadic Arab lifestyle and the caliphs had lived accordingly.

But Damascus was one of the oldest and most cosmopolitan cities of the Middle East. It is reported that Omar once reproached Muawiyah, his appointed governor in Syria, when he observed the pomp and ceremony: "Is this a Persian imperial state, O Muawiyah?" Muawiyah justified the lifestyle by saying that no one would respect him in Damascus were he to live according to the austere lifestyle of Medinah.[87]

The time of the Umayyads was a time when the emerging Islamic state took on imperial characteristics. Not the least of these was the institution of patrilineal caliphal succession.

When Muawiyah named his son, Yazid, as his successor, it shocked the Muslim world. In both Arab and Muslim tradition, leaders were elected by tribal election. They wanted to avoid the sense of dynastic inheritance that was the downfall of so many states. They believed the caliphate to be a bestowal based on tribal loyalty and merit, not an inheritance.[88] But Muawiyah continued the nepotism that had been so problematic for Othman—and that led to another crisis that still has ramifications in the Islamic world today.

As mentioned before, after Ali's death, his eldest son Hasan had been appointed caliph in Kufah. He was a pragmatic man and had negotiated a peace treaty with Muawiyah, which had allowed the Umayyads to begin their prosperity. Hasan died during Muawiyah's reign and many felt that Muawiyah had poisoned him. Husayn, the next son of Ali in line for the caliphate and a very idealistic man, succeeded him and immediately began planning a revolt against the Umayyads. This idea found much fertile ground in the Arabian east due to the way Muawiyah had acted toward Ali and his family. By the time they assembled an army at Kufah, Muawiyah had passed away and his son Yazid directed his governor in Kufah to intercept the forces of Husayn before he could rally a large army and threaten his empire. The governor sent out a large army and met a band of about seventy fighters that were accompanying Husayn at a place called Karbala. Husayn's forces were massacred, and the heads of Husayn and his male followers were impaled on spikes and paraded around as Yazid's forces took the women and one remaining son of Husayn first to Kufah and then to Damascus.

The massacre of Karbala made Husayn a Muslim hero and has defined much of the Shia movement within Islam. However, it also has affected all Muslims to some degree. Husayn is now known as the "prince of martyrs," and the date of his death is commemorated around the world by millions of devout Muslims. He came to represent the simple, austere branch of Islam and its collision with the more political, imperialistic Islam.[89]

However, due to the fact that Muawiyah was a shrewd diplomat and had designs for creating an empire, the Umayyads turned the Islamic empire into a massive one. The attitude of the previous caliphs was summarized by Omar when it was suggested to him that the Muslims needed a fleet of warships: "I will not go to any spot that I cannot reach on my camel." Muawiyah, though, had no qualms about amassing naval forces. Consequently, the Mediterranean Sea became an Islamic lake at the service of Muslim traders and military expeditions.[90]

Muawiyah and his successors launched military campaigns from Basra in the east into Central Asia and made accessions all the way into present-day Uzbekistan. To the south of that the Islamic empire spread into the Indus valley in present-day Pakistan. In the west their military expeditions overthrew, one by one, Cyzicus on the Sea of Marmora, Qayrawan in Tunisia, Algeria, and Morocco along the North African coast.

The Muslim armies then turned north into Spain, conquering Cordova, Malaga, Elvira, and Toledo. By 732 CE their armies had progressed through France halfway to the English Channel before Charles Martel "The Hammer" turned them back in a mid-winter battle at Tours. But even after this they later took Avignon, advanced on Valence and Lyons, spread through Burgundy, and threatened Paris.

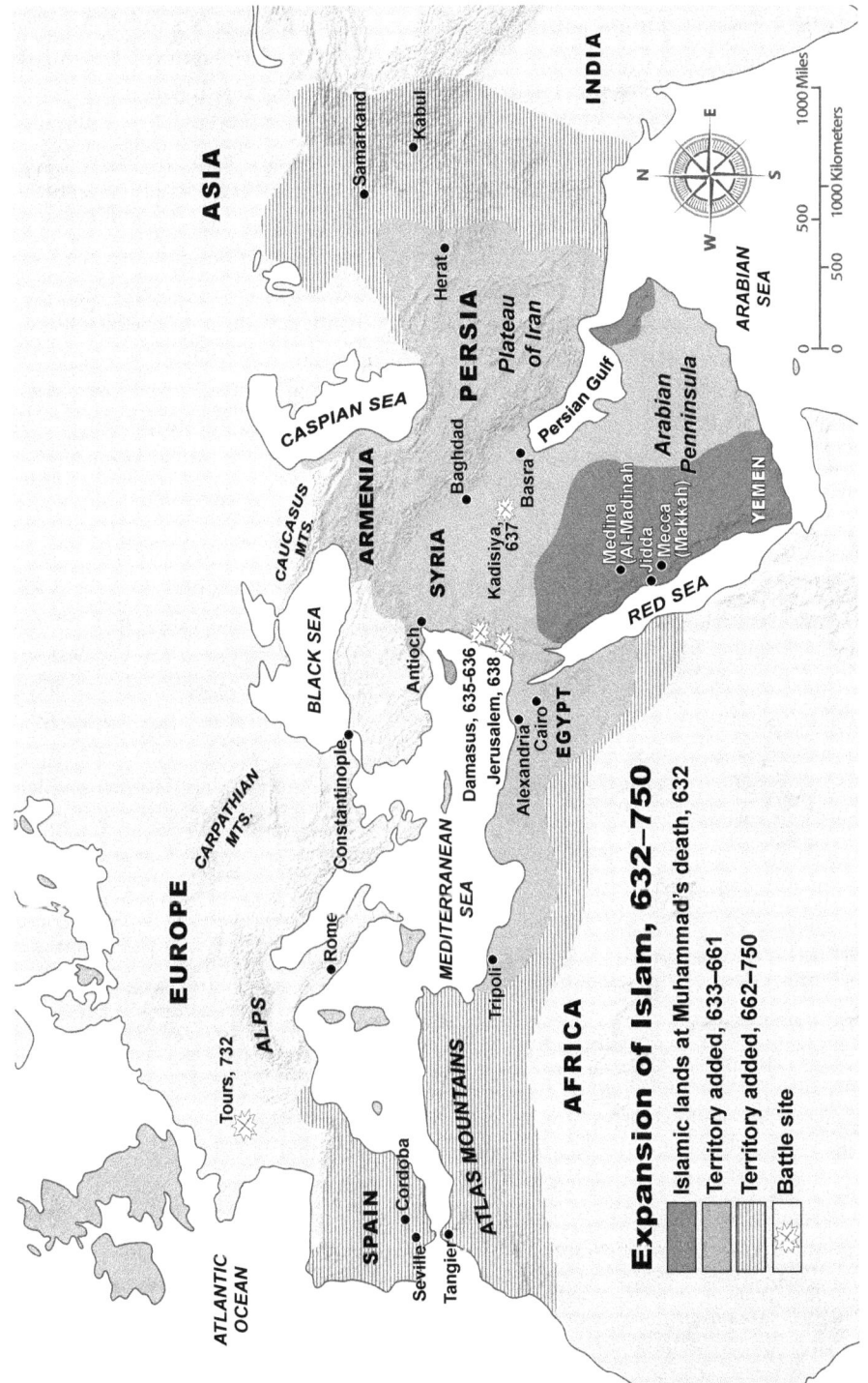

During this time Muslim traders began to carry Islam to China, Southeast Asia, and Africa. By 750 CE, just a little over a century after the death of Muhammad, the Muslim empire extended roughly from Pakistan to Spain, encompassing North Africa, the Middle East, Iran, and Central Asia.

Christendom was alarmed, to say the least, at this upstart religion that had taken hold in many of its oldest areas, places where Christianity had been rooted for centuries. It presented a huge dilemma for Rome and Constantinople that they were now almost surrounded by a mighty empire that would impede any of their designs for expansion. Muslim attacks, although unsuccessful, had been launched even on Constantinople itself during this time, and no Christian countries seemed insuperable from Islamic conquest.

The Umayyads "Arab-ized" the empire—all Persian and Greek officials were replaced by Arabs in the conquered provinces. A new Arab coinage was minted. An extensive postal system was created with a web of routes stemming from Damascus to the provincial capitals. Arabic architecture began to flourish and a base was laid that would later lead to a golden age of learning in the Arab world.[91]

Abbasid Caliphate (750–1251 CE)

The feud between the supporters of Ali and the Umayyads continued until in 747 CE Ali's supporters revolted against Damascus. They proclaimed Abu Abbas caliph in Kufa, and he vowed to rid the world of the hated Umayyad usurpers. On August 5, 750 CE, Marwan II, the last Umayyad caliph, was slaughtered by Abbas' forces along with everyone in his household, except one brother who managed to escape to Spain, where he established an Umayyad kingdom.[92]

Abbas transferred the capital from Damascus to Baghdad, a then little-known village on the banks of the Tigris River in Iraq. This marked a significant change in Islam. The Umayyad caliphate had been Arab culturally and administratively. The Abbasid revolution had been born in Iraq and Persia, and Baghdad was conveniently located with Syria to the west, Arabia to the south, and Persia and India to the east.

It was during this time that Islam began to assimilate the different cultures it had conquered. The Islamic caliphate had become an international one. Harun-ar-Rashid (786–809) is the best-known caliph of this time period, and it was his reign that ushered in a golden age of Islam, whose foundations had been established by the Umayyads. Baghdad became distinguished alike by its wealth, its luxury, its literary brilliance, its schools of learning, and its medical institutions.[93]

The Persians Ali al Razi, ibn Sina and others produced learned works in Arabic. Razi's works on medicine were translated into Latin in Vienna in 1565 and later gained him the reputation of being one of the keenest thinkers and greatest clinicians of the Middle Ages. Astronomy and mathematics flourished; Bagdad's *Bait al Hikmeh* ("House of Wisdom") became world famous. Caliph Al Ma'mun's (813–833) astronomers came very close in estimating the exact circumference of the earth by measuring the length of a terrestrial degree. The Jalali Calendar, originated by the Muslims some 400 years before the Julian calendar, was more accurate than the Julian calendar.[94] As of the tenth century nowhere in the world was knowledge, in all branches of science, so vigorously pursued as in Muslim lands. Their contributions to the world will be analyzed in more depth later in this chapter.

However, the cosmopolitan nature of the Abbasid Empire, which was the main contributor to the empire's success, was also the main contributor to its downfall. The different nationalities represented in the empire began to war with each other, and the empire endured centuries with warring dynasties claiming their right to the caliphate. An example of this was the Turks. In the ninth century Turkish soldiers were brought in to defend the caliph and the capital of Baghdad. Eventually, the Turks took control, and the caliph had to flee from those whom he had brought to protect him!

Finally, in 1258 the Mongols conquered Baghdad and executed the last of the Abbasid rulers. This led to the rise of the Turks and specifically the tribe of Osman in the fourteenth century. This dynasty, now known as the Ottoman Empire, would rule over a huge empire for almost six hundred years and instill fear in the hearts of their European Christian contemporaries. The Ottoman Empire will be more closely examined in the next chapter when examining the prophecy of the fifth and sixth trumpet of Revelation 9.

Again, the reader might be wondering why one needs to examine post-Muhammad Islamic history in this much depth when the Christian is primarily interested in the life and ministry of Muhammad and the role of the Quran. However, even the most casual of readers would notice some trends in Islam when studying the life of Muhammad, the Medinan caliphs, and the subsequent rise of the Umayyad and Abbasid dynasties:

1. One notices that Muhammad and the Medinan caliphs all led an austere lifestyle, and it appears that their highest aspirations were religious in nature. They were committed to this religion of submitting oneself to the God of Abraham and to living according to His will. Political considerations, although necessary, were secondary. However, as exemplified in the struggle between the followers of Ali and Muawiyah with the resulting murder of Husayn, the imperialistic faction of Islam won out over the pious faction. Along with this development came all of the political intrigues that accompany empires. Politics and power gradually came to take primary place in the history of Islam as time progressed after Muhammad. Islam became divided, with competing elements, and religion was used, not to supersede politics (such as Ali did when he refused to abdicate to Muawiyah even though he was outwitted by him politically), but as a tool in the hands of political powers whenever necessary to further the interests of the empire.

2. Greek philosophy began to play a major role in the development and explanation of Islamic theology. As previously noted, Arabic scholars owed much to ancient Greece for the burgeoning culture they were able to create, especially during the time of the Abbasids. However, along with the education and enlightenment of an erudite Muslim class came the dilution of the clear theology with its plain words and literal stories as presented in the Quran. The Quran and its teachings were now seen as needing to be expressed in the vernacular of this learned class if it had

any hope of converting them. Thus, Islam digressed from being a simple religion, which had made it attractive to the masses, to being further removed from the common man.

3. Tradition began to play a much more important role. The Hadith, as it came to be known, was a collection of the sayings of Muhammad. Topics of these sayings range from prophecies about the day of judgment to advice on the minutiae of daily life for a Muslim. There came to be so many of them that Muslims during this time had to verify if they were legitimate or not. Regardless of whether they were legitimate or not, they came to play an increasing role. They still have a huge impact on the practice of Islam. Examples of this would be Muslims' beliefs in regards to clothing, and the supposed seventy virgins that a Muslim inherits if taken from this life in *jihad*. These are beliefs that cannot be supported by the Quran, but they eventually crept into Islam through an acceptance of tradition.

4. Islam went from being a religion oppressed by the Quraysh tribe during the time of Muhammad to becoming the favored religion of a vast, international empire during the time of the Umayyads and Abbasids. Anytime a religion is in the minority it will have a more humble attitude than when it is at the apex of political power. Pride and the desire to dominate, as exemplified in the biblical account of the fall of Satan, is the most insidious temptation for any being or religion. Islam was not immune from suffering the effects of this spiritual disease.

The Christian must be somewhat sympathetic when reading about the historical development of Islam, because it is surprisingly similar to Christianity. The scourges that came upon Christianity when the church began to become more political than spiritual, when the church marred the simple, revealed Word of God by "explaining" it in Greek philosophical terms, when the church began to place the teachings and writings of the early church fathers on a par with Scripture, and when the church ceased to be persecuted and came to political power are well documented facts of its history. The Bible predicted that this would inevitably lead to spiritual decay and forfeiture of God's protection and blessings upon the church.

Spread of Islam
Evidently due to the decline in spirituality in Christendom, Islam, to a great extent, conquered many Christian territories. Bastions of Christianity including Alexandria, Antioch, Jerusalem, Damascus, and the greater part of Asia Minor came under the rule of Islam, with huge portions of the populace accepting the call to submit to God as preached by the followers of Muhammad. And for the most part, those people have remained adherents of Islam for over 1,300 years. So how did Islam conquer so much of Christianity?

Christians tend to think of the rise of Islam as an incursion of rapacious Muslim armies forcing local populations to convert—"or else…." However, even though there was a shift from the austere Medinah caliphs to the imperialistic Umayyads "there was no policy of converting non-Muslims to Islam. The purpose of *jihad* was not conversion, but the establishment of Islamic rule. Nonetheless, partly because of certain disabilities imposed by Islamic law on subjects (mainly the *jizyah*, or poll tax—although they were exempt from the *zakat*, or alms tax levied on Muslims, the *jizyah* was the heavier of the two, particularly for the lower strata of the population) and partly because of Islamic egalitarianism, Islam spread quickly after an initial period during which conversions were even discouraged."[95]

Muslim policies of respect and tolerance for religious minorities are clearly documented well into the eleventh century. Eliyya, the metropolitan of Nasibin (1008–1049), was quoted by a fellow Christian missionary, who himself was hardly sympathetic toward Islam:

> What we believe about the Muslims is that their obedience and love impresses us more than the obedience of the people of all other religions and kingdoms that are opposed to us, whether we are in their land or not, and whether they treat us well or not. And that is because the Muslims regard it as a matter of religion and duty to protect us, to honour us, and to treat us well. And whosoever of them oppresses us, their master, i.e. their prophet, will be their adversary on the day of resurrection. And their law approves of us and distinguishes us from the people of other religions, whether Magians or Hindus or Sabians or the others who are opposed to us…
>
> It is clear also that Muslims, when they have oppressed us or done us wrong, and then have turned to their law … find that it does not praise them for this. So the wrongdoing of the Muslims toward us, and their enmity against us, and their confession that in treating us thus, they are acting contrary to their law, is better for us than the good treatment of others who confess that it is contrary to their law to treat us well.[96]

The *Chronicle of the Seerts*, a history of the Nestorian Christians written perhaps as early as the ninth century by an unknown author, tells of how magnanimous the Muslim victors were to Christians and Jews:

> The Arabs treated them with generosity, and by the grace of God (may He be exalted), prosperity reigned, and the hearts of Christians rejoiced at the ascendancy of the Arabs. May God affirm and make it triumphant.[97]

Many Western scholars, perhaps bemusedly and begrudgingly, acknowledge the superior record of Islam over Christianity in this area of religious freedom:

> On the whole there was more genuine toleration of non-Muslims under Islam than there was of non-Christians in Medieval Christian states.[98]

All scholars, Muslim and Christian, agree that this doesn't mean that there was no bloodshed or instances of forced conversion or injustices *committed* by Muslims. But coercion in matters of religion was forbidden in the Quran, and for the most part, Muslims abode by this maxim for centuries after Muhammad. Even the poll tax for non-Muslims that was instituted by the caliphs could be cited as evidence of this since it would be financially beneficial for the Muslim states if non-Muslims were NOT to convert. While this tax burden would be a motivator for non-Muslims to accept Islam, at least it would have been more voluntary in nature and mitigate the deleterious effects that come with forced conversions.

Historian Peter Brown notes that Muhammad—

> … created a religious empire in Arabia almost exclusively through negotiation…In the first decades of their conquests, the Arabs gained as much by treaty as by the sword: key cities, such as Damascus and Alexandria, fell because the Muslim High Command was instantly prepared to offer generous terms - protection and toleration in return for a fixed tribute.[99]
>
> Peace and tranquility were the lot of those who lived within the walls of the growing Moslem empire. Trade, craftsmanship, scholarship and culture blossomed. "As the storm of the Arab armies rolled over the horizon, the population of the Near East sat back to enjoy the sunshine," … Eventually, the privileges of prosperity diffused to other layers of culture than that of the Arab conquerors. It also offered an economic incentive to conversion. In what might be seen as a giant project of assimilation akin what the United States has been in modern times, the emerging Moslem culture in the Near East became an energetic melting pot for diverse peoples throughout the empire. The door of opportunity was thrown open because "Islam made all its converts equal, whatever their racial origin."[100]

Islam was not as intimidating to Jews and Christians as most Westerners imagine that it was. Rather, it was a simpler, earthier religion (that actually took its holy book seriously) that was based on what we would call the "Judeo-Christian principles" of equality before the law and religious freedom. Jews, for instance, usually fared better under Islamic rule than under Christian rule.[101]

Americans especially should be able to relate to the concept of *jihad* as it was thought of in the early centuries of Islam. *Jihad* was not to impose *shari'a law* by making everyone in the kingdom a Muslim, but instead to spread the rule of law (*shari'a* is just the Arabic word for *law*) that was so lacking in the Christian kingdoms at that time. In much the same way, Americans justify waging war to bring "democracy" to Muslim dictatorships today.

Contributions of Islam

As previously mentioned in this chapter, Islam ushered in a golden age of prosperity in its lands, while Christian lands languished in what is now known as the "Dark Ages." Because this was such an enormous shift for the Arabs to go from being uneducated, primitive nomads to being the leaders of the world in the span of one century, it is worth documenting the positive effects of Islam on the medieval world and the foundation it set for our modern world.

Muslims made huge progress in learning, art, medicine, law, engineering, military arts, business, and the sciences. Muslim scholars brought back to light the works of antiquity and advanced their own theories. Such names as Al-Battani, Ibn al-Baytar, Al-Biruni, Al-Idrisi, Hunayn ibn Ishaq, Al-Khawarazmi, Omar Khayyam, Ibn Rhashud, Al-Razi, Ibn Sin (Avicenna), Abu al-Qasim al-Zahrawi, and Al-Zarqali were all intellects of their time who made important contributions to humanity, but whose names are almost unknown to Christians. One historian describes the true origin of the Renaissance:

> It was under the influence of the Arabian and *Moorish* revival of culture, and not in the fifteenth century, that the real renaissance took place. Spain, not Italy, was the cradle of the rebirth of Europe. After steadily sinking lower and lower into barbarism, Christian Europe had reached the darkest depths of ignorance and degradation when the cities of the *Saracenic* world, Baghdad, *Cairo*, Cordova, Toledo, were growing centers of civilization and intellectual activity. It was there that the new life arose which was to grow into a new phase of human evolution. From the time when the influence of their culture made itself felt began the stirring of new life.[102]

Traditions that quoted Muhammad—"Seek knowledge even in China," "Seek knowledge from the cradle to the grave," "Verily, the men of knowledge are the inheritors of the prophets," and "The ink of the scholar is more holy than the blood of the martyr"—must be cited as a basis for this radical transformation in the Arab world. This is why every Islamic city had public and private libraries; such cities as Cordoba and Baghdad boasted of libraries with more than 400,000 books. It is also known that there were many bookstores in Muslim cities that made a large number of titles available for the residents of Islamic lands to purchase.[103]

As Islam expanded into the centers of learning in Asia and North Africa, it began to translate vast numbers of works from Greek (the language used in such cities as Alexandria) and Pahlavi and Sanskrit (the languages of the Persians and Indians). Arabic thus became a huge repository of the knowledge of antiquity in astronomy, mathematics, physics, and medicine. The works of Aristotle, Plato, Ptolemy, Euclid, Hippocrates, and Galen were thus preserved for future generations to study in Arabic. Hence, Arabic became the most important language of the scientific world for a good portion of the Middle Ages.[104] Some of the contributions of Muslims of that time period will now be examined.

Astronomy

Muslims carefully studied early works on astronomy, such as Ptolemy's and made many new additions. Stars like Aldabaran still reflect their original Arabic names. Muslims were the first to create astronomical observatories as scientific institutions, inventing new machinery to aid scientists in observing stars—the most famous being the astrolabe (which aids in observing the position and in determining the altitude of a celestial body). Ibn Samh even invented a mechanical astrolabe that could be considered the ancestor of mechanical clocks.[105]

Their observations had many practical applications, the most common being the determination of the direction of Mecca, where all Muslims were to face during their prayer times. But they also came to develop almanacs (the word actually being an Arabic word) and very accurate calendars and time-keeping devices. The most accurate solar calendar to this day is the Jalali calendar devised by Omar Khayyam in the twelfth century.

Mathematical Sciences

Al-Khwarazmi was the greatest mathematician of his time (ninth century). He wrote a treatise on arithmetic that brought what is known as Arabic numerals to the West, which eventually replaced the Latin system that then existed in the Christian world. He was also the author of the first book on algebra (itself an Arabic word—as is "algorithm"). Other Muslim scholars developed algebra by successfully solving equations with five unknowns and by classifying algebraic equations up to the third degree.

Other Muslims such as the Banu Musa brothers became experts in geometry. Thabit ibn Qurrah used the method of exhaustion, which laid the foundation for integral calculus. Trigonometry was developed first by Muslim mathematicians such as al-Biruni. A study of the theory of numbers (such as magic squares and amicable numbers) were first studied by such mathematicians as al-Karaji and al-Khujandi.

Physics

Muslims made great contributions in three areas of this field. First, the measurement of weights and objects and study of balance were developed from the original work of Archimedes. Secondly, they developed the theory of impetus and momentum and furthered the work started by Aristotle. Their work helped Galileo in his development. Thirdly, such physicists as Ibn al-Haytham greatly helped to understand the property of lenses in the field of optics; they also discovered the camera obscura, explained correctly the process of vision, studied the structure of the eye, and explained for the first time why the sun and the moon appear larger on the horizon.

Medical Sciences

Since the Quran contains many directives regarding health and hygiene, it is only natural that Muslims would have an interest in studying medicine. Physicians like al-Tabari and al-Razi were the first to synthesize the Hippocratic/Galenic traditions with those of India and Persia. They were some of the first to emphasize clinical medicine and observation and to become proficient in prognosis, psychosomatic medicine, and anatomy. Al-Razi was the first doctor to identify and treat smallpox, to use alcohol as an antiseptic, and to make medical use of mercury as a purgative. His book on medicine was recognized as a medical authority in the West up to the eighteenth century.

The greatest of all Muslim physicians was Ibn Sina, who was even called the "prince of physicians" in the West and who was the final authority on medicine in Europe for six centuries. He discovered many drugs and identified and treated many ailments such as meningitis. However, his greatest contribution was in the philosophy of medicine. He created a system of medicine within medical practice in which physical and psychological factors, drugs, and diet are combined.

Other Muslim physicians are credited with discovering the lesser or pulmonary circulation of the blood and developing the fields of surgery, gynecology, and pharmacology. Muslim cities such as Cairo were known for having reputable, hygienic hospitals where people could get "cutting-edge" treatment for their ailments, including psychological ones.

Natural History And Geography

The vast expanse of the Islamic empire enabled Muslim scholars to study and develop natural history on a large scale. Because of their belief in the biblical flood, they attempted to explain the development of human history and natural history in a way to synthesize their worldview with science. Minerals, plants, and animals were assembled all the way from Malaysia in South Asia to Spain. This enabled them to explain things like the sedimentary nature of the Ganges River basin and the composition of many different types of minerals. They made many contributions in the fields of botany, agriculture, and zoology as they studied animals and tried to make sense of the wonders of God's creation.

Since they traveled so much to administer their empire, and to make the Hajj pilgrimage to Mecca, they studied geography to aid them in these endeavors. Their maps became very reliable and were the basis for Magellan's and Columbus' exploratory voyages.

Chemistry

The very word "alchemy" and its derivative "chemistry" are from the Arabic—*al-kimiya*. Muslims mastered Alexandrian and even Chinese alchemy and made many developments in this field. The alembic instrument (used in distillation) is an Arabic invention (al-anbiq). The mercury-sulfur theory remains the foundation of the acid-base theory of chemistry. Al-Razi's division of materials into animal, vegetable, and mineral is well established. A vast body of knowledge of materials accumulated by Islamic chemists, such as the use of dyes in carpet making and glass design has survived over the centuries in the East and West.

Technology

Muslims assimilated the technological advances of the areas where they spread—the water wheels of the Romans, underground water systems of the Persians, and the use of paper in China, for example—and passed them on to the West. They also made developments of their own, such as new ways of ventilation, irrigation, preparation of dyes, and techniques of weaving, among others. The technology even impressed the Crusaders who took many of the developments they saw with them back to Europe.

Architecture

Muslim architects became skilled in designing new types of buildings. They built domes that could withstand earthquakes and used steel that exhibited great strength in their designs. Such buildings as the "Dome of the Rock" in Jerusalem and the Taj Mahal are exhibits of Islamic architecture. Many of the European designs during the Renaissance were built on theories and patterns exhibited in Cordoba, Spain, during the Islamic rule there.

Learning

The oldest university in the world that is still functioning is the Islamic university of Fez, Morocco. At a time when Europe had almost no universities, centers of learning flourished in the Islamic empire. Much of the Islamic process of education was passed on to Europe through Spain where Christians, Jews, and Muslims lived together peacefully for centuries.

In the eleventh century many Arabic works began to be translated into Latin (often by Jewish scholars who knew Arabic), and gradually the knowledge of the Muslim world, and in turn, the Greek world was passed on to Western institutions of learning that were starting to be established in Europe. Much of the Islamic system was adopted by Western institutions. One example of this is referring to the "chair" of a department and comes from the Islamic tradition of the teacher sitting on his chair (Arabic, *kursi*) in front of the classroom in the *madrasah* (school).[106]

Much of the learning that came from the Muslim world to Europe was due to a German emperor, Frederick, of the Holy Roman Empire in the thirteenth century who was nicknamed the "baptized Sultan of Sicily" (the place he ruled from). He was a most unusual European ruler in that he corresponded with Arab scholars and invited them to Sicily. Latin, Greek, and Arabic became common in Sicily, and he established the first European university by a definite charter—the university of Naples in 1224.[107] Sicily began to prosper, which drew the wrath of the pope in Rome, but Frederick continued in educational and scientific progress and soon became the envy of the other German princes. This revival of learning, flowing from the Muslim world through Sicily into Europe (and specifically Germany) helped create the atmosphere necessary, not only for the Renaissance, but also for the German Protestant Reformation that would occur in the fifteenth and sixteenth centuries.

Saving the Bible?

Even though Muslims made huge contributions to humanity and its progress, a Christian can be even more thankful for the contributions they made in the spiritual realm. Most Christians don't realize the debt owed to Muslims whenever a copy of the Bible is read. In the Middle Ages, as already noted, it was not in the interest of the Christian church for its members to know the Bible, because many of their teachings would have been seen for what they were—deceptions. So the church adopted Latin as its official language and forbade the translation of the Bible into any other language. Conveniently, Latin became less and less spoken in Christian lands, which played right into the hands of a corrupt priesthood in the church.

So, firstly, for Christians in Muslim lands, the fact that the Quran told parts of or even referred to the Bible stories of Adam, Noah, David, Solomon, and Jesus would have given some light to them. Secondly, both Greek and Hebrew were becoming dead languages. The Arab Muslims had a great interest in keeping Greek alive. They were very active in learning Greek and translating works from Greek into Arabic, which eventually saved a knowledge of the Greek language for European Christians, and specifically, the Protestant reformers who were so keen on getting a correct translation of the New Testament.

Additionally, Muslims can be given much credit when it comes to Hebrew. After the destruction of Jerusalem and the dispersion of the Jews into many lands, Hebrew gradually became a dead language. Scholars didn't know how to pronounce words and didn't know which vowels went with which words (since Semitic languages don't print vowels—only consonants). This meant that little by little the rules of Hebrew grammar were being lost to humanity.

However, when the Muslims began to rule, they began working on a compendium of Arabic grammar. Since Arabic is a cognate of Hebrew, the Jews in the Muslim empire decided they wanted one for Hebrew as well. So they worked off of the Arabic vowel structures and gradually began to recover the pronunciations, vowels, and grammatical rules. One biblical scholar says this:

> We owe a great debt to Arabic in the field of Old Testament studies. As soon as Arabic became an imperial language the Jews perceived its close affinity with Hebrew. In the third century of the Hijra [10th century C.E.] the Jews had imitated the Arabs, or rather, the non-Arab Muslims, and submitted their language to a grammatical analysis. The grammar of Rabbi David Qimhi (d. ca. 1235 C.E.), which exercised a profound influence on the subsequent study of Hebrew among Christians, borrows a great deal from Arabic sources. His exegesis, which was founded on his Grammar, is frequently to be traced in the Authorized Version of the Old Testament Scriptures.[108]

It is too easy to be prejudiced against other people groups or religions, and therefore, one must guard against minimizing the actual accomplishments and positive aspects of a religion that it is popular to criticize in this society. Westerners should be very thankful to Muslims with their scientific and literary achievement for helping the world achieve the Renaissance. And Christians should be most grateful that Muslims laid the intellectual and spiritual foundation that helped preserve Scripture, which when translated into our native tongues, in turn helped stimulate the Protestant Reformation. God could have worked through someone else, but He didn't—He accomplished His great designs through the Muslims of the early Middle Ages.

The reader might be wondering, "If Islam was such a great development, what has happened to make it appear as such an oppressive religion today?"

Ibn Hazm and the Doctrine of *Tahrif*

Islam enjoyed this golden age of its scientific, literary, business, and religious achievements and might have enjoyed its preeminence over Christianity (even though it committed some of the same mistakes Christianity had some 500 years before) had it not accepted another baleful teaching: the rejection of the modern Bible as a direct revelation of the God of Abraham.

The eleventh century was the time period when Muslims accepted the foundational belief that they currently espouse: the Bible (Torah, Prophets, Gospels) were direct revelations of God, but they were incorrectly transmitted down through the centuries and were doctored by unscrupulous Christian and Jewish translators to conform to the biases of their beliefs.[109]

It was an Islamic literary tradition dating back to the time of Muhammad to examine the authenticity of the earlier (Jewish and Christian) Scriptures. As mentioned in chapter 6, the Quran is positive toward earlier revelations, but there are a few Quranic texts that have left doubts in the minds of Muslims as to the perversion of the translations of the Bible by Christians and Jews. These texts all relate to the Medinah period of suras.[110]

In Sura 2:75 the Jews were accused of knowingly perverting (*yuharrifuna*) the Word of God after having heard and understood it. The Quran states that some actually, "write the Book with their own hands and then say, 'this is from God'" (2:79). "These transgressors changed (*baddala*) the word from that which had been given them" (2:59). Others corrupt the text by displacing words, changing (*yuharrifuna*) them from their right places (4:46; 5:14) or by "twisting" their tongues and reading it incorrectly:

> There is among them a section who distort (*yaluna*) the Book with their tongues. (As they read) you would think it is a part of the Book, but it is no part of the Book; and they say, 'that is from God,' but it is not from God. It is they who tell a lie against God, and (well) they know it! (3:78)

> Of the Jews there are those who displace the words…and say: 'We hear and we disobey… with a twist (*layyan*) of their tongues… (4:46)

Moreover, the charge of concealment (*ikhfa'*) is charged against the people of the Book. They know the truth as they know their sons, but some of them "conceal" it (2:146; 3:171). One reason the Quran gives for God sending Muhammad is that he was to reveal much of what the people of the Book concealed (5:16). Jews were said to have dismembered the Torah, making it into separate sheets "for show" while concealing much of its contents (6:91). Of Christians it was said that they just completely "forgot" (*nasu*) a good part of the message that was sent to them. (5:15)

Muslim scholars and clerics debated these texts for centuries after Muhammad. They developed what became known as the doctrine of *tahrif*. Some argued that the people of the Book changed the sacred texts themselves (*tahrif al-nass*) and others argued that they had changed only their meaning and/or added their nonbiblical traditions (*tahrif al-ma'ani*).

Obviously, whichever one of these two schools of thought one believed had enormous implications in a Muslim's perception of Jews and Christians. There is a huge difference between accusing the people of Book of intentionally falsifying the manuscripts and the accusation of merely misinterpreting the meaning of the portions of legitimate manuscripts.

In the eighth and ninth centuries, the charge of *tahrif* was usually discussed in Muslim literature in terms of textual misinterpretation, rather than textual corruption. Even where there are hints of textual corruption, it is not laid out in detail.[111]

Also, despite the disparagement of the earlier scriptures, Muslims held that references to the coming of Muhammad were found in them. So Muslims had two contradictory approaches to the Bible: on one hand, some said it was falsified, and on the other hand, they claimed that it foretold their prophet Muhammad's ministry. That would all change in the tenth century with the arrival of Ibn Hazm.

Ibn Hazm (as we will call him—his real name was Abu Muhammad Ali ibn Ahmad ibn Sa'id ibn Hazm ibn Ghalid ibn Salih ibn Khalaf ibn Ma'dan ibn Sufyan ibn Yazid al-Farisi— try putting that name on a passport) was born in Spain in 964 and died in 1064. He was one of the premier Islamic scholars of the Middle Ages. Biographers have described him as a historian, poet, litterateur, lawyer, theologian, moralist, logician, political thinker, psychologist, metaphysician, exegete, and polemicist. He managed during his lifetime to devote scholarly attention to all the branches of Greek and Islamic learning except mathematics.[112]

Ibn Hazm was born into a privileged family in the court of the Umayyad dynasty that had been established in Spain when the Abbasids came to power in Baghdad. Spain's Andalusian culture had flourished as one of the few places of that time where Jews, Christians, and Muslims prospered together. However, at the beginning of the eleventh century the Umayyad Muslim rule was coming to an end and Andalusia was descending into anarchy. With the fall of the Umayyads, Ibn Hazm lost his sheltered status and was subjected to persecution by the new Christian rulers, which even included incarceration. Due to his volatile temperament and the stridency of the expression of his opinions, he spent many years living temporarily in different parts of Spain until the ruling elite (with whom he usually clashed) would cause him to flee elsewhere.

At first Ibn Hazm tried changing Andalusia by involving himself in politics, but he quickly became disenchanted with politics and dedicated himself to scholarly pursuits. By the end of his life it was said that he had composed some 400 volumes of works (with some 80,000 pages), and he became known as the most preeminent scholar ever produced by Islamic Spain.[113]

For the purposes of our study, I will concentrate only on his work in the field of comparative religions. Ibn Hazm was the first Islamic scholar to take the Quranic charge of distortion (*tahrif*) to its most extreme and literal sense. He studied the Bible intensively and compiled a list of why the extant Bible (he studied the Arabic version) could not be considered an inspired Word of God.[114] Ibn Hazm avoided writing about the supposed texts of Scripture that pointed toward Muhammad and concentrated on the passages that he deemed inaccurate and made the Jews and Christians liars and, therefore, inferior to Muslims.

Charges he made against the Bible were that it blasphemes God (citing the example of God participating in the deception of Jacob to gain the birthright); he said it demeans the prophets by recording their sins; he gives examples of arithmetic and historical errors; and of course, he noted that it ascribes unto Jesus divinity, which is only reserved for God.

But these are just a few of the accusations he leveled against the Bible. The accusations are detailed, and he argues them quite eloquently. Some suspect that his main motives were not theological but were socio-political: he was trying to convince his fellow Muslims to not favor Christians and Jews in Andalusia but to return to *shari'a law* and bring about a Muslim golden age once again.[115]

Whatever his motivations were, Ibn Hazm was a transformational character. Theodore Pulcini states,

> Ibn Hazm took the literary tradition centering on the issue of *tahrif* to hitherto unknown levels of detail and rancor. The earliest examples of the *tahrif*-tradition were quite general, making sweeping claims unsubstantiated by specific proofs. However, progressively detailed arguments, replete, with specific examples, were developed by authors through the ninth and tenth centuries C.E. Ibn Hazm represents the apex of this process. Such a detailed exegetical argument for *tahrif* as presented in the *Treatise* was unknown in the centuries preceding and immediately following Ibn Hazm. The *Treatise* was a watershed work in this regard. Furthermore, the combative and vitriolic tone of the *Treatise* certainly set it apart from other works in the *tahrif*-tradition. In short, no other author analyzing the authenticity of the Jewish and Christian Scriptures brought such rigor and antagonism to the task as did Ibn Hazm.[116]
>
> According to a saying of the period, the tongue of Ibn Hazm was a twin brother to the sword of al-Hajjaj, a famous 7th-century general and governor of Iraq.[117]

Although Ibn Hazm may not have intended it, he became the father of the Islamic doctrine of the illegitimacy of the modern Bible as an inspired document. This doctrine has permeated Islam for the last millennium and has served to alienate Muslims from their fellow monotheistic brothers who claim the God of Abraham as their Ruler.

Notwithstanding the fact that the Quran exhorted Muslims to study the previous scriptures, and the fact that Muslims had helped to save the Bible for the first 500 years of the 1260-year apostasy in Christianity, they now went on a course of neglecting the Bible at best, and at worst, utter contempt for it.

So what were the consequences of the discarding of the "previous revelations"? Unfortunately, the gap between Muslims and Christians grew ever larger until it became the chasm that it is today. An example of this is the belief in the virgin birth of Jesus. Early Islamic commentators taught that Jesus was born without a father—this is a belief that would have been shared by Christians and Muslims and could have been agreed upon from the Bible and the Quran. However, many modern Muslim commentators deny that Jesus was born to a virgin.[118] As examined in chapters 6 and 7, there are many doctrines that could have been shared between Christianity and Islam, but Islam left the Bible completely (and began to leave even the Quran) and Christianity had already left the Bible as the sole authority in matters of faith.

Therefore, we witness the sad reality of what happened during the history of the Middle Ages. Both Muslims and Christians were refuting one another's beliefs and attempting to prove each religion's superiority over the other by accentuating the differences rather than comparing the Quran and Bible and coming to agreement over the similarities. Unfortunately, that tone has continued for the most part in both Islam and Christianity up to this day.

It is also interesting to note that until the time of Ibn Hazm Muslims had been relatively sheltered from attacks by Christians. If anything, Islamic governments had had the upper hand in their relations with their Christian counterparts. However, within a little over thirty years of Ibn Hazm's death, and with Islam's subsequent and ever-growing antagonism toward Scripture, the Crusades of the Middle Ages started, and Muslims suffered greatly at the hands of Christians for the next 200 years.

This leads to the next chapter in which the next time period of Muslim dominance will be examined—the Ottoman Empire.

Chapter 9

THE RISE OF THE OTTOMAN EMPIRE AND REVELATION 9

The Ottoman Empire was the next dynasty that would arise in the Muslim world and would threaten the Christian world for the greater part of the next six hundred years (1299–1923 CE). The rise of this dynasty has fascinated historians over the ages. Why did the Ottomans rise to power? They were only one of the many Turkish tribes that had immigrated to present-day Turkey from Central Asia and were warring against the Greek, Armenian, Arab, Jewish, and Kurdish populations that also resided there. The only reason that historians can conceive is a mysterious dream that Osman, the founder of the Ottoman Empire, had while in the tent of an imam:

> He saw that a moon arose from the holy man's breast and came to sink in his own breast. A tree then sprouted from his navel and its shade compassed the world. Beneath this shade there were mountains, and streams flowed forth from the foot of each mountain. Some people drank from these running waters, others watered gardens, while yet others caused fountains to flow. When Osman awoke he told the story to the holy man, who said, 'Osman, my son, congratulations, for God has given the imperial office to you and your descendants and my daughter Malhun shall be your wife.'[119]

This dream, recounted among Ottoman warriors for centuries, breathed life into their forces and gave them a divine mandate to create an empire that stretched over three continents. This empire finally took Constantinople out of the hands of Christians in 1453 CE, putting an end to the Eastern Christian Byzantine hegemony that had lasted since Constantine transferred the capital of the Roman Empire from Rome to Constantinople more than 1,100 years before. The Ottoman Empire, which reached its zenith during the time of Suleiman the Great (1520–1566 CE), caused the papacy and Western Europe to tremble for centuries.

What is of interest to an Adventist about the Ottoman Empire in the study of Muhammad is its direct link to the prophecy of Revelation 9. Beginning in the sixteenth and seventeenth centuries, Protestant reformers such as John Foxe and Isaac Newton (among many) directly linked Muhammad and the Ottoman Empire to the fulfillments of the fifth and sixth trumpets of Revelation 9. The time of Muhammad and the meteoric rise to power of the caliphate was seen as the fulfillment of the fifth trumpet and the rise of the Muslim Ottomans was seen as a fulfillment of the sixth trumpet.

Significantly, the Protestant reformers identified Muhammad as the "fallen star" from the sky that was given a key to the abyss. Of course, any Adventist Bible student understands the spiritual implications if someone is called a "fallen star"—this is making them an equivalent to Satan (Luke 10:18). If Muhammad is a "fallen star," this would significantly shorten our study about the prophethood of Muhammad because the case would be closed.

However, what is very interesting to note is that Adventist pioneers were the first in a long list of reformers (please see Appendix D) who didn't believe Muhammad was a fulfillment of the fifth trumpet. William Miller and Josiah Litch were the first Bible prophecy students who combined the fifth and sixth trumpets, and saw the fulfillment of the fifth trumpet as the rise of the Turks, and the domination of the Turks as the fulfillment of the sixth. This was a radical shift as, in essence, it didn't necessarily implicate Muhammad as the "fallen star."

As early as 1832 William Miller had completely broken with precedence and had combined the five months of the fifth trumpet and the hour, day, month, and year of the sixth trumpet. Using the year-day principle of biblical prophecy (Num. 14:34, Ezek. 4:6), he came to the conclusion that this would be a consecutive period of 541 years and 15 days (150 years of the fifth trumpet and 391 years and 15 days of the sixth trumpet). Even though many expositors had come to this same amount of time for each prophecy, Miller was the first one to combine them and assume that the fifth trumpet referred to the rise of the Turks and the sixth to their period of domination. He started this time period in AD 1298, the date he considered to be representative of the first attack by the Ottoman Turks on the Byzantine Empire, and projected that it would end in 1839.

Josiah Litch, a fellow believer in the Second Advent movement, came to the conclusion in 1838 that the prophecy should begin from the date of the Turks' first battle against the Byzantine Empire that occurred at Bapheum, near Nicomedia, on July 27, 1299. This brought him to 1449 as the close of the fifth trumpet and 1840 as the fulfillment date of the sixth. Litch brought forth as evidence of the fulfillment of these dates the fact that Constantine Palaelogus, a new Byzantine emperor, had asked permission of the Turkish sultan, Murad II, before ascending the throne of the empire. Litch saw this as the end of the "torment" of the Byzantine Empire by the Turks and the beginning of the domination. Constantine's coronation was celebrated on January 6, 1449.

Litch believed that the sixth trumpet would, therefore, end on August 11, 1840. He began proclaiming in 1838 that the Turkish Empire would be overthrown on this date. This was a bold move, to say the least. He was confident enough that this prophecy was yet to be fulfilled that he began to turn people's attention to the events transpiring in the Middle East. And there was plenty going on at that time.

In June of 1839, Mohammed Ali, who was pasha of Egypt and a nominal vassal of the Ottoman sultan, rebelled against his overlord, Mahmud II. The Ottomans attempted to squelch the rebellion and sent their navy to fight against Mohammed; however, this attempt failed and even ended up with the Egyptians capturing the Turkish navy. Mahmud died suddenly, and the ministers of his successor, Abdul Mejid, decided to offer the pashalik of Egypt to Mohammed and the pashalik of Syria to his son, Ibrahim, as a way to bring peace back to the empire. However, when the Western powers of Britain, France, Austria, Prussia, and Russia (all of whom had interests in the Middle East) got wind that there would now be two powers they would have to deal with in the region, they intervened and said that no negotiations should occur between the Ottomans and Egyptians without their approval. Negotiations between the Western and Eastern powers lasted until the summer of 1840. On July 15 of that summer the Western powers signed the Treaty of London, proposing to back with military force the terms that Turkey had set out the summer before. During this time Litch announced that the resolution of this conflict would occur on August 11 as a fulfillment of the sixth trumpet, and that date proved to be an eventful day.

On August 11 the Turkish emissary, Rifat Bey, arrived in Alexandria with the terms of the London convention. The ambassadors of the Western powers also received a communication from the sultan on that day inquiring as to what measures were to be taken in reference to his empire. He was told that "provision had been made" but that the Western powers would inform him later as to what they were. Litch and the advent believers saw in these events a fulfillment of the sixth trumpet in that the independence of the Ottoman Empire was now gone. It was now to be the "sick man of Europe" and play a minor role in European history until its final demise in 1923. Even though many have since attempted to show that this version of prophetic fulfillment was not accurate, these events had a powerful influence on the advent believers as they continued to study prophecy leading them to expect Jesus to come back in 1844. It was to them proof that God was guiding their movement and that they could rely on the Bible's prophecies.[120]

Confidence in this prophecy among Adventist scholars has waned mainly due to the fact that the date of the battle of Bapheum has come into question, with some historians now placing it as late as July 27, 1301. This, in their minds, calls into question the validity of the supposed fulfillment of this prophecy on August 11, 1840. However, there are a few good reasons why this should not shake the initial Adventist confidence in the remarkable fulfillment of this prophecy, which bolstered the new Advent movement of the 1840s:

- The Lord did not reveal to Ellen White at any time during her ministry that this date was not correct, and thereby adjusting the fulfillment date that had been set: August 11, 1840. On the contrary, she clearly states in *The Great Controversy* on pages 334 and 335 that the prophecy had been fulfilled and that it was a landmark moment in the development of the Advent movement. If it had been a mistake and God felt that it was necessary that His people should change their view of this prophecy He had ample time to reveal this to Ellen White from the time of the writing of *The Great Controversy* to the time of her death.

- In researching the date for the battle of Bapheum, there is not wide consensus among historians as to when the battle occurred. While historians now generally accept 1301 as the battle of Bapheum some just say that the Turks arose "around" 1300. Interestingly, when Turkey celebrated the 700th anniversary of the Ottoman Empire they used 1299 as the beginning date.[121]

- To reject this prophecy even if the beginning date was inaccurate doesn't seem like a wise thing to do since we serve an all-powerful God for whom nothing is impossible (Mark 10:27; Luke 1:37). This "mistake" would have been an honest one based on the best historical knowledge that they had from the history books of the day. It wouldn't have made sense for God to fulfill the prophecy on August 11, 1842, without revealing to them the historical inaccuracy of the date they were given by historians. Since He didn't reveal the historical error to the Advent people, it would only make sense to be true to His Word and fulfill the prophecy when it would be expected and highly significant for those who were earnestly seeking Him and His soon return.

So let's now analyze the actual prophecy and why it would make sense that the Ottoman Empire would fulfill Revelation 9. Please acquaint yourself with Revelation 9 before proceeding.

Trumpets

Before delving into the passage one must understand the context of the fifth and sixth trumpets. They are two of the last three trumpets that the angel in Revelation 8:13 proclaims directly before they occur, "Woe! Woe! Woe to the inhabitants of the earth." So it is clear to the Bible student that they predict severe events.

However, one must look at the trumpets in the greater context of Revelation. Revelation starts with a cycle of three sevens: the seven churches, the seven seals, and then the seven trumpets.

The seven churches are portrayed as lampstands (Rev. 1:20). This is understandable since Jesus had told His people, "You are the light of the world" (Matt. 5:14). Revelation 2 and 3 then give the spiritual qualities of the "enlightened" people of God until the end of time. Unfortunately, the church is depicted in these chapters as going from "hard-working" and "persevering" to "losing their first love" and eventually becoming so arrogant and indolent that Jesus threatens to "spit them out" of His mouth by the end of the passage (Rev. 2:2, 4; 3:16).

The seven seals begin in Revelation 6 after a short interlude where John sees heaven and God on His throne, with Jesus as the Lamb and Redeemer of the world glorified and worshiped by the inhabitants of heaven. The seals are then opened up one by one by the Lamb. They describe the overall spiritual condition (not qualities as the seven churches do) of the church. In the seals the church is not represented as a lampstand any longer—the

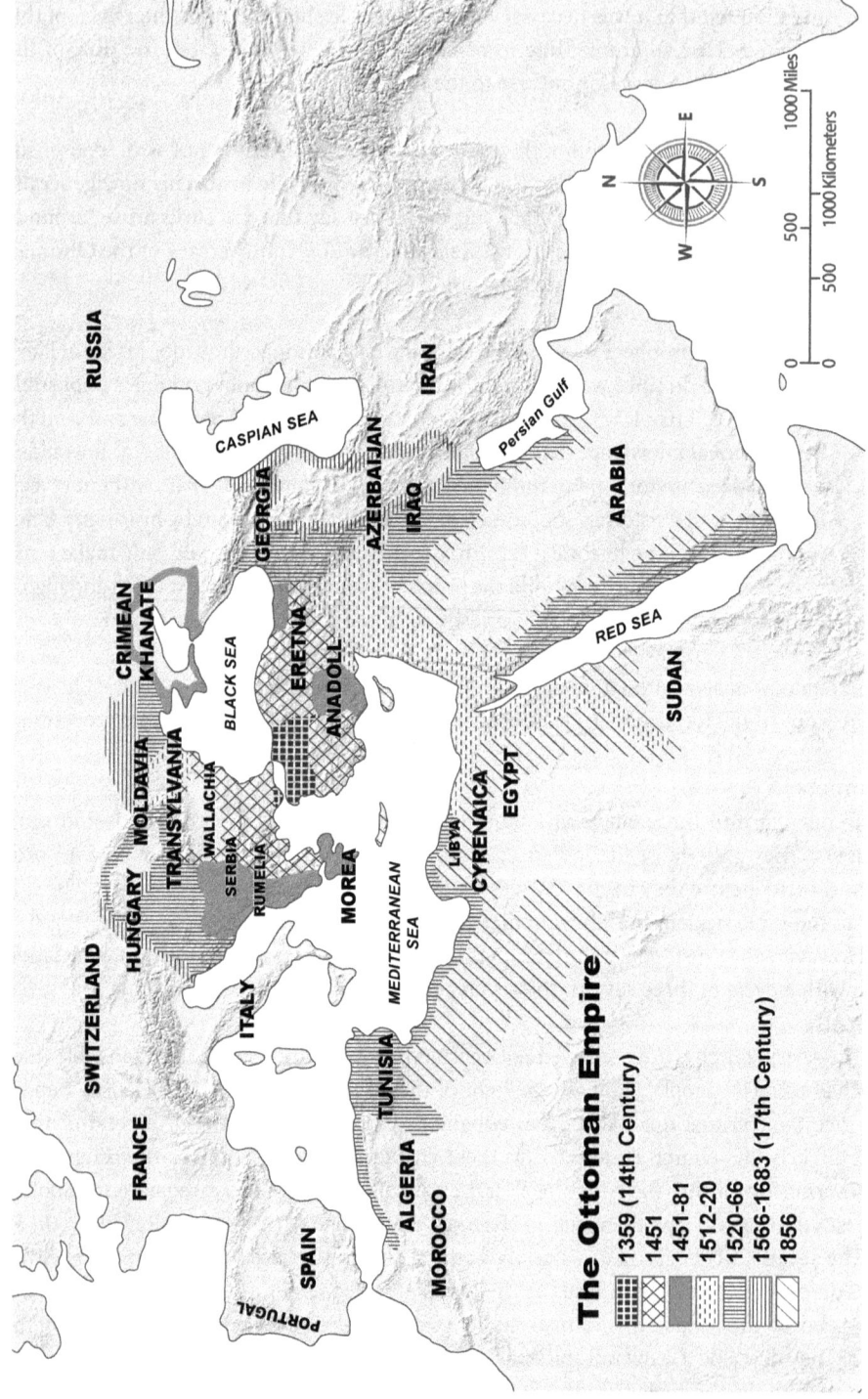

church is now represented as a horse. What would be the symbolic meaning of a horse? Obviously horses are mobile whereas lampstands just "stand" as the name implies.

Horses were used in the first century, when Revelation was written, for war, farming, or traveling; all of these things indicate progress and movement. Without horses, conquering new territories, planting large fields, or visiting other parts of the world and expanding one's worldview would be much more difficult. This also would be fitting since the last words of Jesus to His disciples as recorded in Matthew were a command to go into the world to sow the seed and conquer it for the kingdom of God (Matt. 28:18–20). The seals indicate that the early church did this by representing it as a white horse. However, the horses get increasingly worse—red, black, and then pale—and by the fifth seal there are no more horses—the horses have died!

The fifth seal shows the true nature of the church in the Middle Ages. It shows that instead of getting on their "horse" and conquering the world with the love of Christ and with truth they were busy killing their own fellow Christians—and not just their own group, but the ones who were actually most faithful to God. In the fifth seal there is a chilling prayer by those who suffered at the hands of the church. They cried out, "How long, Sovereign Lord, holy and true, until you judge the inhabitants of the earth and avenge our blood?" (Rev. 5:10, NIV) They were told to wait a bit longer and afterwards John saw the sixth and seventh seals, which delineate the signs leading up to the second coming.

In a brief interlude, John sees the 144,000 and the great multitude in Revelation 7. These two groups were shown to him in answer to the question of the wicked on the day of judgment, "Who can stand?" John is then shown seven angels who are given seven trumpets (Rev. 8:2).

Noteworthy is the fact that the seven trumpets of Revelation 8 and 9 are given in response to another scene that John saw when an angel came to the altar with a golden censer and offered it, along with the prayers of the saints. Very possibly some of those prayers being the prayers we just heard from those who suffered persecution in Revelation 6 during the time of the fifth seal. This means that whereas the seven churches and seven seals were describing the qualities and conditions of God's people, the seven trumpets are judgments against God's enemies, judgments given in direct response to the prayers of the saints. So, instead of reading the trumpets and looking to place blame on the trumpet powers, one must understand that God sent these trumpets as judgments, in answer to the prayers of His people.

Since the book of Revelation is replete with sanctuary language, the student of prophecy must attempt to answer the questions, "Why a trumpet? " and "What role did trumpets play in Israel?" In Numbers 10 God gave the Israelites two silver trumpets upon their exit from Egypt, when they would be experiencing many dangers along the way. These trumpets were also to be sounded for the assembly of the Israelites during religious festivals. And finally, the trumpets were to be sounded "when you go into battle in your own land against an enemy who is oppressing you … Then you will be remembered by the Lord your God and you will be rescued from your enemies" (Num. 10:9).

This promise was fulfilled on many occasions in the Old Testament. Gideon and his band of 300 men blew trumpets and overcame a huge army when God struck fear in the heart of the Midianites (Judges 7). Jehoshaphat and his army were delivered when the trumpeters and singers praised God (2 Chron. 20). Trumpets in the Bible are often associated with God's deliverance, power, and judgments against His enemies (Isa. 27:13; Matt. 24:31; 1 Cor. 15:52; 1 Thess. 4:16).

From this short survey of the biblical meaning of trumpets, the following conclusions applied to Muhammad and the fulfillment of the fifth and sixth trumpets: even if Muhammad was a fulfillment of the fifth trumpet as the early Protestant reformers posited, it means that he was sent by God as a judgment upon Christianity for losing its way.

The same might be said of the Ottomans because a trumpet represents God's deliverance for His people. Many historians acknowledge, "Without the Turk, there is no Martin Luther."[122] Martin Luther himself, although not viewing them as worshiping the same god Christians do, viewed them as "God's rods of chastisement."[123]

Charles V, the most powerful monarch in Europe, who controlled what we now know as Spain, Holland, Switzerland, parts of Eastern Europe, most of Germany, parts of Italy, and some colonies in North and South America, was a devout Catholic and enemy of the Reformation. Right at the time he was scheming to rid Europe of Luther and the German princes who supported the Protestant Reformation, Suleiman the Magnificent marched his Ottoman troops north and laid siege on Vienna in 1530. This terrified all the powers of Europe and diverted the attention of Charles V from the Protestant question. This attack even caused the Protestants and Catholics to sign a truce in 1532.[124] During that time the teachings of the Reformation spread rapidly across Europe, its truths sank more deeply into the hearts of millions, and it became more organized. Thus, God saved Martin Luther and the Protestant Reformation from swift annihilation through a Muslim Ottoman sultan, one known for ruling with justice and magnanimity as the biblical Solomon had.

Sequence of Symbols in Revelation

The sequence of the symbols of Revelation seems to point to the Ottomans as a fulfillment of both the fifth and sixth trumpets. In both the seven churches and the seven seals, there is a chronological order. Adventists have even given approximate dates for the fulfillment of these symbols, for example: 1st church = 31–100 CE; 2nd church = 100–313 CE, etc. While all of the symbols might not have an exact fulfillment on a certain date, like Fitch and Miller believed about August 11, 1840, there is a fluid progression of the description of the symbols and their corresponding fulfillment drawn from history books.

Moreover, within the traditional Adventist interpretation of the seven trumpets, the first four are paired with common elements and are in chronological order:

- 1st trumpet = Roman destruction of Jerusalem (70 CE)

- 2nd trumpet = Destruction of Roman Empire (476 CE)

    Common element = Roman Empire

- 3rd trumpet = Fallen Christianity (313 CE–538 CE)

- 4th trumpet = Darkness of Christian Church (538 CE—Reformation: 1500s)

Common element = Christian Church

This would lead to the conclusion that it would be more accurate to accept what Miller and Litch proposed as the fulfillment of the fifth and sixth trumpet:

- 5th trumpet = Rise of Ottoman Empire (1299 CE—1449 CE)

- 6th trumpet = Domination of Ottoman Empire (1449 CE—1840 CE)

Common element = Ottoman Empire

This interpretation gives the prophecy a fluid progression. On the contrary, by proposing that the rise of Islam from 610–750 CE fulfills the fifth trumpet, not only do the time elements of the prophecy get muddled, but also the progression of the prophecy loses its coherence.

Fallen Star

So who is this "fallen star" that is given a key to the shaft of the abyss and lets out all of the locusts? One must notice a few things when taking up this question:

- There is a significant similarity between the fallen star of Revelation 9 and the angel of Revelation 20. Both came down from heaven and both were given the key to the abyss. In Revelation 20 this angel bound up Satan and locked him away. In Revelation 9 the fallen star opened the abyss and let out smoke and an army of locusts. We would assume that since whoever has the keys to the abyss is an agency that can lock up Satan, then it must be given these keys from God Himself to accomplish some purpose.

- The star is "fallen." This may seem too obvious, but if something is "fallen" then it means that at some point it was "un-fallen" and therefore good. This is why Satan is considered "fallen." There was a time when he was the covering cherub of God and in good graces with God the Father and heaven.

- A better translation of Revelation 9:1 is, "I saw a star out of the heaven *having fallen* to earth."[125] In other words this star had *already* fallen; John did not see him fall at the time of the fulfillment of this prophecy.

- This fallen star of Revelation 9 is called in Hebrew—*Abaddon*, and in Greek—*Apollyon* (verse 11). This seems peculiar after reading the fifth trumpet because those words mean "destroyer." It is clear in verse 5 that God did not give them power to destroy, but "only to torture." So why would this star's name be "destroyer" in Hebrew and Greek, the languages of the Old and New Testaments respectively, when destruction didn't describe his mission? Could this be a reference to the Jews and Christians whom Muhammad referred to as the people of the Book (which was written in Greek and Hebrew) and their misunderstanding of the punishment inflicted by God in answer to the prayers of the true people of God? It seems from the text of Revelation 9 that these are people who are speaking Greek and Hebrew (Bible-readers) who believe that this star has come to destroy them, when in reality God hasn't allowed it to destroy them, but rather to "torture" them in hopes that they will return to Him. In other words, these are people who are out of touch with the designs and workings of God.

The Ottomans appear to be a much better fulfillment of the "fallen"-ness of Islam than the early Muslims. Even to the casual reader of a history book about the Turks, it is apparent that religion, other than Osman's dream that gave them a divine mandate to establish an empire, played a much less significant role than politics. The Ottoman sultans made no pretense of trying to live an austere lifestyle, or to teach and study the Bible—they didn't even conform to the requirements of their own holy book. The Ottomans came centuries after Ibn Hazm, and they believed, as was common in Islam at the time, that the Bible was a mistake-ridden, doctored document corrupted by the people of the Book.

In comparison with the early Medinah caliphs and the Umayyads, the Turks allowed imperialistic principles to supersede the religious principles that had existed in Islam at the beginning of the movement. They, to an unprecedented degree, "politicized" the religious environment by making the religious scholars employees of the state (actually, they technically became part of the army). The interests of the ruling class effectively controlled the religion of the Ottoman Empire.[126] The sultan enforced a strict, religious orthodoxy. The first person to be executed by Suleiman (the sultan at the peak of Ottoman power) was actually Molla Kabiz, who, interestingly enough, dared to suggest that the Quran establishes the spiritual superiority of Jesus over Muhammad.[127] This shows that by this time, Islam had formulated a rigid doctrine in regards to its relationship to the Bible; when presented with an opportunity to find agreement with the teachings of the Quran and the Bible, they relentlessly punished anyone who might pursue this course. It appears that they had fallen from the principles laid out in the Quran for making Allah the final goal and telling the Christians that there is "no contention" between the two groups.

Similarity of Symbols
When analyzing the fifth and sixth trumpets, one sees the following similarities in symbols:

<u>Fifth trumpet</u>	<u>Sixth trumpet</u>
Locusts like horses	Horses like lions
Breastplates of iron	Red, blue, yellow breastplates
Tails and stings like scorpions	Tails like snakes
Could torment people	Could kill people

In these symbols there is a progression of power and viciousness, and the results were progressively worse for the "inhabitants of the earth." In any case, the similarities support the interpretation that the Ottomans would fit the description since it involves the same age and the same power, only with an intensification of power.

We see an intensification of power from 1449 onwards as the Ottomans completely dismantled the Christian Byzantine Empire and conquered Constantinople (the killing of "a third of mankind" in the prophecy as usually interpreted by Adventist scholars), thereby ushering in a golden age for the Ottomans in the next two centuries.

Tails, Fire, Smoke, and Sulfur

Verses 17 and 18 tell us that this power would kill mankind by the plagues of fire, smoke, and sulfur. In both the fifth and sixth trumpet, the powers' "tails" play an important part in torturing and killing. It is a well-known fact that the Ottomans used gunpowder weapons. This is one reason why they were able to conquer so much territory.[128]

Gunpowder weapons are fired from long tubes ("tails"); one of their main ingredients is sulfur, and they produce much "smoke" when "fired." So it is feasible to assume that John saw a figurative battle of the Ottomans and described this phenomenon that was not yet developed during his day. Since the tails play a part in both trumpets, again it would seem that the Ottomans are a better fulfillment of the prophecy by the development of weapons that was occurring right at the time of their ascendency.

Four Angels

In verse 14 the angel releases "four angels" who were bound near the river Euphrates, and they were released to kill a "third of mankind." Since the river Euphrates has its headwaters in Turkey, it makes sense to look to the Ottoman Empire for this fulfillment.

Historians have identified four families that were instrumental in the build-up of the Ottoman Empire since the time of the late fourteenth century: the Evrenosogullari, Mihalogullari, Turahanogullari, and Malkochogullari families. The first two above-mentioned families were Christian families who had converted to Islam in northwest Anatolia. The Malkochogullari were of Serb origin, while the origins of the Turahanogullari are obscure.[129] These families were especially instrumental in helping the Ottoman Empire extend west into Eastern Christian lands. This is also a strong argument that the Ottomans are a good interpretation of the fulfillment, especially of the sixth trumpet.

Conclusion

Solomon encourages the wise to "not move an ancient boundary stone set up by your ancestors" (Prov. 22:28, NIV; see also 23:10). If one's forefathers go through any process in which they examine where a boundary should be, without a new process to determine the faultiness of their thinking, it doesn't seem prudent to start moving it. This interpretation is something that was placed after careful, and in this case, prayerful deliberation. After examining all the historical evidence, it doesn't seem that there is enough evidence to "move the boundary stone" that our pioneers placed in regards to this prophecy over 150 years ago.

When William Miller and Josiah Litch combined the 150 days and "hour, day, month and year" of the fifth and sixth trumpets and arrived at August 11, 1840, BEFORE the fulfillment of the prophecy and then on that actual day something happened that can be interpreted as a fulfillment, this made them unique. This radical interpretation of the prophecy and divine fulfillment gave to the Adventist movement a unique claim as the true expositors of biblical prophecy. A reversion to the old way of interpreting this prophecy does nothing but diminish not only this prophecy, but also the Advent movement as a whole—and especially the alleged prophet of the movement who supported it.

In any case, it appears that the negative attributes applied to Muhammad based upon this prophecy, and his subsequent title of "fallen star" are not deserved. The main point of this prophecy is to show the abject condition of Christianity. Such interpreters don't even understand why God sent the "fallen star," calling him "destroyer" when he was not able to even "destroy." John is clear that even though these woes had come upon this group of people it wasn't enough to make them give up their idol worship and egregious sins (Rev. 9:20, 21).

Some Adventist commentators have seen a reference to the rise of Islam in the prophecy of Daniel 11. I have included my interpretation of the last few verses of Daniel 11 in Appendix C. I believe that there is a reference to extreme, radical Islam and the role it plays in end-time events, but I will not take the time to analyze it in depth here since it doesn't concern Muhammad directly.

Since Muhammad cannot be definitively proclaimed to be the "fallen star" of Revelation 9 (or from Daniel 11), let's turn to the vital task of testing him as a prophet of God.

Chapter 10

The Tests of a Prophet

As stated in the first chapter of this book, a Bible-believing Adventist has only two options when analyzing Muhammad: he was either a prophet or an impostor. There is no room for ambiguity here. The biblical injunction found in Deuteronomy 13:1–5 was clear—if one comes and says that they have had a dream and is a prophet and is found out to be a false prophet, they were to be put to death. The Lord left no doubt in the minds of His people as to the seriousness of the claim of being a prophet of the Lord.

With this in mind, the biblical tests of a prophet will be enumerated:

1. Did the prophet have dreams and visions from the Lord? (Num. 12:6)

2. Did the prophet speak in accordance with previous revelation? (Isa. 8:20)

3. Have the prophet's prophecies come true? (Deut. 18:21, 22)

4. Even if his prophecies came true, did he call people to worship the one true God of the Bible and acknowledge Jesus as Messiah? (Deut. 13:1–5; 1 John 2:22)

5. Were his "fruits" consistent with the "fruits" of the Holy Spirit? (Matt. 7:15–23)

However, before applying the tests, two issues need to be addressed: the role of the Hadith (the traditions and sayings of Muhammad, which are not in the Quran) and the uniformity of God's standards for prophets.

The Hadith

There are three sources from which modern Muslims draw their beliefs: the Quran, the Hadith, and the Sira. These three together make up what Muslims refer to as the *sunnah*, or complete tradition of everything concerning Muhammad.

The Quran is believed to be the direct, revealed word of God; the Hadith are the traditions and sayings of the prophet; and the Sira is the biography of Muhammad. The Quran and its teachings have already been addressed in this book, and if someone wants to read a chronological biography of Muhammad, one can read one of many different versions by modern authors who are constructed from such early Muslim historians as Ibn Ishaq, Waqidi, or Ibn Sa'd.

The Hadith are what Muslims refer to when they want commentary on the Quran (*Arabic: tafsir*), clarification of the context of different suras in the Quran, or instruction on lifestyle issues. They give insights into Muhammad's life and his beliefs on a huge range of issues such as tithing (*zakat*), mortgages, wills, loans, fasting, marriage, divorce, the annual pilgrimage to Mecca (*Hajj*), blood money, counsel for eating, and even cleanliness of restrooms, among many others.

Most Muslims realize that some of the sayings in the Hadith were forged in the early centuries of Islam as a means of influencing public opinion in favor of whatever brand of Islam they were promoting. So determining which ones are legitimate and which are not is a formidable task. Early Muslims also recognized this fact, so a number of individuals began to collect the Hadith, checking each saying's legitimacy.

The most recognized and respected collector of Hadith was the imam Muhammad Ibn Ismail al-Bukhari (810–870). His collection (known as *Sahih Bukhari*) numbered some 300,000 sayings at one point.[130] He was believed to have traveled on foot around the Muslim world checking the veracity of each saying and its chain of transmission (known in Islam as the *isnad*). Ultimately, he chose about 2,000 different sayings as authentic (with repetitions it numbers about 7,000, which covers nine volumes).

However, the fact that they waited over a century to begin this process creates some ambiguity in the process. To illustrate, for an Adventist, it would be analogous to me going around now and checking a "saying" of Ellen White that I heard my friend John Doe state in public once about the inadvisability of grapes being served with peaches for breakfast. He might tell me that he heard it from his grandfather who was good friends with Hiram Edson's grandson who heard Hiram state that he heard Uriah Smith state that one time Ellen White invited him to breakfast where she made that statement. I would then need to check that line of transmission and see if there were many "weak links" (such as Hiram Edson's grandson who left the church and didn't believe in the Spirit of Prophecy, for example).

As one can tell from this small (and strange, I must admit) hypothetical example, this task would be an arduous and inexact science. It makes judging what the prophet said on certain topics almost indecipherable. That, in turn, makes judging Muhammad's prophetic gift more difficult since many things that Muslims believe in today come from the Hadith. A prominent example of this is the belief that a faithful Muslim (usually applied to warriors in *jihad*) will inherit seventy virgins in paradise. This belief comes from the Hadith and not the Quran. Muhammad does describe "beautiful virgins" that Muslims may look forward to in paradise, but nowhere in the Quran is the number "seventy" mentioned.

Another example would be Friday worship. As we have seen from chapter 7, the only holy day mentioned in the Quran is Sabbath, the seventh day. But Muslims all consider Friday their main day of prayer. Again, this is from the Hadith, where Muhammad went to the market to preach on Friday and conduct his "evangelism." That would actually give credence to the idea that he probably observed Sabbath, since most people in largely Jewish Medinah would have been preparing for Sabbath on Friday by doing their shopping.

Thus, the Hadith seriously complicates sorting out truth from error and discovering which were Muhammad's actual teachings and which were merely teachings that later arose in Islam that Muslims then wanted to attribute to the prophet.

Unfortunately, as other Christians who have studied Islam have noted, one of the main problems with Islam now is that, "the Sunna (tradition) is the judge of the Qur'an, and not the Qur'an the judge of the Sunna."[131] This has caused some Western scholars to totally disregard all of the Hadith as spurious additions of tradition to support the different schools of interpretation that arose after Muhammad.[132]

So, for purposes of this book, I will only refer to Hadith that correspond with the Quranic teachings, otherwise I will add the words "allegedly" or "supposedly" when referring to Hadith that don't seem to fit the pattern of revelation from the Quran.

Are God's Standards for Prophets Uniform?

Does God hold every prophet to the exact same standards of conduct? This is a key question when analyzing not only Muhammad but also any prophet. Even after a cursory reading of the Bible and Spirit of Prophecy, it would seem that the answer to this question is "no." This is especially an issue when analyzing "our" prophet—whom Adventists consider to be the only true prophet to appear since the apostle John.

For instance, could Ellen White have had the approval of God had she decided to lead a band of warriors into Connecticut to violently rescue a nephew that had been unjustly jailed by a county sheriff? Probably not—even though one may believe that God didn't reprove Abraham for rescuing Lot by means of violence in the book of Genesis. Could Ellen White have continued her prophetic ministry after having a fellow Adventist's husband murdered so that she could take him as a second husband? Probably not—even though one must admit that David did not cease to be regarded as a prophet, even though a similar situation occurred in his life.

One must allow for God to work in the context of certain religious and cultural milieus. When examining Ellen G. White, Adventists must admit that the context that she worked in was one of the most suitable milieus in the history of the world for religious revival. Ellen White received the prophetic call in a burgeoning country that would become one of the greatest democracies of the world. Rule of law was generally upheld.

The United States of America were founded by people who were wholeheartedly afraid of government-sponsored religion, so religious freedom was granted to all. America was founded by Bible-believing Christians and had already experienced two religious "awakenings" in the eighteenth and nineteenth centuries. A significant portion of the population regularly read the Bible and listened to earnest Bible preachers. She was living and working in one of the most simple, Bible-based, and conservative Christian cultures that the world has ever seen.

An example of this would be the scandal that rocked the presidency of Andrew Jackson a little over a decade before Ellen White's prophetic call. One of Jackson's Cabinet members, John Eaton, war secretary, was accused of consummating his marriage before the wedding—and this caused a national uproar that almost cost Jackson the presidency![133] From what is known of the licentiousness of the cultures surrounding Abraham and his descendants in biblical times, this wouldn't have been a blip on the radar screen; instead, child sacrifices, temple prostitution, and violent political intrigue would have been the norm in those days.

God is an exceedingly merciful God, and He understands where people have come from, and He doesn't expect more than what they can realistically attain given the surroundings into which they were born.

Think again of how modern Adventists might view a new prophet if God called someone today just as He called Ellen White. What would most Adventists say now about a "prophet" who doesn't observe Sabbath and who loves to eat pork? Would they say that this is a prophet of God? I think most would agree that the response of the church would be overwhelmingly negative. However, God gave Ellen White visions for years at the beginning of her ministry under these circumstances. Why? She herself did not know those truths early in her life. He knew that it wasn't realistic even for the prophet to "grow" so quickly. Plus, she would have outdistanced God's people and been so far ahead of them that maybe she would have lost some of them. We see this again and again in history—God condescends to humanity, meets them where they are, and leads them to something better, which culminates in eternal life through the redemption He offered in Christ.

So, the question one needs to ask when addressing the prophethood of Muhammad is, "To whose religious and cultural milieu was Muhammad's similar?" While Muhammad did live after Christ, his context was much more similar to Abraham's than Ellen White's. Bibles in Arabic didn't exist, paganism and superstition abounded, and, of course, that was accompanied by the usual ignorance, licentiousness, and tribal or national warfare.

As we saw in chapter 4, by the time of Muhammad, Christianity, God's chosen vessel to be "salt" and "light" to the world and to lift it from the darkness of paganism, had adopted many aspects of paganism and had descended into that darkness instead of dispelling it.

Muhammad lived almost a millennium before the Renaissance and the Reformation in a time period even Western historians call the "Dark Ages." So when examining his life, modern Christians must temper their judgments with knowledge of the time, not judging him by the light that now exists, nor even the light that existed at the time of Ellen White's call.

With that said, we will embark on our journey of examining Muhammad in light of the biblical tests for a prophet.

Test #1 – Did Muhammad have dreams or visions?

Numbers 12:6 stipulates that a true prophet of God has communication with God through dreams or visions. The Quran makes this claim for Muhammad (2:1–4):

> In the name of God, Most Gracious, Most Merciful. This is the book; in it is guidance sure, without doubt, to those who fear God; who believe in the Unseen, are steadfast in prayer, and spend out of what We have provided for them; and who believe in the Revelation sent to thee, and sent before thy time…

According to Muhammad, he was a prophet of God, not a reformer who listened to others and studied previous writings and came to some new conclusions. The Quran was alleged by Muhammad himself to be a revelation of God to the Arabs in their tongue (13:37; 26:192–206; 41:3, 44; 43:3; 54:17, 22, 32, 40).

In the Quran Muhammad is a specific apostle (Arabic: *rasul*) chosen by God with a message (3:144). If Muhammad had claimed just to be a collector of previous revelations and was proclaiming some "new light" from previous revelations, as Martin Luther or John Wesley did, then one would not have to be so categorical in an assessment of his ministry. But because of his audacious claims, the biblical injunction of Deuteronomy 13 must be applied to him.

Secondly, some Christian commentators make the claim that Muhammad didn't really have visions or dreams but just collected bits and pieces of stories and material as he interacted with adherents to the different religions in the market or around a campfire. Some examples in which he did borrow material from Jewish, Christian, and Zoroastrian sources will be examined later.

However, for the purposes of this chapter, that is an immaterial discussion. Muhammad said that the revelations came from visions, and there is no way of checking that now, just as one can't check whether or not Abraham, Moses, or Paul really had visions.

Ellen White was also accused of not having visions. At worst, critics claimed that she was inspired by demons, while others claimed that she was just an inspired "information-gatherer" from previous revelations, along the lines of Martin Luther and the Wesley brothers. However, during her lifetime, skeptics could actually observe her in vision and check the physical phenomena that accompanied the visions.

There are accounts that Muhammad said that he would hear bells ringing during his visions. Others said that he would have some type of seizure during these revelations. These accounts will have to be relied upon because Muhammad is dead and there is no way to go back and check his pulse or listen for his breath during a vision. Therefore, one must take him at his word and judge him accordingly.

Let's just examine the logic of the argument for Muhammad being an inspired reformer. Would a Christian really want to trust an "inspired reformer" who lies about where he gets information? Shouldn't this be a red flag against treating him as a reformer? If he claimed that he saw Gabriel and heaven in vision, but in actuality, was just relating snippets of "revelations" that he had gathered in the market or around the campfire, then he is a false prophet no matter how good the "revelations" were that he related. The Quran itself roundly condemns such people (2:79; 6:93).

Therefore, Muhammad must be subjected to the tests of a prophet because that was his claim. This leads us to the next test of a prophet.

Test #2 – Did Muhammad Speak According to the Law and Testimony?
Do Muhammad's teachings agree with the Bible's? And do his purported goals for his ministry align with the goals of a biblical prophet? These are the questions that one must deal with when examining his prophethood.

First of all, let us examine the objectives that he believed were given to him by God. It doesn't take a reader of the Quran very long to realize that the day of judgment is the main topic of the Quran. References to the day of judgment are so multitudinous in the Quran that I won't attempt to write them all down here. If the reader looks at all of the references listed in Appendix A, it is abundantly clear that Muhammad viewed himself as one who was calling the Arabs (and tangentially, as the Medinah suras are read, Jews and Christians) to repent and live their lives with the thought that one day they would have to account to their Maker for all of their deeds and beliefs on this earth.

It comes out clearly in reading the Quran that Muhammad considers the following as sins that must be put away before the day of judgment:

- Living life without ever believing one will come into judgment

- Worship of images

- Combining other gods to the God of Abraham

- Forgetting the Sinai covenant and Sabbath observance

- Greed

- Neglecting the poor and widows

- The practice common in Arabia of burying newborn girls alive

- Unbelief in God, Satan, angels, and the afterlife

- Lack of justice in society

- Gambling

- Not observing dietary laws (consumption of alcohol or unclean meats)

- Distortion of the words of Scripture

- Compulsion in matters of conscience and religion

Muhammad believed that he was a help to humanity, and specifically the Arabs, by exhorting them to worship the God of the Bible and be ready to meet Him at the day of judgment. Muhammad also viewed himself as one in a long line of prophets extending back to Adam who had this goal in mind. So one shouldn't expect to find anything in the Quran that doesn't speak "according to the law and the testimony." If anything should be found that is contradictory to that which is delineated in the Bible, then it is obvious that he is an impostor—a false prophet.

If one reads Muhammad's critics' literature, there are four main accusations against his claim of being a prophet: 1) he didn't believe in Jesus as the divine Son of God or His crucifixion, 2) his view of holy war (*jihad*), 3) his view of women as exemplified by his polygamous lifestyle, and 4) discrepancies between the Quran and the Bible. Each topic will be analyzed in turn.

Question 1: The Divinity of Jesus, the Son of God

This issue was addressed in depth in chapter 7, so I will not repeat what has been established previously. First of all, the Christian must admit that the teaching on the divinity of Christ that most Christian denominations espouse can be supported by the Bible, but it isn't so abundantly clear as to not leave doubts even in the minds of some Christians. Bible believing Christians in the time before Muhammad had wrestled with this issue for centuries. Christians, too, of all denominations have wrestled with this topic from the early church up to modern times—even some of the pioneers in the Adventist Church believed Jesus to not be the eternal Yahweh, but a created being.

In the Bible there is seen the tension between Jesus being the Son of Man and totally dependent upon the Father, as humans are, and yet being equal to and even called the eternal Father (Isa. 9:6). So should one expect the Quran to be "clearer" than the Bible in this regard?

Also, it must be noted that Muhammad always pointed to the Bible (including the Gospels) as inspired documents from God. This would mean that a sincere Muslim seeker of truth, when confronted with the dilemma of the divinity/humanity of the person of Christ would automatically be channeled from the Quran to the Bible, where the Christian believes that one can come to truth on this question. There is even one passage in the Quran where God told Muhammad that if he was in doubt as to the meaning of the messages he was receiving from Him, He should consult believers of the Book:

> If thou were in doubt as to what We have revealed unto thee, then ask those who have been reading the Book from before thee: the truth hath indeed come to thee from thy Lord, so be in no wise of those in doubt. (10:94)

This is a very important text to keep in mind when analyzing the truth of any argument from any Christian or Muslim who claims that Muhammad was a divisive character or didn't believe in Jesus. Muhammad himself enjoined his followers and potential converts to study the Bible, where the truth is more clearly portrayed for all who wanted to know the answer to the question, "Who was Jesus?"

By simply studying the Quran one will come to the conclusion that Muhammad had an overwhelmingly positive attitude toward Jesus and will discover that he believed the following about Him:

- Jesus was neither adopted by God as a "son," nor was He God's "fruit of the womb"

- He was not a result of intimate encounters between God and Mary

- He was born as a result of a miraculous conception

- He was of "high rank"

- He was sinless

- He was imbued with the power to do miracles, even bringing the dead to life

- He knew what was going on inside homes, which implies that He possessed Godlike qualities

- He was the Messiah

- He was sent by God to die, and to be raised up

What would Adventists have thought about Muhammad if they were living in Medinah during his time there? Put yourself in their Jewish mindset and read through the above list once again. I think the reader would agree that either a Jew or an Adventist could call him a "Christian."

It was actually known to early Islam that the Jews protested against Muhammad because of his positive views of Jesus. Ibn Ishaq reported that Muhammad said that of all the prophets he was "closest" to Jesus.[134]

Muhammad rejected all titles for himself and probably would have denied being a "Christian" (just as he would probably deny being a "Muslim" today—since he just wanted to be known as a faithful follower of God). But in a modern understanding of the word "Christian," the argument can be made that it could have applied to Muhammad, especially in the eyes of the Jews by whom he was surrounded.

He does make some statements that appear to contradict this, but if the Christian is honest about it, so did Jesus Himself as evidenced when He stated, "I can do nothing by myself..." in John 5:30, even though he was God.

As pointed out in chapter 4, there were many heresies in early Christianity, and one can only speculate which ones Muhammad was dealing with in the Quran. But it certainly appears that he had to deal with the heresies taught by the Collyridians and those teaching elements of full-blown Adoptionism and Modalistic Monarchianism.

Muhammad also appears to believe in the crucifixion. His statements in the Quran seem to be a rebuke to the Jews who thought they had killed the supposed Messiah, Jesus, in that he basically told them, "No, you didn't—God raised Him from the dead." As examined in chapter 6, God is recorded in the Quran as telling Jesus that His plan was for Jesus to die when He was sent to this world.

When understood in the historical context, it appears that the Quran agrees with the Bible in its teaching regarding the Messiah, Jesus. In any case, due to the fact that Muhammad had a very favorable view of earlier Scriptures and pointed Muslims to understand and study them, one can't condemn him for teaching heresy about Christ, since any Muslim with access to the Bible would be instructed to study it just like any Christian.

Question 2: Jihad—"Holy War"

What is "jihad"?

Much is made by Christian commentators about Muhammad's alleged bloodthirsty directives to go out and "fight the infidels" and convert everyone to Islam. This does appear to completely contradict the "turn-the-cheek" teachings of Christ and would automatically implicate Muhammad as a false prophet. However, this topic must be examined in greater depth. First, the meaning of the word *jihad* must be examined.

Jihad in Arabic comes from the verb *jahada*, which means, "to make an effort," "to strive," or "to struggle." The Arabic words *harb muqaddasah* denote "holy war." But this word combination is not used in the Quran. Therefore, one must ascertain what this "striving" that Muhammad refers to is talking about. Not all references to *jihad* in the Quran refer to "holy war." Some of them refer to what we call the "battle against self." An example of this is found in 29:69: "And those who strive [jihad] in our (cause), We will certainly guide them to our paths: for verily God is with those who do right."

Yusuf Ali, when commenting on this text, states, "All that man can do is to strive in God's cause. As soon as he strives with might and main, with constancy and determination, the Light and Mercy of God come to meet him. They cure his defects and shortcomings. They provide him with the means by which he can raise himself above himself. They point out the Way, and all Paths leading up to it."[135]

This type of *jihad*, for the Christian, is equivalent to the warfare motif Paul uses so often. Think, for example, of the injunction to "fight the good fight of faith" (1 Tim. 6:12) or to "contend earnestly for the faith" (Jude 3, 4), referring to fighting against oneself or to fighting to spread or defend faith in the living God in a sinful world. (See also 2 Tim. 4:7; Ephesians 6:10–18). The Christian can agree that this concept of personal *jihad* against oneself and against the powers of darkness is a foundational biblical truth that alerts us to the fact that all humans are players in a cosmic *jihad* (or what Adventists refer to as the "great controversy") between God and Satan. An Adventist would commend Muhammad for teaching this concept.

However, there are also texts in the Quran that deal directly with "striving" for God by going into battle for him. The purpose of this type of *jihad* was to protect the interests of the Islamic community and further the faith. These are the texts that pose a problem for most Christians when examining Muhammad's life. Those texts need to be examined.

Did Muhammad want to fight?

It seems after studying Muhammad's life and examining his practice that he didn't want to take up arms. He viewed himself as a peaceful prophet. He was known for spending hours and days in remote places in prayer. For years in Mecca his followers had either suffered innocently at the hands of the Quraysh or had fled to find shelter in different regions outside of Mecca.

It wasn't until twelve years after he had begun his ministry, when he and the Muslim community became established in Medinah, that Muhammad was convinced by a vision from God that God wanted them to overcome the Quraysh. Muhammad then told Muslims that God could fight their battles for them, but He allowed them to fight to test their faith (47:4).

According to one alleged hadith, Muhammad feared more than anything imams who would misguide his people. Why? He states in the very next sentence, "If the sword is placed in my nation, it will not be raised from them until the Day of Resurrection."[136] If that hadith is reliable, one can say that Muhammad didn't give a "green light" to holy war anytime and anywhere for the sake of God's kingdom and, if anything, feared to allow his followers to resort to violence.

An example of this is given in a hadith. Muawiyah, the founder of the Umayyad dynasty, had commanded his subjects to fight for him and plunder a certain nation. A certain Abdur-Rahmaan was uncomfortable with this and went to Muhawiyah's cousin, Abdullah ibn Umar, and quoted the following Quranic text:

> O you who believe! Eat not up your property among yourselves in vanities: but let there be amongst you traffic and trade by mutual goodwill. Nor kill (or destroy) yourselves; for verily God hath been to you most merciful! (4:29)

Abdullah ibn Umar joined his hands together and placed them on his forehead. He lowered his head for a short while and then he raised it up and said, "Obey him [Muawiyah] in the obedience of Allah and disobey him in the disobedience of Allah."[137]

In the Hadith Muhammad allegedly stated that the day of judgment would not come until, "'thirty Dajjaals [antichrists] appear, each one of them claiming that he is the Messenger of Allah; wealth will increase and flow in abundance; the tribulations will occur; and there will occur tumult and much *Haraj*.' It was asked, 'Which *Haraj*?' He said, 'Killing, killing, killing.'"[138] If this hadith is reliable, one can say that Muhammad didn't condone violence carte blanche, and he was actually grieved that a time would come when violence would be widespread.

Some Christian authors suggest that Muhammad actually moved to Medinah with his followers to prepare for holy war. They come to this conclusion since the words for "holy war" and "emigration" (*jihad* and *hijrah*, respectively) have similar roots.[139] Surah 2:218 is referenced as proof of his intent:

> Those who believed and those who suffered exile and fought (and strove and struggled) in the path of God, — they have the hope of the Mercy of God: and God is Oft-Forgiving, Most Merciful.

There is no historic proof that Muhammad had this in mind when he began his ministry in Medinah, and this Quranic verse doesn't indicate clearly what this "fighting" or "striving" is—is it the battles they fought with the Quraysh, or the daily "evangelistic battles" they were having with the Jews, or was it the fight against self and against their desire for revenge against the Quraysh who had chased them from their hometown? The Quran doesn't clarify this. And history seems to indicate that Muhammad's main goal in immigrating to Medinah was simply to avoid assassination at the hands of his fellow tribesmen.

When did Muhammad allow *jihad*?

When he did agree to fight a holy war? He viewed it as just that—a holy war where the honor of God and survival of a group of believers is at stake. The Quran specifically states that a Muslim cannot fight any battle unless his enemy is fighting against God (2:190, 191, 216, 218, 243, 244); therefore, no war against any people group would be condoned in the Quran unless that group was specifically warring against God and His religion.

> To those against whom war is made, permission is given (to fight), because they are wronged; and verily God is Most Powerful for their aid; (they are) those who have been expelled from their homes in defiance of right—(for no cause) except that they say, 'Our Lord is God'. Did not God check one set of people by means of another, there would surely have been pulled down monasteries, churches, synagogues, and mosques, in which the name of God is commemorated in abundant measure. God will certainly aid those who aid His (cause); for verily God is Full of Strength, Exalted in Might… (22:39,40)

> And fight them until persecution is no more, and religion is all for God… (8:39) (Pickthall)

These texts explain why *jihad* was not only allowed but commanded by God: the Muslims had been persecuted because of their faith, and they were to stop "persecution" and return society to conditions where "religion is all for Allah." Again he cautions: "Fight in the cause of God those who fight you, but do not transgress limits; for God loveth not transgressors" (2:190).

Yusuf Ali again summarizes the moderate Muslim position on this text, "War is only permissible in self-defense, and under well-defined limits. When undertaken, it must be pushed with vigor, but not relentlessly, but only to restore peace and freedom for the worship of God. In any case, strict limits must not be transgressed: women, children, old and infirm men should not be molested, nor trees and crops cut down, nor peace withheld when the enemy comes to terms."[140] It is clear that Muhammad never condoned ruthless, all-out warfare for any reason. It also appears from the Quranic texts that Muhammad only condoned warfare if the existence of true religion was at stake.

But make no mistake about it, as Christian commentators frequently point out, the battles were bloody and the methods of warfare and punishment for the enemies of Islam and traitors to the Muslims were, to our mind, primitive: beheading, stoning, goring, etc. Critics of Muhammad will list some of the following as examples of his ruthlessness:

- Muhammad's commanding of an assassination of a Jewish poet in Medinah, K'ab bin Al-Ashraf, who was antagonistic toward the prophet and Islam[141]

- The deportation of the Banu Nadir Jewish tribe who had conspired to kill the prophet[142]

- The beheading of the whole Banu Qurayzah tribe which had betrayed the Muslims during the Battle of the Trench[143]

- Mistreatment of women captives of war (for example, the tribe of Banu Mustaliq)[144]

While not a complete list, this is a sampling of some of the gruesome incidents that occurred from 622–630 CE as the Muslim armies clashed with the Quraysh and other tribes on the Arabian peninsula. However, the scope of this book does not allow for an analysis of each event.

The main thing that should be analyzed here is whether or not Muhammad spoke "according to the law and testimony." He claims that God gave him this right and, not only that but, commanded him to carry out these military forays. Does this contradict the maxims of the Bible? It certainly seems to directly contradict the teaching of Christ who said, "For all who take the sword will perish by the sword" (Matt. 26:52).

However, Christians believe that this same Jesus, more than 1,000 years before the words in Matthew were recorded, gave the Israelites a set of laws in regards to this exact question in Deuteronomy 20. Muhammad had much in common with this set of injunctions. In order to compare them with the Quran, the biblical rules for engagement in warfare for the Israelites are listed:

- When faced with armies that are larger than the believers', encourage the soldiers by telling them that God is with them and will fight for them (verse 1).

- Commend those who aren't afraid to leave homes and families to fight for the cause of God (verses 2–9).

- In cities that were not granted as an inheritance to the believers, one should offer the opposing side an opportunity for peace; if the opposing party agrees to peace then they become subject to the believers; if not, the Israelites should attack the city, putting all the warrior men to the sword and taking their possessions, wives, and children to be "used" as plunder (verses 10–15).

- In the cities that were granted as an inheritance to the Israelites, they were to put everybody and everything to the sword, not leaving alive "anything that breathes." The reasoning behind this was so that the Israelites would not be tempted to follow the gods of those who might have been spared (verses 16–18).

- When laying siege to a city for a long time, the Israelites were not to cut down the fruit trees so that all survivors would have something to eat later (verses 19, 20)

Judging Muhammad based on these biblical injunctions, the Christian can see many similarities. He always wanted to call people to accept the worship of the God of Abraham and live in peace with them. However, when they didn't and began to oppress him, Muhammad waged war on them. But he rarely went to the lengths the Bible allowed toward the cities that were an inheritance from God for Israel as far as killing "everything that breathes." He tended to spare the Arab and Jewish women and children in his conflicts.

Muhammad did violate this law once. When he alleged that he had knowledge that the Banu Nadhir Jewish tribe in Medina was plotting his death, he sent Muslim soldiers to besiege their portion of the city. After fifteen days of the standoff, Muhammad ordered his soldiers to cut down the date trees in their palm grove. The Jews appealed to him, "Muhammad, you have prohibited wanton destruction and blamed those guilty of it. Why then are you cutting down and burning our palm trees?"[145]

In this context the following verse was revealed in the Quran:

> Whether ye cut down (O ye Muslims!) the tender palm-trees, or ye left them standing on their roots, it was by leave of God, and in order that He might cover with shame the rebellious transgressors. (59:5)

Christian authors view this as a transgression of the law of God and a reason why his revelations were not of God. John Gilchrist compares this situation to a boxer resorting to giving low blows on your opponent in order to win at all costs.[146]

But this analogy breaks down in the sense that the law was given in the Bible, not as a means for pressing your adversary but for preservation of life once God helped you overcome the enemy. In a sense, it was the Muslims who ended up giving themselves low blows in order to overcome their enemies. This would be an odd reason to give for rejecting Muhammad as a prophet since this is not an example of violence toward others, but instead damage he inflicted on himself and his followers.

In any case, Muhammad participated personally in anywhere from six to twenty-seven military conflicts (depending on the Islamic source).¹⁴⁷ So, the main question becomes, "Did God really give a revelation to Muhammad that he could act in accordance with Deuteronomy 20 and not Matthew 26?" If God did make an exception based on the circumstances that Muhammad was facing and He allowed him to live by Deuteronomy 20, then the Christian would have to say that Muhammad was within those guidelines. If He didn't and it was actually Satan inspiring him to fight, then obviously he would have been just another power-hungry, violent chieftain of the Arabian peninsula who happened to be a religious opportunist too.

Question 3: Relationship to Women

It is well known that Muhammad had multiple wives over the course of his lifetime and that the Quran condones polygamy. To the Western, modern mind this reeks of primitiveness, and to the Christian it seems unfeasible that a true post-Christ believer would continue this practice, which has caused so many problems in the world.

However, the overall teaching of the Quran in regards to women must be looked at in the context of Arabia at that time. At the time of Muhammad, women were not highly valued by society. They were almost on the level of possessions, as it had been during the time of the Israelite deliverance from Egypt.¹⁴⁸ The Quran states that at that time for Arabs it was even bad news to give birth to girls:

> And they assign daughters for God!—glory be to Him!—and for themselves (sons, the issue) they desire! When news is brought to one of them, of (the birth of) a female (child), his face darkens, and he is filled with inward grief! With shame does he hide himself from his people, because of the bad news he has had! Shall he retain it on (sufferance and) contempt, or bury it in the dust? Ah! What an evil (choice) they decide on? (16:57–59)

Two things may be noticed from this passage:

- The pagan Arabs believed that angels were "daughters" of God.¹⁴⁹ Muhammad pointed out their hypocrisy in assigning daughters to God, and yet despising receiving daughters from God in their own families.

- There was a tradition on the Arabian peninsula of burying newborn daughters alive in hopes to get a son the next time. The Quran states that those who practiced female infanticide would be brought to justice on the day of judgment (81:8, 9).

So one can see that the society in which he was dealing with in regards to women is much different from Western society today. If Arab fathers were willing to end the life of their own daughters, it shows the value of women in society and how men must have treated them in general.

Muhammad allowed for polygamy, but he placed limits on it. He said that, at a maximum, a man could take four wives, but that in reality a man should not take any more than he was able to take care of:

> If ye fear that ye shall not be able to deal justly with the orphans, marry women of your choice, two, or three, or four; but if ye fear that ye shall not be able to deal justly (with them), then only one, or (a captive) that your right hands possess. That will be more suitable, to prevent you from doing injustice. (4:3)

One must take note of a couple of things in this passage:

- Muhammad starts off his discussion of marriage by mentioning orphans—why would this be? This sura relates to the Medinah period when they were having battles with the Quraysh and were losing warriors, which meant there was a growing number of widows, orphans, and captives of war (who are also mentioned in this passage) in the Muslim camp. Yusuf Ali, in his commentary on the Quran, notes that this injunction was seen as a help to the orphans of the community and that they were doing them "justice" by taking care of those who had lost fathers or husbands.[150] Even then, Muhammad encouraged them to do this only if they had the means to "deal justly" with them. If anything, Muhammad's view of women in this passage is that they are intrinsically valuable and that the men of the Muslim camp should provide "justly" for the women.

- Muhammad is not in this passage *encouraging* polygamy. As was mentioned in the previous point, this was an injunction that arose due to the new numbers of orphans and widows in the Muslim camp. Yusuf Ali again states in regards to this passage, "The unrestricted number of wives of the 'times of Ignorance' was now strictly limited to a maximum of four, provided you could treat them with perfect equality, in material things as well as in affection and immaterial things. As this condition is most difficult to fulfill, I understand the recommendation to be towards monogamy."[151]

In any case, even in this passage, usually roundly criticized by Christians, Muhammad was trying to improve conditions for women by not allowing for an unlimited number of wives and by stating that these wives should be dealt with justly.

This was not the only practice that Muhammad tried to change from the "days of ignorance" in regards to women. Previous to Muhammad, it was a tradition that a stepson or brother would take possession of a dead man's widow or widows along with his possessions.[152] This "inheritance" against a woman's will was forbidden in the Quran (4:19).

One can also see the value Muhammad placed on women in his positions on divorce. There is an alleged hadith stating that divorce is the "most hated" thing for God (Sunna Abu Daud 13:3). From the Quran we see that this issue was a very important one for Muhammad.

One of the tricks that pre-Muhammad Arabs liked to play on women was to treat them very harshly, causing the woman to file for divorce. The men would not consent to be divorced and thereby would not be considered eligible for financial compensation (i.e. they would not have to return the dowry upon divorce). The Quran condemns this practice and states that men should not treat their wives harshly, and should live in peace with them (4:19; 30:21).

Another type of divorce that Arabs resorted to during the "days of ignorance" was referred to as the *Zihar* divorce. In this case an Arab man would say to his wife, "You are to me as the back of my mother." This, according to pagan custom, freed the man from conjugal duties, but didn't free the woman to leave the husband's home, or contract a second marriage.[153] This practice was also condemned in the Quran, and Muhammad stated the obvious—that no woman can be a man's mother except the woman who brought him into the world. Punishment was also laid out in the Quran for the man who attempted to divorce his wife in such a way (58:1–4).

In the Quran rules are given to regulate the financial terms of a divorce. It also establishes a "waiting period" for divorces to be finalized (in hope that reconciliation would take place) (2:226–237; 65:1–7). Special consideration was given to women who were going through a divorce while being pregnant (65:6).

Other examples of Muhammad's elevation of the status of women in his day are:

- Mothers should be honored (4:1; 31:14; 46:15)

- Women can be saved (4:124)

- Men should be protectors of women (4:34)

- Widows should be included as beneficiaries in wills (2:240–242)

- Women are allowed to join the Muslim religion without their husbands (60:10–13)

In the Quran, God is no respecter of sexes: "Whoever works righteousness, man or woman, and has faith, verily, to him will we give a new life, a life that is good and pure..." (16:97).

The Quran likens a woman to a field: "Your wives are as a tilth [field] unto you; so approach your tilth when or how ye will; but do some good act for your souls beforehand; and fear God, and know that ye are to meet Him (in the Hereafter), and give (these) good tidings to those who believe" (2:223).

Muhammad's critics use this text to show how demeaning his attitude was toward women. But in the context of the text, it appears that he was encouraging men to show care unto their wives.

Yusuf Ali comments on this text, "Sex is not a thing to be ashamed of, or to be treated lightly, or to be indulged to excess. It is as solemn a fact as any in life. It is compared to a husbandman's tilth; it is a serious affair to him: he sows the seed in order to reap the harvest. But he chooses his own time and mode of cultivation. He does not sow out of season nor cultivate in a manner that will injure or exhaust the soil. He is wise and considerate and does not run riot. Coming from the simile to human beings, every kind of mutual consideration is required, but above all, we must remember that even in these matters there is a spiritual aspect. We must never forget our souls, and that we are responsible to God."[154]

Another text that has raised eyebrows among Christians is found in 4:34:

> Men are the protectors and maintainers of women, because God has given the one more (strength) than the other, and because they support them from their means. Therefore the righteous women are devoutly obedient, and guard in (the husband's) absence what God would have them guard. As to those women on whose part ye fear disloyalty and ill-conduct, admonish them (first), (next) refuse to share their beds, (and last) beat them (lightly); but if they return to obedience, seek not against them means (of annoyance): for God is Most High, Great (above you all).

The part, of course, that greatly disturbs most Christians is the part about "beating" your wives. This sounds heinous to modern Western Christians. The reader will notice that Yusuf Ali in his translation even added the word "lightly" in parentheses to underscore what moderate Muslim commentators view as something along the lines of a spanking.

While this sounds abjectly primitive to us, Muhammad is writing in the context of trying to prevent a divorce. In the text after this one (35), he states that if all these steps fail that the couple should appoint arbiters from his and her family to attempt to reconcile the two parties. In our day and age, obviously, spanking your wife would not prevent divorce, but cause it. So it sounds woefully primitive to us, but apparently at the time it was viewed as an improvement in the family relations since women had virtually no legal rights and a divorce could be obtained instantly.

One must give Muhammad credit in that he was trying to outline remedial steps for preventing divorce. Other elements of this verse are very much in line with biblical teachings—men are charged with being the protectors of the "weaker" partner, supporting them with their means, and being responsible before God for how you treat your wife (Eph. 5:25–30; 1 Peter 3:7). The fact that Muhammad was attempting to prevent divorce and keep families intact should be applauded even if it seems anachronistic to modern minds. Significantly, there are no recorded incidents in which one of Muhammad's wives claimed that he was physically violent with her.

It is well documented that Muhammad had many wives. Depending on which list one looks at, he had somewhere from eleven to thirteen wives. Contemporary Muslim apologists assert that his many marriages were made for cementing political alliances.

Christians, while acknowledging the political nature of many of his marriages, especially criticize Muhammad as a "demon-possessed pedophile" due to his marriage to six (or seven)-year-old Aisha.[155] According to legend, he consummated the marriage when she was nine (he would have been in his fifties at the time). Oddly enough, he never had to defend this marriage at all in his lifetime, which leads even his critics to admit that this was probably normal practice in seventh-century Arabia.[156]

There is even a Quranic revelation (65:4) regarding waiting periods to tell if pre-pubescent girls were pregnant. Again, this sounds almost absurd to a modern mind, but for the day, it was common practice. From history it appears that Muhammad loved Aisha more than his other wives and that she had a great deal of admiration for him as well. He ended up dying in her tent under her care.

The marriage that Muhammad had to defend himself against criticism for during his lifetime was the marriage to Zaynab bint Jahsh, his former daughter-in-law. She had married Muhammad's adopted son, Zayd bin Haritha. Neither had wanted to marry each other, but Muhammad had insisted upon the union as a political statement—it would prove the equality of all believers, for Zaynab was from a notable family and Zayd was the son of a free slave. God had supported this union with a Quranic revelation (33:6). However, neither was happy with the marriage.

One day Muhammad came to the tent seeking Zayd; however, he was not there, and Muhammad happened to see Zaynab, an apparently beautiful woman, dressed only in her undergarments. She invited him in, but he refused and went back to his tent allegedly saying, "Glory be to God the Almighty! Glory be to God, who causes hearts to turn!"[157]

When Zayd heard this, he thought that he had found his way out of the marriage. So he approached Muhammad numerous times, asking if he would like to have his wife, freeing him to divorce. Muhammad always declined the invitation, telling him to keep his wife and be faithful to God.

In the end, though, Zayd divorced her. This prompted a revelation from God to Muhammad that Zaynab was now to be his wife. This worried Aisha who presumed that Zaynab would now lord her marriage to the prophet over the other wives. Her fears were realized, and this led to much jealousy and bickering among the wives of Muhammad, especially between Zaynab and Aisha, who enjoyed a special relationship with Muhammad.

This marriage also prompted criticism from his peers as to the convenience of this "revelation," and it turned out to be somewhat of a scandal. As in the Bible, Muhammad experienced firsthand the fruits of polygamy—an institution not given by God.

Other criticisms leveled at Muhammad are that the Quran gives sons twice the inheritance as daughters (4:11) and that he allegedly claimed in a hadith that there will be more women in hell than men.[158]

Christians must be careful when criticizing Muhammad for being a misogynist because some accuse the Bible of containing the same attitudes:

- Polygamy, while not being the ideal established in Eden, was permitted by God for Abraham, Jacob, David, Solomon, and many other godly Jewish men

- Such notable prophets as Abraham, David, and Solomon all had their share of "woman problems" in their lives

- Women and children of enemy nations could be taken as plunder or spoil (Deut. 20:14)

- Israelites were able to marry captive girls from foreign nations (Deut. 21:10–14)

- Daughters only received an inheritance if there was no son in the family (Num. 27:1–11)

- Women are the "weaker" sex (1 Peter 3:7)

- Women should submit to their husbands (Eph. 5:22–24)

- Women should learn at church "in quietness" and should not teach or have authority over a man (1 Tim. 2:11–13)

- Women are encouraged to dress modestly, and without expensive adornment (1 Tim. 2:9, 10)

- It is very difficult to find a "righteous" woman (Eccles. 7:28; Prov. 31:10)

One must judge Muhammad (and the Bible prophets, for that matter) based on their historical context and culture of their time. The *Seventh-day Adventist Bible Commentary*, when discussing the divorce law of Deuteronomy 24:1–4 and the application to present day divorce issues, states, "In reality, these verses open to our view the home life of the Jew, in which the taking of a wife was regarded as the acquiring of a piece of property. The husband's authority over his wife was almost absolute. The purpose of the law here announced was to better the lot of Hebrew women. This law, far from establishing a low moral standard, or approving of one, represented a far higher standard than the cruel customs of the time recognized."[159] Overall, when examining Muhammad's apparently archaic teachings in regards to women, one can come to the same conclusion.

Even though a vast majority of modern Western women would balk at living in a Muslim culture, they might actually appreciate living in Muhammad's society during his time if they were choosing between that and the cruel realities of life that existed for women in other cultures of that time.

In fairness, condemning Muhammad based upon his polygamous lifestyle and "women problems" doesn't seem merited when analyzing him in comparison to the biblical prophets. Muhammad's culture and time were much more similar to Abraham and David's time than ours. And Christians do not try to disprove Abraham or David's prophethood because of their polygamous lifestyle, or shortcomings in this area.

Question 4: Discrepancies Between the Bible and the Quran

Number of Divorces Allowed

The Bible states that once a couple divorces and remarries they are under no circumstances supposed to be remarried to each other (Deut. 24:1–4; Jer. 3:1). The Quran allows for a couple to get remarried once after a divorce from another spouse and forbids attempting reconciliation if they divorce each other a second time (2:229, 230). In Deuteronomy the Lord states that this would be an abomination and pollute the land, evidently condemning a practice that was common among other nations.

Even with this law of Deuteronomy 24 there was a school of Jewish thought at the time of Christ that stated that a man could divorce his wife if he found any reason to do so. This included such trivial things as burning a meal or the fact that he found another woman more attractive than his wife.[160] While differing in details, it appears that both the Quran and the Bible gave such a law to prevent men from keeping their wives "on a string" and divorcing them and remarrying them on a whim. They both encourage the parties to try to reconcile, and if things don't work out, to be decisive and move on.

Details Not Recorded in the Bible

It has already been mentioned that the Quran highlights most of the main Bible stories: the fall of Adam and Eve, Noah's ark and the flood, the life of Abraham and his posterity, Moses and the delivery of the Israelites from Pharaoh and the Egyptians, and most notably, the birth and ministry of Jesus the Messiah. However, many Christians are concerned about details in these stories that don't appear in the Bible. Examples of this are:

- One of Noah's "sons" was not saved on the ark (11:42)

- Noah's wife was not "righteous" (66:10)

- Pharaoh's wife was faithful to God and wanted to be saved at the time of the Exodus (66:11)

- The birds and winds were subject to David when he was building the temple (34:11–15)

One must notice a few things about these statements before coming to any radical conclusions. First, none of these details would be considered essential to the salvation of a soul. They are merely details of secondary importance to the main spiritual meaning behind the story.

Second, it does not prove that a prophet is a false prophet simply due to the fact that they might give a few extra biblical details of a biblical story. If Adventists adhered to such a principle, they would have to declare Ellen White a false prophet. She gave details about how Adam looked during his fall, how the knife fell from the priest's hand in the temple right at the time of the crucifixion, and a myriad of other details that one won't find when reading the biblical accounts.

Third, one must attempt to reconcile these stories with the biblical account and not come to the hasty conclusion that if something doesn't sound familiar it must be automatically not of God. For instance, in the case of Noah losing a "son" during the flood, an Adventist will notice that even the *Seventh-day Adventist Bible Dictionary* gives twelve different definitions in the Old Testament of a "son," ranging from your own child, to a cousin, to a kindly form of address from an older man to a younger man.[161]

Since Arabic is also a Semitic language, one would assume that the word "son" could have as many definitions as in Hebrew. This could mean that Muhammad was writing about Noah losing a cousin or just a very close follower who had helped him build the ark and that it was heartbreaking to him. This explanation seems feasible since it seems to be a symbolic description of the event with Noah screaming to his lost "son" through the ark walls while the flood was raging (not the best time to have a conversation).

As for other details, we really don't know the spiritual condition of Noah's or Pharoah's wives or if David did any miracles. So, since they don't contradict the main spiritual themes or doctrines of the Bible—the fall of man and the salvation of God—one must reserve judgment until the millennium when the righteous can have access to the records in heaven. Neither do they contradict facts that actually were revealed in the Bible.

Muhammad's Borrowing From Other Literature

This leads to another group of stories that don't sound familiar to Christians and which cause some to think that Muhammad was really "out there" in his relaying of spiritual stories. Christian author W. St. Clair Tisdall and others have done much research on where Muhammad acquired some of these stories. (*The Original Sources* is the name of Tisdall's book for those readers who would like to study his work more in depth.) The following is a graph that gives a sampling of the stories and imagery that Muhammad used and the possible sources that were extant on the Arabian peninsula in the seventh century:

Story/Description	Quran	Source
Adam's two sons: Conversation between Cain and Abel. Cain kills Abel, and God sends raven to show him where to dispose of the corpse.	5:27–31	Jewish Talmud: Pirqe de Rabbi Eleazer
Abraham smashed one of his Jewish father's idols; kinsmen became so enraged they threw him into the fire; he was miraculously saved by God	21:68, 69	Midrash: Genesis Rabbah
Solomon inviting the Queen of Sheba to come and visit him; how a second hoopoe bird delivered information Jinn and beasts were gathered on Esther	27:17–40	Jewish Targum

Story/Description	Quran	Source
The Harut and Marut story is one from the Jewish Talmud where they, as angels, asked God permission to come down to earth, but they succumbed to temptation and God punished them in Babylon	2:102	Jewish Talmud
Legend of Christian "Companions of the Cave" (also called the Christian legend of Seven Sleepers)	18:8–25	European tale
Story of birth of Mary and her early life with Zechariah	19:16–35	Proto-evangelium the priest James the Less
Jesus was able to speak in his cradle	3:46	Arabic Infancy Gospel
Jesus was able to make a clay item into a live bird, along with healing powers	5:110, 111	Gospel of Thomas the Israelite
Descriptions of Paradise: righteous will be adorned with "bracelets of gold and pearls"	22:23	Multiple Persian sources/Zoroastrain sources
"dressed in fine silk and rich brocade"	44:53, 54	
"recline on green cushions and rich carpets of beauty"	55:76	
"will sit on thrones encrusted with gold and precious stones"	56:15–17	
share in "dishes and goblets of gold" on which would be "all that the souls	43:71, 73	
could desire, all that their eyes could delight in" including an	55:66, 68	
"abundance of fruit" along with "dates and pomegranates." There	56:21–36	
they will enjoy the "flesh of fowls, any that they may desire."	3:198, 136	
Paradise consists of "gardens with rivers flowing beneath"; in it are	47:15, 16	
"two springs pouring forth water in continuous abundance" along	76:13, 14	
with "rivers of milk of which the taste never changes; rivers of wine,	13:35, 36	

Story/Description	Quran	Source
Descriptions of Paradise: a joy to those who drink; and rivers of honey pure and clear.	78:31–34	Multiple Persian sources/Zoroastrain sources
That wine is "free from headiness" so that those who drink it will not	37:48–50	
"suffer intoxication therefrom." There will be "voluptuous women	44:54–56	
of equal age," those of "modest gaze, with lovely eyes," "fair	76:19–22	
women with beautiful, big, lustrous eyes." Righteous will be with such "chaste maidens."	52:20–24	

These borrowings "prove" to many Christians that Muhammad was a false prophet and just had political designs in the creation of a new religion, synthesized from the religions of the areas he was about to conquer. Bible-believing Christians can obviously find dissimilarities with Scripture in some of these accounts. But before condemning Muhammad as a false prophet one must be very careful and look at the experience of Adventists.

First of all, haven't Adventists faced similar accusations against their prophet? Didn't the church even have to hire a copyright lawyer to analyze the charges of plagiarism against Ellen White? Many hold that a prophet must be almost infallible. Ellen White herself taught that not every word and punctuation mark was from God, but that the ideas and thoughts were inspired of Him, and He left the prophet to write down the inspiration in his own words, sometimes using the religious ideas, stories, writings, and language of his time.

Second, for an example of the concept of thought inspiration, the Christian may learn much from Jesus' teaching and ministry. Did He ever borrow ideas or stories that were common among the people of His day, which we find strange at best, or heretical at worst? One doesn't need to look further than Luke 16:19–31 and the story of the rich man and Lazarus.

Jesus, in this passage, uses language that is extremely strange to a modern Christian—that Lazarus was carried "into Abraham's bosom." He then proceeds to tell how the rich man was being "tormented" in hell. For Adventists, this is not just strange language, but it contradicts what the rest of Scripture teaches about the mortality of the soul, including Abraham and his "bosom," hell, and the day of judgment. So why would Jesus, the divine Son of God, pick a story like this that has contributed to many Christians believing in false doctrines? The *Seventh-day Adventist Bible Commentary* makes the following statement:

> One of the most important principles of interpretation is that each parable was designed to teach one fundamental truth, and that the details of the parable need not necessarily have significance in themselves, except as 'props' for the story. In other words, the details of a parable must not be pressed as having a literal

meaning in terms of spiritual truth unless the context makes clear that such a meaning is intended. Out of this principle grows another—that it is not wise to use the details of a parable to teach doctrine. Only the fundamental teaching of a parable as clearly set forth in its context and confirmed by the general tenor of Scripture, together with details explained in the context itself, may legitimately be considered a basis for doctrine.[162]

Later on in the article it mentions that other non-Adventist commentaries agree that the details of this parable are not to be used for defining doctrine but that they were merely commonly held Jewish beliefs of the time.[163]

The point is that if Christians should not attempt to discredit the divinity of Jesus based on the details of a "heretical" parable, neither should one condemn Muhammad for usage of spiritual stories that were contemporary for him without examining the spiritual truths that he was attempting to teach using the language and stories that were prevalent on the Arabian peninsula at the time.

I will take one example from the list above that may appear dubious to Christians—the "Companions of the Cave" story related by Muhammad. This is a story about a number of boys from Ephesus who fled persecution during the time of the Roman Emperor Decius (249–251 CE) and took refuge in a cave not far from the city. When their enemies discovered them, they barricaded the entrance to the cave, leaving the boys to perish from starvation. As the story goes, God put the boys to sleep indefinitely.

One hundred and ninety six years later, during the reign of Theodosius II, a shepherd found the cave and opened it up. The boys awoke at that instant and related their story to the shepherd. They then went into the city and were amazed to find that Christianity had ceased to be persecuted and was now the main religion of the empire. When they visited a shop, they found the storekeeper very skeptical about their story. So they produced a coin with Decius on it.

As the story goes, the boys were radiating with so much celestial brightness that the townspeople called for the emperor to come and examine the boys and see the cave where they had "slept." When he arrived and entered the cave, he believed in their story, upon which the boys died immediately.

The emperor, Theodosius, claimed that God had given him this as a testament to the doctrine of the immortality of the soul.[164] The story had become popular among Christians of the time, apparently as proof of this false doctrine.

Tisdall and other Christian commentators use this as an example of Muhammad's false claim of prophethood: that he said that God revealed to him this story about the boys in the cave, and that Muhammad believed it actually happened. (In Tisdall's opinion, it is just a "silly tale").

So why would God include this apparently fallacious tale in the Quran? According to the tradition of the Hadith, some pagan Meccan Arabs came to test Muhammad's claim of inspiration, and they asked him if he could reveal how many boys there had been and how many years they had been in the cave (since these were both disputed points among those who told the story). Muhammad said that he would answer them on the next day.

That night he received the revelation recorded in Sura 18. He came back and he never stated how many boys there were, but did say that the boys were those who had faith in God, and that God had blessed them, put them to sleep for a "number of years" and then He "roused them" to "test them" (10–13). Then Muhammad draws the conclusion, "Nor say of anything, 'I shall be sure to do such and such tomorrow' without adding 'so please God'" (23, 24).

Although he says that they stayed "three hundred years and (some) add nine," he tells the Muslims,

> Say: 'God knows best how long they stayed: with Him is (the knowledge of) the secrets of the heavens and the earth: how clearly He sees, how finely He hears (everything)! They [the boys in the cave] have no protector other than Him; nor does He share His Command with any person whatsoever. And recite (and teach) what has been revealed to thee of the book of thy Lord: none can change His words, and none wilt thou find as a refuge other than Him. And keep thy soul content with those who call on their Lord morning and evening, seeking His face; and let not thine eyes pass beyond them seeking the pomp and glitter of this life; nor obey any whose heart We have permitted to neglect the remembrance of us, one who follows his own desires, whose case has gone beyond all bounds'. (26–28)

Muhammad does not get into a long argument about the time they spent in the cave or how many boys there were. Even though he says that the boys were there 309 years, from verse 26 it appears that he might just be quoting what others stated about the story (because 300 was a number that had been used previously—and some believed up to 372 years) since he tells the Muslims to say "God knows how long they stayed" when asked this question.

In stark contrast to the spin given this story by Christians as a proof of the immortality of the soul, Muhammad gives it as sign of the vanity, shortness, and unpredictability of life. He challenges the pagans that were challenging him to be content with studying the revealed things of God in the "Book" and, if one reads from verses 29–31, he tells of the day of judgment. In other words, God is saying here, "Don't worry about the silly details of this story. The main thing is that I can put you to sleep and rouse you from your sleep. You need to live your life with the thought that one day you will have to give an account of yourselves to God." Yusuf Ali says that this parable "refers to the brevity, uncertainty and vanity of life; to the many paradoxes in it, which can only be understood by patience and the fullness of knowledge; and to the need of guarding our spiritual gains against the incursions of evil."[165]

I give this as an example because when I read Tisdall's book his accusation toward Muhammad about this story of the cave bothered me more than any of his other accusations. It was especially disconcerting when I read that Christians used this tale as proof of the immortality of the soul. I couldn't understand why Muhammad who, as we studied in chapter 6, didn't espouse or teach the immortality of the soul in the rest of Quran would include such a tale as supposed inspiration from God.

But after studying the context, and the actual story in the Quran, I found it had a completely different spiritual meaning than what was assigned by Tisdall. And from the Quranic story it isn't clear what actually happened—were the boys actually asleep for many years or just a few years? Were they dead (since death is like a sleep), sleeping, or did God just give them strength to hide from their persecutors for a long time? Would God have allowed them to die and then resurrect them to show His power over death much as we believe He did in Jerusalem when Jesus was resurrected? These questions are not answered in the Quran.

Simply, Muhammad says that God revealed that He did something with these boys and that He is the only One who knows the details of this story; we should just be content with studying the clear revelation that He has already given.

If one were to go through each reference Tisdall makes to the "borrowed" literature, which Muhammad used, it would be a book in and of itself. But it is clear that Adventists, just as the *Seventh-day Adventist Bible Commentary* warns in regards to biblical interpretation, must not get "hung up" in the details of stories or religious language that Muhammad uses in the Quran. On the contrary, one must look at the primary teaching and the spiritual principle that each story or parable espouses.

After doing that, one notices the fact that, while they sound strange to our ears, in each of these stories—Jesus speaking in his crib, palm trees feeding Jesus and His parents, Jesus making clay birds come to life, Solomon "ruling the wind," and Mary being under the tutelage of Zechariah—these Bible characters are lifted up in the Quran as being inspired of God.

The stories about Jesus are especially striking since they set Him apart from all of the other Quranic characters. An example of this is the story of Jesus "speaking from the cradle." Ibn Ishaq tells us that the Christians of Najran had come to Muhammad telling him of the story of Jesus speaking "from the cradle and that this is something that no child of Adam has ever done."

They also used the story of Jesus making clay objects come to life to prove His divinity.[166] To this day when Arabs want to prove the uniqueness of someone, they talk about that individual having "spoken in the cradle."[167] So the fact that Muhammad used these stories in the Quran actually suggests that he believed what the Christians of Najran told him. So instead of using this story, as many Christians do, to show that Muhammad was a false prophet, it actually can be used to show, according to our definition of the word, that Muhammad was a "Christian."

Christians must admit that prophets such as Jesus, Paul, and Ellen White all "borrowed" material, and that therefore a prophet cannot be condemned on these grounds. Neither may a prophet be condemned for the details of parables contemporary to them, which they use in teaching spiritual lessons.

Based on these understandings, we can conclude that neither Muhammad's main theme of worshiping the God of Abraham in this life and preparation for the day of judgment, nor any of the other teachings that were examined in chapter 6 are contradicted by any of this borrowed material. More importantly, the great themes of the Bible, and even its revealed details remain intact.

Interestingly enough, the accusation that Muhammad merely copied or told others' stories was one that he faced when he was still alive. In Sura 16 it is recorded that his detractors claimed that only a "human being" had related to him these revelations (103). According to Ibn Ishaq, his detractors thought that Muhammad received his "revelations" from Jabr, a Christian slave, at whose booth in the market Muhammad used to sit. Others mention Yasara, another slave who was a Christian, with whom Muhammad used to spend time. Then, of course, there was Khadijah's cousin, Waraqah, who was known to be a Christian.

Waraqah was well versed in the Bible and had even copied the Gospels in Hebrew. He was the one who encouraged Muhammad to follow the prophetic call and assured him that the call was of God.[168] So it is true, even according to Islamic sources that Muhammad had contact with some Christians. And it is well known that he lived among many Jews in Medina, so he had contact with what one would term "Bible-believers."

However, in answer to this accusation put forth by his contemporary detractors, a revelation was given by God refuting it and stating that the Quran was revealed by the Holy Spirit (16:102). One thing one can say for sure is that there was no known translation of the New Testament in Arabic, so Muhammad would not have been able to gain information from reading it, or to compare whether or not a story was from the canon or an apocryphal source. So, Muhammad must be taken at his word until there is further proof that his revelation is contrary to previous revelation.

Conclusion for Test #2

After studying these four main objections, one can't definitively prove that Muhammad didn't speak according to "the law and the testimony." A case can be made that he did.

Most Christian critics don't bring up the objections of *jihad*, his position toward women, and the supposed discrepancies of the Quran with the Bible because one can argue that these would not have been valid arguments for a contemporary of Muhammad living in Arabia at that time.

Most of his critics believe that he was a false prophet because they say he didn't believe in the divinity of Jesus and His crucifixion. However, after having studied the many false teachings within Christianity at the time of Muhammad, and having seen his actual words about Jesus and His death from the original Arabic, it is difficult to agree with this objection, also.

Test #3 – Have his prophecies come true?

This is a difficult one to judge because Muhammad didn't make many prophecies in the Quran concerning the future, with one main exception—the day of judgment and the resurrection. Obviously, one can't say as of yet that this prophecy has been fulfilled, but Adventists certainly hope it will be, since it is a main feature of their faith as well! I think there is enough biblical evidence to believe in these truths and to "hope for what is not seen," that neither Muhammad nor Adventists will be disappointed in this prophecy. And this is the dominant theme of the Quran.

So, what are some of the other prophecies that Muhammad made? In Sura 30 Muhammad states the following:

> The Roman Empire has been defeated-in a land close by; but they, (even) after (this) defeat of theirs, will soon be victorious-within a few years. With God is the decision, in the past and in the future; on that day shall the believers rejoice… (30:2–4)

Muslims believe this prophecy was given in Mecca about the sixth or seventh year before the Hijra (615–616 CE). In order to understand this prophecy, the historical context in which it was given must be understood.

Arabia was located between two great, international empires—the Byzantine Empire headquartered in Constantinople and the Persian Empire. Although the Arabian peninsula was never truly conquered by either empire, due to their proximity both exerted an influence on the life of the Arabs. The Arabs, including the Quraysh tribe of Mecca, tended to favor the Zoroastrian Persians over the Christian Byzantines.

Muhammad, in this text, claims that the "Roman Empire" had been defeated (Muhammad and the Muslims usually referred to Constantinople as "Rome" since it had replaced Rome as the capital of the Roman Empire since the time of Constantine)—and this was true. The Persians, under the leadership of Khusrau Parwiz (an adopted son of a previous Byzantine emperor, Maurice) had defeated the Byzantine emperor, Heraclius, in battles for Aleppo, Antioch, and Damascus in 611 CE. In 614–615 CE Jerusalem fell to the Persians, which was a major defeat to the Christian Byzantines—to lose the "holy city." The city was burned and pillaged, with the Jews and pagan Arabs siding with the Persians. The Persian priests claimed it was a great victory for Zoroastrianism, and the general feeling among non-Christians was one of elation. In the succeeding years after this great victory, the Persians raided Egypt, Libya, and even made it through Asia Minor almost to the gates of Constantinople.

To most observers of the time, it looked as if the Byzantine Empire had almost reached its end. However, in this Quranic passage Muhammad claimed that this victory was short lived and that the Byzantines ("Roman Empire") would be victorious in a few years. And that is exactly what happened.

Heraclius, even though faced with a desperate situation, didn't give up; instead, knowing that the Persians were weak at sea, he conceived a brilliant plan, which included his superior naval power. He transported his army through the Aegean Sea to launch a surprise attack on the Persians just south of the Taurus Mountains. A decisive battle was fought, and the Persians were routed. They still had a large force in Asia Minor so Heraclius rushed home to Constantinople, made a treaty with the Avars, and they collaborated to keep the Persians at bay near the capital. He then led three campaigns in 623, 624, and 625 CE along the southern shore of the Black Sea and was victorious, securing Asia Minor up to the regions of Kars and Trabizond.

From this vantage point he was able to proceed through the Christian Armenian kingdom and launch strikes into the very heart of the Persian Empire. A decisive battle was waged near Mosul along the Tigris in December 627 CE, and Heraclius and the Byzantines prevailed. Heraclius celebrated his triumph in March 628 CE, and peace was then declared between the two empires.[169]

If Muhammad really stated this prophecy before the Hijra during his time in Mecca, this would be a stunning fulfillment of prophecy, for it seemed to the world that the Byzantines would be overcome by the resurgent Persians. But within one decade the fates of the empires would be completely reversed, with the "Roman" Byzantines expanding in power and the Persians in decline.

In an odd twist of fate, both empires suffered tremendous losses in territory and prestige in the seventh century, not at the hands of each other, but instead, at the hands of a new Arabian Muslim empire that would arise around the followers of Muhammad.

Another prophecy made in the Quran is a reference to a famine that enveloped Mecca. There is a reference to a "smoke" (or "mist") that God would send upon the inhabitants of Mecca as punishment for the Quraysh's unbelief (44:10, 11). Some commentators also combine this warning with the "distress" of Sura 23:75 as foretelling a great famine that occurred in Mecca around 630 CE. Other historians mention another famine around 618 CE. Both of these suras were written while Muhammad was still in Mecca, so they could have foretold either of these events before they happened.

Muslim historians have recorded that the second famine was especially severe, and say that the residents of Mecca even began to eat bones and carrion.[170] While it is not clear from these texts that a famine was intended, since Muhammad didn't use that exact word, it is clear that the Quran states that this "penalty" was placed upon the Meccans since God had sent them an apostle and they had rejected his message.

The Quran went as far as to predict that even though God would punish them, this would not be enough to bring these proud polytheists to repentance (44:12–15). With that in mind, it would make more sense if this prophecy related to the famine of 618 CE since it is known that the Quraysh continued to fight Islam for twelve years before Muhammad returned to Mecca, turning it into the center of Islam.

This prophecy may not be considered a very clear one, and some skeptics may doubt its reference to a famine; however, the spiritual principles here are similar to biblical ones, that God punishes His people in hopes that it will have the effect of bringing them to repentance.

Muhammad states in the Quran that every people group is allotted a certain "time" by God and that God owns time (7:34; 10:49; 11:104; 14:10; 15:4, 5; 67:26). From these texts one can conclude that Muhammad believed in the concept, which Adventists also espouse, of prophetic time periods in which God grants nations a probationary time to bring them to repentance.

Prophecies of the Hadith

I will now briefly cover the prophecies of the Hadith. I cannot go into the details of each prophecy; that would have to be the topic of another book, since there are many of them.

Muslims themselves dispute the chains of communication by which some of them were transmitted, and some of them are obviously fabrications because they contradict the revelations of the Quran. I will only touch on the main themes of prophecies given in the Hadith because, as previously mentioned, it is almost impossible to declare authoritatively which hadith are legitimate and which are not.

Some of the things that Muhammad allegedly prophesied, which occurred during the first few centuries of Muslim rule are:

- Abu Bakr would be the first caliph, and there would be eleven true caliphs after him

- The Muslim conquest of Egypt, and the Persian and Byzantine Empires

- The murder of the caliph Omar

- The trials of the caliph Othman

- The thirty years of the Muslim caliphate with the rise of the Umayyad dynasty following

- That Hasan, the son of Ali, would make peace between two large groups of Muslims

- That Islam would reach to India and China

- The Muslims would fight the Turks

- That his generation would be the best Muslim generation with succeeding generations getting worse

Other alleged prophecies of Muhammad concerned individuals of his time and their fate in Muslim battles. However, I will not focus much attention on these, because it is very difficult to tell if Muhammad actually predicted these or if they were concocted by Muslims who used them for their own or their Islamic sect's political gain. I will leave these to Islamic studies experts to determine if they are valid, because, of course, if someone thought them up a hundred years or so *after* Muhammad passed away, and after the events had occurred, they would naturally be very accurate prophecies!

Muhammad has allegedly made another whole genre of prophecies recorded in the Hadith. Those concern the end of times before the second coming of Jesus and the day of judgment. Muhammad allegedly prophesied the following:

- Islam would divide into sects and become very evil

- There would be a lack of knowledge, and ignorance of the Quran would be widespread
- Islam would return some day "new and strange" as it began
- Every hundred years God would need to send a reformer to the Muslims
- Fifteen evils would exist on the earth immediately preceding the day of judgment:
    1. Spoils of war hoarded by some members of society only
    2. People will steal things that were left with them as a trust
    3. *Zakat* (like a tithe) will be taken from people against their will and be a burden
    4. A man will obey his wife, but
    5. Will disobey his mother
    6. A man will treat his friend well, but
    7. Will be harsh and distant with his father
    8. Voices will be raised in mosques
    9. The leader of a people will be the basest individual among them
    10. A man will be honored because his evil is feared
    11. Alcohol will be imbibed
    12. Silk will be worn (by men)
    13. Female singers will be used
    14. Musical instruments will be used
    15. The last of the nation will curse the first
- Muslims will enter paradise first
- Predominantly the poor will be in paradise—they will enter before the rich

- Most dwellers in hell will be women

- The Mahdi—a family member of Muhammad—will come and fill the world with justice and fairness right before the second coming of Jesus. However, there are some hadiths that claim that the Mahdi actually is Jesus, the son of Mary.[171]

- The Arabs will become extremely wealthy (have a "mountain of gold") and will compete with one another in building large mosques and tall buildings

- Iraq, Syria, and Egypt will be "denied" their currency (overrun by another political power)

- People will come to Islam in throngs and leave it in throngs

- Muslims will love to fight with the sword; there will be much killing on the earth

- People will want to die because of evil on earth

- There will be earthquakes and great rainfall

- Thirty false prophets will arise after him

- The most evil generation will directly proceed the last day

- Homosexuality will abound

- Last generation will not promote good or forbid evil

- There will be six signs showing the nearness of the hour (day of judgment):

  1. Death of Muhammad

  2. The conquering of Constantinople

  3. Death that will kill Muslims like sheep

  4. An abundance of wealth and discontentment with it

  5. A trial that will not leave a single house from the Arabs except that it enters it

  6. A battle with the Romans ending with a truce

The Tests of a Prophet

- Ten signs will come before the day of judgment

    1. Smoke (some say between East and West—for forty days)

    2. The antichrist must come (Dajjal)

    3. The beast

    4. The rising of the sun from the West (appears to be sign for close of probation)

    5. Descending of Jesus, son of Mary

    6. Gog and Magog must come

    7. Three *khasf* (swallowing of earth)—Khasf of East

    8. Khasf of West

    9. Khasf of Arabian peninsula

    10. Last sign—great fire from East to direct all people to gathering place

- The Romans will have the greatest numbers before the day of judgment

- The conquering of Jerusalem will be bad for Medinah; then there will be a "massacre" that will lead to the conquering of Constantinople, which will lead to the appearance of the antichrist

- The antichrist will:

    1. Come after three years of hardship sent by God

    2. Not be able to enter Medinah, and when Jesus dies he will be buried in Medinah

    3. Be "one-eyed," white, radiant, and with curly hair and have *kafara* (unbeliever) written on his forehead (every believer will be able to read this regardless of whether he is illiterate or not—so it is a cryptic message); first will appear as king, then prophet, then God Himself

    4. Come at a time when religion and knowledge of religion is weak

5. Have a mountain of "bread" to give his followers at a time when there is scarcity of food

6. Cause "rain" to fall, and with devils will raise the dead to life

7. Call the river "Paradise"—"Fire"; and river of "Fire"—"Paradise"

8. Claim to be the Lord; but is a liar

9. Besiege Muslims who have taken refuge near "Shams" (present-day Syria); Muslims will be divided into three groups

10. Will remain on earth for forty days—one day will be like a year, another like a month, and another like a week; this is about one year, two and a half months.

11. Will be killed by Jesus at His appearance, who appears as a result of prayers of Muslims

- Jesus, son of Mary, plays a very prominent role in these prophecies, and according to the Hadith:

   1. He kills the antichrist and Gog and Magog

   2. He "smashes the cross" and "kills the pig"

   3. He descends near to Damascus with brown complexion and head dripping with water

   4. He ushers in a new age of peace where lions will graze with camels, leopards with cows, wolves with sheep—and children will play with snakes and not be hurt

   5. He will remove the *jizyah* (poll tax on non-Muslims)

   6. All will come to believe in Him

   7. Kaba will be destroyed and Hajj will not be performed any longer[172]

Obviously, some of the hadith appear dubious, since they even contradict the Quran. The best example of this is the hadith that states that Jesus will die and be buried next to Muhammad. This contradicts the Quran, which states that Jesus will come back again before the day of judgment. It seems contradictory that God "raised up" Jesus after His death on earth, but then Jesus has to come back before the great day of judgment at the end of time and die here on this earth, while supposedly bringing in a new age of peace at the very time when the righteous are supposed to inherit eternal life.

Interestingly though, this hadith was only mentioned by one person, whereas, for example, the hadith about Jesus killing the antichrist and Gog and Magog is attested to by numerous hadiths.[173] One can imagine though why the latter hadith would have been accepted through the centuries as Christians and Muslims began to war with each other with each attempting to prove the superiority of their own religion.

Even though I have neither the space in this book nor the expertise to adequately judge which hadiths are legitimate, it is worth noting that many of Muhammad's prophecies given in the Hadith have come true and/or resemble what Adventists believe the Bible teaches about the end of times. His statements about the end of times deal with "the beast," "Gog and Magog," the decadence of the last generation, the Laodicean condition of believers (not forbidding evil or promoting good), and the occurrence of natural disasters. These all sound very similar to what one would hear in an Adventist evangelistic campaign.

Muhammad doesn't spare his own people, predicting that many of them will apostatize and revert to paganism, all the while becoming extremely wealthy and building tall buildings. If he did predict these things, one can say, upon examining modern Islam and the Arabs of the Middle East, that his predictions have come true.

Again, even if some of the hadiths in regards to Jesus were concocted, He is still the hero of the last days even in the Hadith. He is the one who ushers in a new age of peace, kills the antichrist, and is the deliverer of the true people of God. We also notice that, while some of the prophecies sound a bit strange to us, many of the same cryptic symbols appear in these prophecies as in the Bible: Gog and Magog, the beast, the antichrist, divisions of religion (Babylon), and Jesus' deliverance of the saints.

Of course, modern Muslims give these prophecies a different spin, attempting to prove that Jesus will come to show that He is only a prophet, not the divine Son of God. But the hadiths themselves don't lend themselves to this interpretation, unless one wants to see things that way.

Have Muhammad's prophecies come true?

I don't claim to be an expert, able to analyze the authenticity of either the Quranic revelation or the hadiths of Muhammad; however, upon investigating Muhammad's authenticity as a prophet, I must admit the following:

- If Muhammad foretold in the Quran of the resurgence of the Christian Byzantine Empire and their conquest of the Persian Empire while he was in Mecca, this prophecy was fulfilled.

- If Muhammad really did predict, as stated in the Hadith, the coming of the antichrist and a beast, the second coming of Jesus which would destroy these powers, a time of violence, wickedness and disasters, and a time when the Arabs would become wealthy, build tall buildings and apostatize from the faith, then these are all prophecies that either have been fulfilled, or as Adventists believe, will be fulfilled in the future.

- If Muhammad really saw in vision the great day of judgment, the resurrection of the dead, the reward of paradise to the faithful people of God, and the punishment of the wicked in hell—Adventists also believe that these are biblical teachings, fulfilling one of the signs of a true prophet. These are the most prominent themes in the Quran. One will be struck, when reading the Quran for the first time, how often the themes of judgment and a real heaven and hell appear. And Adventists agree that these are real prophetic concepts, of which believers are awaiting the fulfillment.

Test #4 - Did Muhammad call people to worship the one true God of the Bible?
The fourth test comes to us from Deuteronomy 13:1-5. That is to say, that even though all of these prophecies came true maybe Satan inspired him, since he is an astute student of Bible prophecy and can "predict" some things that God will do in the future. The Christian must check and see if Muhammad through these prophecies called mankind to worship the God of the Bible, and repent of worshiping any god except Him. So one must analyze the Quran's god and check to see if it is the same one of the Bible.

Many well-meaning Christians assume that the Allah of the Quran is not the God of the Bible and refuse to use this name for the God of the Bible. Ironically, this belief only persists in non-Arabic lands. Arab Christians consistently use the word "Allah" to signify the God of the Bible. In Arabic the word for "god" is *ilah*. To signify "the God" the definite article *al* is added to *ilah* to come up with *Allah*.

Even the Quraysh recognized that there was "the God"—they just had 359 other gods to go with Him in the Kabah in Mecca. So, it makes sense that Muhammad dedicated so much space in the Quran to condemning taking "partners" for "the God." Muhammad's message was that there was only "the God"—all other gods were false.

Most scholars acknowledge that Allah stems from the Aramaic *elah*—which also was the root for the Hebrew *eloah* (singular) and *elohim* (plural), terms that are used in the Bible to designate "god," "gods," and "God."

Oddly enough, the Arabic Allah has a much firmer biblical foundation for a designation of "God" than the English "God." The English word "god" has pagan Germanic roots to *Gott*—a designation for Odin, the chief Teutonic deity, who lives on top of the world and procreates with his blonde, blue-eyed goddess wife of love, fertility, and beauty, Freya. However, this stops no English speakers from using this pagan-originated word to designate the God of the Bible. In the same way, Arab Christians, Jews, and Muslims have all designated the God of the Bible Allah for the past 1,400 years. So, there is no foundation upon which a Christian can say that Muhammad was calling on the Arabs to worship another god simply due to his usage of the word Allah.

The accusation that Muslims worship a god other than the one that Christians or Jews do is not a new one. From the time Muhammad began to draw a following, the people of the Book began to accuse this new sect. In Sura 2:139 Muhammad tells the Muslims to say the following when conversing with Jews and Christians on this topic:

> Will ye dispute with us about God, seeing that He is our Lord and your Lord; that we are responsible for our doings and ye for yours; and that we are sincere (in our faith) in Him?

In Muhammad's words he was not calling people to the worship of a new god, but rather leading them back to the religion that was given by God starting with Adam, Noah, and Abraham in Genesis and continuing through the New Testament. The next text in the Quran helps to clarify this point:

> Or do ye say that Abraham, Ismail, Isaac, Jacob and the Tribes were Jews or Christians? Say: Do ye know better than God? Ah! Who is more unjust than those who conceal the testimony they have from God? But God is not unmindful of what ye do! That was a people that hath passed away. They shall reap the fruit of what they did, and ye of what ye do! (2:140, 141)

Muhammad believed that just claiming a name for oneself, in this case, "Jew" or "Christian," didn't prove one had the "chosen" religion. One's fruits had to go along with the calling. It is interesting that in his mind Abraham wasn't a Jew or a Christian, even though an Adventist Christian would consider him both a Jew and a Christian.

So here one gets insight into Muhammad's viewpoint of why God would inspire him and not continue to work through Christianity. Muhammad states that they had "concealed the testimony they have from God" (Sura 5:18). Muhammad blamed both the Jews and Christians for not sharing the Word of God that had been entrusted to them. In Muhammad's mind they had lost their missionary spirit and had continued to lead sinful lifestyles.

After working as a pastor in a part of the world not very far from where Muhammad lived, I think I can understand what he was trying to say. It was offensive to me to see so many Christians take the name of Christ yet know so very little about the Bible and be so corrupt and pleasure-loving right in a Christian part of the world near to the Arabian peninsula.

I once had a man tell me how much he disliked Muslims and how he was so proud that even babies from his country were Christians from the time they were in their mothers' wombs. I didn't want to tell him, but I actually found the Muslims from the country he was referring to a more humble, friendly lot than the Christians from his country. But once nations accept a certain religion they often forget the essence of that religion with time. So it becomes a hereditary, cultural trait and not a personal spiritual exercise.

Muhammad also picked up on this and rebuked both Jews and Christians for forgetting that they are not genetically superior because of their religious heritage, but that they are entrusted by God with His revelation, and He expects them to live accordingly. Muhammad's view in this matter is much closer to an Adventist's view of the spiritual nature of the calling of God than to that held by most modern Jews and Christians (or for that matter, modern Muslims).

The Quran paints a picture of a God who:

- Is the Creator of the earth, the heavens, and all that is in them

- Inspired the prophets of the Bible

- Sent Jesus as the "gospel"

- Forgives sin and punishes unrepentant sinners

Most Christians who accuse Muhammad of worshiping another god state that the god of the Quran is vengeful and merciless and that Muhammad (like Adventists) preached a legalistic message of salvation by works. However, in reality, the same tension exists in the Quran as in the Bible: God is simultaneously a just God who will eventually destroy sinners and a merciful God who forgives sin and rewards the righteous.

It is true that Muhammad painted a very clear picture for the Quraysh of their fate in hell, but he also encouraged believers to come to the God of Abraham, for He is "most merciful and most gracious." Sura 3:135, 136 states:

> And those who having done something to be ashamed of, or wronged their own souls, earnestly bring God to mind, and ask for forgiveness for their sins, - and who can forgive sins except God?- and are never obstinate in persisting knowingly in (the wrong) they have done - for such the reward is forgiveness from their Lord, and Gardens with rivers flowing underneath,- an eternal dwelling.

The Quran shows that we are saved by God's grace, which accompanies salvation with a necessity to obey God:

> I would, if I disobeyed my Lord, indeed have fear of the penalty of a mighty day. On that day, if the penalty is averted from any, it is due to God's mercy; and that would be (salvation), the obvious fulfillment of all desire. (6:15, 16)

Muhammad states that obedience to God is required for salvation, but that salvation is only due to God's mercy. An Adventist can actually empathize with Muhammad because most Christians say the same thing about him that they say about Adventists. Yet they both believe in a God who saves mankind by His grace and is going to judge them by their works.

So, the accusations against Muhammad are as groundless as they are against Adventists—the Bible and the Quran both make it abundantly clear that one is saved by grace and grace only; *but,* if obedience (*islam*—submission) to God is not a result of our religion, God will not save us into an eternity where rebellion and sin will never exist again.

There is nothing in the Quran that would suggest that Allah is a different god than the One talked about in the Bible. Christians, Jews, and Muslims living in the Middle East for over a thousand years have agreed that their "Allah" is the same god in the Old Testament, New Testament, and Quran; they just don't agree with each other's theology about that God.

Test # 5 – Were the "fruits" of Muhammad's life consistent with the "fruits" of the Holy Spirit?

Jesus gave us this test in Matthew 7:15–23. He stated that the Christian would be able to tell if someone was sent by God if their "fruits" were consistent with the fruits of the Holy Spirit.

So did Muhammad exhibit fruits of the Holy Spirit as defined in Galatians 5:22, 23— love, joy, peace, patience, kindness, goodness, faithfulness, gentleness, and self-control? It depends on whom you listen to. Historically, Christians have accentuated his vindictive and violent traits—assassinations, commands to go to war, raids, etc. However, to be objective, Christians must recognize that one could paint Moses, Samuel, David, and Solomon in very dark tones if one wanted to turn a blind eye to their spiritual calling and the body of work that they produced in the course of their lives.

There is another completely different side of Muhammad that Muslims accentuate. Muslims describe him as one whose "heart was filled with intense love for all humankind irrespective of caste, creed, or color."[174] He was someone who "had the opportunity to strike back at those who attacked him, but refrained from doing so."[175] He was someone who "spoke of mercy for humankind."[176] As one of his companions described him, he was "neither rough nor harsh. He is neither noisy in the markets nor returns evil for evil, but he forgives and pardons."[177] Another companion said that he was "more bashful than a maiden in her seclusion."[178] He was not a "reviler or a curser nor obscene."[179] One of Muhammad's servants stated that he was always treated with the utmost kindness: "So I served the prophet at home and on journeys; by Allah, he never said to me for anything which I did: 'Why have you done this like this?' or, for anything which I did not do, 'Why have you not done this like this?'"[180] Christian critics of Muhammad don't deny these characteristics and admit that there was a great deal of "charm" and "personal magnetism" in his character.[181]

Even Christian critics marvel at the dedication that he exhibited to his cause. One such critic, John Gilchrist, states, "Mohammed never wavered in his belief in his own mission, nor, what is more extraordinary, in his belief as to its precise nature and well-defined limits."[182]

Gilchrist states again,

> One of the best evidences of his subjective sincerity is the almost fanatical devotion of his companions to his mission. With only a few exceptions, those nearest to him, once converted, stood with him through triumph and defeat, trial and setback, poverty and persecution.[183]

Muir states,

> It is strongly corroborative of Muhammad's sincerity that the earliest converts to Islam were not only of upright character, but his own bosom friends and people of his household, who, intimately acquainted with his private life, could not fail otherwise to have detected those discrepancies which ever more or less exist between the professions of the hypocritical deceiver abroad and his actions at home.[184]

The devotion of Abu Bakr who was a leading man of Mecca and known to be an upright man is also considered as one of the greatest signs of the relative uprightness of Muhammad's character for his time.[185] Gilchrist comes to this conclusion,

> Even before his claim to prophethood Muhammad was highly esteemed for his integrity and earned the title al-Amin, 'the Trustworthy'. Judged relatively by the standards of his day, he appears to emerge without reproach.[186]

Even though Muhammad didn't always refrain from violence, one of the greatest acts of magnanimity in victory was exhibited by him when he entered Mecca triumphantly after more than a decade of exile and bitter fights with the rulers of Mecca. He commanded all of his Meccan soldiers to refrain from revenge upon entering their hometown or when coming into contact with those who had taken their possessions and caused them years of suffering. It would have been very easy to give in to the temptation to punish those under whom they had suffered persecution for over a decade. But it was an example of graciousness in victory and "turning the other cheek" that succeeding Muslim rulers could emulate, as did Saladin who acted likewise in recapturing Jerusalem from the Crusaders more than 500 years later.

Since we are honestly investigating Muhammad's claim that he was a prophet, we can bring the following fruits forward as arguments for his prophethood:

- He was pious, spending much time in prayer
- He was considerate toward the poor and orphans
- He was considerate toward women
- He attempted to bring fairness and jurisprudence to his people
- He was not vengeful
- He was peace-loving at heart

- He encouraged learning and inspired in his followers a desire to improve themselves

- He united people around a simple form of worship

Most Christian critics don't deny that Muhammad was a relatively just man. Their contention against him being a true prophet doesn't stem from a comparison of his behavior toward his contemporaries but rather with his claim that he was a prophet for all mankind. They don't really go into much depth in analyzing his prophethood due to the fact that it appears to them that he denies the divinity of Christ and His crucifixion.[187] Therefore, they discard his claims of being a prophet right away without looking at the overall body of his work and the fruits of his labor.

I also would be remiss were I not to mention the fruits of his labor. What Muhammad accomplished during his lifetime and the effects he had on future generations of Arabs and Muslims is phenomenal. Muhammad united a plethora of warring tribes and religions and made a fairly monolithic and monotheistic religion and empire in just one century. He led them from rank polytheistic paganism to a belief in and submission to the one true God. It is one of the greatest success stories of all time for any religion or kingdom.

Muhammad's success would be analogous to somewhere like present-day Afghanistan, a loosely connected group of tribes led by warlords, converting to a new religion, and within a century overtaking all of Asia, not only conquering other lands, but taking heretofore uneducated groups of people and making them the most enlightened, technologically advanced, and educated people on the planet.

Muhammad's fruits, as examined in chapter 8, are plenteous. His nation became the most enlightened group of people in the world at the time, and made great achievements in literature, medicine, mathematics, the sciences, language, architecture, and government. One can actually argue that Muhammad's fruits include the Renaissance and the Protestant Reformation, which were made possible by the revival of learning in northern Europe, carried there through Sicily by Muslim scholars.

It was the children of Ishmael that kept the ancient Greek language alive and helped the Jews to regain their Hebrew language, which in turn made it possible to have the trustworthy translations of the Bible that modern Christendom now possesses.

It was the Muslims who during the seventh to eleventh centuries offered sanctuary to dissident groups such as the Nestorians and showed the world the blessing of religious freedom. Christians can thank Muslims that they offered a conscience to Christianity of the Middle Ages in calling them to repent of their idol-worship. Without the voice of the Muslims, many Christians would probably not have had the fortitude to protest the pagan, polytheistic, idolatrous practices that were quickly overtaking Christianity.

Without the rise of Islam, it is difficult to imagine what the modern world would be like. Who would have risen up and stopped the spread of that mighty power which Bible prophecy calls the "antichrist"? Would the two most populous countries on the planet, China and India, have succumbed to the "beast"-power of Revelation (which would have meant that half of the world's population now would have been adherents to that power)?

Who would have risen up at the time of Martin Luther to offer a diversion to those bent on eradicating the "Protestant heresy" from Europe, preventing them from accomplishing their purpose? Surely, God could have raised up other nations to accomplish His will, but one is constrained to admit that in the scope of the great controversy between God and Satan Islam played a critical role in favor of the side of truth.

So, far from discarding Muhammad as a prophet and disparaging him and his character, one must give him his due. Adventists are indebted to our spiritual cousins on the Ishmaelite side of the family for setting the foundation for bringing the world to the condition that it is today in which it is possible to have an end-time movement called to uphold religious freedom and proclaim a message to all peoples of the world.

In any case, even though the "fruits" of modern-day Islam don't appear to be in line with biblical standards, the vast majority of Muhammad's Christian critics acknowledge that one can't disprove Muhammad's prophethood based on bad personal character or evil "fruits" of his own life.

Chapter 11

WAS MUHAMMAD A TRUE PROPHET?

After this review of Muhammad's life and ministry, his teachings and prophecies as outlined in the Quran, biblical prophecies concerning the time period of Muhammad, and the historical context of his time, one must come to some decisive conclusion to the question—"Was he inspired by God?"

One of the problems that Adventists encounter when analyzing Muhammad is that they can't fully agree with the vast majority of either of the camps that are studying and judging him. On one hand, an Adventist can't agree with Muslims who almost deify Muhammad, stating that he was infallible and insisting that he is the great model for humanity's behavior and that everyone should emulate him as the greatest and last prophet. They even go as far as stating that all other prophets (including Jesus) will disclaim the privilege for "Intercession" on the day of judgment and will confer it upon Muhammad,[188] which, obviously, goes against what the Bible teaches.

On the other hand, Adventists can't agree with the non-Adventist Christian commentators who "prove" that Muhammad was not of God, but themselves believe that the Christian church never fell into complete apostasy and don't believe there is anything wrong with worshiping icons or statues, Sunday observance, erroneous conceptions of the immortality of the soul, eating unclean foods, or drinking alcohol (all stances that Adventists agree with Muhammad on).

Since we do not go to great lengths to either deify or vilify Muhammad, Adventists should be able to make an objective assessment of his prophethood. For this final assessment, I will rely heavily on the Bible and the writings of Ellen White, whom Adventists believe was given the Spirit of Prophecy that would prepare a people to meet Christ at the end of time.

Did the Bible Prophesy that Muhammad Would Arise?

The Quran states (Sura 7:157) that there is a biblical prophecy concerning Muhammad. Modern Muslims insist that the Bible foretold that a prophet would arise by the name of Ahmad (which they claim is a variant for the name of Muhammad). They attempt to prove that Jesus foretold him when He prophesied of a Comforter coming for the believers in John 14 (see Appendix E for a detailed discussion on this topic). Obviously most Christians cannot agree that this is a prophecy relating to Muhammad since it is usually interpreted as referring to the outpouring of the Holy Spirit starting at Pentecost and foretelling that the Holy Spirit would never leave the true believers in Christ. So would there be any other prophecies that would foretell Muhammad in Scripture? There are a couple of possibilities.

Joel 2

This is a prophecy which states that at the "end of time" God will give "young men" and "old men" visions and dreams. The context of this prophecy was one of judgment. Joel describes in detail the coming heavenly army on the "day of the Lord" and the absolute necessity to repent and prepare for this day. In Acts 2 the apostles interpreted the outpouring of the Holy Spirit at Pentecost as a fulfillment of this prophecy.

Adventists also interpret this prophecy as being fulfilled in Ellen White's prophetic gift. Who are we to say that God could not have fulfilled this prophecy through one of His devout followers on the Ishmaelite side of the family?

One needs to be careful since the Bible proclaims that God pours out His Holy Spirit on whomever He determines (1 Cor. 12:11). If what Muhammad stated was true—that Gabriel did appear to him and that he had visions of inspiration—then this prophecy was fulfilled.

Revelation 2:13–18

Jesus gives a stern warning here to the church of Pergamum and is revealed as the One bearing a "two-edged sword." This is an allusion to Scripture itself—Jesus is the Revealer of Scripture and it is called a "double-edged sword" (John 1:1–3; Heb. 4:12). Adventists traditionally have interpreted this to be a description of and a message to the church from the time of Constantine up to the starting point of the 1260-day prophecy (313–538 CE).

In no unclear terms the believers of Pergamum were told to repent and quit eating food sacrificed to idols, practicing immorality and tolerating Nicolaitans (thought to be those in the church who encouraged lawlessness under a guise of grace and freedom). Jesus is clear that He would come and "fight against them with the sword of My mouth" (Rev. 2:16). So was the message heeded—did Christianity repent?

One has to look no further than the message to the church of Thyatira (538–1500s CE) in the next section of the chapter to see Jesus' words, "I gave her time to repent of her sexual immorality, and she did not repent" (verse 21). He proceeds to say to these unrepentant believers that He would "kill her children with death" and then they would know that "I am He who searches the minds and hearts. And I will give to each of you according to your works" (verses 23).

So who fought against the church of Thyatira with a "double-edged sword"? Some commentators would probably lean toward small minority Christian groups that protested against the papacy during the Middle Ages such as the Albigenses, Waldenses, Bogomils, Passagians, Sabbatati, Cathari, and the Picards.[189] However, most of these groups were rather small and mainly appeared in history starting in the eleventh and twelfth centuries.

Those groups did form some type of resistance against medieval Christianity, but they were only minute blips on the radar in comparison with the overwhelming expansion of Islam, which completely surrounded Rome and Constantinople and kept them from expanding aggressively to the continent of Asia. Consider the article on the medieval church in the *Seventh-day Adventist Bible Commentary* describing the religious milieu of the sixth century:

> The 6th century witnessed a remarkable increase in papal power ... it was the removal of these German tribes [Vandals, Ostrogoths] that, in no small measure, opened the way for the development of papal power, and prepared for the imposing pontificate of Pope Gregory I, called "the Great," from 590 to 604. Gregory systematized church ritual and promoted monasticism, which was gradually becoming popular in the West ... he was vitally interested in missionary activity ... he became virtually the civil governor of Rome and its surrounding territories, practically replacing the weak Ravenna, who was supposed to govern Italy for the Byzantine emperors. From then on, despite weak popes, the papacy continued to grow in power, while the influence of the emperor became less and less in the West and finally vanished.[190]

The subtitle in the commentary directly following the above paragraph is "Rise of Mohammedanism." From history one can determine that no one group of people instilled more fear into the hearts of European Christians during the Middle Ages or inhibited more of the missionary activities of Rome and Constantinople than the followers of Muhammad. Whole crusades were organized by the Europeans to fight against them. Competing European monarchs reconciled with each other to present a united front to the Muslims. And even though they had some success against the Muslims, in the last 1,400 years they have never been able to completely retake the lands that the Muslims took from them.

The case could actually be made that God allowed the devil to control Christianity and even gave up the true Christian groups to Satan's whims for 1260 years (Rev. 6:11) since all of the minority groups within Christianity were either eradicated by Christian armies, chased out of the empire, or severely limited, as seen with the Waldenses, who resorted to a hermit's lifestyle in the caves and rugged valleys of the Alps. God had told the church of Pergamum that they were living "where Satan dwells" (Rev. 2:13). So even though the Bible-believing Christian groups were faithful to God, their influence was severely limited by the reigning apostasy in mainstream Christianity.

However, this cannot be said about the Muslims. At no time during the Middle Ages did they come under the control of Christian Europe. They were a continuous nuisance to any pope or monarch that served in Europe and the first and foremost check of the Christian missionary activity that was introduced by Gregory. And Muhammad appeared on the scene with his first alleged vision only six years removed from the death of pope Gregory "the Great."

The Muslims were not only a military check against the power and missionary work of Christian Europe, but they were a voice of conscience to the true Christians in Christianity. A great example of this is the iconoclastic controversy that raged in the medieval church. Everywhere Muslims went they reprimanded Christians for worshiping statues and icons since they, along with the Jews, considered this a clear violation of the commandments of God. And they not only reprimanded the Christians, but every chance they had, they attempted to destroy the images and icons. For sincere believers in Christianity this seemed to be a call to repentance, and soon there were many voices in Christianity calling for a cessation of this "idol worship"—they came to be known as iconoclasts.

The iconoclastic controversy became so great in Christianity that the church was forced to convene the second Council of Nicaea in AD 787 to make a judgment in this matter. Prior to the council the pope made it known that Western Christianity desired image worship to continue, and, as expected, iconoclasm was condemned as heretical at the council and all Iconoclast bishops either yielded to the decision or were deposed.

However, the controversy didn't end at Nicaea; eventually the Eastern part of Christianity adopted the veneration of only two-dimensional representations, while the West accepted two- and three-dimensional. This became one of the issues that contributed to the schism between Eastern and Western Christianity.[191] It is worth noting in this discussion of Muhammad that the Christian church had the opportunity to repent and obey the commandments of God due to the voice of conscience that came from the desert of Arabia.

Could it be that when the Bible foretold that Jesus would come with a "double-edged sword" and fight against the apostate elements in God's church that this was a reference to the rise of Islam and its conquests, which blocked the missionary activities of apostate Christianity? It appears that this interpretation could fit the symbolic description given by God of what transpired in the Middle Ages.

Psalms 84:5–7

While this psalm doesn't refer directly to Muhammad, it is worth mentioning that some Christian and Muslim scholars have seen this as a reference to those in Islam who would worship the true God. In these verses it talks about believers on a pilgrimage through the "Valley of Baca" where springs of water appear for them in the desert as they go "from strength to strength" until they appear before God on the day of judgment.

Some Muslim scholars say that Mecca, the site of Islamic pilgrimage, used to be called "Baca."[192] According to Ibn Ishaq, Mecca possessed a sterling reputation for morality in antiquity and thus acquired this name:

> Mecca did not tolerate injustice and wrong within its borders and if anyone did wrong therein it expelled him; therefore, it was called 'the Scorcher,' and any

king who came to profane its sanctity died on the spot. It is said that it was called Bakka because it used to break the necks of tyrants when they introduced innovations therein.[193]

Unfortunately, this hallowed place of pilgrimage that commemorated Abraham's and Ishmael's construction of an altar to God was taken over by corrupt and unjust tribes such as the Jurhum, Khuza'a, and finally, in the days of Muhammad, his own Quraysh tribe. Pilgrims came to be abused and exploited and the ruling elite of Mecca became greedy and arrogant.

Could this be a prophetic vision that David had that there would be many pilgrims on the true path from Abraham's Ishmaelite side? It is safe to say that it could be, although it is not in the scope of this book to dig into the text and go into a detailed analysis of the etymology of these words. Many translators have translated "Baca" as "weeping" or "balsam tree" and as most commentators agree, no one is sure what the word means.

Muslim legend tells us that Abraham journeyed to Mecca (or 'Baca') to visit his son Ishmael and that they erected an altar there. If that is true, David could have had a prophetic vision of Muhammad calling his spiritual cousins to come back to the worship of his one true God, to repent of their immoral, corrupt ways, and to make Mecca a place where the faithful remnant people of the God of Abraham could again make spiritual pilgrimage on the way to the heavenly Zion.

What Does Ellen White Say About Muhammad?

If, as some Christians claim, Islam is the great antichrist that was to come, and is "enemy number one" for the Christian, Adventists would naturally expect God's end-time prophet to write quite extensively on this topic to warn Christians to beware of it and stand firm until the second coming of Christ.

Mrs. White did write very extensively on the antichrist power—apostate Christianity. She penned hundreds of pages (including most of a whole book—*The Great Controversy*) dedicated to documenting the history, errors and biblical remedies for God's main enemy on earth over the last 1700+ years. But she wrote almost nothing about Islam. She wrote only one paragraph on this topic:

> Mohammedanism has its converts in many lands, and its advocates deny the divinity of Christ. Shall this faith be propagated, and the advocates of truth fail to manifest intense zeal to overthrow the error, and teach men of the pre-existence of the only Saviour of the world? O how we need men who will search and believe the word of God, who will present Jesus to the world in his divine and human nature, declaring with power and in demonstration of the Spirit, that 'there is none other name under heaven given among men, whereby we must be saved.' O how we need believers who will now present Christ in life and character, who will hold him up before the world as the brightness of the Father's glory, proclaiming that God is love![194]

This statement must be analyzed before moving on:

- She must not have had many visions about Muhammad or Islam considering the paucity of counsel given on how to relate to this religion. In fact, in this statement there is nothing that would seem "revealed" to her in vision. It was and still is common knowledge among Christians of all denominations that Muslims deny the divinity of Christ. This doesn't appear to be "new light" for any Christian of any denomination since most Christians believe this to be an error in the light of Scripture.

- Mrs. White refers to the religion as "Mohammedanism" and not "Islam." While this was common for Christian writers of her day, Christians, including Mrs. White, accurately describe what Islam has become for many Muslims—the "cult of Muhammad." Unfortunately, for millions of Islam's adherents it has ceased to be the religion of Islam that the Quran promotes—to bow oneself in submission to the God of Abraham—and has become an adherence to the alleged traditions of their prophet. Since Muhammad thought there should be a reformer for Islam every hundred years, and since he himself referred to Jesus as the Messiah multiple times, is it not possible that he might have given his approval to such a statement?

- Ellen White makes no statement about the "falseness" of this religion—she only points out that they have an error that is in desperate need of correction. Could not the exact same thing be said of most of Christianity, which believes in the divinity of Christ, but rejects the law of God? Does any Adventist say that Christianity is a false religion, based on false prophets when discussing the numerous false beliefs taught in modern Christianity? Absolutely not—it is only the errors that need to be corrected. One doesn't discard the whole religion based on those errors. One could infer from her silence about other aspects of the religion that God saw fit to encourage Adventists to work with Muslims primarily on this one question, especially since it is the core question of salvation. But as has been seen in previous chapters, Adventists have a lot in common with Muslims (as taught in the Quran): the Sabbath, state of the dead, great controversy, sin, law of God, dietary habits, and a serious devotional and prayer life. Perhaps God, in His infinite wisdom, didn't see fit to condemn the whole religion, since, as Muhammad claimed, it was a continuation of the faith given to mankind by the God of Abraham.

Would the Bible or Ellen White Allow for Another Post-biblical Prophet?

This is not a new question among God's people. God had to remind the Israelites who thought they had a monopoly on truth that, "I revealed myself to those who did not ask for me; I was found by those who did not seek me" (Isa. 65:1, NIV). Spiritual arrogance continued to be a problem even in the Christian era, resulting in the council at Jerusalem recorded in Acts 15. It is difficult for anyone who is part of what they consider to be a "chosen" religion to accept prophets from outside of their group or even a new prophet arising from within. A study of Bible history should caution all believers to approach this subject with a certain amount of humility.

Ellen White does not directly address the topic of other prophets in the Christian era. However, she does make the following statement about the time of Christ:

> Outside the Jewish nation there were men who foretold the appearance of a divine instructor. These men were seeking for truth, and to them the Spirit of Inspiration was imparted. One after another, like stars in the darkened heavens, such teachers had arisen. Their words of prophecy had kindled hope in the hearts of thousands of the Gentile world.[195]

How could these men foretell the appearance of Christ if the Spirit of God had not given them the "gift of prophecy"? These were men who were not part of the "chosen religion," yet God saw fit (apparently due to the lack of missionary zeal on the part of Israel) to let them also drink from the cistern of prophetic insight, and foretell some of His greatest acts in history. Joel 2:28 and Acts 2:17 are very clear that the Holy Spirit will be poured out on "all people."

The Bible tells us that the one true God doesn't want even one person to perish, but all to come to a knowledge of salvation (John 3:16; 2 Peter 3:9; Luke 15). How much more would He care for a whole nation, or ethnic group such as the Arabs, the descendants of Ishmael, whom He had promised to bless?

So the Christian shouldn't find it surprising that during the time when most Christians had wandered far from God that He should inspire men of other nations, especially someone who considered himself a direct descendant of Ishmael. Earlier in this book the blessing that God gave Ishmael and his descendants due to their relation to Abraham was discussed. Would it not be appropriate that God would raise up a prophet among this blessed people when their "cousins," the descendants of Isaac, had colluded with paganism and Satan to oppress the Bible, the true followers of God, and even supplant God Himself?

If one listens to Muhammad, it appears that this was God's purpose. Muhammad stated that he was sent to warn the Arabs in Arabic and prepare them for the day of judgment. In addition, he was to call Christians and Jews to repent of their sins. He affirmed the Bible as a true revelation and claimed that God told him to establish a monotheistic faith in the God of Abraham on the Arabian peninsula. It seems that the case can be made that God might do something along these lines during the 1260 years of prophecy, a period of deep apostasy that He underlined seven times in Scripture.

Did Muhammad Believe He Was the Last of the Prophets?

Muslims claim that Muhammad was the last (and the best—including Jesus) prophet that God will call until the end of time. This obviously would be a serious consideration in an analysis of his prophetic gift since Adventists believe that God promised in Joel that the gift of prophecy would be with the believers until the end of time. So the question remains,

"Did Muhammad believe that he was the last inspired prophet before the second coming of Jesus?" Muslims take the text found in the Quran that states:

> Muhammad is not the father of any of your men, but (he is) the apostle of God, and the seal of the prophets: and God has knowledge of all things. (33:40)

This text was given in response to some Muslims who didn't agree with one of Muhammad's revelations—apparently his revelation about Zaid's divorce from Zaynab (verse 37). The context is God's directive to the Muslims to not complain against Him and His messenger, Muhammad, and God's decisions that are revealed to him.

Muhammad is called in this text the "seal" (*khatm* in Arabic) of the prophets. This word in Arabic is used to indicate a sealing of some sort—"seal," "signet," "stamp," and "postmark" are all possible translations of this word in modern Arabic.[196] The first thing that may be clearly noted is that nothing is mentioned in this text (or in the entire Quran, for that matter) about Muhammad being the "last" of the prophets.

Secondly, one must try to understand what a "seal" or "stamp" is. According to *Webster's Dictionary* the main meaning for "seal" (other than the marine animal) is "something that confirms, ratifies, or makes secure." Synonyms for this word include "guarantee" or "assurance."

It is true that *Webster's* also gives a meaning for "seal" as "something that secures—as a wax seal on a document ... and must be broken to be opened that thus reveals tampering."[197] So yes, a seal can close a document, but it doesn't automatically preclude it from being sealed again, or opened and connected to another official document. There is no text in the Quran that suggests that God could not break such a seal. Interestingly, if one follows this spiritual analogy, it can be seen from the book of Revelation in the Bible that only Jesus is able to open up seals (Rev. 5:5).

However, from the context of this passage and the general teaching of the Quran, the most feasible meaning for this text is that Muhammad viewed himself as confirming, ratifying, and making secure the previous revelation that was given by God to His people, from the time of Adam.

One is left to guess whether Muhammad believed that there would be more prophets after him. But there are plenty of texts (as we have already seen in chapter 6) that make it abundantly clear that he viewed himself to be included in the long list of those whom God called in the Bible to be His messengers.

Difficulties in Understanding the Quran

One of the arguments against the inspiration of the Quran is that it is an incoherent text that is difficult to understand. However, I have had many people tell me the same thing about the Bible. The Spirit of Prophecy states the following on this topic:

> The difficulties of Scripture have been urged by skeptics as an argument against the Bible; but so far from this, they constitute a strong evidence of its divine inspiration. If it contained no account of God but that which we could

easily comprehend; if His greatness and majesty could be grasped by finite minds, then the Bible would not bear the unmistakable credentials of divine authority. The very grandeur and mystery of the themes presented should inspire faith in it as the word of God.[198]

It is true, the Quran is not "easy reading," but, for the most part, neither is the Bible. Any truly God-inspired document would be difficult enough to stimulate study in order to glean the treasure contained within the separate parts; only then can they be laid out in a coherent, unified manner. Likewise, until the Quran is studied in-depth, with its teachings being systematically organized, one must not make any superficial judgment. Thus a high level of difficulty would not be a good reason to dismiss any piece of literature as uninspired.

Weaknesses Of Muhammad

The reader might be thinking, "How can somebody that lived such a primitive lifestyle with so many sins be considered a prophet?" It is interesting that Mrs. White actually brings this argument up when discussing the Bible prophets:

> The lives recorded in the Bible are authentic histories of actual individuals. From Adam down through successive generations to the times of the apostles we have a plain, unvarnished account of what actually occurred and the genuine experience of real characters. It is a subject of wonder to many that inspired history should narrate in the lives of good men facts that tarnish their moral characters.... The inspired writers did not testify to falsehoods to prevent the pages of sacred history being clouded by the record of human frailties and faults....
>
> It is one of the best evidences of the authenticity of the Scriptures that the truth is not glossed over nor the sins of its chief characters suppressed.... How many biographies have been written of faultless Christians, who, in their ordinary home life and church relations, shone as examples of immaculate piety.... Yet had the pen of inspiration written their histories, how different would they have appeared. There would have been revealed human weaknesses, struggles with selfishness, bigotry, and pride, hidden sins, perhaps, and the continual warfare between the spirit and the flesh....
>
> Had our good Bible been written by uninspired persons, it would have presented quite a different appearance and would have been a discouraging study to erring mortals, who are contending with natural frailties and the temptations of a wily foe. But as it is, we have a correct record of the religious experience of marked characters in Bible history. Men whom God favored, and to whom He entrusted great responsibilities, were sometimes overcome by temptation and committed sins, even as we of the present day strive, waver, and frequently fall into error. But it is encouraging to desponding hearts to know that through God's grace they could gain fresh vigor to again rise above their evil natures; and, remembering this, we are ready to renew the conflict ourselves.[199]

It is interesting to note that Muslims at the time of Muhammad recorded uncomplimentary fragments of his life, something that modern Muslims tend to minimize or completely disregard. Many Muslims now have the conception that a prophet should be a "perfect example" and "infallible"; this is one reason they give for disregarding the Bible—"How could David, a prophet, commit murder?" Or "How could Abraham lie?" are samples of questions they ask. However, an Adventist view is just the opposite.

A candid history that doesn't gloss over the weaknesses and sins of the prophets is one of the trademarks of real inspiration. It is a bit of a paradox, but in arguing how "weak" and "sinful" Muhammad was, one is not actually disproving his ministry, but actually giving a reason why his ministry might be authentic (of course, if his teachings line up with biblical teaching).

"But Muhammad was so violent…"

So how could a prophet of God be so violent in the post-Christ era? First, one needs to understand why the prophets of the Old Testament era were so violent. This is what Ellen White states in regard to this when discussing the situation that Saul and Samuel were dealing with in the Old Testament:

> But the Lord sent His servant with another message to Saul. By obedience he might still prove his fidelity to God and his worthiness to walk before Israel. Samuel came to the king and delivered the word of the Lord. That the monarch might realize the importance of heeding the command, Samuel expressly declared that he spoke by divine direction, by the same authority that had called Saul to the throne. The prophet said, "Thus saith the Lord of hosts, I remember that which Amalek did to Israel, how he laid wait for him in the way, when he came up from Egypt. Now go and smite Amalek, and utterly destroy all that they have, and spare them not; but slay both man and woman, infant and suckling, ox and sheep, camel and ass." The Amalekites had been the first to make war upon Israel in the wilderness; and for this sin, together with their defiance of God and their debasing idolatry, the Lord, through Moses, had pronounced sentence upon them. By divine direction the history of their cruelty toward Israel had been recorded, with the command, "Thou shalt blot out the remembrance of Amalek from under heaven; thou shalt not forget it." Deuteronomy 25:19. For four hundred years the execution of this sentence had been deferred; but the Amalekites had not turned from their sins. The Lord knew that this wicked people would, if it were possible, blot out His people and His worship from the earth. Now the time had come for the sentence, so long delayed, to be executed.[200]

Many Christians have a hard time reading these types of passages in the Old Testament and justifying violence against unbelievers, but God only uses this method when the situation calls for it. Mrs. White is very clear that God only allows this type of execution for a people group who are emboldened idol worshippers who would, if not destroyed, wipe out the true people of God from the earth. A failure to do so in obedience to the command of God is a rejection of His will; in this case, Saul's negligence in not destroying the nation that God had designed for him to exterminate cost him the kingship of Israel and led to the anointing of David. Later in the story, after Saul had spared the Amalekite king's life, Mrs. White comments:

> An act of justice, stern and terrible, was yet to be performed. Samuel must publicly vindicate the honor of God and rebuke the course of Saul. He commanded that the king of the Amalekites be brought before him. Above all who had fallen by the sword of Israel, Agag was the most guilty and merciless; one who had hated and sought to destroy the people of God, and whose influence had been strongest to promote idolatry. He came at the prophet's command, flattering himself that the danger of death was past. Samuel declared: "As thy sword hath made women childless, so shall thy mother be childless among women. And Samuel hewed Agag in pieces before the Lord."[201]

What would modern commentators say about Samuel, an otherwise peace loving, mild, sensible prophet, who condemns a wicked king to a gruesome death and commands that a whole nation be obliterated? It is difficult enough for the Western, contemporary, postmodern mind to even conceive of God giving an order directly to a person or favoring one religion, not to speak of giving an order to execute someone who doesn't believe the same way. So one would expect modern Christians to have problems with both the Old Testament and Muhammad—and they do. However, this is something that Adventists do believe—God does "choose" people and fight for them against their enemies. In the same chapter in *Patriarchs and Prophets*, Mrs. White comments that when Jonathan and his armor-bearer were able to defeat the Philistine army that the "angels fought by their side"[202]—a claim that Muhammad also made when describing his military victories.

> Those nations that rejected the worship and service of the true God were to be dispossessed.[203]

This situation is strikingly similar to Muhammad's: a command of the Lord to wipe out an idolatrous people, the institution of a government that would promote the monotheistic worship of the God of Abraham, and angels helping believers rout armies much larger and more professional.

If anything, Muhammad was more lax than the injunctions found in Deuteronomy 13:12–18 about how to deal with idol-worshippers—he didn't always obliterate everybody in the towns he fought against. It is recorded that many times he took captives and their livestock and possessions as plunder. But, it would be a strange day for a Christian to accuse Muhammad of being a false prophet because he wasn't violent enough! The level of violence that Muhammad attained didn't equal the violence of the Mongol raids, the Crusades, or the global wars/genocides of the twentieth century.[204]

Unity of Both Testaments
Some argue that after Christ and His teachings that it is inconceivable that a prophet would resort to using methods that had been done away with at the cross. However, unlike most Christians, Adventists see a unity in the way God deals with people in both testaments.

> The Old and New Testaments are linked together by the golden clasp of God. We need to become familiar with the Old Testament Scriptures. The unchangeableness of God should be clearly seen; the similarity of His dealings with his people of the past dispensation and of the present, should be studied. Under the inspiration of the Spirit of God, Solomon wrote, "That which hath been is now: and that which is to be hath already been; and God requireth that which is past."[205]

So the question one must answer is, "Would God use an Old Testament style of dealing with prophets and nations in the post-Christ era?" If Muhammad was a fulfillment of Joel 2 and Revelation 2, the case could be made that God did deal with Muhammad and the nations on the Arabian peninsula in much the same way as he dealt with the nations through the prophets of old, since the situation was very similar to that in Samuel's time. Even John Gilchrist, who rejects Muhammad as a prophet, admits that the spirit of Muhammad "may compare favorably with Judaism but is considerably inferior to the spirit of true Christianity."[206]

The Argument of History
As already examined in this book, the Muslims played a key role in the history of the Middle Ages. They confined apostasy to Europe and checked the missionary zeal belatedly begun with Gregory the Great. They conquered huge portions of Christian empires and brought a simpler, more pious religion, and they gave more religious freedom to dissident groups than the Christian empires they supplanted. They acted as a conscience to the medieval church in reminding them that disregard of God's law was a sin, that monasticism was not of God, and that statue and icon worship were both still idol worship. They kept before the world the truths that denying religious freedom to others is wrong, that the veneration of Mary, and the subsequent heresies about a "Trinity" of the Father, Son, and Mary were heretical, and that they needed to be more concerned with pleasing God and getting ready for the day of judgment than arguing over philosophical theories. Muslims stimulated learning and the development of the arts and sciences. They preserved a knowledge of ancient Greek and Hebrew, which motivated the church to preserve the original manuscripts of the Bible. They set the intellectual foundation for the Renaissance, which helped pave the way for the Reformation. Their military endeavors usually, though often unwittingly, supported Protestants' cause against the Catholics.

A Christian who believes in a mighty, omniscient God believes that "all things work together for good to those who love God" (Rom. 8:28). He should not think differently when discussing Muhammad. Isaiah 54:16 and 17 states that it is even God who "create[s] the destroyer to wreak havoc" and that His purpose is to strengthen us so that "no weapon forged against you will prevail, and you will refute every tongue that accuses you" (NIV). If God had not intervened, Muhammad and his followers could have been exterminated multiple times: a Christian encouraged Muhammad to accept the call of God when he believed himself to be demon-possessed; a Christian king offered refuge to the early followers of Islam; Jewish tribes rescued him and his followers from Mecca by inviting them to Medinah; and the Quraysh had multiple opportunities to exterminate this nascent religion at the battles of Badr, Uhud, and the Trench, but somehow with an outnumbered, unskilled, rag-tag group of believers they conquered more accomplished foes and Muhammad came out victorious.

If God had seen fit for Muhammad and his religion to perish, there were many opportunities to withdraw His hand of protection. It is striking when reading the history of Muhammad and early Islam how quickly they grew from a small band of monotheists in just one city, to a mighty empire that shook the world.

Muslims rarely lost military encounters. The ones they did lose were usually, in their minds, due to their unfaithfulness to the command of God (just as the Israelites of the Old Testament). Even when they lost, it was not a major loss or a blow to the overall strategy of establishing Islamic rule. No one could stand against them. They captured territory from more powerful Christian rulers and have never given it back. They only lost again to Christianity the Iberian peninsula. The rest of the former bastions of Christianity—North Africa, the Middle East, and Turkey have been predominantly Muslim for over a thousand years.

Why couldn't Christians overcome them if the Christians were truly of God and the Muslims of Satan as so many contemporary Christians paint the picture? Deuteronomy 28:1–14 says that if believers are faithful to God all of their enemies will be utterly defeated before them and that they will be the head and not the tail. Upon reading the history of the world from 610 CE–1000 CE, who was faithful to God according to the characteristics put before us in Deuteronomy 28?

The Bible-believing Christian is constrained to admit that the Muslims would have been the "faithful" ones whom God was blessing. They were the "head" in every area to the Christian establishment "tails": military might, science, literature, languages, mathematics, business, jurisprudence, societal structure, unity, religious freedom, etc. It is hard to name any human endeavor from that time period which Christians did better than Muslims. Could this be the "blessing" of Satan?

Would this fit in the Adventist prophetic understanding? Adventists believe that the papacy is the fulfillment of the antichrist power foretold in Daniel and Revelation. And yet many Adventist commentators apply the fifth trumpet of Revelation 9 to Muhammad and state that Satan raised up Muhammad to "punish" the medieval church. The question must be asked—does Satan fight against himself? Jesus was confronted with a similar situation when people accused Him of driving out demons with the power of Satan. Jesus said that "any kingdom divided against itself" will come to ruin (Luke 11:14–23, NIV).

Muhammad was accused from his earliest years of ministry of being of Satan, but his main line of argument was, "Why would Satan want this revealed?" The same question must be asked today: why would Satan fight against monasticism, idol worship, spiritual pride, heresies about Christ, false conceptions of the state of the dead, even the changing of the law of God? These were all developments in Christianity that Adventists teach that Satan himself insidiously inspired. We must ask ourselves the question, "Why would Satan inspire Muhammad to oppose what he inspired in the first place?"

When we study the 1260-day prophecy of Daniel and Revelation, we notice that the prophecy shows there would be a place in the "wilderness" that God had prepared for His true church. If one listens to some modern Adventist commentators, they make it seem as if God were powerless during this time and Satan was all-powerful. However, Ellen White has counseled, "Let us not talk of the great power of Satan, but of the great power of God."[207] "It is true that Satan is a powerful being; but, thank God, we have a mighty Saviour, who cast out the evil one from heaven. Satan is pleased when we magnify his power. Why not talk of Jesus? Why not magnify His power and His love?"[208]

Sovereignty of God

Something greater is at stake in this issue of the prophethood of Muhammad—the sovereignty of God. Somehow, it is easy to study the Middle Ages and come to the conclusion that Satan overcame the church and God went on hiatus from 538 CE to the beginning of the Reformation in the fourteenth century and Satan just had a heyday and was able to act on his every whim.

This fatalistic approach continues to this day when many Christians talk about Muslims—"maybe probation is up for them," "they are just a cursed lot"—and they come to the conclusion that the problem is all with Muslims because they don't "become Christians." Then Satan, Muhammad, restrictive Islamic governments, and the ignorance of Muslims are all blamed for the lack of missionary success.

Many Adventists have a defeatist attitude when it comes to looking at Islam today with its history, and yet they speculate that "someday" God will open up the door miraculously to "finish the work" among Muslims. But why is God obligated to act in the way Adventists expect? Have Adventists forgotten that God's hand has always been involved in surprising ways in human affairs? In the words of Dr. Kenneth Oster:

> If we could only disentangle ourselves from the stranglehold that Satan has thrown around us and get a cosmic perspective of events, we would be reassured to find out that we need not be molested and shoved around by Satan. Rather, we would see the guiding hand of God.[209]

As Mrs. White reminds Adventists, if the veil were pulled back, we would see, "behind, above, and through all the play and counterplay of human interests and power and passions, the agencies of the all-merciful One, silently, patiently, working out the counsels of His own will."[210]

To illustrate what a difficult thing this is to do, ask yourself, "When is the last time that I heard an Adventist praise God for the rise of Islam in the seventh century, or for the fact that modern Islamic governments are very restrictive of Christian missions?" But, if one believes in the sovereignty of God, this can actually be done. I believe that I have laid out enough historical facts in this book that, even if you don't believe that God inspired Muhammad, that you must agree that the Muslims made a fairly large contribution to God's side in the great controversy from the seventh to the sixteenth centuries. With this principle we must even look at the difficult situations that exist in the Muslim world today and see in it God's almighty hand and His blessing.

When one accepts the sovereignty of God, a truly joyous life can be lived in faith because "all things work together for good to those who love God" (Rom. 8:28). The rise of Islam and its continued dominance over a major part of the world should be no exception to this belief.

How Can So Many People be Led Not to Believe in the Divinity of Christ by a Prophet?

We have seen in the history of Islam that Muslims have not remained completely true to the teachings of the Quran and that many diverse theories on a number of topics, especially about Jesus, have been promulgated in the Islamic world. An interesting development that we are witnessing now is that millions of Muslims are actually coming to an understanding of Jesus as the Savior of the world through the Quran. There are now more groups coming to Christ in Islam than ever before. As of July 2013 there were sixty-four groups of Muslims of over 1000 members and 100 places of worship that have come to Christ.[211] There are approximately five million Muslim believers in these groups. Missiologists have polled a sampling of these groups and have asked them what were the largest factors for their journey to a belief in Christ. The overwhelming factor in the Muslims' turning to Christ was the Quran. Almost 65 percent of them stated that the verses about Jesus in the Quran played a role in their changing their minds about the divinity of Christ.[212] This new movement of Muslims studying the Quran and coming to a biblical belief about the Messiah would be consistent with Muhammad being an inspired individual.

How Can Islam be So Bad Now if Muhammad Was of God?

Some readers might be wondering how anyone can claim Muhammad was of God when present-day Islam is in such disarray and so heretical. The Christian needs not look further than the history of Christianity to answer this question—how can Christianity be so "Babylon"-ish if Jesus was of God? It has happened time and time again in the great controversy that Satan redoubles his efforts to lead people astray who are actually on the right path.

The fact that parts of Islam are so diabolical now may be an argument in favor of its original authenticity. For instance, why aren't there more Buddhist or Sikh terrorists? Could it be that Satan expends more time and energy on Islam than other religions? While this would only be speculation since it is impossible to record the number of demon-hours spent on influencing religions, one can look at history and examine things that can be observed empirically.

Here are some mistakes made by Islam in the centuries after Muhammad:

- After the death of Muhammad, Muslims gradually came to let politics hold sway over their religion instead of vice versa. (An example of this would be the acceptance of Friday as their "holy day" to contrast themselves with the Jews who observed Sabbath and the Christians who observed Sunday.)

- The traditions about the prophet came to hold equal authority with the Quran itself, and some would even say they occupy a superior position to most Muslims today.

- The Quran came to be interpreted by commentators, who were affected by their religious and philosophical training, in order to explain it to the intelligentsia of the world, which resulted in cerebral theological controversies.[213]

- The Arabic version of the Quran became the "only version" acceptable for the true Muslim (even though today Arabic is spoken by no more than 20 percent of all Muslims as a native tongue).

- The Bible eventually came to be despised in Islam as being a corrupt document that is unworthy of study.

- Intellectual and religious freedom was gradually extinguished, which resulted in a dearth of knowledge and learning.

Compare now the histories of Christianity and Islam. Has the Christian church made any of the mistakes that Islam has? It is an irony of ironies to see that the Christian church has not made just "any" of those mistakes, but all of them!

- After the death of Jesus, Christians gradually came to allow their politics to hold sway over their religion instead of vice versa (for example: accepting the day of sun worship as their "holy day" to distinguish themselves from Jews).

- The traditions of the "church fathers" were placed on an equal level with the Bible, or even superior to it.

- The church fathers began to explain the Bible in philosophical terms, which led to cerebral theological controversies.

- The Latin version of the Bible became the only version of the Bible allowed and could only be interpreted by Latin-educated priests since the masses didn't know Latin.

- The Old Testament was gradually considered anachronistic, and the study of it was neglected even more than the New Testament.

- Intellectual and religious freedoms were gradually removed from the Christian realms of the empire in the name of "protection" of the people from heresies, which resulted in a dearth of learning and education.

Even when looking at the timeline of both religions one sees that both of them had periods of "purity" and expansion for about 300 years and about a 1,000 years of "darkness." Christianity finally awoke from its stupor after a millennium of obscurity. When examining the Muslim world of the early twenty-first century with the appearance of encouraging signs such as the "Arab Spring," protests against dictators, and an increasing numbers of voices from within Islam calling for intellectual and spiritual revival, the Muslim world appears to be set for a "Reformation"-type, transformational moment after its millennium of slumber.

Summary of the Tests of a Prophet

Did Muhammad have dreams and visions? It appears from historical sources and from Muhammad himself that he did.

Did he speak according to the law and the testimony? Overall, yes. As was seen, his one law about the remarriage of a previously married couple does differ from the Old Testament law. However, in an odd twist, his law would probably be more palatable to most Adventists than the Old Testament law—since the Adventist Church has no position on remarrying a former spouse, but would probably not prefer that someone do it five or six times. Chapters 6 and 7 looked at the many similarities between biblical and Quranic teachings.

Have his prophecies come true? It appears that some have, but as admitted in chapter 12, this is one area that really needs more study.

Did he call people to worship the one true God? Yes, he did call people to a worship of the God of Abraham, as even most Arab Christians believe.

Did he believe in the life, death and resurrection of Jesus as the Messiah foretold in the Old Testament? When one reads the original Quran, it appears that he did.

Were his "fruits" those of a true prophet? Most Christian critics of Muhammad admit that his "fruits" are not an argument against his prophethood.

So, as in any court case, defining a possible motive is the key element to winning any trial. What would have been possible motive on the part of God for inspiring a prophet on the Ishmaelite side of the family during a time when Isaac's side had gone into apostasy will now be examined. If God called Muhammad, why might He have done so, according to this theory?

Saving Monotheism?

Not even all Christian scholars have believed Islam was a pernicious development. Arnold J. Toynbee in his book *Civilization on Trial* argues that Muhammad didn't come to fight against the Bible or Jesus but rather to fight "with the Christian Church, which had captivated Rum [sic] [the Byzantine, or Eastern "Roman" Empire] by capitulating to pagan Greek polytheism and idolatry. From this shameful betrayal of the revelation of the One True God, Islam had retrieved the pure religion of Abraham. Between the Christian polytheists on the one side and the Hindu polytheists on the other there again shone the light of monotheism; and in Islam's survival lay the hope of the world."[214]

As Dr. Kenneth Oster writes, monotheism "is a high mountain that must be scaled, not a valley into which man naturally slithers."[215]

Outside of the three great monotheistic faiths—Judaism, Christianity, Islam—only three times in known history have nations worshiped in a monotheistic religion.

The first was Akhenaten, otherwise known as Pharoah Amenhotep IV of Egypt, who went directly against the wishes of a powerful priesthood and established a new Egyptian monotheistic religion. It was the first time in history that an attempt was made to establish a monotheistic religion in a kingdom by the will of one idealistic ruler. However, it only lasted while he was alive. The priests reverted back to the old religion as soon as he was gone.

The second occasion was when Zarathustra of Iran in the sixth century BCE introduced what we call Zoroastrianism and its monotheistic belief in the god Ahuramazda. Persian royalty only evoked this god for a few centuries, but already by the fourth century BCE, as new gods were added, it was no longer a monotheistic religion.

The third occasion was in the fifteenth century AD when Guru Nabak created Sikhism in the Punjabi region of the Indian subcontinent as a monotheistic offshoot of Hinduism. Although it officially proclaims to still be a monotheistic religion that teaches the oneness of God, many observers still consider it to be a polytheistic religion because of their practices of observing Hindu holidays and rituals.

For some reason, humans, when left on their own without the God of heaven, always end up in polytheism. It has been this way for the Egyptians, Assyrians, Babylonians, Persians, Greeks, Romans, and every other people group that has dwelt on earth. When humanity discards a knowledge of the true God, Satan insinuates his substitute.

There have been only three that have been recorded where somebody dared to even attempt it in about 6,000 years of earth's history—and the most successful attempt was for a century and a half.

Only Judaism, Christianity, and Islam have had any staying power in promulgating a monotheistic religion. So the question is, "Why?" A Christian certainly would never argue that Judaism isn't a God-inspired religion—since Christians believe that their movement is merely the continuation and completion of Judaism. Obviously, Christians believe that Christianity, while barely being able to be described as a monotheistic religion for over a thousand years as examined in this book, was still a God-inspired religion. Couldn't one argue that the existence of Islam as a monotheistic religion for 1,400 years is a fairly good argument in favor of it being a God-inspired religion?

Islam, in contrast to Judaism, its cousin monotheistic religion, has not only been maintained by a significant group of people but has spread to many people groups around the world and expanded much like Christianity has. Don't Christians believe that God preserved the Jews for over 1,200 years as a monotheistic religion before Christ? Yes, they had rocky moments with God and ended up rejecting His will for them, but they still have residual blessings from God (Rom. 11:1). And they didn't automatically lose their monotheistic aspect that God had designed for them to have.

Though Adventists believe Christianity was in apostasy for 1,260 years, it didn't cease to be upheld by God as a true monotheistic faith (by the true remnant among her, at least). Adventists would have no problems admitting that Christianity and Judaism were God-inspired religions and therefore they would be able to "scale the mountain" and overcome the proclivity for humans to descend into polytheism. But why would the same thing not be said about Islam?

If Christians believe that Muhammad was not a God-inspired person, they would have to admit that he is the absolutely most influential non-inspired person that has ever graced the face of the planet. He would only be the fourth person in the history of the planet even to attempt establishing a monotheistic religion—and he would be, by far (1,200 years and over a billion adherents to his religion) the most successful at it.

How did Muhammad "scale the mountain" of polytheism like no one who has ever lived apart from the God of heaven has? Some might say that Satan can also "scale some mountains." While that is true, then why has he never been able to do it with anybody as successfully as he did with Muhammad?

This, then, leads back to the Bible. Finally one comes to the conclusion that it is only by analyzing the movement as a whole, taking Muhammad through the tests of a prophet, and testing what is good and what is evil, with the help of the Holy Spirit, that the believer can correctly judge his prophethood.

Even strong Christian critics of Muhammad, such as John Gilchrist, have marveled at his dedication to preaching monotheism to a pagan people and have given him credit for his determination.[216] One of Muhammad's critics states about him and his failed attempt to preach to the polytheists of Tayif when, as a result, he was almost stoned to death:

> There is something lofty and heroic in this journey of Mahomet to Tayif; a solitary man, despised and rejected by his own people, going boldly forth in the name of God, like Jonah to Nineveh, and summoning an idolatrous city to repent and support his mission. It sheds a strong light on the intensity of his belief in the divine origin of his calling.[217]

The Hanifs

One interesting development on the Arabian peninsula in the early seventh century that historians and theologians who have studied Muhammad have noticed is a movement of Hanifs. Ibn Ishaq reports that there were four reformers who refused to worship all of the gods that had been accumulated by the Arabian tribes—they were Waraqah ibn Asad, Ubaidu'llah ibn Jahsh, Uthman ibnu'l Huwairith, and Zaid ibn 'Amr. All of them were relatives of Muhammad. They collectively decided to go in search of the one true God—the god of Abraham.

This led them to different countries to inquire of other tribes and nations. Waraqah, the cousin of Khadijah, who was already mentioned as being the Christian who confirmed that the first vision Muhammad saw was from the God of Abraham, ended up accepting Christianity.

Ubaidu'llah accepted Islam once Muhammad began to preach in Mecca, and later fled to Abyssinia when the persecution in Mecca became intolerable. He converted to Christianity there and died as a Christian in Abyssinia.

Uthman went to Byzantium and became a Christian there.

Zaid didn't convert to Christianity but ended up staying in Mecca and rejecting the prevalent religion of his hometown; he became known as a *hanif*.

In Hebrew (and Syriac) this word, *hanif*, means, "to conceal, to pretend, to lie, to be a hypocrite." But in Arabic it means, "to limp or walk unevenly." Undoubtedly it was intended to be a reproach to these reformers, but they evidently came to accept it as the moniker of their movement to find the religion of the God of Abraham and to reject the religion of their polytheistic tribesmen.[218]

Eventually, it appears that the persecution against Zaid became so relentless that he moved out of Mecca to Mt. Hira where he lived until his death five years before Muhammad received his prophetic call. As legend has it, Muhammad received his first vision in the cave Zaid previously inhabited.

There are not many historical references to this group. They are only known through the very earliest biographers of Muhammad—Ibn Ishaq and Ibn Hisham. There is one recorded poem in which Zaid is quoted as saying:

One Lord or a thousand Lords
Shall I worship? Are things then partitioned out?
I have abandoned Allat and 'Uzza' altogether:
Thus doeth the hardy, the patient man.
Therefore I worship neither 'Uzza' nor her two daughters,
Nor do I resort unto the two idols of the Banu 'Amr.
Nor do I worship Ghanam, though he was a Lord to us
At the time when my intellect wandered.
I marvelled: both during the nights are there marvellous things
And during the days, which he that seeth clearly understandeth.
For God hath often destroyed men,
Whose condition was immorality.
And others hath he preserved by proving a nation:
Therefore doth He rear up from them the little child.
And among us a man stumbleth: one day he recovereth,
As the branch that drinketh rain is refreshed.
But I serve as my Lord the Merciful One,
That the forgiving Lord may forgive my sin.
Preserve ye therefore the fear of God, your Lord
when ye preserve it not, it shall not perish.
Thou shalt see the pure: gardens are their abode:

And for the unbelievers is Hell-fire blazing:
And in life is disgrace, and that they should die:
That with which their breasts shall be oppressed shall they meet.[219]

Hanifs had seven characteristics that distinguished them from their fellow Arabs:

1. the prohibition of killing infant daughters by burying them alive, according to the cruel custom of the Arabs of the time

2. the acknowledgment of the unity of God

3. the rejection of idolatry and the worship of Al-Lat, Al-'Uzzá, and the other deities of the people

4. holding to the promise of future happiness in paradise or the "garden"

5. the warning of the punishment reserved in hell for the wicked

6. the denunciation of God's wrath upon the "unbelievers"

7. the application of the titles *Ar Rahman* (the Merciful), *Ar Rabb* (the Lord), and *Al Ghafur* (the Forgiving) to God[220]

These elements all became part of the religion of Muhammad. The Quran states: "Abraham was not a Jew nor yet a Christian; but he was true in faith, and bowed his will to God's (Which is Islam), and he joined not gods with God" (3:67).

A couple of things must be noted about this verse:

1. The word that is translated by Yusuf Ali as "Christian" is *Nasraaniyan*. This word denoted someone who was from the district of Nasara where many Christians lived on the Arabian peninsula. So, this doesn't mean that Muhammad was stating that Abraham didn't believe in Jesus (since Muhammad himself believed in Him and referred to Him as the "Messiah"). Likewise, Abraham was the father of the Jews and so predated both groups. Further, Muhammad is clarifying that Abraham wouldn't be in agreement with the religious movements identified with Judaism or Christianity of that time, nor would he have become involved in arguments about religion (since that is the context of the previous verses).

2. Yusuf Ali took some liberty when translating the next portion of the text when he translated that Abraham was "true in faith and bowed his will to God's and he joined not gods with God." The original only states that Abraham was "a *hanif* Muslim and was not from among the polytheists (*mushreekeen*)." It was clear to

those who were listening to him what a *hanif* was (as well as the term, *Muslim*). This text simply meant that Abraham would have approved of Zaid's and the Hanif's positions (as well as Muhammad's), for he was not into arguing about doctrinal stances and was not a polytheist—he was a true follower of God.

One Reason for God to Call Muhammad

An Adventist should be somewhat sympathetic to Muhammad and the early *Hanifs* since Adventists believe that God called a prophet to aid a fledgling movement in the nineteenth century, which was calling the world to repentance and belief in the Creator God of the universe. Would it not be a valid reason for God to call Muhammad to aid a fledgling group of monotheists who were anxious to adhere to the true religion of Abraham? If one were to describe the situation on the Arabian peninsula—the corrupt, polytheistic, hedonistic Arabs being the dominant group with a few tribes of contentious Jews who couldn't even get along with each other, and then add in some groups of Christians who believed in the divinity of Mary and/or the non-divinity of Jesus, with other pagan beliefs which had been incorporated in medieval Christianity—and then give Adventists the choice of which group they would want to join: the pagans, Jews, Christians, or *Hanifs*—which group would they choose?

I tend to think that the majority of Adventists would side with the *Hanifs*—the group that tends to live out in the country and pursue spirituality and faithfulness to God. Would it really be out of the realm of possibility to think that God would help a group like this by giving direct revelations in order to uphold and bolster this movement and spread it to other nations?

I ask the reader to consider if it is so far-fetched for God to, in essence, repeat the story of Genesis 16–25—when He called a recalcitrant pagan (Hagar-Ishmael/Muhammad) to become a powerful nation (twelve tribes of Ishmael/Islam) and drink from the water of life while wandering in the desert in answer to a prostrate descendant of Abraham, bowing in prayer, when the church (Sarah/Christianity) is not walking in faith with its god? As the old adage goes, "history repeats itself." It could appear that the sad history of Sarah/Hagar has been replayed in the last 1,700 years.

So How Could Christians be so Wrong About Muhammad if He Was of God?

An Adventist shouldn't be too surprised that Christianity can err so flagrantly—most Christian teachers and leaders attack us in the same way over our beliefs about the Sabbath, state of the dead, and the sanctuary. God's true believers have ever been in the minority.

Just as in the issue with the Sabbath, there are some objective reasons why Christianity could hold such opinions about Islam:

- Muhammad and his followers have been considered by Christians as the avowed enemies of their religion for over a millennium. The Roman Catholic and Orthodox churches lived in terror of Muslim armies from around 700 CE to the 1800s when the Ottoman Empire began to decline. Islam has been the historical enemy of the Christian church, so one can see why it would be considered extremely odd for a Christian to even attempt to justify Muhammad.

- Islam over the centuries has gotten away from the original teachings of the Quran and introduced things that truly aren't consistent with God's revelation: refutation of the divinity of Jesus, infallibility of Muhammad, Friday worship, seventy virgins for fallen *jihadists*, temporary marriages, etc. These doctrines are purported to have come from Muhammad, so to any devout Christian it would seem that he was a false prophet.

- The Quran and much of the Hadith have not been readily available for research by Christian theologians and scholars until the last century. So through the Middle Ages Christians, overall, just relied on what Muslims said about their religion without being able to "check the facts" in the actual documents. It is no coincidence that in Christian circles a more positive genre of literature about Muhammad has accompanied a more careful study of the Quran itself. This should be welcomed by Adventists as a means to a clearer understanding of our Muslim "cousins."

- Since Islam has adopted such an intolerant attitude toward other religions in modern times, all too often it is convenient for Christians to not "turn the other cheek." We have often adopted much the same attitude toward them as they have toward Christians. This cannot be justified by the teachings of Jesus in the Bible, but, unfortunately, it is a fact of life in the sinful world that we as Christians live in.

- Adventists believe that Christianity has gotten many things wrong. Why should one be surprised that it didn't understand Muhammad when it accepted doctrines such as belief in the immortality of the soul, monasticism, Mary as the "God-bearer" and "intercessor" for humanity, Sunday worship, combining of church/state with its accompanying persecution, violence, wars, etc.? It really shouldn't surprise Adventists at all that Christianity could error in regards to Muhammad.

- There is a misunderstanding of the divine mission given Islam, which would be consistent with what has been uncovered so far in this book. In fact, it seems prophesied in Revelation 9 where the fallen star (the Ottoman Empire) is called "destroyer" in Greek and Hebrew (the languages of the "people of the Book"), but hadn't been given by God the right to destroy—only to "torture."

Mrs. White warned the people of God of the dangers of prejudice:

> We learn from the sacred word that the people of God are still in danger from the devices of their archenemy. Satan stands ready to aim his shafts at the unguarded soul, and he will lead astray all who will give heed to his deceptions. Many who imagine that they have a sincere zeal for the honor of God, have permitted Satan to control their minds, and are accomplishing his purposes. Few understand the terrible power of prejudice, of envy and jealousy, when once they take possession of the soul.[221]

Notice that she was directing this counsel to the people of God—not the world. Prejudice—whether it be racial, religious, or political—is an insidious monster that destroys love and community, and according to God's prophet, it exists within the walls of the church. We must be extremely careful not to let our discussions about Islam, Muhammad, and the Quran be guided by our biases and prejudices rather than humble, honest, spiritual, and intellectual inquiry.

Have Other Christians Come to This Same Conclusion?

Actually, historically it is not anomalous to come to the conclusion that Muhammad was a prophet of God. It has already been documented in this book how Christians that lived in Muslim lands well after Muhammad's time were very happy to be included in a Muslim empire.

During the life of Muhammad, there were a few instances of Christians accepting the prophethood of Muhammad. As already noted, Waraqah, his wife's cousin who was a Christian and well versed in the Bible, accepted him as a prophet. The king of Abyssinia accepted the reading of the Quran as a sign that the Muslims were fellow believers in God and Christ and so protected them from the Quraysh.

Another story is told by Ibn Ishaq about a time when twenty Christians came to visit Muhammad in Mecca. (They were either from Najran or Abyssinia.) Their intent seems to have been to check the authenticity of this new prophet in Arabia. A portion of the Quran was read to them, and they were reported to have tears in their eyes after having heard the revelation. They believed in him as a prophet and went home.[222]

Another story is told of a delegation from Najran comprising sixty people who came to visit Muhammad when he was in Medinah. They were allowed to pray with the Muslims in the mosque, although they faced east and not toward Mecca. After the prayers they had a long theological discussion. The Christians finally decided to keep their religion, but they accepted Muhammad as a prophet, and even asked him for help in settling their disputes. Muhammad obliged and sent them a mediator from among the Muslims.[223]

As Geoffrey Parrinder points out, "Christians and Muslims, when they were true to the spirit of their founders, were close to each other."[224]

Many of the early Muslim writers were well versed in the Bible. Tabari, a well-known early Muslim author, quoted the Bible extensively and regarded it as inspired.[225] But centuries of political contention, the Crusades, the Inquisition, and the overall hostility between the two groups took its toll.

However, Adventists can be thankful that in these "end times," especially in the last 100 years, more Muslim authors are writing on the topic of the Bible and Jesus, and more Christian scholars and missionaries are reading the Quran (which wasn't translated or distributed widely in European languages until the 1900s) and trying to understand Muslims.

So things are looking better as to the future of Islamic-Christian relations. Could it be that we are living in the period of history where God will unite the children of Ishmael with the children of Isaac by a message that will prepare the world for the day of judgment? And could it be that the devil is working hard amongst the children of Ishmael to promote extremist, violent groups of them to scare off their spiritual brothers, and thwart the grand plan of God?

Conclusion

I hope that you have enjoyed this process of analyzing Muhammad and his claim to be one of God's prophets. It is like a Western style trial in a court of law. You are the jury and I have tried to be the defense attorney for Muhammad. He stated that he was a prophet, and because he is one of God's beloved children, he deserves a defense. I don't believe that I have "proved" that Muhammad is a prophet, because this matter is a question of faith. And after all, matters of faith can't be "proved" 100 percent—they remain matters of faith, which is belief in the unseen (Heb. 11:1–3).

The decision of whether or not he was a prophet is yours to make. And after all, isn't that the Protestant *modus operandi*? A Protestant shouldn't take anybody else's opinion of any issue without a careful, open-minded assessment of every claim in light of the entire Bible. Doesn't everyone have to appear before God on the day of judgment individually and answer for their convictions and actions (2 Cor. 5:10)? If we rejected something good or true simply because it wasn't discovered by our own church, or pastor, or family, it would be particularly embarrassing to face God, since He gave us time and opportunity to search out that truth and know it individually. The Protestant follows the Bible's injunction to "test everything" (1 Thess. 5:21).

I will end this book by quoting from two passages in the Quran. The first one is the first prayer recorded in the first sura (the most famous and most recited of all texts in the Quran):

> In the name of God, Most Gracious, Most Merciful. Praise be to God, the Cherisher and Sustainer of the Worlds; Most Gracious, Most Merciful; Master of the Day of Judgment; Thee do we worship, Thine aid we seek. Show us the straight way, The way of those on whom Thou hast bestowed Thy grace, Those whose (portion) is not wrath, and those who go not astray.

This is a beautiful prayer that if prayed with sincerity, God has promised He will honor (see James 1:5). And thus will He guide all of His children into the straight path—both from the side of Isaac and from the side of Ishmael.

The second quote is what Muhammad counseled Muslims to say to the Christians they would encounter:

> For us (is the responsibility for) our deeds, and for you, for your deeds. There is no contention between us and you. God will bring us together, and to Him is (our) final goal. (42:15)

May the God of Abraham, Ishmael, Isaac, and Jacob help us all keep our eyes on Him and follow Him in His advancing light.

Appendix A

A Concise Concordance to the Teachings of the Quran

Abyssinian Invasion (570 AD)

- Allah thwarted the plan of the king with a flock of birds (105:5)

Abraham

- Abraham was the father of the faithful, along with his sons Ismail, Isaac, and Jacob (Muslim, Hanif) (2:123–135; 3:95; 19:40–50; 21:67–74; 29:22–30)

- Abraham was not Jewish or Christian, he was faithful to Allah (Hanif)—a "friend" of Allah (3:67; 4:125; 6:161; 37:83–113)

- The closest people to Abraham are those that do as he did (Muhammad and all believers) (3:68, 69; 22:76–78)

- Story of Abraham and his father, Azar, and how he was not an idol worshipper (6:74–83; 21:51–65; 26:69–104)

- Prayed for forgiveness for his father (9:114)

- When it became apparent that his father was an enemy to Allah, he disassociated himself from him (9:114)

- Was compassionate and patient with his father (9:114)

- Birth of Isaac foretold (11:69–73)

- Abraham pleads for Lot (11:74–83)

- Lot's wife and destruction of Sodom and Gomorrah (15:51–77)

- Prayed for city (Mecca) and for believers who would pray, believe in Allah, and receive forgiveness in the day of judgment (14:35–41)

- Abraham was a nation in and of himself, member of the righteous, a model for us (16:120–124)

- Idol worshiping relatives and neighbors attempted to throw Abraham into a furnace of fire, but God delivered him (37:91–98)

- Surrenders his son as a sacrifice to God—as a trial (37:101–111)

- Allah ransomed Abraham's son with a great sacrifice (37:107)

- Isaac blessed because of Abraham, described as a prophet from among the righteous (37:112–113)

- Abraham, Isaac, and Jacob were men of "power and vision" (38:45)

- Abraham only worshiped Him who made him and left a legacy for his followers (43:26–32)

- Abraham was an example for us; he did not make friendships with unbelievers, and he appealed to them to leave their idols (60:4–6)

Adam and Eve

- Adam and Eve were placed in a garden and taught all things by Allah (2:31–34)

- Allah told Adam not to eat from a tree and transgress against Him (2:35)

- Story of their creation from the clay (15:26–44)

- Angels were instructed to prostrate themselves before Adam and Eve; all did, except Iblis (Satan) (15:29–44)

- Satan vowed to make evil attractive to them and to mislead all mankind (15:39)

Allah, Characteristics of

- Allah is most full of grace, most forgiving (1:1; 3:89, 155; 5:74, 98, 101; 6:12, 54; 9:117, 118; 10:107; 16:47; 17:44, 66–70; 34:1, 2; 41:43; 48:14; 49:5; 60:4–7; 67:2; 85:14)

- Allah is the Lord of the world, He is mighty (1:2; 2:20, 29, 106; 3:109, 165, 189; 5:120; 9:16; 85:12–16; 114:1–3)

- Allah is master of the day of judgment and will judge the righteous and unrighteous—He knows the day of judgment (1:4; 2:85, 177; 6:12, 57; 43:85)

- Allah is the straight way, and He guides and protects the sincere in the straight way (1:6; 2:142, 186, 257; 3:101; 10:25; 24:46; 28:56)

- Allah does not pour His wrath upon those who follow Him (1:7; 2:207; 3:152; 16:128)

- He is forgiving and merciful to those who seek forgiveness (4:110)

- Allah provides for all of His children, and we should return unto Him some of our money (2:3, 245, 261–271; 4:58)

- He returns to the man who loans to Him many times over (2:245, 261)

- He sees when you spend for others or pay a vow (2:271)

- Allah can veil people's hearts and blind them, leave them in darkness (2:7, 17, 257)

- Allah is the Creator (2:21; 4:1; 6:1–3, 95–102; 7:54; 10:3–7, 34; 11:6, 7; 13:1–3, 16; 14:10; 25:59; 29:60–62; 31:10, 11; 32:3; 85:13)

- He created all things in six days (7:54; 10:3; 11:7; 25:59; 32:3)

- Allah created man from clay, then decreed a term and a specified time (6:2)

- He created both men and women from one soul (4:1; 39:6)

- He shaped us in the womb (3:6)

- He preserves all things and sends rain to cause new growth (2:255; 7:57, 58; 11:6; 29:63; 31:10, 11; 35:13; 85:13)

- All things belong to Allah (23:84–90)

- He made seven heavens (2:29; 67:3)

- Allah will raise the dead, and they will return to Him, and He will reward them (2:28, 112, 212, 258, 259; 36:12; 42:9; 46:33; 85:13; 86:5–8)

- Allah is all-knowing; He can read hearts—nothing is hidden—He knows everything in heaven and earth (2:29, 215; 3:5, 29, 121, 153, 154, 180; 4:39, 63; 6:18, 58, 59, 73, 115; 9:105; 10:61; 28:69; 29:5; 31:22–30; 33:2; 35:38; 41:47; 49:13; 57:3; 58:7; 67:13; 84:23; 87:7)

- Allah knows your secret, what you make public, and what you earn (6:3; 3:29)

- He knows what you spend for others (2:215; 4:37–39)

- He keeps a clear record of everything on earth (6:59; 10:61)

- He views the most righteous as the most noble (49:13)

- We were without life and Allah gave us life (2:28, 187)

- Allah promises forgiveness (2:268, 284)

- Allah is our only Helper; He delivers us from disasters (2:107; 3:126, 150, 175; 6:63–67; 8:9, 10; 9:116)

- We are to worship Allah because He is the Creator; He said, "Be," and it was (2:117, 255; 4:1; 6:73; 10:55; 16:40; 35:3; 42:11)

- Partners assigned to Allah are actually jinn, His creatures (6:100)

- Allah is the God of Christians, Jews, and Muslims; and a true Muslim is sincere in Allah (2:139)

- Allah will choose as His objects of mercy those whom He wishes (2:212; 3:26, 27; 3:129)

- Allah decides which religion is right in the judgment (2:105, 113; 3:55, 128)

- Allah is close to His followers (2:186; 34:50)

- Allah will listen to every supplication from His followers; He can be trusted (2:186, 214; 3:122, 159–161)

- Allah does not slumber or sleep (2:255)

- Allah loves purity and cleanliness (2:222)

- Allah does not place a burden on the soul that is greater than it can bear (2:286; 7:42; 23:62)

- Every soul will only bear its own burden (35:18)

- Allah is everywhere, in the East and the West (2:115, 142; 73:9)

- There is one god—Allah—and no other (2:163, 177, 255; 3:2, 18, 62; 4:87; 14:52; 16:1; 17:41–44; 28:70)

- Truth only comes from Allah; He is only One to show truth; He will decide who is right in the end (3:60; 5:105; 6:57; 10:35; 34:26)

- Allah is God of "bounties" (mercies) unbounded (3:74)

- Allah frustrates the wicked (3:127)

- Allah fixes our days in writing (3:145; 6:60)

- Allah loves those who are firm and steadfast in the faith, those who ask forgiveness (3:146)

- Allah tests believers (and unbelievers) (3:166, 186; 29:1–10; 34:21)

- Allah never harms those who serve Him; He never wishes injustice for His servants (3:182; 40:31)

- Allah guides us; He wants to show us the ordinances of those who went before us (4:26–28)

- Allah doesn't like proud, vain people—people who spend of their wealth to be seen by others or are stingy, don't believe in the last day, or are companions of Satan (4:36–38)

- Allah is never unjust (8:51)

- Any good deed He doubles (or multiplies) in His grace (4:40)

- Allah is mightiest in power and punishment (4:84, 131–134; 67:1–7)

- Jews say, "The hand of Allah is chained." But rather, both His hands are extended; He spends however He wills (5:64)

- Allah is the only God; He doesn't allow people to worship any other gods; if they do, they worship Satan who deceives them (4:116–120; 19:65; 28:88)

- Allah knows the unseen (27:65)

- He knows the future (27:65–67)

- Allah is the goal (or destination) of all believers; they will be returned to Him (2:285; 5:48, 105; 8:24; 10:4, 56; 24:42; 35:18; 39:7, 44; 40:3; 50:43; 60:4; 88:25)

- Only He knows the true results of preaching the message (5:109)

- He is invisible, yet sees all (6:103)

- He is omniscient, sees all (6:103)

- Allah opens "hearts" or "breasts" to His truth; He knows hearts (6:125; 31:23)

- Allah never commands us to sin or commit immorality (7:28)

- He is the best planner (8:30; 13:42)

- He helps those who have quality of faith, not quantity of believers (9:25–27)

- He gives life and causes death (9:116; 10:31, 56; 16:70; 44:8)

- Allah has the "secrets" of heaven (11:123)

- He has control over His affairs, decrees (12:21; 13:30, 31; 35:11)

- Allah watches every soul all the time; He knows all things (13:32–34, 42; 14:42–50; 41:36)

- He keeps His promises to those He sends and will "back up their warnings" (14:42–51)

- He has created the heavens, and the animals, and sustains them with life (15:16–25; 16:1–21; 21:15–24, 30–33; 22:61–64; 24:40–45; 25:45–50; 27:59–66; 36:37–40; 39:5; 43:84–87; 57:5)

- Favors of Allah cannot be counted (16:18)

- All creation, in heaven and on earth, worship Allah as Creator and obey Him (16:49, 50; 17:43, 44)

- One thousand years are as one day for Him; He just delays judgment (22:46–48)

- Allah is the Light of the heavens and earth and reveals Himself in parables (24:35)

- Allah's light is like oil in a lamp in a niche (24:35)

- Allah's light shines like a pearly star, lit from a blessed olive tree (24:35)

- Allah is glorified when His light is in places of worship where prayers are offered (24:35–38)

- Allah is Lord of Mecca, and He made it sacred (27:91)

- Allah's promise is true (22:47; 31:9)

- Allah is full of knowledge and wisdom and power (33:1; 34:48; 48:4–7; 57:2)

- Allah doesn't need us (has no needs); we need Him; He could get rid of us all (35:15–17; 39:7; 47:39; 60:6)

- Allah is the best listener of prayers (37:75)

- Allah has no companion (wife), so how could He have a son? (6:101)

- Allah has no "children," in context of angels being daughters (37:149–166)

- What Allah wills, no one can change—mercy or punishment (harm) (39:38)

- He has the only right of intercession (39:43, 44; 53:26)

- He has the keys of heaven and earth (39:63)

- Allah is never unjust with His people (41:46)

- Allah created the world so that none may be wronged, but rewarded for what they deserve (45:22)

- Allah created the earth for an appointed time, or term (46:3)

- There is no God but Allah; we need to ask Him for forgiveness; He knows how we all "dwell in our homes" (47:19)

- Allah reveals Himself, forgives and punishes whom He wills (48:14)

- He is closer to man than man's jugular vein (50:16)

- Allah gives life and death (50:43; 57:2)

- Men making Allah into a woman is not "fair" (53:21–25)

- All things belong to Allah (53:31)

- He is free of need (22:64)

- Allah knows us in the womb (53:32)

- All will perish on earth (or the sea), except the face of the Lord, which is full of majesty, bounty, and honor (55:26–30)

- All creation is dependent upon Allah (55:29; 67:15–29)

- Allah is the First and the Last; He knows the end from the beginning (53:25; 57:3; 92:13)

- Allah has the following fifteen characteristics: The only god, omniscient, most gracious and merciful, only source of peace, guardian of faith, preserver of safety, exalted in might, irresistible, supreme, the Creator, evolver, bestower of forms and colors, most beautiful "names," worshiped, most wise (59:22–24)

- Allah is the One and Only God—eternal, absolute— doesn't "beget, nor is He begotten"; there is no one like Him (112:1–4)

- Allah is my refuge as Lord of the dawn, from the mischief of witchcraft, and all evil created things (113:1–5; 114:1–6)

- Allah is King, God (Judge), Lord of all mankind (114:1–3)

- The judgment is Allah's and He is the swiftest of accountants (6:62)

Angels

- The importance of believing in angels (2:177, 285)

- Allah appointed to us guardian angels (6:61, 62; 13:11)

- Allah created the *jinns* (6:100)

- *Jinns* deceive people with "flowery deceptions" and join the devils among men in opposing the prophets (6:12)

- *Jinns* will be devoured in fire, appear in judgment (37:158)

- Thousands of angels can help us, as in the battle of Badr (8:9)

- Angels are sad when unbelievers die (8:50)

- Angels are only sent for "just causes" to help the righteous, not to try to prove truth to unbelievers (15:7, 8)

- Angels only obey Allah's commands (19:64)

- Angels are not "daughters of Allah" as Arabs claimed, but are just servants of Allah (37:149–166; 43:16–20)

- Those who "sustain the throne" sing praises and glory to their Lord (40:7; 41:38)

- Angels praise Allah and pray for the forgiveness of inhabitants of earth (40:7; 42:5)

- Angels take souls at death, smite "faces" and "backs" at death (8:50; 47:27)

- Allah has two angels by His side: one to note good deeds and one to note bad deeds (50:17–19)

- Naming angels with feminine names does no good (53:26, 27)

- Some *jinns* listen to the Quran and agree with it and are on the right path and worship Allah, others have not agreed and don't worship (72:1–15)

- Nineteen angels are "guardians of the fire"; it is a fixed number (74:30, 31)

- "Sent forth" ones (angels or winds) separate, blow together, and spread a message abroad of justification or warning (77:1–6)

- Some "tear out" with violence, some bring out good gently (79:1–5)

- Angels write down all your deeds and know all that you do (82:10–12)

- Bad records: *sijjin*; good records: *illiyin* (83:10–19)

- Angels and the Spirit came down during "night of power" (97:1–4)

Backsliders

- Backsliders will be punished as unbelievers (2:208–211, 217; 3:63, 86, 90, 91, 104, 105)

Baptism

- The need to be baptized by Allah; Allah is the true baptizer (2:138)

Battle of the Trench

- Story depicted of enemies' attitude, Muslims' lack of courage and Allah's intervention—command to be strong and fight (33:10–20)

Bedouins

- Are stronger in disbelief and hypocrisy, less likely to recognize the limits of what Allah has revealed (9:97)

- Most give grudgingly, some give as a means of closeness to Allah (9:98, 99)

- Who remained behind, excuse themselves, "Our families occupied us, so ask forgiveness for us" (48:11)

- Said with their tongues what was not within their hearts; they assumed with pleasure that the Messenger and believers would never return (48:11, 12)

- Predicted that the bedouins would be given another chance to face a people of great military might and that they would gain much booty (48:16–20)

Bible/Scriptures That Predated Muhammad/Holy Writings

- The importance of studying the books from Allah (2:121, 285; 3:119; 10:37)

- Allah's revelation through Muhammad confirms earlier scriptures (2:4)

- If in doubt, "then ask those who have been reading the Scripture before you" (10:94)

- Allah sent the Book (Bible) in truth to judge between them, as mercy (2:213; 4:105; 6:91; 7:52, 196; 16:64; 42:17)

- "We revealed the message, so ask the people of the message [i.e. former scriptures] if you do no know" (21:7)

- True believers will attempt to understand the spiritual meaning of the book, not argue (3:7; 7:190–200)

- The Book is the truth (42:18)

- Those who believe the Book are fearful of it, unbelievers are impatient of it (42:18)

- Allah chose Adam, Noah, Abraham, Ishmael, Isaac, Jacob, Moses, and Jesus as messengers to reveal His will, also David, Solomon, Job, Ezekiel, Aaron, Elijah, Elisha, Zechariah, John, Joseph, Jonas, and Lot (3:33, 84; 4:163–166; 6:83–86; 17:55; 19:50–60; 21:78–86; 57:26)

- Truth only comes from Allah—He is the only One to show truth (3:60; 5:105; 6:57; 10:35)

- He who doesn't believe in the "books" of Allah, and His prophets have gone far astray (4:136)

- Those who reject some of Allah's apostles and accept others are truly disbelievers (4:150–152)

- The Quran was given to protect the Bible (5:48; 10:37)

- The Quran explains the former scriptures, about which there is no doubt (10:37)

- Even if Allah had sent down a book, people wouldn't have believed; they would have wanted an angel, or wanted "old" messengers (6:6–10; 37:168–182)

- Those who reject Muhammad would have rejected other apostles of Allah; those who accept are righteous (6:31–40)

- Revelation is to give good news and to warn (6:48, 92; 12:111)

- The Quran confirms previous revelation (6:92; 10:37; 11:17; 12:111; 20:98–104)

- A witness from the children of Israel has testified to something similar (to the Quran) and believed (46:10)

- The scriptures of Moses came before the Quran (11:17)

- None can change the words of Allah (6:115; 10:64; 18:27; 50:29)

- Some didn't accept God's signs, saying they were just tales of the ancients (6:25; 8:30–2)

- Every people group is sent an apostle or messenger (10:47)

- For each period of human history, a Book is revealed (13:38)

- Allah is the mother of the Book (13:39; 43:4)

- Allah sent messengers and prophets to every nation (15:10, 11; 16:36; 43:5–7)

- Many prophets, sent among the former people, were ridiculed (43:6, 7)

- The Book was given to Moses to guide the children of Israel—foretold their captivity and the destruction of the temple (17:2–10; 28:43, 44)

- God gave the children of Israel the Scripture, and judgment, and prophethood (45:16)

- All words of Allah cannot be recorded (18:109)

- If the sea were ink, it would be exhausted before the words of my Lord were (18:109)

- Allah is the Light, and He reveals Himself in parables (24:35)

- All nations that rejected Allah's revelation were destroyed (25:34–44)

- Before the Quran came the revelation of God to Moses as guidance, to lead by mercy (32:23; 46:12)

- The scripture of Moses is a confirming book in an Arabic tongue (46:12)

- Earlier prophets had revelation to "give light" and clear signs (35:25)

- Allah gave the Book to Moses and the children of Israel to guide them on the straight path (32:23; 37:114–122; 40:53)

- Nothing was said to Muhammad that God's previous messengers had not already said (41:43)

- Prophet (Rasool) can not harm or help; he can only pass on what Allah reveals to him (72:20–28)

- There are "books held in high honor" (commentators say it is Quran), with instruction, written by hands of scribes—honorable, pious, and just (80:11–16)

- Allah reveals "in degrees" so that people don't forget (87:6)

- Messages about the wicked being destroyed and the righteous rewarded is in the former scriptures of "Abraham and Moses" (87:18, 19)

Cain and Abel

- Story of Cain and Abel (5:27–31)

Covenant

- Allah took a covenant from those who received the Scripture that they must make it clear to others and not conceal it (3:187, 188)

Christianity, Growth of

- Allah supported those of the children of Israel who believed in Jesus, the son of Mary, and they became dominant (61:14)

Creation, History of the Beginning of the World

- Allah is the Creator of everything in heaven and earth (2:21, 255; 4:1; 6:1–5, 95–107; 10:3–7, 34; 11:6–8; 13:1–3, 16; 14:10; 23:84–90; 25:59; 29:60–63; 31:10, 11; 35:11–14; 85:13)

- Created everything in six days (7:54; 10:3; 11:7; 25:59; 32:3; 50:38–40; 57:4)

- Allah shaped us in the womb (3:6)
- Begins creation and then repeats it (10:34; 29:19; 85:13; 30:27)
- No woman conceives or gives birth except with His knowledge (35:11)
- Mankind was once one single nation (2:213, 4:1; 10:19; 39:6; 49:13)
- Allah creates you in three darknesses (39:6)
- Nature is a sign from Allah; teaches us truths about Allah (2:164; 3:190, 191; 16:65–81; 23:16–22; 30:22–30; 50:6–15)
- Creates animals to generate milk for man's use (16:66, 67)
- Creates honey for man's healing (16:68, 69)
- Brought forth a tree from Mt. Sinai producing oil and food to eat (23:20)
- New creation: more sure than the first (50:5–15)
- Process of creation of man (23:12–16; 40:67)
- We are to worship Allah because He is Creator; He said, "Be" and it was (2:117, 255; 4:1; 6:73; 10:55; 16:40; 35:3; 36:82; 40:68; 42:11)
- Allah created all—will make new creation; He is the reason for worship (29:19, 20; 40:61–68; 51:47–60; 56:57–74; 82:6–9; 88:16–20)
- All creation, in heaven and on earth, worships/exalts Allah as Creator (16:49, 50; 17:43, 44; 22:61–64; 27:59–66; 43:84–87; 57:1, 5; 59:1; 62:1)
- Created man from nothing (19:67)
- Allah created all people/languages/colors/sleep/mates—all people belong to Him (30:22–30; 67:23)
- Produced for mankind: hearing and vision and hearts (67:23)
- Created both *jinn* and mankind to worship Him (51:56)

- Allah created us by breathing into us His spirit, started us with clay and then brought us from "fluid" (a sperm-drop) (32:4–10; 35:11; 36:77)

- He perfected everything He created (32:7)

- Allah created all things in pairs (36:33–36; 42:11; 78:8)

- Story of creation of Adam and rebellion of Satan (38:71–88)

- Creation of heavens and earth, even a greater thing than creation of man; most men don't understand it (40:57; 79:27–33)

- Earth was created in two days, and its sustenance in four more days, and seven firmaments in two days (41:7–12; 65:12)

- Creation is a sign from Allah (42:29)

- If Allah could do first creation, He can do second new creation (50:6–15)

- Creator is able to give life to the dead (75:36–40)

- Allah created everything in "proportion and measure" (54:49)

- The command of creation was a "single act" (54:50)

- Created man, taught him speech, created sun, moon, herbs, trees, the "balance of justice," *jinns*, etc.; therefore, don't disregard Allah or deny His favors (55:3–25)

- Allah created life and death, lower and upper heavens, stars (67:1–5)

- Creation displays no inconsistency (67:3, 4)

- Allah created seven heavens, moon, sun, and humans in stages (2:29; 67:3; 71:14–17)

- Allah created male and female (75:39)

- Allah has made man from "mingled" sperm and showed him the "right way" and made him strong (76:1–5, 28–30; 77:20; 80:17–32)

- Allah created man from a "drop emitted" that proceeded from between the backbone and the ribs (86:5–7)

- Allah created eyes, tongues, lips for man (90:7–10)

- As surely as God acted on Mt. Sinai, He has created man in the "best of molds" ("best of stature") (95:1–4)

- Created man from clay, then decreed a term and a specified time (6:2)

- Created both men and women from one soul (4:1; 39:6)

- Preserves all things, sends rain to cause new growth (2:255; 7:57, 58; 11:6; 29:63; 31:10, 11; 35:13; 85:13)

- All things belong to Allah (23:84–90)

Charity

- Give charity before death approaches, for never will Allah delay when the soul's time has come (63:10, 11)

- Spend from what Allah has given you (63:10)

David

- Was one who repeatedly turned back to Allah (38:17)

- David was given a kingdom, strengthened and given wisdom and discernment in speech (38:17–20)

- Mountains and the birds united with him in repeating praise (38:18, 19)

- Story of two disputants coming to David for decision—he always turned to Allah and was given much power and wisdom by Allah (38:15–26)

Day of Judgment (See also Last Day, Second Coming of Christ, or Resurrection)

- Allah is master of the day of judgment (1:4)

- Knows day (hour) of judgment (43:85)

- The decision is only for Allah, the best of deciders (6:57)

- We are to live with the thought in mind that we will meet our Lord, Allah, to whom we belong, when He comes with clouds of angels (2:45, 46, 210; 7:172–174)

- Allah will choose as His objects of mercy those whom He wishes; Allah decides which religion is right in the judgment (2:105, 113, 212; 3:26, 27, 55, 128, 129)

- Allah will not speak to or purify the wicked on the day of the resurrection (2:174; 17:45–52; 19:65–70)

- Say, "Perhaps it will be soon" (17:51, 52)

- Allah will judge those who have been given more signs (privileges) harsher (7:1–10; 45:8–10)

- Righteous will be elevated on the day of judgment; wicked will be humbled, destroyed (2:212; 20:104–112; 27:87–90; 29:50–65; 30:41–45; 34:3, 4; 36:51–58; 40:15–20; 74:9–15; 77:13–48; 79:34–41; 88:1–16; 101:1–8)

- Believer who does righteousness will fear neither injustice nor deprivation (20:112)

- All will come to Him humbled on the day the horn is blown (27:87)

- One blast alone will bring all together before God (36:53)

- Will be a difficult day, not an easy one for disbelievers (74:9, 10)

- Deniers will not speak, nor be permitted to make excuses that day (77:34–36)

- Light scales versus heavy scales on that day (101:4–11)

- Allah will gather everyone together on one day (3:9, 25, 185; 4:87; 10:28, 45; 19:65–98; 25:11–25; 27:83; 45:26)

- Day about which there is no doubt (3:9, 25; 4:87; 45:26)

- Righteous will be separated from the worshipers of other gods on the gathering day (resurrection) (10:28; 19:68–72)

- Allah has the power to bring the living out of the dead, bring from dust (3:27; 20:55; 22:5–7, 66; 23:16; 30:11–19, 40; 36:12; 41:39; 43:11; 71:18; 86:8)

- Truth only comes from Allah; He is the only One to show it; and He will decide who is right in the end (3:60; 5:105; 6:57; 10:35; 34:26)

- Wealth and family or profession of religion will not help a person on the day of judgment (3:116; 4:123; 86:10)

- Unbelievers and those who are arrogant will have a terrible, painful, humiliating punishment; they will be terrified (3:176–178; 4:56; 16:21–25; 22:1–4; 27:87; 37:21–37)

- Allah will punish those who hold on to His gifts (3:180)

- Allah will punish those who have not kept His covenant (3:187; 4:37; 16:95)

- Those who received the Scripture but refused to make it clear to others and hid it will receive a painful punishment (3:187, 188)

- Allah will save the righteous from shame on the day of judgment; He will help them (3:194, 195; 27:87–93; 40:51)

- Allah doesn't like proud, vain people—people who don't believe in the last day (4:36, 38)

- Those that don't love Allah will want to hide from Him when He appears (4:42)

- Who will plead on behalf of unrepentant sinners in the day of judgment? (4:109; 10:27; 30:13; 40:18)

- Only Allah can intercede on behalf of mankind during the day of judgment (32:4; 39:44; 45:19)

- To those who fear the day of judgment, their only help or intercessor will be from Allah (6:51, 70)

- Angels' intercession will avail nothing; only He who is approved by Allah (53:26)

- It will be a day when the "trumpet will be blown" (6:73; 20:102; 27:87; 36:51–53; 39:68; 50:20; 78:18)

- On that day of the blast hearts will tremble and eyes will be humble (79:6–9)

- Mountains will pass as the passing of clouds (27:88; 78:20)

- Trumpet will be blown and many will fall dead; then it will be blown again and at once they will be standing looking on (39:68)

- When the horn is blown, that is the day of carrying out the threat (50:20)

- "The hour" of the day of judgment is known only to Allah—it will come unexpectedly (7:187)

- None will reveal the time (of the hour) except Him (7:187)

- The hour has come near, and the moon has split as a sign (54:1, 2)

- Signs and information are sent as a deterrence (54:1–5)

- There will be no way out for unbelievers on the day of judgment, even if they gave all the possessions in the world as ransom (10:54–56; 39:47–52)

- Will judge schisms of children of Israel, all religious disputes (10:93, 94; 39:31, 46)

- If God delays judgment and shows favor to wicked, they become proud; they become bolder as the day of judgment approaches (11:8–10; 21:1–15)

- Judgment is for an "appointed time" (11:104; 18:59; 29:5, 53; 38:78–81; 54:3; 78:17; 79:42–44 [limit or finality])

- God does not bring judgment for "one wrong" if community is likely to repent (11:117)

- Some will just be misled by others and still be condemned in judgment (14:21)

- Earth will be changed into "different earth" and the heavens as well; the mountains will be swept away (14:48; 27:88; 52:9–11; 73:14; 78:20; 84:3)

- A scroll, a book, a register will be presented to all with their deeds written in it on the day of judgment (17:11–14; 18:45–49; 36:12)

- Allah does not pour out His wrath until He sends a messenger to warn a community (17:15–17; 28:59)

- Allah will destroy all nations before the day of judgment; all nations will be judged (17:58, 71, 72)

- Only the "one" who receives permission from Allah on day of judgment can intercede (19:87; 20:109; 34:23)

- The day of judgment will be very fair for everyone—everyone bears own guilt (21:47; 29:12, 13; 34:25; 38:28)

- None can bear the burden of another (39:7)

- Allah records every good deed and takes it into account (21:94, 22:66–70)

- The day of judgment "will come and will fulfill what is written in Psalms 'the righteous will inherit the earth'"—heavens rolled up like scroll (21:104, 105)

- Allah will judge between Jews, Christians, Sabians, Muslims, polytheists, and Magians (22:16–18)

- In the day of judgment it will appear as if we were on earth for only a day or so (23:112–115)

- The wicked will blame false teachers and wish that they had accepted the right path on day of judgment (28:63–67; 34:51–54)

- The wicked, in terror, will claim that they believe (34:51–53)

- The deeds we have done and not done are recorded in a clear register (36:12)

- Allah will judge between us in truth (34:26)

- Will condemn most of world for worshiping *jinns* (34:39–41)

- Allah should destroy everyone for their wickedness, but He gives an "appointed time" to repent (35:42–45)

- Allah does not change or alter His methods (35:43)

- On the day of judgment Allah will "seal" the mouths of the wicked, but their deeds will testify to their beliefs (36:65)

- Two trumpet sounds will be sounded on the day of judgment; the books will be opened; witnesses (prophets) will be called forward; and the glory of God will shine (39:68–70; 69:11–18; 74:8; 78:18)

- The righteous will praise Allah for being faithful to His promises and giving them heaven (39:74)

- The wicked don't believe in judgment and are bold; they want it to come right away (42:16–18)

- On the day of judgment believers in Islam will have no fear and will have a rich reward; terrible punishment will befall evildoers (43:68–80)

- Only those who bear witness to the Truth have power of (or can benefit from) "intercession" (43:86)

- No one can help someone in the day of judgment were it not for the mercy of Allah (44:41, 42)

- Those who think wickedness will be rewarded like righteousness make a grave mistake (45:21)

- The wicked will be hostile toward faith even at the day of judgment (46:6–8)

- There will come a day when all will "bow the knee" to Allah; the wicked will realize their mistake, that only Allah is worthy of praise (45:25–37)

- The wicked wait for the "hour"; it will come "all of a sudden," even though Allah has sent "tokens" (indications) of judgment, but they didn't listen (47:18)

- Every soul will come to judgment, and with it a driver and witness (50:21)

- All who transgressed, forbade what was good, cast doubts and suspicions, and worshiped another God besides Allah will be thrown into hell (50:20–29)

- At the resurrection, the One who calls will be quite near (50:41)

- To rend asunder the earth and resurrect the dead is quite "easy" for Allah (50:44)

- Judgment will come as surely as there was a mountain of revelation, inscribed decree, scroll unfolded, and much frequented "fane" (house) canopy raised high (52:1–7)

- Allah has promised a second resurrection (the other "next" creation) (53:47)

- The day of judgment is approaching (53:57)

- Judgment is close at hand, moon is "cleft asunder," but the wicked say it is magic (54:1–5)

- For the wicked, the day of judgment will be a "hard" day (54:8)

- Every matter, small and great, is on record—nothing is secret (54:53)

- The sky will be rent asunder and become red; everyone will stand before the judgment seat (55:37–46; 56:1–6; 69:16; 73:18; 77:9, 10; 84:1–6)

- There will be three classes on the day of judgment—those on the left hand, right hand, and closest to Allah—on thrones; from older and newer (from former and later peoples) (56:7–21, 39, 40; 69:18–37)

- Among your wives and children are enemies, so beware of them (56:14)

- Your wealth and your children are but a trial (56:15; 63:9)

- Tale of one righteous and one wicked man on the day of judgment and their reactions (64:17–37)

- On the day of judgment the heaven will split open and the throne of your Lord will appear above, supported by eight angels (69:15–17)

- The righteous will be given his record in his right hand and will be pleased to read it and for others to see it and his reward (69:19–24; 84:7–9)

- Man given his record in his left hand (or behind his back) will wish he had not been given his record or the reward based on it (69:25–31; 84:10–15)

- The wicked in hell will be inserted into a chain of seventy cubits (69:32)

- For us the day of judgment seems far off, but for Allah, to whom 50,000 years are as a day, it is close at hand (70:4–7) (the extent of the day is 50,000 years)

- Don't judge—Allah will judge all at the day of judgment (73:11–14)

- The wicked will be destroyed because they were greedy, denied the day of judgment, weren't kind, believed Allah's messages to be "magic," and didn't pray (74:15–45)

- Allah will assemble human bodies in "perfect order" at the resurrection (75:1–4)

- Man will be a witness against himself, even if he presents his excuses (75:13–15)

- Allah made man from sperm, made them male and female; He can raise the dead, which no magician can do; the day when no sun or moon will exist (75:24–40)

- On the day of judgment, Spirit and angels will stand in the ranks at the throne of Allah and only will speak when Allah allows them (78:38)

- Only the One who is most merciful will speak on the day, and he will speak what is correct (78:38)

- Unbelievers will wish to be made into "dust" (78:40)

- It will be a day of "agitation"; the hearts of the wicked will be in agitation, and they will wish to be in a "former state"—dust (79:6–12)

- There will be a deafening noise, a man will flee from his own family, and some faces will be "beaming" (80:33–42)

- The day of judgment will call forward falling stars, sun disappearing, and raging earth, mountains removed, graves opened; the scrolls will be laid open and every soul will know what he has done (81:1–14; 82:1–5)

- The day of judgment is the "day of entrance" to bliss for the righteous or fire for the unrighteous (82:15; 88:1–26)

- The day of judgment, who can explain it except to say that no soul will have power, all commands will be from Allah (82:17–19)

- The day of judgment when the righteous will laugh at those who used to laugh at them while they are sitting on thrones (83:29–36)

- Allah is the one who punishes, not prophets, at the day of judgment (88:22–26)

- When your Lord comes with the angels, rank upon rank, the earth will be leveled—pounded and crushed (89:21–23)

- Allah is the wisest (most just) of judges (95:7, 8)

- Men will cry out about the earth on the day of judgment, and if anyone has done "atom's weight" of good or bad, it will be revealed (99:1–8)

Day (One)

- One day with Him is as one thousand years which we count (32:5)

Death

- Never will Allah delay death for one to change his ways, give charity, and be among the righteous when his time has come (63:10, 11)

Elijah

- Elijah was one of Allah's true messengers; he decried worship of Baal (37:123–132)

Elisha

- Elisha is listed in the company of the good (38:48)

Fasting

- Decreed on you that you may become righteous (2:183)
- Month of Rahmadhan (2:185)
- Equal number of other days for the sick or travelers (2:185)
- Test of the beginning of night or day: a white and black thread (2:187)
- Sexual relations are allowed on the night before the fast (2:187)

Fitrah (the natural inclination to worship the Creator)

- God created people to worship Him, incline toward the truth, follow the true religion (30:30)

Forgiveness

- Allah does not forgive association of or joining of other gods with Him, but He does forgive lesser sins (4:116)

Form(s) or Principles of Religion

- The whole creation worships Allah (2:116)

- The form of religion is not important, only that which is from Allah (2:120)

- True religion comes through Abraham, Ishmael, Isaac, Jacob, the tribes, Moses, and Jesus (2:136)

- People should aim for good, and Allah will bring us together (2:148)

- Seek Allah with patience and prayer (2:45, 153, 155)

- Importance of having a lowly spirit when seeking God (2:45; 7:55; 23:2)

- Following the religion of the Jews or Christians after the revelation of Allah will leave you with no helper or protector (2:120)

- Questions about things not revealed may lead to doubt and then unbelief (5:101, 102)

- Don't associate with those who make fun of Allah's revelation or treat religion as amusement (6:67–70)

- Wear beautiful apparel for time of prayer, but not excessive (7:31)

- Should "remember the Lord" in morning and evening, praise Allah (7:205; 33:41–48; 60:6)

- Those nearest the Lord prostrate themselves in worship, exalting Him (7:206)

- Wait on Allah (11:122)

- Prayer without faith (by unbelievers) is futile (13:14)

- Reward was promised to those who migrated for faith (16:41–44; 22:58)

- Should not boast about tomorrow; say "Insha Allah" (18:23, 24)

- Importance of praise to Allah numerous times of day and night (20:129-133; 52:48, 49)

- Sacrifices should be brought near Mecca with a clean heart (22:26–33)

- Punishment for adultery is 100 lashes for both (unmarried fornicators) (24:1, 2)

- Punishment and rules for those who accuse someone of adultery (24:4–11)

- Etiquette for entering homes that are not your own (24:27–29)

- Secret meetings are of the evil one (58:10)

- Danger of making close friendship with enemies of Allah (unbelievers, those who drove them out of their homes); however, Allah can do miracles and change their hearts (60:1–13; 62:7–17)

- Story of stingy (or unbelieving) owners who were not generous with Allah and destruction of their garden (68:15–34)

- Only name of Allah should be invoked at "place of worship" (72:18, 19)

- Witchcraft condemned (those who "blow on knots") (113:1–4)

Rules of True Religion

- Importance of bowing down in worship to Allah (2:43; 7:206)

- Establish (regular) prayer (2:3, 43, 110, 177, 238; 3:61; 8:3; 11:114 (regular); 17:78, 79; 27:1–3; 58:13)

- Eat what is lawful and good, not unclean meat, blood, swine, or meat of dead animals (2:168–176, 3:93; 5:88)

- The importance of taking care of orphans (2:177, 215, 220; 4:2, 6, 8, 36; 93:9–11; 107:2)

- The importance of fulfilling contracts (2:177)

- The importance of justice for slaves (2:177; 4:36)

- The importance of taking care of your family (2:177, 215)

- If we differ in beliefs among ourselves, we should refer the matter to Allah and His apostle, best to believe in judgment (4:59–66)

- Whoever helps in a good cause becomes a participant; and whoever helps in evil, also becomes guilty (4:85)

- By very careful when judging somebody who greets you in peace (4:94)

- Punishment for waging war against Allah and His apostle—death, crucifixion, maiming, or exile (5:33)

- Punishment for theft—amputate hands, both male and female; Allah will forgive if they repent (5:38–40)

- Stone altars and divining arrows are but a defilement from Satan (5:90)

- The importance of taking care of wayfarers (2:177, 215; 4:36; 93:10; 107:3)

- The penalty for intentional murder is death; unintentional, compensation (2:178; 4:92, 93)

- The importance of leaving wealth for parents, family in case of death, and rules for dividing (2:180, 4:7–12)

- The importance of fasting (to learn self-restraint), of anger, or of appetite (2:183)

- Not to do kind deeds to be seen by men; when we give in secret, Allah will reward us (2:264–266, 274)

- To lend without interest, put contracts in writing; better to give in charity (2:275–283, 3:130)

- Trade is allowed by Allah, but interest is forbidden (2:275)

- Bribery is a sin (2:188)

- Ramadan is a month of fasting (2:185)

  - Do not fight during Ramadan, it is great sin, but averting people from the worship of Allah is a greater sin (2:217, 218)

  - Ramadan is intended for ease and not for hardship (2:185)

  - Substitute an equal number of other days if traveling or ill (2:185)

  - Permissible to go to your wives on the night before the fast (2:187)

- - Eat and drink on the night before the fast until the white thread of dawn becomes distinct from the black (2:187)
  - Complete the fast until night, and have no relations with women during the day, while you are at the mosques (2:187)
- Fight for the honor of Allah; fight enemies of Allah only if they fight against Allah (2:190, 191, 216, 218, 243, 244)
- *Fitnah* (religious oppression) is worse than killing (2:191, 217)
- *Hajj* and *umrah*, pilgrimage to Mecca (2:196–203; 3:96, 97; 22:26–30)
  - During certain months (2:197)
  - No sexual relations, no disobedience, and no disputing during *hajj* (2:197)
  - Substitutes prescribed for those prevented from *hajj* pilgrimage (2:196)
  - Take provisions, but the best provision is fear of Allah (2:197)
  - Seeking profit during *hajj* is allowed (2:197)
  - Eat of the sacrificial animals and feed the miserable and poor (22:28, 36)
  - Fulfill your vows and perform *tawaf* around the ancient house (22:29)
  - Place of sacrifice of animals is at the ancient house (22:33, 34)
  - Meat and blood of the sacrifices will not reach Allah, but what will reach Him is your piety (22:37)
- Drinking and gambling are sins (2:219)
- We should praise Allah (27:93)
- Marriage should only be with believers (2:221; 24:32)
- Believers should be cautious with whom they associate, not take unbelievers as allies or intimates (3:28, 118)
- Men should not approach their wives during their menstrual period (2:222)

- Be cautious in taking oaths (2:224, 225)

- Rules of divorce: fairness for women [two just witnesses required, must provide for her, a term is granted for reconciliation, breastfeeding, etc.] (2:226–237; 65:1–7)

- Father required to support his wife and child while she nurses, up to two years (2:233)

- Widows should be given their maintenance for one year, without being turned out, and included in the will (2:240–242)

- Should consult before making a decision, then keep the decision firm (3:159)

- Be patient and persevere, endure, and remain stationed; Allah will prosper those that believe in Him and do this (3:200)

- Should honor our mothers (parents) (4:1; 31:14; 46:15)

- Men should only marry as many ladies as they can take care of, up to four, in a just manner (4:3)

- Dowry should be given as a free gift (4:4)

- Don't give property to weak minded people, be kind to them though (4:5)

- Rules of inheritance (4:6–12, 18, 33)

- Adultery should be punished, both parties, unless they repent and correct themselves (4:15, 16)

- Do not kill yourself (4:29)

- We should not be jealous and "eat up" other's properties except in mutually beneficial business (4:29, 30)

- Avoid the major sins, and God will remove the lesser ones (4:31)

- Should pray with a clear mind (no intoxication) and with a clean body (4:43)

- A courteous greeting deserves an equally or even more courteous response (4:86)

- Keep oaths, and expiation for breaking an intentional oath (5:87–89)

- Avoid gambling and intoxicants, they are Satan's ways to avert you from remembering Allah and from prayer (5:90, 91)

- Rules for eating game from land and sea during *ihram Hajj* (5:93–98)

- Rules regarding last will and choosing honest witnesses (5:105–108)

- Eat only that upon which the name of Allah has been mentioned and which has not been forbidden by Allah (6:118–121)

- One-fifth of spoils of war go to Allah, the Prophet and his near relatives, orphans, the needy, and the traveler (8:41–44)

- Treaties should be honored—only the treacherous break them (8:55–58; 9:1–9)

- A time is outlined when not to make treaties with "pagans" because they are treacherous (9:1–20)

- Twelve months in year; four are sacred (9:36, 37)

- *Zakat* for poor, needy, those employed to administer funds, to bring in new believers, to free those in bondage and debt, and wayfarers (9:60)

- True believers in the Torah, the Gospel, and the Quran:

    - Are repentant

    - Are worshippers

    - Are praisers

    - Are travelers

    - Bow and prostrate

    - Enjoin what is right

    - Forbid what is wrong

    - Observe the limits set by Allah

    - Give good tidings to the believers (9:111, 112)

- Heaven, a peaceful final home, is the reward for those who:

  o Fulfill the covenant of Allah

  o Do not break the contract

  o Join that which Allah has ordered to be joined

  o Fear their Lord

  o Are afraid of the evil of [their] account

  o Are patient, seeking the countenance of their Lord

  o Establish prayer

  o Spend from what God has provided them secretly and publicly

  o Prevent evil with good (13:20–24)

- Believers should be careful to limit their gaze (for both men and women) and guard their private parts (24:30)

- Believing women should dress modestly, covering their "adornment," except to their close male relatives, and uphold sexual purity (24:30–34)

- Do not compel your slave girls into prostitution (24:33)

- Assist your slaves to regain their freedom (24:33)

- Allah is merciful to prostitutes who are forced into prostitution (24:33)

- Attend meetings that require collective action; do not leave without permission (24:62–64)

- Should not raise voice—it is like the braying of a donkey (31:19; 49:2)

- Allah has prepared great reward for both men and women who are:

  o Muslim

  o Believing

- Obedient
  - Truthful
  - Patient
  - Humble
  - Charitable
  - Fasting
  - Guarding their private parts
  - Remember Allah often (33:35)
- These can expect a transaction [i.e. profit]:
  - Those who recite the Book of Allah
  - Establish prayer
  - Spend privately and publicly out of what God has provided them (35:29, 30)
- Should respect leader (apostle) and not raise voice above him (49:2–4)
- Do not "turn your cheek" or walk exultantly, self-deluded, boastful (31:18)
- All believers are brothers (49:10)
- Treat all brothers with respect and resolve quarrels; be fair in dealings and don't spy upon or backbite a brother (49:8–13)
- Difference between submitting and believing is faith (49:14, 15)
- Believe in Allah, His apostle, and give "charitably" (57:7; 58:13)
- Leave trade when prayer is called on Friday, and proceed to the remembrance of Allah (62:9)
- Pray at night, not all night, but many hours (73:1–4)

- He has certainly succeeded who:
  - Purifies himself
  - Mentions the name of his Lord, and
  - Prays (87:14, 15)

Gog and Magog

- Allah bans any nation (city) that he has destroyed from appearing again; prophecy of the last day (21:95–97)

Gospel

- Allah gave Jesus the Gospel (5:46)
- Confirms the Torah (5:46)
- Contains guidance and instruction for the righteous (5:46)
- People of the Gospel should judge by what Allah has revealed therein (5:47)

Grace

- Allah does not pour out His wrath upon those who follow Him (1:7; 3:152; 16:128)
- We were without life and Allah gave us life, and He forgave us (2:28, 187, 268, 284, 286)
- Only Allah can forgive sins and make our conduct right (3:135, 193; 14:10; 33:71; 39:53; 42:25)
- Allah was very gracious and "turned" to Adam and Eve as they worked the land for their livelihood (2:37)
- There is no compulsion in religion (2:256; 10:99–103)
- Allah does not place a burden on the soul that is greater than it can bear—every soul can only bear its own burden (2:286; 7:42; 23:62; 35:18)
- The human heart tends to deviate from Allah—we need grace to overcome it (3:8)

- Allah is kind to those who serve Him and will forgive their sins and evil (3:30, 31, 89, 135, 136; 4:110; 9:104; 13:6; 22:50; 23:116–118; 42:19; 46:31)

- Allah is a God of "bounties unbounded" (3:74)

- Allah will not forgive those who have "sold" their faith (3:77)

- By Allah's grace we became "brothers" and united and saved (3:103)

- Believers' faces will be "lit up" by the grace (mercy) of Allah (3:107)

- Believers should desire (like a race)(hasten to) forgiveness of Allah (3:133)

- Allah loves those who are firm and steadfast (3:146)

- Allah rewards those who ask for forgiveness of sins (3:147, 148)

- The best reward for believers will be the presence of Allah himself—He will save (3:195; 9:22)

- Allah guides us because we are weak; He wants to show us the ordinances of those who went before us (4:26–28)

- Allah wants to accept your repentance (4:26–28)

- Allah is never unjust, any good deed He doubles (multiplies) (4:40; 8:51)

- If it were not for Allah's grace (favor), we all would have fallen into the clutches of Satan (4:83)

- Grace is given now—judgment comes at the day of judgment (6:12–17)

- Allah opens "hearts" or "breasts" to His truth; He knows the heart (6:125; 31:23)

- Allah never changes one's grace (favor bestowed) unless people change what's in their souls (8:53, 54)

- Allah will show mercy to those who strive for faith with goods and "person" (9:20, 21)

- Allah accepts repentance from His servants (9:104)

- Those who show constancy, patience, and work righteousness shall be forgiven (11:11)

- The Lord is full of forgiveness for the people despite their wrongdoing (13:6)

- He invites you that He may forgive you of your sins, and He delays you [i.e. your death] for a specified term (14:10)

- If Allah were to punish the world, not a single living creature would be left—he gives us a time of grace (16:61–65)

- Allah is full of grace (bounty), but most people are ungrateful (27:73; 33:73)

- Wind and rain are a sign of Allah's mercy (30:46–53)

- Allah is most forgiving (15:49; 24:22, 62; 33:35; 35:41; 39:53; 110:3)

- We should pray to Allah and trust in (hope for) His mercy (39:9)

- Do not despair of the mercy of Allah (39:53)

- Allah forgives all sins (39:53)

- Allah is subtle (i.e. gentle) with His servants (42:19)

- Allah sends His grace (provision) in "due measure" (42:25–27)

- Allah forgives when we bring upon ourselves misfortunes (42:30)

- The mercy of Allah is better than amassed wealth—Allah has prepared something better than the wealth of this world (43:32–35)

- The revelation of Allah is a mercy to mankind (44:2–6)

- No one can help someone in the day of judgment were it not for the mercy of Allah (44:41, 42)

- Allah will accept the "best deeds" and turn from their ill deeds those who honor their parents (46:15–16)

- Allah will remove all "ills and improve condition" of those who work deeds of righteousness (47:2)

- There is no God but Allah; we need to ask Him for forgiveness; He knows how we all "dwell in our homes" (47:19)

- Allah granted a great victory—forgave sins, gave peace, and guided on the straight way (treaty at Hudaibiya) (48:1–4)

- Allah will grant forgiveness and a great reward to the righteous (48:29; 74:56)

- By Allah's grace, sin becomes hateful to us (49:7)

- Allah has endeared to you the faith and made it pleasing to you (49:7)

- Righteous people don't sleep so much; they are praying for forgiveness (51:15–18)

- Allah grants everything—laughter, tears, death, life, wealth, satisfaction (53:43–48)

- Allah is most kind and merciful to us (57:9, 28)

- Allah sends clear evidence that He may bring you out from darknesses into the light (57:9)

- People of the Book should know that Allah's grace is given by Him, not by them; He gives it to whom He wills (57:29)

- We should seek Allah's grace (forgiveness) (73:20)

- Some were disputing about the "great news"—soon they will find out (78:1–5)

- The righteous will be given food and drink to their heart's content for what they used to do (77:43)

- By the night visitant, and star of piercing brightness, all souls have a "protector" over them (86:1–4)

- Allah has granted a "delay" to the wicked so that they might repent (86:17)

Greediness

- Withholding what Allah has given is not better for them, especially on the day of judgment (3:180)

Health

- We are to eat what is lawful and good, not unclean meat, blood, swine, or "dead animals" (2:168–176; 5:88; 16:114–118)

- Bring the Torah and recite it regarding lawful foods (3:93)

- Drinking and gambling are great sins—greater than any benefit (2:219)

- One should avoid intoxicants, Satan's tools to avert you from Allah and prayer (5:90–94)

- Do not eat meat that Allah forbids (6:116–121; 16:115)

- Eat only that upon which the name of Allah has been mentioned, and which has not been forbidden by Allah (6:118–121)

- Exception for eating forbidden foods: only under compulsion of necessity (6:119)

- Many mislead others to transgress by their appetites unchecked by knowledge (6:119)

- Foods prohibited to Jews are still prohibited (6:146; 16:118, 119)

- Do not eat to excess (6:141, 142)

Heaven—Life After Death

- Belief in life after death (2:4; 6:27–32; 13:35; 57:20–24)

- Those who don't love Allah are afraid of death (2:19; 3:150, 151)

- The righteous will inherit a garden fed by rivers (2:25; 3:15, 133, 136; 4:57; 7:42, 43; 9:72; 15:45–50; 16:31; 22:22–26; 32:15–22; 35:28–37; 37:40–50; 38:50; 51:15; 52:17–20; 54:54, 55; 65:11; 68:34; 70:35; 74:40; 85:11)

- Allah rewards those who ask for forgiveness of sins (3:147, 148)

- Allah gives life and death (3:156–158)

- Allah rewards those who do right and refrain from doing wrong (3:172; 11:115; 14:23; 46:14)

- Allah rewards those without measure who believe in His apostles and in Him and give of their wealth and "persons" (3:179; 9:88; 41:30–32)

- Those who say that there is no life after death (resurrection) stray from the right path and will be punished by Allah (6:27–30; 23:63–77; 32:10–11; 34:6–9)

- Approval of Allah is greater than life (9:72)

- One needs to value the afterlife more than this life (14:3; 40:39; 74:53–55)

- One day the earth will be replaced with another earth and the heavens as well (14:48)

- The home of the hereafter is greater than the good of this world (16:30)

- Righteous believers will be adorned with bracelets of gold and pearls and garments of silk (22:23; 35:33)

- Rewards those who do good deeds and trust in Allah, in path of Islam (29:58, 59)

- This life is just vanity in comparison with eternal life (29:64–68)

- Neither fatigue nor weariness touches any therein (35:35)

- Allah has prepared mansions for the righteous (39:20)

- The righteous will be in rich garments of silk and brocade, dressed in fine clothes, have big, beautiful eyes, and not taste death (only the first) (44:51–58)

- Allah will marry the righteous to fair women with large eyes (44:54; 52:20)

- Rivers of paradise flow with pure water, milk, wine, and honey, and much fruit is there (47:15)

- Allah takes away all ills (misdeeds) when righteous enter paradise, which is the highest achievement for man (48:5)

- Allah rewards those who keep their oaths with Him (48:10)

- People who deny the afterlife are in a confused state (50:5)

- If Allah could do first creation, He can do second new creation (50:15)

- Paradise will be brought near to the righteous (50:30–35)

- The righteous will sit on thrones, lined up, facing each other; have positions of honor (52:20; 54:54, 55)

- Believing families will live happily in paradise; they will be reunited (52:21)

- They will enjoy eternal life with "companions, with big and lustrous eyes" and sit on thrones (52:20; 56:22, 23)

- The righteous will praise Allah for saving them and being so merciful to them in heaven (52:26–28)

- Heaven will contain all kinds of delights: two springs, fruits, trees, virgins, red and green carpets to lie on (55:48–78; 56:34–40)

- Allah will reward all with "companions," virgins, among fruitful trees, with water flowing constantly nearby and fountains of "wine" made with ginger (56:24–39; 76:6–25; 83:20–28)

- Allah will give life to the earth after its "death" (57:17)

- The desires of the righteous will be fulfilled, and they will have full-breasted "companions of equal age" (78:31–37)

- Described and contrasted to hellfire (88:1–20)

- The path to bliss will be smooth for the honest who fear Allah, give in charity, and desire His presence; they will be satisfied (92:1–7, 17–21)

- For the person whose scales are heavy (with good deeds) (101:6, 7)

Hell—Destruction of the Wicked

- Wicked will be punished, destroyed by fire— those who resist Allah; they will abide therein eternally (2:24, 39, 165–167; 3:10–12, 131, 151, 185; 4:14, 55, 56; 5:86; 8:14, 36; 13:18; 16:29; 18:102–108; 22:18–22; 35:36, 37; 38:56–64; 39:72; 40:10–14; 47:12; 52:15, 16; 54:46–48; 55:43, 44; 56:44–51; 76:4; 82:14–19; 87:12, 13; 104:4–9)

- Those who do evil will be found there, and those who rejected the Quran (4:120, 121; 10:41–47; 18:105; 39:24–27; 41:15–29; 58:5–7)

- What can Allah gain from your punishment if you are grateful and believe? (4:147)

- No chance to return when made to stand before the fire; if returned to this life, they would go back to the forbidden (6:27–29)

- Conversation of those who want water in hell—reasons for Allah putting them there (7:48–53; 67:7–13)

- "Many" shall be in hell—both wicked men, *jinns*, and those who don't acknowledge God's signs; they will be driven there in groups (7:175–181; 39:71, 72)

- Those who made a covenant with Allah that if He blessed them they would serve Him, but broke it, will be punished (9:75–80; 10:21–23)

- Demons and wicked will be in Hell together (7:179; 11:119; 19:68–70)

- Wrongdoers will be gathered around hell, and left in it, on their knees (19:68–72)

- The wicked will want to return to life to accept the right path, but it will be too late; he would even offer his children as sacrifices (23:99–111; 39:53–63; 70:11–17)

- Cannot be ransomed, either by wife, brother, or children (70:11–15)

- Wicked will want double punishment from Allah for their leaders (33:67, 68; 41:29)

- Hell is an abode for those who lie about Allah (39:32)

- Conversation of those who were "weak" with those who led them to the fire (40:47–50)

- Criminals in hell will cry, "O Malik, let your Lord put an end to us!" He will say, "Indeed you will remain" (43:74–77)

- Is for those who reject the knowledge of Allah, even though He sends His signs (45:7–10)

- Wicked will receive just penalty, especially those who turned away from religion of parents (46:16–20)

- Many wicked cities have already been destroyed by Allah for their sins (47:13)

- Wicked will receive "boiling water" that will destroy their bowels (47:15; 56:42; 78:24, 25)

- Allah will punish hypocrites, polytheists, and all those who imagine evil about Allah, both men and women (48:6)

- Allah will punish wicked in "degrees"; Allah gives them "respite" for a long time, but punishment will come (68:44, 45)

- Nineteen angels guard the fire (74:30, 31)

- It lets nothing remain and leaves nothing (74:28, 29)

- A place for transgressors, they will dwell there for ages with nothing cool to drink, just boiling fluid and foul purulence (55:43, 44; 78:21–30)

- Hell is brought "face to face" with mankind at the coming of Allah (89:23)

- Wealth will not profit the greedy who believe in a lie when they are destroyed (92:8–12, 14; 111:1–5)

- The wicked will be thrown into a pit where there is fire (101:9–11; 102:6)

- The wicked will admit they were warned before being thrown to the blaze (67:8–11)

- The wicked will admit their sin (67:11)

- Those in hell cannot die or live (35:36; 87:11–13)

Holy Spirit

- Allah sends His Spirit to His servants to warn of the day of "mutual meeting" (40:15)

- Allah strengthens His believers and writes "faith" in their hearts, just like Jesus with "spirit from Himself" (2:87, 253; 58:22)

- Muhammad not a "forger" as some claimed—Holy Spirit inspired him (16:101, 102; 17:85–88)

- Revelation compared to winds, flowing, distributing (51:1–5)

- The Spirit and the angels will ascend to Him in a day, which is like "fifty thousand years" (70:4)

- On the day of judgment, the Spirit and the angels will stand in ranks at the throne of Allah and will only speak when Allah allows them—except for one whom Allah permits (78:38)

- The Spirit and the angels came down during "night of power" bringing peace until the emergence of dawn (97:3–5)

Hud (a prophet to Aad, Arabian peoples, fourth generation from Noah)

- Messenger from the Lord of the worlds to the people of Aad, his own city (7:65–69)

- Story of preaching and rejection of prophet (7:65–72; 11:50–60; 23:33–44; 26:123–140; 41:13–20; 46:21–26; 51:41–43; 53:50; [Noah's time, general] 69:3–7; 89:6–8)

- People of Aad saw a cloud approaching their valleys; it rained as a painful punishment, destroying everything, leaving nothing of them but their dwellings—disintegrated ruins (46:24–25; 51:41, 42)

- Story of Luqman (Sura 31)

- Denied afterlife, received warning (50:12–14)

- Destroyed by a screaming, violent wind imposed upon them for eight nights and seven days in succession (69:6–8)

Hypocrisy

- God hates believers who say what they do not (61:2, 3)

- Hypocrites are apprehensive lest a sura be revealed about them, revealing what is in their hearts! (9:64–66)

- Have locks upon their hearts, and do not reflect upon the Quran (47:24)

- Believers who turn pale as death when a sura is sent down mentioning fighting have a disease in their hearts (47:20)

- Started because they disliked what Allah sent down (47:26)

- "We will obey you in part of the matter" (47:26)

- Mark of the wicked would not be clearer than their speech (47:30)

- Believers, why do you say what you do not do? Allah hates that greatly (61:2, 3)

Iblis (or Iblees)—see Satan

Injeel—(see Gospel or Bible)

Intercessor Before Allah

- No intercessor except by His permission (7:3)

- Only one to whom the most merciful has given permission and has accepted his word (20:109)

- Only by Him who had taken from the most merciful a covenant (19:87)

- Who will plead on behalf of unrepentant sinners in the day of judgment? (4:109; 10:27; 30:13; 40:18)

- Only Allah can intercede on behalf of mankind during the day of judgment (32:4; 39:44; 45:19)

- On the day of judgment, the Spirit and the angels will stand in ranks at the throne of Allah and only will speak when Allah allows them—except for one whom Allah permits, and he will say what is correct (78:38)

- To those who fear the day of judgment, say that your only help or intercessor will be from Allah (6:51, 70)

- Angels' intercession will avail nothing—only he who is approved by Allah (53:26)

Inspiration

- Righteousness is believing in Allah and the Book and the prophets (2:177)

- Woe to a prophet who says his writings are from Allah, but they are not (2:79)

- None is more unjust than one who claims his own writings are from Allah, leading wrongdoers to punishment; he will be punished with humiliation (6:93)

- Those who reject Muhammad would have rejected other apostles of Allah; those who accept are righteous (6:31–40)

- Revelation is to give good news and to warn (6:48, 92; 12:111)

- Those who reject some of Allah's apostles and accept others are truly disbelievers (4:150–152)

- Reveals Himself, forgives and punishes whom He wills (48:14; 62:3)

- Revelation compared to winds, flowing, distributing (51:1–5)

- Can those who mimic Muhammad write down such revelations that he wrote? Are they gods? They will be punished. Only Allah can reveal such things (52:30–52)

- The prophet (Rasool) can not harm or help; he can only pass on what Allah reveals to him (72:20–28)

- Allah reveals "in degrees" so that people don't forget (87:6)

- Muhammad did not know if what God promised was near or for a future period of time (72:25–27)

Ishmael

- Named in the company of the good, the outstanding, and the righteous (3:84; 38:48, 49)

Islam

- Allah's true religion is Islam (submission to His will) (3:19, 83–85; 39:12; 61:9)

- Muhammad is the messenger of Allah (48:29)

- Those with Muhammad are forceful with disbelievers and merciful among themselves (48:29)

- Their mark is on their faces from prostration in prayer, as described in the Torah (48:29)

- Allah helped Muhammad in a miraculous way in his battle with Mecca (3:13)

- Muslims should challenge Christians with a message to submit to Allah (3:20)

- Bakkah (Mecca) was the first house of God (3:96)

- Allah was graceful and sent an apostle to teach them scripture and wisdom (2:151; 3:162–164)

- All who obey Allah and the prophet will be in good company in the afterlife—with the prophets, the steadfast affirmers of truth, the martyrs and the righteous (4:69, 70)

- Those who depart from the way that the prophet taught will be condemned to hell (4:115)

- Those who believe in the Quran (Book) will guard [maintain] their prayers and believe in the afterlife (6:92)

- Those who divide Islam into sects are not Muslims (6:159, 160)

- We are to sacrifice everything to Allah (6:161–163)

- Stories of prior nations are told to teach lessons (7:101, 102)

- Allah helped Muslims in the Battle of Badr and all the lessons that go with it (sura 8)

- True believers trust completely in Allah, and their hearts "tremble" when they talk of Allah (8:1–2)

- When His verses are recited to them, it increases them in faith (8:2)

- The believers who joined the Muslims—their past was forgiven (8:38–40)

- Four requirements of those who attend mosque: believe in and fear Allah, believe in the last day, regularly pray, and practice charity (9:18)

- Other guidelines for the believer (9:112; 13:22; 14:31; 33:35; 35:29; 87:14, 15)

- Allah will punish those who make fun of this religion and forgot Noah and other nations Allah destroyed (9:64–70)

- One needs to be willing to leave home and family to fight with one's wealth and one's life for the cause of Allah (9:80–88)

- He who builds a mosque to disunite believers is not a true Muslim but a hypocrite, a liar (9:107)

- Allah tested (and punished) previous generations; now He is testing Muslims to see how they will behave (10:13, 14)

- Allah, to whom Muslims bow, is the same God as the God of Christians and Jews (29:46)

- Some men argue about Allah without a Book to guide them (31:20)

- When revelation from Allah comes, we should not say that we will just "follow the ways of our fathers" (31:21)

- Whoever submits himself completely to Allah and does good has found the best way ("he has grasped the most trustworthy handhold") (31:22)

- Islam is no "bringer" of a new-fangled doctrine (46:9, 10)

- One who disbelieves in it must beware lest something similar happens as occurred with the children of Israel (46:10)

- Treaty at Hudaibiya was great victory for Islam, even though Allah could have destroyed unbelievers (48:18–29)

- Never will you find in the way of Allah any change (48:23)

- Arabs, before Muhammad, were in a "discordant doctrine" and deluded (51:8, 9)

- Three goddesses—Lat, Uzza, and Manat—are not true "gods" (53:19–23)

- Allah took from the tribes around and gave possessions to Islam so that they could bless wayfarers and orphans (59:7)

- The faithful love the emigrants God sends to them and give them preference over themselves, even though they are in privation (59:9)

- A Muslim should hasten to prayer on the day of assembly, leaving all business behind, then disperse and rejoice after the meeting (62:9–11)

- Believers should spend from what Allah has given them before death approaches, for death will not be delayed for them to change their ways (62:10, 11)

- When Allah grants victory and people enter the religion in "crowds," praise Allah and pray for His forgiveness (110:1–3)

Israelites or Children of Israel

- Allah made a special covenant with Israel and bestowed His favor on them (2:40, 47, 211; 45:16–18)

- Remember to fulfill the covenant God made with Israel, and Allah promises to fulfill His covenant to Israel (2:40)

- Allah told the children of Israel, "Fear only Me" (2:40)

- The Lord, Allah, delivered His people from the hand of the oppressor, Pharaoh (2:49)

- Allah divided the Red Sea for His people and drowned Pharaoh's army (2:50)

- Allah took Moses away for forty nights and talked to him directly; the Israelites sinned greatly against Him, but Allah forgave them (2:51)

- Israelites wanted to see Allah face to face otherwise they wouldn't believe (2:55)

- Allah sent manna to the Israelites, but they rebelled (2:57)

- Moses struck the rock to give water miraculously to the Israelites, and there gushed forth twelve springs of water (2:60; 7:159–162)

- Israelites grumbled about the food they were given in the wilderness (2:61)

- Israelites were rejected because they would not believe in His signs and messengers (2:61)

- Story of sacrifice of a heifer for an unknown murder (2:67–73)

- Story of Israelites asking for king, but not fighting for God (2:246)

- Story of King Saul, David, and Goliath (2:247–251)

- Jews killed the prophets before Muhammad and demanded signs from them (3:182–184)

- Story of Moses, Caleb, Joshua and curse for forty years wandering in wilderness (5:20–26)

- For the Israelites, killing one person was like killing the whole people, saving one, like saving the whole people (5:32)

- Not good to ask questions in unbelief like Israelites (5:101–104)

- Ten Commandments were given to Moses on tablets, in which are instruction and explanation for all things (7:143)

- Moses threw down the tablets when he saw the golden calf (7:150)

- God forgave those who sinned at the golden calf but afterwards repented and believed, because He is forgiving and merciful (7:153)

- Later Moses' anger cooled, and he took up the tablets (7:154)

- In the tablets' inscription was guidance and mercy for those who fear God (7:154)

- Story of golden calf and rebellion in desert (7:148–156)

- Allah gave them a good land, yet they began to have schisms (10:93)

Jesus

- Allah said, "O Jesus, indeed I will take you [cause you to die] and raise you to myself…" (3:55)

- Allah said to Jesus, "I will … purify [i.e. free] you from among those who disbelieve, and make those who follow you superior until the Day of Resurrection" (3:55)

- Allah sent apostles and then Jesus, the son of Mary, as messengers (2:87, 285)

- Jesus was strengthened by the Holy Spirit, was of a high rank (2:87, 253; 5:110)

- The Jews should have recognized that Truth which was revealed to them of old (Jesus), but they rejected it (2:87–89)

- True religion comes through Abraham, Ishmael, Isaac, Jacob, the tribes, Moses, and Jesus (2:136)

- Jesus was sent by Allah as the "Gospel" (3:3; 5:46)

- John came to confirm "a word" from Allah (3:39)

- Jesus was honorable, abstaining, and a prophet from among the righteous (3:39)

- Allah sent "a word" from Himself; His name is the Messiah, Jesus, the son of Mary (3:45; 4:171)

- Mary was a virgin; Allah created Jesus by saying "Be" (3:47)

- Jesus would be held in high esteem in this life and the next and by the heavenly hosts (3:45)

- Jesus was "righteous" (3:45)

- Jesus spoke to the people in childhood and maturity (3:46; 5:110)

- Allah taught Jesus the "Book, Wisdom, the Law, and the Gospel" (3:48; 5:110)

- Jesus had the ability to heal and bring life to inanimate and dead objects (3:49; 5:110)

- Jesus' miraculous powers were a "sign" to the children of Israel (3:49; 5:110)

- Jesus was all-knowing—at least had supernatural knowledge (3:49)

- Jesus came to "attest" to (to confirm) the law and make things that were forbidden, not forbidden (lawful) (3:50, 81)

- Jesus showed the "straight way" (3:51)

- Jesus called on people to worship Allah, not Himself; He said, "Indeed Allah is my Lord, and your Lord, so worship Him" (3:51, 79)

- Disciples of Jesus were "Muslims" and followed the messenger (Jesus) (3:52, 53)

- Jesus found unbelief in the world and gathered to Himself followers (3:52)

- Unbelievers plotted Jesus' death (3:54)

- Allah "took" Jesus (caused Him to die) and raised Him to Himself (3:55)

- Allah will justify Jesus (3:55)

- Allah will make Jesus' followers superior to those who don't believe in the resurrection (3:55)

- Jesus was similar to Adam in that He had a supernatural birth, created by God's word (3:59)

- Jesus never commanded people to worship angels (a human) (3:79)

- Jesus wasn't killed by the Jews; Allah raised Him up and took Him up (4:156–159)

- Don't say Trinity ("three"); Jesus was created by the word of Allah, who sent a soul to Mary (4:171)

- Christ disdains it when people don't worship Allah (4:172)

- Never would the Messiah disdain to be a servant to Allah (4:172)

- Jesus confirmed the law sent before Him, the Torah (5:46)

- Allah gave Jesus the Gospel (the *Injil*) in which was guidance and instruction for the righteous (5:46, 47)

- People of the gospel judge by what Allah has revealed therein (in the Torah and the Gospel) (5:46–47)

- Whoever does not judge by what Allah has revealed is of the defiantly disobedient (5:47)

- Allah is not Christ, son of Mary; that is certainly disbelief (5:72)

- The Messiah said, "O Children of Israel, worship Allah, my Lord and your Lord" (5:72)

- Christ was Apostle (not but a messenger); He ate food along with His mother (5:75)

- Jesus and Mary were favored by Allah (5:110)

- Spoke in childhood and maturity (5:110)

- Knew the book (writing), wisdom, law (Torah), and the gospel (5:110)

- Made a clay bird come to life, and people resurrect, healed blind and lepers by permission from Allah (5:110)

- Allah inspired the disciples of Christ; they are Muslims (5:111)

- Disciples of Christ were more interested in earthly food than spiritual (5:112–115)

- Jesus never stated, "take me and my mother as two deities beside Allah" (5:116, 117)

- Jesus was a witness over His disciples until He was taken up; now Allah is the observer over them and a witness of all things (5:117)

- Jesus appears in a list of " the righteous" (6:85)

- How can Allah, the Creator, have a Son (*walad*) when He does not have a companion? (6:101, 72:3)

- Some say, "Allah has taken a son." But He is free of need. They have no authority for that claim (10:68; 18:4, 5; 19:35, 88, 91, 92; 23:91; 25:2)

- If Allah had wanted to take a Son, He could have chosen from what He creates whatever He wills (25:2; 39:4)

- Jews say, Ezra is the Son of Allah; and Christians say, the Messiah is the Son of Allah. May Allah destroy them, disbelievers, deluded. They take priests (monks) and rabbis (scholars) as their lords instead of the Messiah, the son of Mary, and Allah and His light. Imitate polytheists of ancient times (9:30, 31)

- Story of Mary at the fig tree, Jesus providing figs for her, and Jesus speaking as a "babe" (19:23–30)

- Jesus said:

    o "I am the servant of Allah" (19:30)

    o "He has given me the Scripture" (19:30)

    o He has "made me a prophet" (19:30)

- ○ "He has made me blessed wherever I am…" (19:31)

- ○ He has "enjoined upon me prayer and zakat as long as I remain alive" (19:31)

- ○ He has made me "dutiful to my mother…" (19:32)

- ○ "He has not made me a wretched tyrant" (19:32)

- ○ "Peace is on me the day I was born and the day I will die and the day I am raised alive" (19:33)

- ○ "And indeed, Allah is my Lord and your Lord, so worship Him. That is a straight path" (19:36; 43:63)

- ○ "I have come to you with wisdom, and to make clear to you some of that over which you used to differ…" (43:63)

- ○ "So fear Allah, and obey me" (43:63)

- ○ "I am the messenger of Allah to you confirming what came before me of the Torah…" (61:6)

- ○ And I am "bringing good tidings of a messenger to come after me, whose name is Ahmad" (61:6)

- "That is Jesus, the son of Mary—the word of truth" (19:34)

- Jesus will judge between "sects" who differ among themselves (19:37)

- Gave "son of Mary" and Mary as signs; gave them rest on "high ground" (23:50)

- Took from Jesus "the son of Mary," (and Abraham, Noah, etc.) a "special covenant" that He may question the truthful about their truth (33:7, 8)

- Allah made a "difficult way" for those who associate others with Allah—the religion of Abraham, Moses, Noah, and Jesus; there should be no divisions in this religion, but it should be established (42:13)

- Arabs wanted to dispute that their "gods" were better than Jesus (43:57, 58)

- He was (no more) than a servant, favored of Allah—an example to the children of Israel (43:59)

- Jesus was a "sign" for knowledge of the hour (of judgment) (43:61)

- Jesus came to make clear some points that were disputed (43:63)

- Jesus was a true worshipper of Allah, pointed to the straight way (43:64)

- Followers of Islam should say, "If Allah had a 'son'—we would be the first to worship Him" (43:81)

- Allah sent Jesus, son of Mary, and bestowed on Him the gospel and ordained in hearts of followers "compassion and mercy" (57:27)

- Jesus said that He was "apostle" ("sent") of Allah with glad tidings and predicted a messenger to come named "Ahmad" (61:6)

- Jesus invited His disciples to be "helpers" in the cause of Allah (61:14)

- Allah is the one and only God, eternal, absolute; He doesn't "beget, nor is He begotten," no one is like Him (112:1–4)

Jihad

- To fight for the honor of Allah; fight enemies of Allah only if they fight against Allah (2:190, 191, 216, 218, 243, 244)

- All should be ready to fight *jihad* in order to protect the oppressed (4:71–76; 9:38–42)

- We should not fear man, only Allah; we should fight for justice (4:77)

- Fight those that are fighting against you; if deserters desert you don't fight them if they won't fight you (4:88–91)

- Those who fight to protect Islam are of a higher rank than those who don't (4:95, 96)

- People should leave homes to protect themselves from persecution; they will find a spacious place (4:97–100)

- Instructions for prayer during fighting (4:100–104)

- Seek Allah with all of your might and strive in His cause (5:35)

- When the enemy approaches in organized fashion (Zahfan), don't turn back; believe and fight on and Allah will fight too (8:15–20)

- Turning your back in battle against unbelievers is to return with anger from Allah upon him—his refuge is hell (8:15–16)

- Pray much and be humble and organized when enemies attack (8:45–48)

- Fight with all your strength, but be ready to make peace with those who want to make peace (8:59–64; 9:5)

- Prisoners of war should not be taken by a prophet until a massacre has been inflicted on Allah's enemies and the land subdued (8:67; 47:4–6)

- Tell prisoners of war that Allah has something better for them (8:70, 71)

- Motives of worldly gain for fighting should be severely punished, but Allah is merciful (8:67, 68)

- Consume what you have taken of war booty as lawful and good (8:69)

- Those who came to Medinah after the battle of Badr were to be accepted as brothers (8:72–75)

- Allah will grant mercy to those who strive with might with their goods and "persons" (lives) (9:20, 21, 38–59; 61:3)

- Those who are unwilling to fight for the cause are condemned, those who are poor or ill are not (9:94–99)

- Should fight with Quran against unbelievers with all might (25:51–60)

- Allah will not let "deeds" be lost of those who are slain in war; they will be admitted to the Garden (first year, *Hijra*) (47:4–6)

- Allah could fight against the unbelievers himself, but He allows His followers to do so to test them (47:4)

- Allah aids and is protector of those who accept Him and fight for Him (47:8–11)

- The righteous should be ready to sacrifice for the cause; the wicked have a "disease in heart" and don't want to suffer (47:20–22)

- Allah will not forgive those who turn others from the true path and die fighting against it (47:34)

- Allah loves those who are just; don't fight against those who don't fight against you; treat them justly (60:8)

Job

- Was a pattern of patience and endurance and faith (38:41–48)

John the Baptist

- Story of Zechariah (Zacharias) asking Allah how a barren woman could have a son (19:1–15)

- Story of John the Baptist preceding Jesus (3:38–41)

- Sign given to Zechariah was that he would be dumb for three days and nights (3:41; 19:10)

Jonah

- Was righteous; story of being swallowed by fish, repenting, and being spit on shore to preach to 100,000 men or more (37:139–148; 68:47–52)

- Should not be like Jonah and run away from duty (68:48)

Joseph

- Story of Joseph (12:1–111)

Jugular Vein

- God is closer to man than his jugular vein (50:16)

Judgment (see also Day of Judgment)

- God will be just, He will wrong no one, sinners only wrong themselves (10:23, 44)

- Unbelievers will bear witness against themselves (7:35; 41:19–22)

- Wicked will admit their sin (67:7–11)

- Before entering hell, each will admit that messengers of warning came to them (39:71, 72)
- For all there are degrees of reward or punishment (46:19)
- Enemies of Allah: their hearing, their eyes, and their skin will testify against them (41:19–23)

Lot

- His story, calling for repentance, destruction of Sodom and Gomorrah (26:160–175; 27:54–58; 29:26–35)
- His disgust for homosexuality, and the men's disgust for his purity (7:80–82; 26:165–167; 27:54–56; 29:28, 29)
- Was righteous; "old woman" left behind (37:131–137)
- His "brothers" denied afterlife, received warning (50:12–14)
- Story of Lot and decadence (homosexuality) of his city and destruction by Allah (7:80–84; 15:60–77; 51:24–37; 53:53, 54; 54:33–40)
- Wicked men blinded by the angels (15:72)
- Lot's wife—an example of unfaithfulness (26:170, 171; 27:57; 66:10)
- Cities were destroyed by a rain of clay stones (7:84; 15:74; 54:34; 26:173; 27:58)
- People of Sodom suffered an abiding punishment (54:38)

Kabah

- Allah made the "Sacred House" (5:97)

Last Day (see also Day of Judgment)

- Righteousness requires believing in the last day (2:177)

Mark of Believers

- Mark will be seen on the forehead of believers: from prostration in prayer (48:29)

Mark of Unbelievers

- If Allah willed, you would know them by their mark, but you will surely know them by the tone of their speech (47:30)

Marriage (see also Women)

- Examine believing women as to their faith, and if proven faithful, do not return them to the disbelievers, but marry them after giving them their due (60:10)

- Hold not to marriage bonds with disbelieving women (60:10)

Mary

- Mary was a devout follower of Allah: "We breathed into her body" (66:12)

- Mary received special grace from Allah (3:35–37, 42–44)

- Mary was a virgin; Allah created Jesus by saying "Be" (3:47)

- Mary was a supporter of truth (5:75)

Mecca (Makkah)

- The first house of worship established for mankind was that at Bakkah (3:96)

- In a vision believers were promised, "You will surely enter … in peace with your heads shaved without fear" (48:27)

Michael

- Whoever is an enemy to Michael and Gabriel; Allah will be his enemy (2:98)

Monasticism

- Allah didn't invent it; it was invented by Christians. Allah placed love and compassion in the hearts of Jesus' followers, and they didn't pursue what pleased Allah (57:27)

Monks and Scholars (or Priests and Rabbis)

- Are taken as lords besides Allah and the Messiah, son of Mary (9:30, 31)

- Monks and scholars devour the wealth of people unjustly and avert from the way of Allah (9:34)

- Monks and scholars hoard silver and gold and spend it not in the way of Allah (9:34)

Moses

- Story of Moses (the Muslim) (7:101–156; 10:74–92; 11:96–101; 23:44–49; 26:10–68; 40:21–27; 51:38–40; 79:15–26)

- Tablets inscribed by Allah were given to Moses and contained instruction and explanation for all things (7:145, 154)

- Among the people of Moses is "a community which guides by truth and by it establishes justice" (7:159)

- Sent to enlighten his people (14:5, 6)

- Moses was given nine signs, and people still didn't believe him (17:101–104; 27:7–17)

- Story of impenitent youth (18:60–82)

- Story of being hid in the river, his call, deliverance from Pharaoh, and the sin of Samiri with the golden calf at Sinai (20:8–98; 28:1–42)

- Story of Korah (Qarun) and his followers and their rebellion (28:76–82; 29:38–40)

- Moses and Aaron were blessed by Allah and given a Book to lead them in the straight path (37:113–122)

- Through Moses Allah gave the children of Israel the Scripture as guidance and a reminder for those of understanding (23:49; 40:53, 54)

- Sermon by a believer who concealed his faith before Pharaoh (40:28–45)

- Moses was sent to rebellious people as a sign; drowning of Pharaoh's army as punishment (14:5, 6; 43:46–56; 51:38–40; 79:15–26)

- Punishment for Egyptians and Israelites should be a lesson for Quraysh (44:17–29; 54:41–48; 85:17–20)

- Pharaoh denied afterlife, received warnings, and was punished (50:12-14; 69:9, 10; 73:16; 89:10)

- Moses begged the people to listen to him and warned that Allah doesn't guide rebellious (61:5)

- Wife of Pharaoh was faithful and wanted to be saved (66:11)

Mosques

- Should only be maintained by believers (9:17, 18)

- Allah is glorified when His light is in places of worship where prayers are offered (24:35-38)

Muhammad

- Allah's revelation of truth and righteousness came through Muhammad (2:4, 177, 252)

- His role was just to proclaim the message: warn (every people), give good tidings, and recite the Quran (5:99; 7:188; 13:7; 27:91-93; 33:45, 46; 34:28; 35:24; 36:1-5; 48:8; 73:15; 88:21)

- Those who reject Muhammad would have rejected other apostles of Allah; those who accept are righteous (6:31-40)

- Muhammad is no more than an apostle of Allah, a mere man (3:144; 18:110; 25:1-10; 48:29)

- Punishment for waging war against Allah and His apostle: death, crucifixion, maiming, or exile (5:33)

- Muhammad was mentioned in Scripture (7:157)

- Muhammad was given for all of mankind (7:158; 21:107-112)

- Allah is strict in punishment with those who fight against His apostle, e.g. Battle of Badr (8:13; 9:61-63)

- Turn not a "deaf" ear to the apostle of God (8:20-23)

- Zealously taught people whom he didn't want to perish (9:128)

- Was content with having as his witness Allah and those who know the "Book" (13:43)

- Was sent to teach his people in their language, enlightening them so that they would do good deeds (14:4)

- Was accused of being mad and a sorcerer (15:6; 43:30)

- Was not a "forger" as some claimed; the Holy Spirit inspired him (16:101, 102; 17:85–88)

- Allah took him on a tour to "farthest mosque" (17:1)

- Aisha and the accusation of adultery (24:11–20)

- Three commands given by Allah to Muhammad:

    o "I have only been commanded to worship the Lord of this city, who made it sacred and to whom belongs all things.

    o "I am commanded be of the Muslims,

    o "and to recite the Quran" (27:91, 92)

- Could not read or write; if he had been able to, people would have doubted that the Quran was from Allah (29:47, 48)

- Closer to his people than their relatives; his wives are their mothers (33:6)

- Was a "pattern of conduct" for his people (33:21)

- His wives were offered a divorce or promised rich rewards in eternity if they were devout Muslims and sought Allah, but double punishment for immorality (33:28–34)

- Was commanded by Allah to marry wife of his adopted son, Zaid (33:37)

- Not father of your men, but "seal of the prophets" (33:40)

- Should not enter the prophet's house without permission, stay to socialize after a meal, or marry his wives after his death, ever (33:53–55)

- Was blessed by Allah and His angels (33:56)

- Called "a mad poet" by those unwilling to leave the worship of their idols (37:36)

- Came with the truth and confirmed the previous messengers (37:37)

- Did not have knowledge of what was discussed in heaven, just was given revelation (38:65–70)

- Muhammad was himself instructed to ask forgiveness for his sin (40:55; 47:19)

- Nothing was said to Muhammad that God's messengers had not already said (41:43)

- Believers should obey Allah and obey Muhammad (47:33)

- Muhammad was sent so that people would honor Allah and praise Him every "morning and evening" (48:9)

- Was sent to reprimand the desert Arabs who "lagged behind" and call them to defend Islam (48:11)

- Muhammad was called to proclaim the praises of Allah (52:48, 49)

- Can those who mimic Muhammad write down such revelations that he wrote? Are they gods? They will be punished. Only Allah can reveal such things (52:30–49)

- By the Star that "goes down," Muhammad is not led astray or misled (53:1, 2)

- Muhammad didn't speak because of His desire to speak (53:3–5)

- Description of Muhammad receiving revelation by Lote tree; true revelation (53:4–18)

- Invites all to believe in Allah, and has taken your "covenant" (57:8)

- All who reject Muhammad and Allah will be punished (58:5)

- Was sent by Allah to "unlettered" men to explain Scripture and wisdom, sanctify them, and rehearse signs (62:2)

- Was to reveal by "pen" and "record" revelation, was not "mad" or "possessed" (63:1–7; 68:1–15, 51, 52; 69:38–52)

- Was a real apostle; if he wasn't Allah could have cut off his artery (69:38–52)

- Advice for his "consorts" (wives); his family was to have a higher standard; Allah was their protector (66:1–7)

- His message was not one of a "possessed" man or from Satan, even the planets, night, and dawn testify to the truthfulness of his message (81:15–29)

- Allah didn't forsake Muhammad but found him as an orphan, took care of him, made him self-sufficient, and promised an even better afterlife (93:1–8)

- Allah promised Muhammad relief from all burdens and commanded him to turn all attention to Him; Allah raised him to high esteem (94:1–8)

- First call of Muhammad to proclaim and call sinful man to repentance and turn to Allah (96:1–19)

- Muhammad revealed to him the Quran in that "Night of Power." It is better than a "thousand months" (97:1–5)

Nature

- Nature is a revelation from Allah (2:164; 3:190; 13:2–4; 45:3–5)

- Obeys God (16:49, 50)

Nicknames

- Do not call each other by offensive nicknames (49:11)

Night of Power

- Angels and the Spirit came down on the night of power (97:1–4)

- Better than a thousand months (97:3)

- Peace it is, until the emergence of dawn (97:5)

Noah

- Story of preaching and rejection of prophet, Noah (7:59–64; 10:71–73; 11:25–49; 23:23–30; 26:105–122; 40:5; 51:46; 54:9–15; 69:10–12)

- Built the ship under the observation and inspiration of God, but mocked by the eminent ones of his people (11:37, 38; 23:27)

- Loaded two of each creature and the few who believed into the ship (11:40; 23:27)

- Noah lost a son who refused to come aboard, to his great sorrow, in spite of his appeals to Allah (11:42–47)

- God opened the gates of heaven, and the springs of the earth burst, and the waters met in a great flood (54:11, 12)

- Flood with waves like mountains (6:6; 11:40–44)

- The people denied him, so Allah saved him and those who were with him in the ship (7:64; 10:73)

- Allah saved him on a construction of planks and nails (54:13)

- Noah sailed under Allah's observation, who left it as a sign for any who will remember (54:14, 15)

- He was a devout man; we are all his descendants; Allah listened to his prayers (17:3; 21:76, 77; 37:75–82)

- Was a sign for unbelievers for 950 years (29:14, 15)

- Allah could have destroyed everyone but had mercy (36:41–44)

- Wife of Noah, example of unfaithfulness, betrayed God's righteous servant—as did Lot's wife (66:10)

- Was a reminder for after generations of a judgment to come (69:11, 12)

- Noah warned people publicly and secretly (71:1–20)

- Pleaded with Allah not to leave any worshippers of Wadd, Suwa, Yaguth, Yauq, nor Nasr, otherwise they would continue to mislead people (71:21–28)

- People of Noah's time were destroyed because they were defiantly disobedient (51:46)

Obedience

- All creatures and the angels do what Allah commands them (16:49, 50)

- Obey Allah and obey His messenger: you have been clearly notified (64:12)

Parables

- Believer and unbeliever: recognize God as the source of wealth, be content with what we have; Allah is best reward (18:32–44)

- Spider: like those who take protectors other than Allah (29:41–44)

Paradise (see also Heaven)

- Those who repent, believe, and do righteousness will enter paradise (19:60, 61)

- Dwellers in paradise will hear no ill speech, only peace, with provision morning and evening (19:62, 63)

- On the appointed day the earth will be replaced with another earth, and the heavens as well (14:48)

- Gate keepers will welcome those who feared their Lord, "peace be upon you; you have become pure; so enter it to abide eternally therein" (39:73)

- Those who enter the gate to paradise will say, "Praise to Allah, who has fulfilled for us His promise and made us inherit the earth…" (39:74)

- The righteous will see the angels surrounding the throne, exalting with praise their Lord (39:75)

People of the Book—Jews and Christians (of Muhammad's time)

- Allah is the God of Christians and Jews, and a true Muslim is sincere in Allah (2:139)

- People should aim for all that is good, and Allah will bring them together (2:148)

- Allah sent the Book (Bible) to allow us to judge between the people as guidance and mercy to people who believe (2:213; 4:105; 6:91; 7:52; 7:196; 16:64; 42:17)

- Can't agree about their teachings because of envy of one another (2:213; 3:19; 45:17)

- Muslims should challenge Christians with a message to submit to Allah (3:20)

- If the people of the Book submit to Allah, their religion is right (3:20)

- Some said they will not burn, but for a "few days," because they are deluded in their religion (2:80, 3:24)

- They will not fare well on the day of judgment because they were deceived and sold the covenant for a small price (3:25, 77)

- People of the Book should come to common agreement with Muslims (3:64)

- People of the Book argue about Abraham and other topics that they have little knowledge about (3:65, 66; 11:110–113; 45:16, 17)

- Some of the people of the Book desire to lead true believers astray (3:69; 4:44, 113)

- People of the Book have clothed truth with falsehood even though they had knowledge (3:70–72)

- There are some honest people of the Book, some dishonest; it depends on their "fruits" (3:75–77, 110, 113)

- There are those who "distort the Scriptures with their tongues" while they read it, knowingly adding their words and claiming they come from Scripture; these people obstruct the path to Allah (3:78, 98–101; 11:15–24)

- If a person listens to one faction of the people of the Book, he will become an apostate, those who believe in superstition and false objects of worship (*jibt* and *taghut*) (3:100; 4:51–55)

- True believers believe in Allah and the last day, forbid what is wrong, and do good deeds (3:113, 114; 9:71)

- The apostates have transgressed "beyond bounds" and have rejected and killed God's prophets (3:112)

- Those who received the Scripture but refused to make it clear to others and concealed it will receive a painful punishment (3:187, 188)

- There are people of the Book who believe in Allah, and Allah will reward them (3:198–200; 11:15–24; 98:1–8)

- Some distort the meaning of the Book and introduce lies (4:46, 50)

- Call for them to believe in what was given them and Muhammad before they get punished like Sabbath-breakers (4:47–50)

- If we differ in beliefs among ourselves, we should refer the matter to Allah and His apostle - best to believe in judgment (4:59–66)

- Hypocrites turn away from the prophet; need to admonish them and speak a word to save their souls (4:63)

- Don't associate with hypocrites, those who make light of serious messages (4:136–145)

- Jews had foods made "unclean" which were formerly clean, as punishment because they practiced usury and hindered people from coming to Allah (4:160–162)

- Some Jews will be saved, those who pray and practice charity (4:162)

- Judge the Jews fairly (5:42)

- Why do they come to Muslims when they have the Torah, their own law, before them in which is the judgment of Allah? (5:43)

- Some Jews are avid listeners to falsehood; their lips say they are believers, but the heart does not (5:41, 42)

- Allah sent down the Torah in which was guidance and light—that is the Scripture of Allah (5:44)

- People of the gospel should judge by what Allah has revealed therein; if not, they rebel (5:47)

- God could have made "one people," but they "will not cease to dispute" (5:48; 11:118; 42:8)

- People of the Scripture should all run to all that is good (5:48)

- Don't take the Jews and the Christians as protectors or allies; most are rebellious and hypocritical; they try to get Muslims to follow heresy (5:51–57)

- Why don't the rabbis and (Christian) religious scholars teach their people not to utter forbidden things and eat forbidden foods? (5:63)

- Had they stood by the law and the gospel, they would have had their iniquities blotted out (5:65, 66)

- Among them (Christians and Jews) there is a moderate (acceptable) community (5:66)

- "O People of the Scripture, you are standing on nothing until you uphold the Torah, the Gospel, and what has been revealed to you from your Lord" (5:68)

- Among the Jews, Sabeans, and Christians, those who believed in Allah and the last day and did righteousness will have no fear or grief (on the judgment day) (5:69)

- The children of Israel didn't believe there would be a "trial" or any resulting punishment, so they rejected God's apostles (5:70, 71)

- Should not "exceed bounds" of their religion beyond the truth; they rejected the advice of David and Jesus and were cursed because they disobeyed and continually transgressed (5:76–78)

- Christians are the closest to Muslims because they are not arrogant, and among them are men devoted to learning and who have renounced the world (5:82)

- Those strongest in enmity against the believers (Muslims) are the Jews and the pagans (5:82)

- True Christians recognize the truth of Islam and will receive paradise (5:83–86)

- Among the "people of Moses" there are those who guide by truth, and by it establish righteousness (7:159)

- Some good/some bad—bad say that "all will be forgiven" (7:169–171)

- People who inherited the Book followed vanities, so the covenant of the Book was taken from them, and they study what is in the Book (7:169)

- Fight against those of the people of the Book who don't believe in Allah, nor the last day, nor prohibit things prohibited by Allah, nor acknowledge the religion of truth—until they willingly pay the poll tax (*jizyah*) (9:29)

- Jews call Ezra a son of God, and Christians say Jesus is the Son of God—may Allah destroy them because the Jews and Christians take priests and rabbis as lords in derogation of Allah and the Messiah, the son of Mary—they are imitating the pagans of old (9:30, 31)

- Priests and rabbis misappropriate (devour unjustly) the wealth of people and hoard (or bury) gold and silver; they will be branded with it in the fires of hell (9:34, 35)

- After the prophets, their posterity missed prayers, and followed after their lusts; they will be condemned (19:59)

- "We sent before you [O Muhammad] men to whom we revealed the message, so ask the people of the message [i.e. the former scriptures] if you do not know" (21:7)

- Quran clarifies most of the questions among the children of Israel (27:76)

- Many people of the Book recognized the divine authority of the Quran and will be given their reward twice (28:51–55; 29:47)

- Muslims are commanded, "Do not argue with the people of the Scripture except in a way that is best" (29:46)

- Muslims are commanded to say to the people of the Scripture, "We believe in that which has been revealed to us and revealed to you. And our God and your God is one; and we are Muslims [in submission] to Him" (29:46)

- Some Jews (people of the Scripture) who fought against the Muslims during a battle were overcome by Allah (33:25–27)

- Some descendants of Abraham and Isaac do right, others do not (37:109–113)

- Allah conferred favor upon Moses and Aaron and gave them the explicit Scripture and guided them in the straight path—peace be upon them (37:114–120)

- Their doubts in the book of Moses (jealous animosities) gave rise to their differences (41:45; 42:14)

- Muslims are to call them to faith; they believe in the same Book; there is no contention between them; Allah is the final goal (42:15)

- Muslims are commanded to invite the followers of Abraham and Moses and Jesus, saying:

    - "I have believed in what Allah has revealed of Scripture, and
    - "I have been commanded to do justice among you.
    - "Allah is our Lord and your Lord.
    - "For us are our deeds, and for you are your deeds.
    - "There is no argument between us and you.
    - "Allah will bring us together, and
    - "To Him is the destination" (42:13, 15)

- Sects after Christ began to disagree with each other; they will have terrible punishment (43:65–67)

- Monasticism was invented by Christians and wasn't given by Allah; many of them are rebellious transgressors (57:27)

- People of the Book should know that they have no power whatever over the grace of Allah; it is given by Him, not by them; He gives it to whom He wills (57:29)

- Story of the tribe of Banu Al-Nadir and their treachery with the "hypocrites of Medinah" and Allah's punishment upon them (59:1–17)

- Jews who had the Torah but did not take it on are pictured like a donkey that carries huge tomes, yet they are not friends of Allah, and don't repent (62:5–8)

- If "they" had continued on the right way, Allah would have poured out on them "rain in abundance" (72:16)

- Allah set nineteen angels as guardians of the fire as a "trial for unbelievers" in order that the people of the Book would arrive at certainty and the believers would increase in faith (74:31)

- Were waiting for "clear evidence" and made "schisms" after seeing this evidence (98:1–4)

- Were commanded to worship God, devote themselves, pray, give charity—that is true religion; those who do this are the "best creatures," those who don't are the "worst creatures" (98:5–7)

- Are standing on nothing until you uphold the Torah, the Gospel, and that which was revealed to you (5:66, 68)

- Among them are a moderate community (5:66)

- If in doubt, Muhammad said to "ask those who have been reading the Scripture before you" (10:94)

People of the Book (Future/Prophetic)

- Allah will bring forth a people He will love and who will love Him (5:54)

- Allah will bring forth a people humble toward the believers, powerful against the disbelievers (5:54)

- Allah's people will strive in the cause of Allah and not fear the blame of a critic (5:54)

- Allah's true people will:

    o Establish prayer

    o Give *zakat*

    o Bow in worship (5:55)

Poets

- It is those straying in evil/the deviators who follow them; in every valley they roam, they that say what they do not do (26:224–226)

Polytheists

- Cling steadfastly to their gods (25:41, 42)

- The one who takes as his god his own desire (25:43)

Prayer

- Importance of establishing prayer (2:3, 43, 110, 177, 238; 3:61; 8:3; 11:114 (regular); 17:73–81; 27:1–3; 58:13)

- Allah will listen to every supplication from His followers; He can be trusted (2:186, 214; 3:122, 159–161)

- Each (religion) has a direction toward which it prays (2:148)

- Sample prayer for forgiveness and salvation (3:191–194)

- Should pray with a clear mind (no intoxication) and with clean hands and body (4:43)

- When to pray: at the two ends of the day and at the approach of the night (11:114)

- When to pray: from the decline of the sun until the darkness of the night, at the dawn, and from the night (17:77–79; 76:25, 26)

- When to pray: the hours of the night are more effective for concurrence and more suitable for words (73:1–6)

- Allah is the best listener of prayers (37:75)

- Prayer restrains us from shameful and unjust deeds; we need regular prayer (29:45; 73:1–6)

- The righteous devote themselves to prayer, respect each other's wealth, believe in the day of recompense, fear displeasing Allah, and are chaste; their testimony is true, and they carefully maintain prayer (70:22–35)

- Prayer without faith (of unbelievers) is futile (13:14)

- Instructions for prayer during time of war (4:100–104)

- Instructions for washing before prayer (5:6)

- Seek the means to approach Allah, do your duty to Him, strive with all of your might in His cause so that you may prosper (5:35–37)

- Pray much and be organized when people attack (8:45–48)

- Arise to pray in the night—the best time for words (73:1–6)
- Not all can pray half the night, so do what you can (73:20)
- Praise Allah numerous times of the day and night (20:130, 132; 52:48, 49)
- When prayer is called on *Jumu'a* (Friday) proceed to the remembrance of Allah and leave your trade (62:9)
- When the Friday prayer is concluded, disperse, seeking from the bounty of Allah, and remembering Allah often (62:10)
- What is with Allah (in prayer) is better than a diversion or a transaction, for Allah is the best of providers (62:11)

Predestination/Free Will

- When the people deviated, Allah caused their hearts to deviate (61:5)
- Allah helps those whom He wills, and hardens whom He wills (14:4)

Probation

- Extension of time only reveals the truth of what God has promised (19:75)
- Counts out to the wicked only a limited number, so be patient (19:84)
- "I will give them time" (7:182, 183)

Promise (God's)

- Allah does not fail in His promise (3:9)
- Promise of Allah is truth (10:55; 40:55)

Prophecy

- To every people there is a certain time appointed; no one can stop it or hurry it (7:34; 10:49; 11:104; 14:10; 15:4, 5)
- Allah sends "winds" of mercy and good tidings and will raise the dead to life (7:57, 58)

- After Rome's defeat by the Persians, Allah will give victory to the Romans within three to nine years, and Muslims will rejoice (30:1–5)

- No generation should boast; Allah will punish every generation if it rejects Allah's prophets (30:5–10)

- Prophecy about famine in Mecca; doubted in prophethood of Muhammad (44:9–17)

- Knowledge of time belongs to Allah (67:26)

Prophets

- All apostles had one message—worship the one true God, Allah (21:25–29)

- All prophets have been persecuted, including Muhammad (22:42–45)

- Allah chooses angels and men as His messengers (22:75–77; 42:51)

Quran

- The Quran was given to protect, confirm, and further explain the Bible (5:48; 10:37; 28:48–50)

- When the Quran is read, those present should be quiet and listen (7:204)

- Increases the faith of true believers (9:124–127)

- The Quran confirms previous revelation (6.92; 10:37; 11:17, 20, 133; 35:31; 46:10–12)

- It is a book of wisdom to warn unbelievers to repent (10:1, 2; 11:1–5; 12:2; 17:105–111; 18:2; 31:1–8; 32:2; 36:1–11; 38:1; 41:2–4; 84:20, 21)

- Allah sent the Scripture in truth, confirming the Scripture that came before it, and guarding it in safety (5:48; 46:9–12)

- The Quran was given to declare that there is one God and that God has no "partners" (6:19–26)

- Given to the reader so they might not claim ignorance of the two scriptures sent before it (6:155–157)

- Revelation of Allah to confirm Bible and explain it; it makes "things" clear; it is a sign (10:37; 15:1; 20:133; 35:31; 40:2; 43:2–4; 46:30, 31)

- The Quran provides guidance and mercy to help lead Muslims to healing, from darkness to light (10:57; 14:1; 26:1–9; 27:1–5; 42:51–53)

- Book of truth to guide the righteous (10:108, 109; 13:1; 17:9, 10; 38:29; 39:1, 2; 43:43–45)

- The Quran is a book whose verses are perfected and then presented in detail from (the) wise and acquainted (11:1, 2)

- It is not forged; it is a revelation of Allah (11:13, 14; 25:1–9; 27:6; 28:85; 55:1, 2)

- The Quran is revealed in Arabic for a specific people and is easy to understand (13:37; 26:192–199; 41:3, 44; 43:2–4; 46:9–12)

- Has parables, is a good word, like good tree (14:23–27)

- Allah gave seven grand verses, oft-repeated and the great Quran (15:87)

- Those who reject this sign will be sent to hell (17:90–100)

- Those given knowledge before the Quran, upon hearing its verses recited, fall on their faces weeping and it increases them in humble submission (17:107–109)

- Recite the Quran in prayer—but not too loudly, or too softly (17:110)

- A reminder to those who fear Allah, Creator of heaven and earth (20:1–8)

- Sent down in Arabic to perhaps help them avoid sin or remember (20:113)

- Was revealed gradually so that people could accept it (25:32–34)

- Quran is mentioned in the scriptures of the former peoples, and it is recognized by the scholars of the children of Israel (26:196, 197)

- Was only revealed to Arabs; non-Arabs wouldn't have accepted it (26:198, 199)

- Was not revealed by demons; they would not have wanted to reveal it (26:208–213)

- Importance of reciting, as much as you can, for your own sake (27:92; 73:4,20)

- Revelation of Allah is a mercy to mankind (44:2–7)

- By the clear Book, it has made distinct every precise matter (44:2–4)

- Revelation of the Book is from Allah and full of wisdom and power (45:2)

- Arise in the night to recite the Quran and pray (73:1–6)

- Recite what is easy for you of the Quran (73:20)

- The Quran was made easy for remembrance, but will any remember? (54:17, 22, 32, 40)

- The Quran is similar to the revelation of God to Moses; it was promised to "reach" Muslims in Arabic (32:22, 23; 46:12)

- Was sent because the Arabs had no "Book" or "messenger" beforehand (34:44)

- Nothing was said to Muhammad, that God's messengers had not already said (41:43)

- Was sent to warn "mother of cities" (Mecca) in Arabic (42:7)

- Is "in the mother of the Book," that is, in the "presence" of Allah; it is full of wisdom (43:4)

- Arab critics asked why the Quran was not revealed to leading men of the "two chief cities"—Mecca and Taif (43:31)

- Reflect upon the Quran, unless there are locks on hearts (47:24)

- Can't be touched by "unclean" people, is guarded, enjoyed by those who are righteous and will be in heaven, but the deniers will be in scalding water, burning in hellfire (56:78–96)

- Allah sent the Book for clear evidence, the "balance" for justice and iron for military might (57:25)

- Had the Quran been revealed on a mountain, that mountain would "cleave asunder" to it (59:21)

- There are "books held in high honor" (commentators say it is the Quran) with instruction, written by hands of scribes, honorable, pious, and just (80:11–16)

- It is a glorious tablet preserved (85:21, 22)

- A word that distinguishes good from evil just as earth helps vegetation, not for amusement (86:11–16)

- Was not revealed in the same way as to Moses, but no less inspired (28:48–50)

Quraysh

- A call for them to worship the one true God (105:1–4)

Religious Freedom

- Allah could have bound everyone and kept them from sinning, but He didn't (36:66, 67)

- Messengers of Allah can preach revelation, but they can't force men's wills (39:41)

- The Quran was revealed in truth; he who receives guidance benefits his own soul, while he who strays injures his own soul—you are not a manager over him (39:41)

- There is no compulsion in religion, the right way has become clear from the wrong (2:256)

- Allah could have made everyone on earth believe; then will you compel people to become believers? (10:99–103)

- Do not insult those who invoke other than Allah (6:108)

- Be patient over what they (unbelievers and deniers) say and avoid them with gracious avoidance (73:10)

- "Leave with Me the deniers, those of ease, and allow them respite a little"—punishment will come from God (73:11–14)

- Woe to those who persecute (and burn) people, believers in God; there place is the fire of hell; stars in the sky are witnesses against them (85:1–10)

- Believers should not worship false gods of unbelievers but say to disbelievers, "For you is your religion, and for me is my religion" (109:1–6)

- Even Muhammad was not a controller over others—he was only a reminder (88:21, 22)

Repentance

- Adam received words from Allah, and Allah accepted his repentance (2:37)

- Repentance accepted by Allah is for those who do wrong in ignorance and then repent soon after (4:17)

- Not acceptable from those who do evil deeds right up to their death then claim to have repented (4:18)

- Not for those who die as disbelievers (4:18)

- He who repents and does righteousness does indeed turn to Allah with repentance (25:71)

- Allah brings good news to those who repent (39:17)

Resurrection

- Indeed, on the day of resurrection you will be resurrected (23:16)

- There will be regret over what they neglected on that day (6:31)

- Allah will resurrect the dead, then they will be returned to Him (2:28, 212; 6:36)

- Will recreate His believers as their reward (10:4)

- Cheaters will be resurrected for a tremendous day when mankind will stand before the Lord of the worlds (83:1–6)

- Likened to the wind, which brings rain to a dead land, giving it life (35:9)

- On the day of resurrection the wicked will be sent back to the severest of punishment (2:85)

- The resurrection day is the day the horn/trumpet will be blown (20:101, 102)

- Allah will surely assemble you for the day of resurrection, about which there is no doubt (6:12)

- Allah will raise the dead, and they will return to Him, and He will reward them (2:28, 112; 8:28; 36:12; 42:9; 46:33; 85:13; 86:8)

- Rewards will be given to every soul only on the day of resurrection (3:185)

- Say, "Perhaps it will be soon" (17:51, 52)

- The wicked will emerge from the graves like locusts spreading (54:6–8)

Rewards (See also Heaven/Hell)

- Reward is incumbent upon Allah for one who emigrates due to persecution (4:100)

Righteous (People Who Are)

- The righteous will not be afraid, nor will they grieve (2:38)

- Worship your Lord, who created you that you may become righteous (2:21)

- The righteous submit their face in Islam, have faith, and work righteousness—repent, confess, believe, change their ways, pray, recite the Quran, and do good (2:82, 112, 160; 3:89; 4:17, 18; 10:9, 26; 23:57–61; 28:67, 83; 73:20; 84:25; 103:3)

- The righteous are:

    - The patient in poverty, hardship, or battle

    - The true

    - The obedient

    - Those who spend

    - Those who seek forgiveness before dawn (2:177; 3:17; 22:35)

    - Those who become fearful when Allah is mentioned

    - When His verses are recited, it increases them in faith

    - Those who rely upon their Lord

    - Those who establish prayer, sleep but little at night, and in the hours before dawn ask forgiveness and recite the Quran

- Those who spend from what God has provided them
- Those are the believers, truly (8:1–4; 25:64–67; 51:16–19; 73:20)
- Those who walk on the earth in humility
- Those who, when the ignorant speak harshly to them, respond with "Peace!" (25:63)
- Those who do not desire exaltedness or corruption (28:83)
- Those who teach each other truth and advise each other to patience (103:3)

- To be righteous, you need to give from what you love (3:92)
- Allah tests the believers (and unbelievers) (3:166, 186; 29:1–10; 34:20, 21)
- The most noble among you in the sight of Allah is the most righteous (49:13)
- They will drink from the gushing spring of Kafur (76:5, 6)
- They give food to the needy, the orphan, and the captive only for the countenance of Allah (76:8, 9)
- They feed the poor without desire of reward or gratitude (76:9)
- The righteous will be rewarded with a garden and silk, reclining on couches with no sun or cold (75:11–13)

Righteousness/Law of God/Godliness

- Allah is the straight way, and He guides and protects the sincere in the straight way (1:6; 2:142, 186, 257; 3:101; 10:25; 24:46; 28:56)
- Importance of learning "righteousness" (2:21, 177; 16:90–95)
- Some who say they believe in Allah and the last day do not (really) believe (2:8)
- Importance of being charitable (give *zakah*) to wayfarers, kindred, and Allah (2:43, 110, 177, 195, 254; 3:17; 8:1–3; 16:90; 22:35; 30:37–40; 51:19; 73:20)

- Righteousness includes:
  - Believing in Allah
  - Doing righteous deeds (14:23)
  - Establishing prayer
  - Giving regular charity
  - Bowing with those who bow (2:43, 110; 23:4, 9)
  - Seeking help through patience and prayer
  - Being humbly submissive to Allah (2:45)
  - Believing in Allah, the last day, the angels, the Book, and the prophets (2:177)
  - Spending in the way of Allah, and
  - Doing good, indeed Allah loves the doers of good (2:195, 254)
  - Leaving all sin, open and secret (6:120)
  - Justice
  - Good conduct
  - Giving to relatives, the needy, and the traveler,
  - Abstaining from immorality,
  - Bad conduct, and
  - Oppression (16:90; 30:38)
  - Humble submission during prayer (23:2)
  - Guarding one's private parts (23:5–7)
  - Being attentive to their trusts and promises (23:8)

- o Sleeping but little at night, but reciting the Quran and asking forgiveness in the hours before dawn (51:16–19; 73:20)

- Not only studying Scripture, but practicing true godliness will be rewarded (2:44; 3:17; 14:23–27; 16:95–99)

- Seek help with patience and prayer—it is difficult except for one who comes with humble submission (2:45; 7:55; 23:2)

- There are different kinds of hearts for God—hard like rock, soft and can be opened, hardened by choice, impenitent (2:74, 264; 39:22)

- Do not trade an afterlife in paradise for the pleasures of this life with hell for a reward (2:86; 3:14, 15; 17:18–22)

- Allah will test the believer's faith with trials; need to persevere (2:155–157, 177, 214; 3:140–142; 47:31)

- Love for Allah will overflow from those who serve Allah (2:165)

- To reject Allah is to be devoid of wisdom (2:171)

- We should not do kind deeds to be seen by men; when we give in secret, Allah will reward us (2:264–266, 274)

- The best thing we can do in this life is be near to Allah, better than possessions or pleasures (3:14)

- Be self-controlled, patient, speaking only good words (3:17; 17:53; 41:35; 74:7; 103:3)

- Surrender completely to Allah (3:102; 73:8)

- "Wounds" are the same among believers, all are tried by Allah, He will find martyrs among those who believe (3:140)

- All good comes to you from Allah; evil comes from our own souls (4:79)

- He who obeys God's messenger (Rasul) obeys Allah (4:80; 24:51–56)

- Do not plead for those who are not righteous; they can't hide their actions from Allah (4:107)

- One who exhorts another to good works, reconciliation, especially, has a great reward from Allah (4:114; 103:3)

- Fight for justice, witnesses for Allah, even against yourself or relatives, for the rich or the poor (4:135)

- Don't follow your own inclination as a witness lest you be unjust; neither must you distort testimony or decline to give it (4:135)

- Superstitious beliefs of Arabs—fathers were destroyed for lack of knowledge (5:101–104)

- To those without faith, their deeds seem pleasing (6:122)

- God covered Adam and Eve with raiment to cover their shame, but the raiment of "righteousness" is the best (7:26)

- God sends suffering and adversity to produce humility toward Allah (7:94–100)

- Worst "beast" in the sight of God is to be deaf and dumb and not listen to His messages (8:20–24)

- Allah loves those who purify themselves (9:108)

- Build on your building on righteousness, and not on a sandbank ready to collapse into hell (9:107–109)

- Those who fulfill their covenant with Allah will be saved (13:18–27)

- Allah will guide to Himself whoever turns back to Him (13:27)

- Remembrance of Allah brings tranquility to the soul (13:28)

- Don't sell "covenant" of Allah for a miserable price—staying with Him is the best reward (16:95)

- Blood and meat of sacrifices will not reach Allah, but piety will for thus you glorify Allah (22:37)

- Be kind to parents, but if they try to discourage you from the straight path, obey Allah (29:8)

- Prayer restrains us from evil deeds; we need regular prayer (29:45; 73:1–6)

- Praise to Allah should be on our lips at all times, morning and evening, noon and night (30:17–19)

- Our skin shivers and our hearts tremble at His word (39:23)

- Patiently persevere; do not let those with no certainty of faith shake your firmness (30:53–60; 40:77; 46:13, 35)

- Allah didn't give a person "two hearts"; things don't become that way just because you say they do; you should call people by their real names (33:4, 5)

- Do justly to close friends (33:6)

- Righteous works must follow a person's words to raise them to God (35:10)

- Those who receive understanding should also receive admonition from Allah (39:9)

- No man can serve two quarreling masters, so we need to dedicate ourselves to Allah (39:29; 73:8, 19)

- Allah allows people to grow old, to learn "wisdom" (40:67)

- When Satan tempts you, seek refuge in Allah (41:36)

- Repel evil with what is "better," and thereupon your enemy will become your devoted friend (41:34)

- He who works righteousness benefits his own soul; he who does evil harms his own soul (41:46; 45:15)

- The best way is the way of forgiveness when offended, even if one can defend/avenge himself (42:38–43)

- To those who receive guidance, Allah gives more light, piety, and restraint (47:17)

- Allah asks believers to be generous and give of our possessions to the cause; everything belongs to Allah, who is free of need (47:36–38; 57:10–20)

- If you loan Allah a goodly loan, He will multiply it and give you a noble reward (57:11, 18)

- Muhammad was sent so that people would honor Allah and praise Him every "morning and evening" (48:9)

- Righteous people don't sleep so much; they are praying for forgiveness and giving from their property to the petitioner and the deprived (51:15–19)

- The righteous will weep and repent/fall prostrate; they will not just laugh at Allah's warnings (53:60–62)

- Story of the hypocrites wanting to borrow light from the righteous at the day of judgment, but it is too late; a door will be closed behind them as they return for their own light because they have not followed Allah or been generous with him (57:11–20)

- The righteous devote themselves to prayer, respect each other's wealth, believe in the day of recompense, fear displeasing Allah, are chaste, fulfill their promises, and are upright in their testimony (70:22–35)

- Tolerate the deniers; Allah will judge all on the day (73:11–14)

- Allah is the Lord of righteousness and the Lord of forgiveness (74:56)

- Keep your garments unstained, shun all abominations, and don't expect worldly gain (74:1–6)

- Allah has shown two "highways"—one of virtue (freeing the bondman, giving food in a day of privation and taking care of the poor and orphans, that included believing and advising others to patience and compassion) that is as difficult as breaking through a difficult pass, and the other one that is of disbelieving His signs (90:11–20)

- Whoever wills among you may take a right course, (yet) no man can will, except that Allah wills (81:26–29)

- To purify the soul is true success, just as the sun, earth, moon, day, and night all glorify Allah (91:1–10)

- Man becomes "abased to the lowest of the low" except for them that believe and do righteous deeds (95:5, 6)

- Since Allah has granted the "fountain," turn to Him in prayer and "sacrifice" (108:1–3)

Ridicule

- Do not ridicule other people (49:11, 12)
- Women should not ridicule other women (49:11)
- Same category as spying, backbiting, and negative assumptions (49:12)

Sabah (town in Yemen)

- Story of people who rejected Allah's message of the hereafter (34:22–26)

Sabbath

- Transgressors of the Sabbath were told by Allah, "Be apes, despised" (2:65; 7:163–168)
- People in a city by the sea were tested by Allah, sending fish lifting their heads above the water, but only on the Sabbath; they did that which was forbidden (7:163, 165, 166)
- Allah cursed the Sabbath breakers (4:47)
- Allah made a solemn covenant with His people at Sinai not to transgress the Sabbath, but they transgressed (4:153–155)
- Allah has sealed the hearts of those who broke the covenant of the Sabbath because of their disbelief (4:155)
- Sabbath was made (strict) for those who disagree (as to its observance); Allah will judge between them (16:124)

Salih (A Prophet to the People of Thamud, after Aad Was Destroyed; see also Thamud)

- Story of preaching and rejection of prophet, Salih, whereupon three days later, as Salih predicted, an earthquake took them unawares, yet Salih was preserved (7:72–79; 11:61–68; 26:140–159; 27:45–53; 29:36–38; 69:3–7)

Satan (Iblis or Iblees)

- Allah commanded the angels to "worship" (serve) Adam and Eve, but Satan was proud and refused to prostrate himself (2:34; 7:15; 15:26–44; 17:61–65; 18:50; 20:116–127; 38:71–75)

- Satan caused Adam and Eve to leave the garden and their state of happiness (2:36)

- Satan is a clear enemy to man (2:208; 12:5; 17:53; 35:5–7; 43:62)

- Satan works in opposition to Jesus; one averting man from God, the other bringing signs and knowledge of the hour (43:61–63)

- Satan enjoins immorality, evil, and wrongdoing (2:168–169; 24:21)

- In revenge against God, Satan swore he would sit in wait for mankind on the straight path, and come to them from every side (7:16, 17; 38:82, 83)

- Story of the creation of Adam and rebellion of Satan (38:71–88)

- Satan (the evil one) tries to make us afraid of his supporters, but we need only fear Allah (3:175)

- Worship of any other god is to worship Satan (4:116–120)

- Satan deceives people with his promises and arouses desire in them, but his promises are only delusions (4:120)

- Satan admits God promised people the promise of truth in judgment (14:22)

- Satan admits that he promised people a lie and betrayed them on the day of judgment (14:22)

- Satan, on judgment day, says, "Do not blame me; but blame yourselves, I cannot be called to help you" (14:22)

- Satan taunted God, "You will not find most of them (mankind) grateful" (7:17)

- Story of Satan's fall, and the fall of Adam and Eve (7:10–25)

- Satan said to God, when asked why he refused to bow to Adam, "I am better than him. You created me from fire and created him from clay" (7:12; 38:75, 76)

- Satan swore by Allah to Adam and Eve that he was one of the sincere advisors (7:21)

- When Satan attacks and you are tempted to think evil, flee to Allah, remember Him, and at once you will have insight (7:200, 201)

- Satan is the leader/patron/ally of the wicked today (16:63)

- Seek Allah's protection from Satan when reading/reciting the Quran (16:98)

- Satan is called "the expelled" or "the rejected one" (7:18; 16:98; 38:77)

- He has no authority over those who have believed and rely upon their Lord (16:99, 100)

- Satan's fate is in the fire of hell (7:18; 18:50–54; 38:82–85; 59:16, 17)

- Satan tries to destroy the prophets' messages by inserting Allah will not allow it—He will cancel/abolish what Satan throws in; thus Satan tries to make "schisms far" (22:52–57)

- The wicked will complain on the day of judgment that Satan deceived them, or that a friend led them astray when they knew the Message, and they will wish they had taken the path with the Messenger (25:25–31)

- The evil one is a traitor/deserter to man (25:29)

- The evil ones descend on those who pass on hearsay and are liars and slanderers (26:221–227)

- Demons (*jinn*) cannot see the unseen; they carry on doing their work, but they will receive penalty (34:14)

- Satan and his angels do not have access to the exalted assembly in heaven (37:1–11)

- Satan and his angels are repulsed/repelled from the exalted assembly, pelted from every side (37:8–9)

- Satan and his angels were given respite/reprieve until the day the "dead are raised"—the day of recompense (7:14, 15; 38:71–86)

- He swore against Allah, "By Your might, I will surely mislead them all, except among them, Your chosen servants" (38:82, 83)

- Satan says to man, "Disbelieve," but then he disassociates himself from the disbeliever (59:16)

- Called the "whisperer" who withdraws after he whispers—whispers into hearts of all mankind (114:4, 5)

- He is a clear enemy; you must not worship him (36:60)

Second Coming of Christ

- Heaven will split open with emerging clouds, and the angels will be sent down in successive descent (25:25)

- On that day those who disbelieved and disobeyed the Messenger will wish to be covered by the earth (4:42)

- On that day Allah will bring from every nation a witness, and will bring you as a witness against these peoples (4:41)

Shu'aib (prophet to Maydan)

- Story of preaching and rejection of Shu'aib and destruction by earthquake of Maydan (7:85–93; 11:84–95; 26:176–191; 29:36–38)

- Urged his people to give full measure and weight in justice, not to deprive the people of their due, and not to commit abuse on the earth after its reformation, or spread corruption (7:85; 11:85; 26:181–183)

- Taught the people of Maydan that Allah's ways are best, if they were believers, and left the choice to them saying, "But I am not a guardian over you" (11:86)

- Warning: "Do not sit on every path, threatening and averting from the way of Allah those who believe in Him, seeking to make it seem deviant" (7:86)

- Earthquake left them prostrate in their houses on the "day of the black cloud" (7:91; 26:189)

Sin

- Allah can veil people's hearts and blind them, leaving them in darkness (2:7, 17, 257)

- Human hearts tend to deviate from Allah (3:8; 13:1)

- Children of Allah who believe in Him need forgiveness for sin; they pray for it, and for protection from the punishment of the fire, and they do not knowingly persist in what they have done (3:16, 17, 135)

- Who can forgive sins except Allah? (3:135)

- Every soul has committed evil (3:30)

- Every soul that commits a sin commits it only against himself (4:111; 10:44)

- If anyone earns a sin and blames the innocent for it that is a flagrant sin in addition (4:112)

- Fear Allah to determine "good" from "evil" (5:100)

- Good and evil are not equal, though the abundance of evil may impress you (5:100)

- People will be judged because they "ceased not" from sinning (6:49)

- Avoid all sin—open or secret—God will pay for the deeds you have "earned" (6:120)

- There are four things Allah forbids: shameful deeds, sins against truth or reason, assigning "partners" to Allah, and saying things about Allah that you have no knowledge of (7:33)

- Allah never commands us to sin or do anything shameful (7:28)

- Excuses are not acceptable for sin: "We found our fathers doing it," and "Allah has ordered us to do it" (7:28–30)

- Those who are denied heaven are ones who "hinder" men from the path of Allah and seek to make His way seem deviant (7:45, 86)

- He who invents a lie about Allah, or denies His signs, will never prosper (10:17, 69)

- Ingratitude to our Creator is a sin (23:77–82; 27:73; 36:77–83)

- We should overcome evil with good; Allah is our refuge (23:94–96)

- None is more unjust than the one who invents untruth about Allah even as he is being invited to Islam (61:7)

- Even the "more" righteous have been given "vast" forgiveness (53:32)

- Allah knew you as fetuses in your mothers' wombs, so do not claim yourselves to be pure (53:32)

- Sin is a "straying of the mind," and "mad"-ness (54:47)

- Inventing falsehoods against Allah is the greatest sin (61:7)

- Sinners turn from right, hide from Allah behind wealth and other people, and are willing to sacrifice their loved ones (70:11–18)

- Sinful man is impatient and fretful when evil comes, proud and miserly when good comes (70:19–21)

- Sinful men are "violent" and love wealth and show their ungratefulness to Allah by their deeds (100:1–11)

- Rivalry for "piling up" possessions detracts from good things (102:1–4; 104:2)

Sins

- Exchanging the covenant of Allah for a small price (3:77, 187; 16:95)

- Withholding (greedily) what Allah has given them of His bounty (3:180)

- Refusing to witness or make the Scripture clear to others is a sin of omission (3:187, 188)

- Associating anything with Allah (4:36)

- Spending wealth to be seen by people (4:38)

- Not believing in Allah nor in the last day (4:38; 69:33)

- Stinginess and concealing what Allah has given of His bounty (4:37)

- Disbelief in the words of David and Jesus (5:78)

- Wine and intoxicants (6:90, 91)

- Gambling (5:90, 91)

- Killing one's children for fear of poverty (6:137, 140; 17:31)

- Eating to excess (intemperance) (6:141)
- Eating forbidden foods:
  - dead animals
  - blood
  - flesh of swine
  - food dedicated to other gods (6:145)
  - animals of uncloven hoof
  - fat—except that which adheres to certain parts (6:146)
  - game killed in the state of *ihram* (5:95)
- Receiving the Scripture, but refusing to make it clear to others and concealing it (3:187, 188)
- Worshiping anything other than Allah (17:23)
- Not caring for parents (17:23, 24)
- Spending wastefully (17:26–27)
- Not encouraging the feeding of the poor, or neglecting to speak a gentle word to them (17:26, 28; 69:34)
- Unlawful sexual intercourse (17:32)
- Killing a soul that Allah has forbidden (17:33)
- Pride—walking on the earth exultantly (17:37)
- Taking as his god his own desire (45:23)
- Loving the immediate, and leaving (neglecting) the hereafter (75:20, 21)
- Love of wealth, accumulating wealth and children (100:8–11; 102:1–6; 104:1–4)

- Love of pleasure (102:8)

Sleepers in the Cave (Ephesus)

- Allah knows what is best and right in this story (18:6–26)
- They remained in the cave for three hundred years and exceeded by nine (18:25)

Solomon

- Story of Solomon, the Queen of Sheba, and her conversion to Allah (27:15–44)
- Solomon said that God had taught them the language of birds, who worked for him and communicated message to and from him, especially a *hoopoe* (27:16–25)
- Solomon was a very wise ruler; God put the wind at his command as well as evil ones—every kind of builder and diver (38:30–40)
- Story of building the temple—*jinns* and winds subject to him (34:12–14)

State of the Dead

- Martyrs are not dead, they are alive, but you perceive it not (2:154)
- Those killed in the cause of Allah are not to be thought of as dead; they are alive, receiving sustenance and good tidings of favor from Allah (3:169–171)
- Everyone shall have a taste of death (3:185; 21:35; 29:57)
- At death, Allah's guardian angels take him and do not fail, so all "return to Allah" (6:61, 62)
- No one is eternal, if *rasools* (apostles) are destined to die, how much more the disbelievers (21:34–41)
- "We did not grant to any man before you eternity" (21:34)
- Those in the grave can't be made to hear us, but Allah can make any to hear that He wills (35:22)
- There is only a "first death" for believers (37:59)

- Death is compared to a sleep (39:42)

- Allah takes the souls at death, or during their sleep (39:42)

- All become dust at death (50:3)

- The spirit of man "reaches collar bone" (upon exiting) (75:25–30)

- For those who awake at the day, it will seem as if they had tarried just "one evening" or (at most) the following morn (79:46)

- The day of judgment is the day of entrance to bliss fire for righteous and unrighteous (82:13–15)

- At death humans are hidden and lost (i.e. disintegrated) within the earth until recreated (32:10, 11)

Ten Commandments

- Allah gave Moses the Scripture and the "criterion" for telling right from wrong on Mt. Sinai, and a security (peace) for those who fear the hour (2:53, 87, 93; 3:3; 21:48–50)

- The Torah was given for guidance and light, the prophets were submitted (Muslims); if anyone does not judge by them, he is an unbeliever (5:44, 45)

- The story of Allah writing them for Moses on the tablets of all things as guidance for believers (7:142–145)

- Allah ordained laws for him in the tablets, in all matters, both commanding and explaining all things (7:145)

- Moses was commanded: "Take and hold these with firmness, and enjoin your people to hold fast by the best in the precepts" (7:145)

Thamud

- Rejected message from Allah; they preferred blindness over guidance; so the thunderbolt of an earthquake struck them, leaving them corpses (15:80–86; 29:36–38; 41:17; 51:43–45; 53:51; 54:23–32; 64:1–6; 85:18; 89:9)

- Allah sent a she-camel as a trial for them; instead of caring for her, they hamstrung her (17:59; 54:27–29; 91:11–15)

- Denied afterlife, received warning (50:12–14)

Tithe (*Zakat*)

- Allah provides for all of His children, and we should return unto Him some of our money (2:3, 245, 261–271; 4:58)

- Who is he that will loan to Allah a beautiful loan that God will double into his credit and multiply many times? (2:245; 57:11, 18)

- Those who spend their wealth in the way of Allah are like a seed that grows seven spikes, and on each spike is a hundred grains (2:261)

- Do not give to be seen by others; that invalidates your charities (2:264)

- Those who give to please God are like a high field that produces well with a downpour or even with a drizzle (2:265)

- If you conceal your charitable expenditures and give them to the poor, He will remove from you some of your misdeeds (2:271)

- Give secretly and in public; you will not grieve or fear; you will have your reward (2:274)

- Allah asks believers to be generous and give of our possessions to the cause—everything belongs to Allah (47:36–38; 57:10–20)

- Allah rewards those without measure who believe in His apostles and in Him and give of their wealth and "persons" (3:180; 9:88; 41:30–32)

- Proper uses for *zakat*: for the poor, the needy, those employed to administer funds, for new believers/or for bringing hearts together, for freeing those in bondage and debt, and for wayfarers (9:60)

- Believe in Allah and His apostle, and give out of that whereof He has made you heirs (57:7; 58:13)

Torah

- Sent down by Allah (5:44; 6:154)
- In it is guidance and truth (5:44)
- Basis for the judgment of Allah (5:43, 44)

Trinity

- Allah is not one of "three" gods (5:73)
- Jesus never stated, "Take me and my mother as two deities beside Allah"—He always commanded to worship Allah (5:116, 117)

Truth

- His word is the truth (6:73)
- Promise of Allah is truth (10:55; 40:55)
- Allah dashes truth upon falsehood, and it destroys falsehood (21:18)
- Allah is the truth (22:62)

Tubba (A People of Yemen)

- Were destroyed because of their wickedness (44:37–40)
- Denied afterlife, received warning (50:11–14)

Will of God

- Never say of anything, "I will do that tomorrow," without adding, "if Allah wills" (18:23, 24)
- When you forget (to say "if Allah wills), call your Lord to mind and say, "I hope that my Lord will guide me ever closer than this to right conduct" (18:24)

Witnessing

- Allah wants us to openly declare the truth—plain message—tell our story (2:160; 16:82)

- Only Allah knows the true results of preaching the message (5:109)

- One day there will be a true witness raised/resurrected from among all peoples (16:84–89)

- Invite all to true path with wisdom and the best arguments/beautiful preaching, execute punishments fairly, be patient—patience is from Allah (16:125–128)

- Proclaim the "good news" to all that "do right"—sacrifice isn't what God wants, but piety and a new heart/character (22:37)

- Refusing to witness or make the Scripture clear to others is a sin of omission (3:187, 188)

Wicked, The

- Allah sent poverty and hardship to nations before that perhaps they might humble themselves, but Satan made their sinful practices "alluring" (6:42, 43)

- When poverty and hardship failed to lead people to humble themselves, Allah opened to them the doors of every good thing, but forgetting their former hardships, they just rejoiced in what they were given—then they were called suddenly to account and were destroyed (6:44, 45)

- If God delays judgment and grants the wicked favors, they become proud and mock His judgments (11:8–10; 30:33)

- If God gives the wicked a taste of mercy, then withdraws it, they despair and blaspheme (11:9; 30:36)

- Allah made mankind one brotherhood/community/religion, but mankind has divided into sects, proud of what they have (21:92, 93; 23:52–54)

- Men that have no "book of enlightenment" argue about Allah without knowledge—for them is disgrace in this world and a burning fire on the day of resurrection (22:7–10)

- Some men serve Allah "on an edge," but when trials come they turn their faces against Him—they lose both this world and the hereafter (22:11–14; 30:33–37)

- The wicked are like the darkness in a vast ocean, waves upon waves, with layers of darkness so deep a man can hardly see his hand (24:40)

- The wicked deny that there will be a judgment; they will be punished (25:10, 11; 34:3–5)

- The wicked deny that there will be a resurrection (27:67–70)

- The wicked follow their own lust and divide religion into sects and change it (30:28–32)

- Oppressed sinners will blame their arrogant oppressors for their unbelief, but the arrogant will deny forcing them or being responsible for their fate; they will refute each other's words, but all will confide regret when they see the punishment (34:31–33)

- The wicked refuse to believe any revelations from God (34:31)

- Usually the wealthy deny God's revelations; it is not a sign of God's pleasure; the wealthy stray from God; the poor seek Him, but not sincerely (34:34, 35; 41:47–51; 42:48)

- Allah can't guide those who thinks their alluring, evil deeds are good; He gives them over to an evil "companion/devil" (35:8, 9; 43:35–40; 61:7)

- The tree of Zaqqum is fruit for the wicked; terrible fruit followed by scalding water (17:60; 37:62–68; 44:43–47; 56:51–54)

- The wicked deny "signs" of Allah, are ungrateful, and don't repent (46:4–10)

- The wicked are those who turn people from the true path of Allah (47:1)

- The wicked follow vanities/falsehood (47:3)

- Wicked hearts have been "sealed" by Allah, and they ask those who receive Muhammad's instruction, "What did He say just now?" (47:16)

- Allah makes the wicked "deaf and blinded" (47:23)

- The wicked are those who receive light, and turn away from it because they dislike what Allah sent down, and say, "We will obey you in part of the matter" (47:25, 26)

- Allah could show who the wicked are, but believers will know them by the tone of their speech (47:30)

- Allah makes the deeds of the wicked who attempt to turn people from the true path of "no effect" (47:32)

- The wicked who desire rewards in this life get their rewards only in this life (53:29, 30)

- The wicked rush about (following base nature); there will come a day of resurrection when their rushing will do no good (70:36–44)

- Allah calls to the wicked, but they become obstinate, even when He promises to bless them (71:6–14)

- The wicked hear about the day of judgment/resurrection, but to no effect; they continue to do wrong, do not pray, and do not give charity—they will condemn themselves (75:1–31)

- Those "sent forth" have messages of justification or warning, and indeed what is promised will occur (77:5–7)

- One who thinks himself without need is less likely to be spiritually purified than a blind man who comes striving earnestly (80:1–16)

- Woe to those who defraud their brothers; they will be called to account on the day when mankind will stand before the Lord of the worlds (83:1–6)

- The wicked prefer this life to the next (87:16)

- Allah tests people with wealth; people say that they are honored when they have wealth, and cursed when they don't. But no! It is because you love wealth more than your fellow man (89:14–20)

- You love wealth with immense love; because you don't take care of the poor and orphans and you consume the inheritance of others, on the day when earth has been leveled, you will say, "I wish I had sent ahead for my (future) life" (89:14–20)

Women (and Wives)

- Rules of divorce: fairness for women (witnesses required, need to provide for her, term mandated for reconciliation, etc.) (2:226–237; 65:1–7)

    o Husband may not abstain from relations with a wife more than four months (2:226, 227)

    o Waiting time before a woman may marry again is at least three periods (2:228)

    o Must not disguise a pregnancy discovered during the waiting period (2:228)

    o Husband has first right to remarry her during that time if he wants reconciliation (2:228)

    o Women shall have rights similar to the rights against them, according to what is equitable—but men have a degree of advantage over them (2:228)

    o Divorce is allowable only twice: after that the parties should either hold together on equitable terms or separate with kindness (2:229)

    o Man must not take back any gift he has given to his wife, unless she wishes to give something for her freedom (2:229)

    o Divorced women are due maintenance on a reasonable scale (2:241)

- Mothers may nurse their infants two full years; the duty of supporting them rests fully upon the father or his heir (2:233; 31:14)

- Parents who wish to hire a substitute to nurse the child may if they pay the nurse fairly (2:233)

- Widows must wait four months and ten days, then they are free to do whatever they wish with themselves—within the just and reasonable ways (2:234)

- Widows should be included in a will: a minimum of one year's maintenance and residence (2:240–242)

- Honor your mothers (parents) (4:1; 31:14; 46:15)

- Men should only marry as many ladies as they can take care of, up to four (4:3)

- Dowry should be given as free gift (4:4)

- Women should not be treated with harshness but with fairness in dowries and all dealings (including divorce) (4:19–21, 127–130)

    - Men are forbidden to inherit a woman by compulsion (4:19)

    - Husbands must not make life miserable in order to take back part of what he gave—unless she commits a clear immorality (4:19)

    - Men must live with women in kindness (4:19)

- Women who are forbidden for believers to marry (4:22–25)

- Should marry fairly with chastity, not out of lust (4:24)

- Can marry slave women, but need to practice self-restraint (4:25)

- Men are protectors of women because God has given the one more strength than the other and because they support them from their means (4:34)

- Righteous women are devoutly obedient (4:34)

- Righteous women guard that which they should during their husband's absence (4:34)

- Rules for punishing errant wives (4:34, 35)

- Women, like men, can be saved in heaven if they do righteous deeds while having faith (4:124)

- Pagan Arabs called angels "daughters of Allah," although having a girl was bad news for them (16:57–59; 43:16)

- A sign from Allah is that He gave you mates that you may live in tranquility with them, and He placed between you affection and mercy (30:21)

- Waiting period for divorce required; no more than four wives (permission from Muhammad was needed for more) (33:49–52)

- Should cover themselves when going outside so that they may be known (as chaste believers) and not be molested (33:59)

- "Chaste" women will be in Heaven beside men of equal age, as promised for the day of account (37:48, 49; 38:52, 53)

- "Zihar" divorces are not allowed (calling your wives your "mothers")—punishment will be given for such offenses before they may touch each other again (58:1–4)

- If a woman becomes a believer and joins the Muslim community, examine her faith, and if she is found to be a believer, don't send her back to an unbelieving husband, but pay dowry for her (60:10)

- Hold not to marriage bonds with disbelieving women, but refund their payments and let them go equitably (60:10)

- If women want to become Muslims, allow them, and pray for their forgiveness if they pledge not to associate anything with Allah, nor to steal, nor to kill their children, nor to slander, intentionally forging falsehood, nor to commit adultery, and that they will not disobey you (Muhammad) in any just matter (60:11–13)

- Burying female infants condemned (81:8–14)

Worldly Life

- A worldly life is only amusement and diversion (6:32; 47:36)

Zakat (see Tithe)

Zul-Qarnain (King)

- Story of his conquest (Gog and Magog mentioned) (18:82–101)

- In the company of the good (38:48)

Appendix B

SON OF GOD:
"A Word Study in both the Quran and New Testament"

by Edwin Dysinger
(as on the General Conference Adventist Muslim Relations CD)

Introduction

We probably would be safe in saying that the single greatest contention between Christians and Muslims is over the position of Jesus to God. One of the important areas of disagreement has been over the Christian/Biblical concept of the 'sonship' of Jesus to God.

This word study examines the meanings and usage of the Arabic and Greek words used for *Son* in the Quran and the New Testament. Specific attention is paid to words translated *Son* when used in connection with either God or Jesus. The author does not expect that this simple study can resolve an issue as complex as this one, but it is hoped that it can add some perspective to the discussion on the *Sonship* of Jesus and the wider discussion on the position of Jesus to God.

The meanings of Arabic words were obtained from the *Hans Wehr Dictionary of Modern Written Arabic*. Occurrence of the words in the Quran was determined by doing a word search for the Arabic words using *Alim Islamic Software*. For the New Testament, listings under the entry *Son*, in *Strong's Concordance* were reviewed and Strong's definitions of the Greek words were used. The author recognizes a potential weakness here in not having done word searches for the Greek words, but assumes that in this case there are probably few other words, besides 'son', that they could have been translated into. The author would be grateful for any correction, addition or insight that others more familiar with Arabic or Greek could provide.

The study will begin with the words used in the Quran, giving definitions and then examining usage. It then moves on to the words used in the New Testament dealing with them in a similar fashion. It finishes with some conclusions.

The Quran

In the Arabic used in the Quran, there are two primary words for *son*. These are *Walad* and *Ibn*. We will first look at the definitions of *walad* and *ibn*, then at their use in the Quran in connection with God and Jesus.

Definitions

<u>Walad</u>. Most Arabic words are derived from root words composed of 3 consonants, with variations in voweling, prefixes, and suffixes, creating a host of words with related meanings. The root of *walad* is *walada (wld)*.

The meaning of *walada* (the root word) is: to bear (a child), give birth (to); to beget, generate, procreate; to bring forth, produce.

The meaning of *walad* (the word we will research in the Quran) is: descendant, offspring, scion; child; son; boy; young animal, young one; (colloquial) progeny, offspring, children.

Other related words from the root *walada* are: *wilada*—parturition, childbearing, childbirth, birth, confinement, delivery. *maulid*—birthplace; birthday; anniversary, birthday of a saint. *walid*—procreator, progenitor; father, parent. *walida* - mother; parturient woman, woman in childbed. *muwallida*—midwife. etc.

<u>Ibn</u>. The meaning of *Ibn* is: descendant, scion; offspring, son (of a people or nation): *Ibn Adam* (son of Adam) a human being; *ibn al-balad* (son of a locality) local inhabitant, native; *ibn al-harab* (son of conflict) warrior, soldier, bellicose; *ibn sabiil* (son of the road) a wayfarer, wanderer; *ibn hamsiin sana* (son of 50 years); 50 years old; etc.

In comparing the definitions of these two words, we see that they both carry the meaning *descendant, offspring, scion, son*. But in the case of *walad* we can see that its meaning is limited to these definitions in a stricter sense. The root and other related words amplify this, in that they all have something to do with procreation, birth or generation. *Ibn* on the other hand carries, in addition to the strict meanings mentioned above, possibilities for much broader, figurative or metaphorical usage as in *ibn al-balad* and *ibn sabiil*.

Quranic Usage

Let us now see how these two words are used in the Quran in relation to Jesus and God. We will begin with *walad*.

References to *walad*

The word *walad* appears in at least 18 verses of the Quran in connection with either Jesus or God. These references are as follows (see appendix 1 for the verses written out in full):

        2:116
        3:47
        4:171
        6:101

10:68
17:111
18:4
19:35, 88, 91, 92
21:26
23:91
25:2
37:(151), 152
39:4
43:81
72:3

On examining these verses, we see that every one of them (except 3:47 which is referring to Mary's having a son) is a denial that God could have a *walad*. He is above procreation with a consort (6:101; 72:3) He is above begetting a *walad* or having any other children (6:100, 101; 19:35, 91, 92; 17:111; 37:151–153). In at least two places it is clear that the argument is directed also to pagan Arabs who believed that angels were daughters of God (6:100, 101; 37:151–153). He has no other partner or god with Him (17:111; 23:91; 25:2).

Another significant verse relevant to this, even though it does not use the word *walad* is 112:1–4 which reads as follows:

1. Say: He is Allah, the One;

2. Allah, the Eternal, Absolute

3. He begetteth not, nor is He begotten;

4. And there is none like unto Him.

In verse 3 the words translated 'begetteth' and 'begotton' are *yalid* and *yulad*. They are from the same root as *walad* and refer to physical procreation. These verses are making the same argument the *walad* verses make.

We can conclude by summarizing these '*walad*' verses to say that God is above begetting or fathering children in the normal human fashion. He has no wife or son or daughter or any other god in partnership with him. The argument is against the pagan idea of gods procreating; the teaching of Mary, the Mother of God; and some Trinitarian teaching that makes the Trinity appear more like three co-equal gods than one indivisible God.

References to *Ibn*

The word *Ibn* occurs at least 23 times in the Quran in connection with either Jesus or God. These verses are as follows (See appendix 2 for the verses written out in full):

2:87, 253
3:45
4:157, 171
5:18, 46, 72, 75, 78, 112, 114, 116
9:30, 31
19:34
21:91
23:50
33:7
43:57
57:27
61:6

We find that with two notable exceptions (5:18 & 9:30), all of the above verses use the word *ibn* in reference to Jesus being the son of Mary. In Arab tradition, a son is called, for example, *Yusuf ibn Ahmed* which means 'Yusuf, son of Ahmed', Ahmed being the father. The Quran in recognizing that Jesus had no earthly father, calls him *Aisa Ibn Mariam*, or 'Jesus, son of Mary.' This is unusual in that the author is not acquainted with any other figure in Arab history or tradition who is called 'the son of his mother'.

So, we find that the word *ibn* is not used by the Quran in reference to Jesus' father, but it is used in reference to His mother.

The only exception to this is found in 9:30:

> The Jews call Uzair a **son** of Allah and the Christians call Christ the **son** of Allah. That is a saying from their mouths; (in this) they but imitate what the unbelievers of old used to say. Allah's curse be on them: how they are deluded away from the truth!

In the Arabic, the expression for Christ the son of Allah is *Al Masih ibn Allah* or 'the Messiah, son of God.' This is a recognition that Christians use the word *ibn* rather than *walad* in referring to Jesus being the Son of God (more on this when dealing with the NT).

The phrase that follows is significant; *(in this) they but imitate what the unbelievers of old used to say.* It seems clear that this is reference to the arguments we saw above regarding *walad*. It is a denial of the pagan concept of God participating in procreation with consorts or humans, having sons or daughters or any other partners. In other words, it identifies the Christian concept of 'son (*ibn*) of God' with the pagan concept of 'son (*walad*) of god'. It does not recognize that the Christian usage of *ibn* might be in a figurative or metaphorical sense rather than a strict sense of sonship.

5:18 reads as follows:

> (Both) the Jews and the Christians say: "We are **sons** of Allah and His beloved." Say: "Why then doth He punish you for your sins? Nay ye are but men of the men

He hath created: He forgiveth whom He pleaseth and He punisheth whom He pleaseth: and to Allah belongeth the dominion of the heavens and the earth and all that is between: and unto Him is the final goal (of all)."

Here we find Jews and Christians calling themselves 'sons (*abnau* - plural of *ibn*) of God'. The Quran deals with this in a manner consistent with all the other references to sonship with God. It obviously understands them to be claiming that they are gods and it makes the point that they are *but men of the men He hath created* rather than gods. Again, we find the Quran denying the pagan concept of gods in partnership with God, while at the same time not recognizing that a figurative or metaphorical interpretation of *abnau* could be possible.

The New Testament

From the Greek of the New Testament, there are four words which are translated *son* in the English KJV. These are (using Strong's numbers): *431 Anepsios*; *3816 Pais*; *5043 Teknon*; and *5207 Huios*.

Definitions

431 Anepsios means 'a cousin' or 'sister's son'.

3816 Pais: perh. from 3817; a boy (as often beaten with impunity), or (by anal.) a girl, (gen.) a child; spec. a slave or servant (espec. a minister to a king; and by eminence to God): - child, maid (-en), (man) servant, son, young man.

3817 Paio: a prim. Verb; to hit (as if by a single blow and less violently than 5180); spec. to sting (as a scorpion): - smite, strike.

5043 Teknon: from the base of 5098; a child (as produced): - child, daughter, son.

5207 Huios: appar. a prim. word; a "son" (sometimes of animals), used very widely of immed., remote or fig. kinship: - child, foal, son.

Usage

<u>431 Anepsios</u>. This word is only used once (Col. 4:10), not in connection with Jesus, so we will not deal with it further.

<u>3816 Pais</u>. This word is used 3 times in the NT (John 4:51; Acts 3:13, 26).

John 4:51 referring to the Nobleman of Capernaum, "And as he was now going down, his servants met him, and told him, saying, Thy **son** liveth."

This verse obviously does not refer to Jesus.

Acts 3:13 "The God of Abraham, and of Isaac, and of Jacob, the God of our fathers, hath glorified his **Son** Jesus; whom ye delivered up, and denied him in the presence of Pilate, when he was determined to let him go."

Acts 3:26 "Unto you first God, having raised up his **Son** Jesus, sent him to bless you, in turning away every one of you from his iniquities."

These two verses do refer directly to Jesus. But while the KJV translates *pais* as 'son' in these two verses, it is important to note that the NKJV, the RSV, the TEV, the NEB, and the NIV all translate *pais* as 'servant'. There seems to be some consensus among modern Biblical Greek scholars that this is a better and more accurate translation.

We thus feel comfortable in saying that these two words (*431 Anepsios & 3816 Pais*) are not important to our discussion of the 'sonship' of Jesus.

<u>5043 Teknon</u>. This word occurs 14 times in the New Testament.

> Matthew 21:28
> Mark 2:5; 13:12
> Luke 2:48; 15:31; 16:25
> I Corinthians 4:17
> Philippians 2:22
> I Timothy 1:2, 18
> II Timothy 1:2; 2:1
> Titus 1:4
> Philemon 10

In each case, it is used in the sense of a parent, an elder or an authority speaking to a child, or one who is under the influence of one who is greater. It is used by a father in reference to his son, it is used by Jesus in reference to a man he had healed, in the story of the rich man and Lazarus it is used by Abraham in reference to the rich man, it is used by Paul in reference to Timothy, Titus and Philemon.

In only one place is it used in reference to Jesus, and that is in Luke 2:48 where his parents had just found the boy Jesus in the temple after three days of searching. His mother said to him, "**Son**, why have you treated us like this? Your father and I have been anxiously searching for you."

It seems that *teknon* is somewhat comparable to *walad*. They both refer to the child who is produced by his parents, in other words, the literal offspring. And both; *teknon* perhaps more so, but it is also true of *walad*; can be used by an elder or authority figure to refer to someone they are relating to as their child, or under their influence. It is interesting to note that the only time *teknon* is used in the NT in relation to Jesus is in reference to his mother, just as the only time *walad* is used in the Quran in relation to Jesus is in reference to his mother (apart from the many times it is used in denial of God having a *walad*).

5207 Huios. All remaining references to *son* in the NT are translated from this word. This word is used without exception by both writers of the gospels and epistles to refer to the 'sonship' of Jesus. From both the meanings of the words and from their usage, it seems that *huios* is remarkably similar to *ibn*. Both can refer to a literal or physical son, but both are often used in a figurative or metaphorical sense. The NT is consistent in using *huios* in referring to Jesus and the Quran admits that Christians use *ibn*, rather than *walad*.

Conclusion

1. We see that the whole 'sonship' argument in the Quran is based on the word *walad* and the concept of physical procreation that accompanies this word. We see that this is an argument against pagan ideas—that God would have consorts, that He would procreate through consorts or humans, that He would thus have sons and daughters. We see that even when the Quran recognizes that Christians use the word *ibn* in describing Christ's 'sonship' to God, it falls back on the argument against the pagan (*walad*) concept of 'sonship' with God. We therefore assume that either: a) Muhammad was addressing his arguments to 'Christians' who had perverted the true Biblical/Christian understanding of God and had assumed pagan concepts, clothing them with Christian terminology (something that we do recognize happened in history), or b) Muhammad was ignorant of true Biblical/Christian teaching in this regard.

2. We recognize that there seems to be some correspondence in meaning and usage between the Arabic *walad* and the Greek *teknon*. There also seems to be some correspondence in meaning and usage between the Arabic *ibn* and the Greek *huios*. While this correspondence may not be complete, we can see that it is close enough to be significant. The correspondence between *ibn* and *huios* seems to be stronger than the correspondence between *walad* and *teknon*.

3. We see that the Quran and the NT seem to have some agreement in the language they use in referring to Jesus as 'son of God'. The Quran denies that Jesus is a *walad* from God. The NT does not claim that he is a *teknon* from God. The Quran admits that Christians use *ibn* in referring to Christ's sonship, and we see that the NT is consistent in using *huios* in reference to Christ's sonship.

4. Since the words *ibn* and *huios* can be used in both a literal as well as a figurative or metaphorical sense, we cannot claim that the use of these words proves that the figurative or metaphorical sense is the correct one.

    But we can make an inference that the figurative or metaphorical sense is correct since in both the Arabic as well as the Greek, a more literal word is available (*walad* and *teknon*) and since the Quran denies that Jesus is a *walad* from God and the NT does not claim that he is a *teknon* from God.

Since the Quran and Bible do not teach that Jesus is a literal (*walad* or *teknon*) son of God, and since the words *ibn* and *huios* are used in both the Quran and the NT to describe the Christian understanding of 'sonship' the distinct possibility remains that Christian/Biblical 'sonship' is based on the metaphorical or figurative rather than literal meanings of *ibn* and *huios*.

For Further Study

As was mentioned in the introduction to this study, this study does not expect to resolve the debate between Christians and Muslims regarding the position of Christ. While we hope that it adds some important perspective to this debate, we recognize that there are still important issues remaining that must be addressed, such as the divinity/humanity of Jesus.

Appendix C

A POSSIBLE INTERPRETATION OF DANIEL 11

The prophecy of Daniel 11 had never really intrigued me until I read *God Cares*, volume 1 by Mervyn Maxwell. I had always thought that Daniel 11 was too difficult to understand and too detailed to really comprehend the events foretold in this chapter. Dr. Maxwell, however, showed how the first twenty or so verses were fulfilled in great detail, and I was amazed at how accurately God can predict the future. Maxwell stated, though, that after the first few verses most commentators disagree about the fulfillment of this prophecy.

Then I happened to read what Ellen White said about the study of Daniel 11 in the ninth volume of *Testimonies for the Church*. She states that "the world is stirred with the spirit of war. The prophecy of the eleventh chapter of Daniel has nearly reached its complete fulfillment. Soon the scenes of trouble spoken of in the prophecies will take place" (p. 14) After reading this comment I began to study Daniel 11. I have always appreciated the historical method of interpreting prophecy because it seems to me to be the most "common-sense" way of studying God's dealings with humanity. God sees the whole picture and is involved in a personal way with the history of our planet. To make God seem ignorant of the "current events" that have shaped the world, as we know it, does God an injustice. The fact that Adventists have interpreted God's prophecies with a history textbook in hand is a sign to me that we serve a God of love who cares for His creation and keeps a watchful eye upon them wherever they go and whatever they do in the course of the earth's history.

What makes a study of Daniel 11 very pertinent to us today is that God saw that we would be here this long in a "delay" and that nothing surprises Him. This study has satisfied my question of "Why didn't God put anything in prophecy that relates to events of the twentieth century that have so radically effected the world we live in, such as the creation of Israel, World War I and II, the Cold War/Soviet Union, or the War on Terror with radical Muslims. I was pleasantly surprised to find in my study what I perceive as God's prophecy of these modern events that have played so great a role in world affairs in the last century. What was absolutely astounding to me is that Ellen White counseled the church to study this prophecy on the very next page after she described a 9/11-type scenario that the Lord showed her in a vision (see *Testimonies for the Church*, vol. 9, pp. 11–13). This seems to me to be a call to the church of the end times to study this prophecy.

Daniel 11:40–45
For the purposes of this study I am assuming that the interpretation as set forth in Mervyn Maxwell's book *God Cares*, volume 1 is the standard Seventh-day Adventist interpretation of verses 1–19 in which the Persian/Greek/Seleucid/Ptolemaic dynasties and their exploits and battles are described in great detail.

From verses 20–39, I also assume, as Maxwell does, that these texts describe the history of the Christian church from the time of Christ (times of the "tax collector"—verse 20) to the end of the apostasy of the Christian church during the Middle Ages. During these verses one sees many similarities with the power described in Daniel 7. It is not a stretch of the imagination to see the apostate Christian church described in this chapter with the king of the North (apostate Christianity) making war with the king of the South (the exploits of the Crusades against the Muslims of the East and South) and setting his "heart against the covenant" and "exalting and magnifying himself" above every god (verse 36) as he set aside God's law and the Bible for its traditions.

This prophecy sets forth even in greater detail the absolute apostasy that the Christian church reached during this 1260-year prophecy, which is so noteworthy because Jesus mentions it seven times in prophecy (Dan. 7:25; 12:7; Rev. 11:2, 3; 12:6; 12:14; 13:5)! So I will not deal with verses 20–39, as it seems just to flesh out the previous prophecies in Daniel that describe the attitudes and exploits of fallen Christianity during this stunning 1260 years of rebellion against God on the part of His church.

Time of the End
That leads us to verse 40 where Daniel closes off the last passage of the chapter by saying that these next events will occur during the "time of the end." Traditionally, for Adventists this has meant the time period starting after the collapse of the papacy in 1798, and the fulfillment of Daniel 8:14 in 1844. Since William Miller started the Advent Movement, which is known as an "end-time" movement, in the decade around 1830, one would expect the following verses to have reached their fulfillment beginning in the early 1800s. This would also be logical considering the progression of the prophecy of Daniel 11 starting with Persia leading up to the end of the apostasy of Christianity.

King of the North
The king of the North in Daniel 11, if one accepts the interpretation of Maxwell, has been a metamorphosis of powers located to the north of Jerusalem. It started out as the Persian dynasty, changed into the Greek empire, and turned eventually into the Seleucid dynasty. It then morphed into the Imperial Roman Empire and then the Roman Catholic Church.

In 1798 another power shift occurred as Europe entered the Industrial Revolution. Power in the West had gradually been transferred from a dictatorial papacy to the arising democratic French/British/Italian governments of Europe, with the eventual addition of a small country-turned-superpower, the United States of America.

So when one thinks of the "king of the North," one doesn't necessarily think of any one power. In one word the "king of the North" of Daniel 11 is the "West" (as it is referred to in modern times) and the power(s) that rules Western civilization. Adventists believe from the other prophetic writings of Daniel and John in Revelation that this will eventually include a revived Catholic Church with the help of the United States of America and Europe.

King of the South

Since the "king of the North" is what is known as the "West," then the "king of the South" would have to be what is known as the "East." From the times of Greece, the enemies of the "West" and those that were to be conquered were the inhabitants of North Africa/Middle East/Oriental East—places south of Israel. From this geographical area the Egyptians, Ptolemies, Syrians, and Vandals, the Muslim Arab conquerors, and the Turkish Ottoman Empire have come onto the prophetic stage of Daniel 11. These powers have always caused Western rulers concern and overt fear and have been the subjects of their armed conquests. Over the course of history they have generally been referred to as "pagans" and "infidels." Even some Adventist commentators consider the "king of the South" as atheism due to this characterization. However, for this paper, the king of the South will be the power that aligns itself against the "West."

King of the South Engaging the King of the North in Battle

Verse 40 tells us that at the time of the end the king of the South will "engage him [the king of the North] in battle" (NIV). So who had been engaging the West in battle for centuries by the "time of the end"? The Ottoman Empire seems like the best answer.

The Ottoman Empire grew from a small Turkish tribe headed by Osman in the early fourteenth century AD to an empire that in the 1500s covered all of the Balkan Peninsula, much of the Middle East, and parts of Hungary, northern Africa, and even parts of Russia. They had put an end to the Byzantine Empire when they conquered Constantinople in 1453, and had made Europe tremble when they made it almost to the gates of Vienna in 1529.

The Roman Catholic Church and the Holy Roman Empire had done all they could to keep the Muslim Ottomans out of their territory—and the sultans of the Ottoman empire had proved to be a worthy counterbalance for power in the medieval world to the predominantly Christian European West.

However, it was at the "time of the end" as the events that led to the demise of apostate Christianity were unfolding and God was preparing a power that would be able to nurture His end-time church to finish His work on earth (Rev. 13:11) that the king of South began to be "stormed" in attacks by the king of the North.

It is true that the Ottoman Empire had been declining in power since 1571 when European fleets defeated the Ottoman navy in the Battle of Lepanto near Greece. However, in 1774 the Turks lost a six-year war to Russia and were forced to allow Russian ships to pass through the Straits—the channel that connects the Black Sea with the Mediterranean. In 1783 they ended up even losing the Crimea to Russia. But, by and large, the Ottoman Empire was still intact when the 1260-year prophecy of Daniel and Revelation came to an end in 1798.

So what did God have in mind when He showed Daniel that the king of the North would "storm out against him with chariots and cavalry and a great fleet of ships" (verse 40, NIV)? God foretold that this king would "invade many countries and sweep through them like a flood" (Ibid.). What happened to the Ottoman Empire during the 1800s?

"The Sick Man of Europe"

The 1800s are when the Ottoman Empire came to be known as by Europeans as the "sick man of Europe." This is the time when the Ottoman Empire officially ceased to be a world power. Although the Ottoman Empire still existed until 1923 when Kemal Ataturk replaced it with the republic of Turkey, the 1800s were the years when the empire ceased to evoke fear in the hearts of her enemies.

In 1821 Greek revolutionaries revolted against the Ottoman Empire and forced it to sign the treaty of Adrianople (Edirne) in 1829, which recognized the independence of Greece and gave Russia the control of the mouth of the Danube River. After this the Turks fought a series of wars with Russia in which they lost most of the Balkans. In 1830 it also lost Algeria to France.

In the late 1830s our Adventist pioneers (specifically Josiah Litch) studied the fifth and sixth trumpets of Revelation 9 and came to the conclusion that the Ottoman Empire would lose its power on August 11, 1840. As already covered in this book, the Adventist pioneers believed that this was accurately fulfilled, which helped stimulate the nascent Adventist movement. In any case, historians have documented extensively that the Ottoman Empire was "sick" and was on the verge of passing into oblivion.

The Invasion of the King of the North

The Bible predicts the invasion of the king of the North in the following way in Daniel 11:41–43:

> He shall come into the glorious land. And tens of thousands shall fall, but these shall be delivered out of his hand: Edom and Moab and the main part of the Ammonites. He shall stretch out his hand against the countries, and the land of Egypt shall not escape. He shall become ruler of the treasures of gold and of silver, and all the precious things of Egypt; and the Libyans and the Ethiopians shall follow in his train. (RSV)

This is an amazingly accurate prediction of what happened to the countries that were formerly in the Ottoman Empire from 1840 to the present day.

"Egypt Shall Not Escape"

The prophecy names specifically Egypt as a country that would not escape and that would have its "gold" and "silver" and "all of the precious things" of this ancient country ruled by the king of the North. That is exactly what happened. After Muhammad Ali's hopes of creating a regional superpower (he had won military battles before 1840 over Arabia, Greece, Sudan and Syria) were squelched by Great Britain, France, Russia, and Prussia in the treaty of London, these powers decided that Egypt would be a good place to do business.

A French firm built the Suez Canal from 1859–1869, and the government of Egypt agreed to let the firm operate the canal for ninety-nine years. However, in 1875 the Egyptian government was facing bankruptcy after wild spending, and they were forced to sell all of their shares to the British. In 1876 the government appointed two British and French officials to manage its financial affairs. In 1881 the people couldn't handle the foreign influence anymore and revolted against the French and British. The British finally quelled the revolt and took over Egypt in 1882. Egypt remained under British control for the next forty years.

This was a general trend of the countries of the former Ottoman Empire. Great Britain took Cyprus in 1878. France seized Tunisia in 1881. By the time of World War I when the Ottomans sided with Germany and lost the war, the Europeans had carved up the whole empire. Britain took Iraq, Palestine, Jordan, and Tanganyika in the early 1900s.

During this time France took Syria and Lebanon. Italy ended up taking Libya and Ethiopia (called Nubians) (verse 43 actually lists these two countries separately and says that they would be in "submission"—a telling sign that these two countries would have the unfortunate fate of "submitting" to the same power—the fascist dictatorship of Italy's premier, Mussolini).

The European powers called these newly acquired territories "mandated territories." However, in verse 41 Daniel says that even though the king of the North would invade the "glorious land" (that is, the Middle East—where Israel was) that the neighbors of Israel—"Moab, Edom and the leaders of Ammon"—would be "delivered" from the hand of the king of the North. That is what happened. All the above-mentioned countries ended up obtaining independence from these powers in the following years:

1922—Egypt

1923—Modern Turkey created

1932—Iraq

1946—Syria, Jordan, Lebanon

1947—Libya and Ethiopia

1948—Palestine

1962—Algeria

Although the king of the North had attempted to take over the former Ottoman Empire, the countries were "delivered" from his hands.

The Prediction of the Creation of Israel
An interesting detail in this prophecy is the prediction that the king of the North would come into the "glorious land"—what is called the Holy Land today. Daniel also predicted in verse 41 that "tens of thousands" (RSV—some translations "many countries") would fall due to the decision to enter this land. This was fulfilled to some degree by the conquests of the Western nations as they took over the countries of the Ottoman Empire—but it is difficult to imagine that this prophecy would not include the most controversial event of the twentieth century in the "Holy Land"—the creation of the state of Israel in its historical territory. This was a decision that the British came to after World War I when they drafted the Balfour Declaration that gave Britain support for the creation of a Jewish "national home" in Palestine without violating the rights of non-Jews who lived there. However, there was not enough international support for it until after World War II, thirty years later when the rest of the world discovered the horrific details of the Holocaust. It was only then that in 1948 the state of Israel was created with the intent of providing a homeland for the Jews of all nations of the world.

Since then there have been numerous wars, conflicts, peace talks, treaties, realigning of borders, and terrorist attacks where, literally, tens of thousands have lost their lives due to this decision of the West to take away some of the Arabs' land and give it to the Jews. To this day, it is the defining moment in Western-Christian/Eastern-Muslim relations. Muslim inhabitants of these former Ottoman countries are still bitter over the king of the North's desire to "extend his power over many countries" (verse 42, NIV), which Daniel foretold.

Prophecy of the Threats of Nazism and Communism
Verse 44 of Daniel 11 goes on to tell us that there would be "reports" from the east and the north that will "alarm" the king of the North and cause him to go out in a "rage" to "annihilate" many (NIV). This continues to describe the series of power shifts that occurred in the world during the "time of the end."

The interesting thing about this prophecy is that the king of the North would be "alarmed" at reports from the "north" itself. How could the king of the north be afraid of something from the north? Daniel seems to say that some of the new "alarming" enemies of the king of the North (with their menacing "reports") would be from the North itself! It is amazing that that is exactly what happened. Two world wars were fought with Germany (one of the former powers of the king of the North) and a fifty-year long Cold War was fought with another player of the king of the North—Russia. The Nazi regime of Hitler and the Communist regime of the Soviet Union were the two most dreaded powers in the Western world from the 1930s to the turn of the twenty-first century.

Without these two powers, the Western nations of the United States (the newest addition to the king of the North power—which quickly became the most powerful), Great Britain, and France would not have had the motivation to come up with the amazing technological developments that helped to protect the West from those regimes. It is interesting that Daniel predicted that this would cause the king of the North to go out in a "rage to destroy and annihilate many" (verse 44, NIV). It is easy to look back on history and see the development of weaponry that has so dramatically increased since the beginning of the 1900s before World War I was fought. Relatively simple methods of warfare were replaced by sophisticated machine guns, tanks, airplanes, helicopters, and eventually nuclear weapons that could in a real way fulfill Daniel's prophecy that the West would be able to "annihilate many."

It is clear now for us to see why Ellen White would say in the early 1900s that "the world is stirred with the *spirit of war*. The prophecy of the eleventh chapter of Daniel has nearly reached its complete fulfillment. Soon the scenes of trouble spoken of in the prophecies will take place" (*Testimonies for the Church,* vol. 9, p. 14, italics added). The Lord had predicted in this chapter that tens of millions of people would go to their graves in wars with the modern weapons that would be used in the wars of the twentieth century.

Threat of Radical Islam

Also in verse 44 Daniel states that the king of the North would not only hear "alarming reports" from the north, but also from the "east." This would take us in the prophetic view of history up to today. For most of us who grew up with the threat from the "north" of the Soviet regime, it was a welcome sight to see the much-feared Soviet Union fall apart in the early 1990s.

For almost a decade the West lived without fear of a mortal enemy—that is, until 9/11 when the West was brought to its knees by a handful of "Eastern" warriors for their faith. The ensuing years have seen the king of the North go out in a "rage" to "annihilate" the new enemy: radical Muslims intent on terrorizing the West.

It is hard to call it a coincidence that Ellen White wrote about the importance of studying this prophecy on the very next page after she was shown in vision by the Lord skyscrapers that were on fire in New York City. It is equally difficult to think that something like the War on Terror would be something that God would overlook in prophecy. This conflict is quickly becoming the factor uniting most of the governments of the earth, and it may well set the stage for the last attempt of Satan to unite his kingdom against God's people. Truly the West is still alarmed at the reports from the messengers of Al-Qaeda and other threatening movements in the East.

The Final Stand

Verse 45 of Daniel 11 states that the king of the North will "pitch his royal tents between the seas at the beautiful holy mountain" (NIV). We are helped by Revelation 13 and the corresponding prophetic ministry of Ellen White to understand what this term means. Adventists believe that God foretold a time when Satan will make one last attempt to unite the world under his banner of rebellion. This prophecy tells us that the king of the North will play a lead role in this union. Adventists believe that there is a time when the United States and apostate Christianity and Europe, in unison, will lead the way in trying to establish their "mark," not allowing anyone to "buy or sell" unless they give obedience unto this united power (Rev. 13:14–17). This prophecy in Daniel 11:45 confirms that interpretation and says that Satan will try to unite the "seas" (nations) and establish authority on the beautiful, holy mountain (Jerusalem and Mount Zion).

This prophecy again shows us that the coming conflict will be a mix of religion and politics in that the king of North is a political power but is said to be "pitching his royal tents" between the people and God's mountain—that is, they will be a hindrance to true spirituality, which people will have to overcome to find the "way of truth" as it is in Jesus.

But Daniel comforts us with these words, that the king of the North will "come to his end, and no one will help him" (verse 45, NIV). The next verse, chapter 12:1 tells us that it is at this time that Michael (Christ) will "arise" and will come to the aid of His people—that is, He will come back and deliver them at His second coming to earth.

Conclusion

If this interpretation of prophecy is correct, then the following conclusions can be made:

1. All the prophesied events that are found in this chapter have already taken place with the exception of the last stand of the king of the North against God and his final destruction at the second coming.

2. Nowhere is there mentioned anything here about a third conflict, a worldwide *jihad* with Islam, which some Adventist commentators see in Daniel 11. The only mention of Islam in the prophecy would be the references to "reports from the East" and the worldwide "war on terror" with Islamic extremists.

Appendix D

Application of Year-Day Principle, by Centuries, to Respective Trumpet Periods

KEY TO NATIONALITY OF WRITERS:
A—American; B—British; D—Dutch;
F—French; G—German; I—Italian.
S—Scottish.

TIME KEY:
391 days (lun) = 360+1
396 days = 365+30+1

No.	Expositor	Nationality	Date of Pub.	Fifth Trumpet	Sixth Trumpet	Period Length Years	Days
I. Prior to Reformation							
1	Joachim of Floris	(I)	1190	5 months=150 yrs			
	(First to apply year day principle and first to apply to Mohammedans)						
2	Brute of Britain	(B)	1391	5 months=150 yrs			
3	Luther, Martin	(G)	1545		Sixth Trumpet is Mohammedanism		
II. Sixteenth Century							
1	Foxe, John	(B)	1586	606-756	1051-1573		
2	Napier, John	(S)	1593	1051-1203	1300-1696	396	
III. Seventeenth Century							
1	Downham	(B)	1603	630-780	1300-1696	396	
2	Brightman, Thomas	(B)	1609	830-980 (630-780)	1300-1696	396	
3	Pareus, David	(G)	1618	606-756	1300-1696	396	
4	Mede, Joseph	(B)	1627	830-980 (953-1055)	1057-1453	396	
5	Goodwin, Thomas	(B)	1639	830-980	1453-1849	396	
6	Huit, Ephraim	(A)	1644	606-756	1302-1697	395	
7	Parker, Joseph	(A)	1646		1259-1649 (1376-1800)	390	
8	de Launay, Pierre	(F)	1651	Saracens	Turkish Invasion		
9	Poole, Matthew	(B)	1666	830-980	1057-1453 (1300-1699)	396	
10	Jurieu, Pierre	(F)	1687	622-772	1300-1696	396	
11	Cressener, Drue	(B)	1689	637-787	1062-1453	391	
12	Knollys, Hanserd	(B)	1689	(150 Yrs.)	(391 "odd days")	391	
13	Lloyd, William	(B)	1690	(150 Yrs.)	1302-1698	396	
14	Newton, Isaac	(B)	1691	637-9036(300)	1063-1453	391	
15	Horchen, Heinrich	(G)	1697	622-1057	1057-1452	396	
16	Beverley, Thomas	(B)	1698		1055-1453	391	(+15 days)
IV. Eighteenth Century							
1	Fleming, Robert	(B)	1701	622-772	1057-1458	391	
2	Baxter, Richard	(B)	1701	(150 Yrs.)	1300-1696	396	
3	Brüsskin, Conrad	(G)	1702	606-756	1057-1453 (Turks)	396	
4	Vitringa, C.	(D)	1705	Saracens (150)	1301-1697 (1062-1453)	396	
5	Whiston, William	(B)	1706	612-827			
6	Mather, Increase	(A)	1709		1300-1699	396	
7	Daubuz, Charles	(B)	1712	612-762	1386- (1356-		
8	Henry, Matthew	(B)	1712	627-779	1675-1453	396	
9	Anonymous	(B)	1719	(150 Yrs.)	1057-1453	396	
10	Newton, Thomas	(B)	1755	612-762	1281-1672	391	
11	Durham, James	(B)	1764		(Period of Time)	391	
12	Gill, John	(B)					
13	Kershaw	(B)	1780	629-779	1301-1697	396	
14	Wood, Hans	(B)	1787	630-780	1650-		
15	Scott, Thomas	(B)	1791	612-762	1281-1672	391	(+15)
16	Osgood, Samuel	(A)	1794	622-772	997-1388 (1297-	391	
17	Winthrop, James	(A)	1794	"150 yrs."	"391 years"	391+	
18	Woodhouse, J. G.	(B)	1794		1055-1453	391	
19	Bicheno, James	(B)	1799	606-756	1302-1697	391	(+16)
20	Kett, Henry	(B)	1799	612-762			
V. Nineteenth Century							
1	Mitchel	(B)	1800	622-772	1300-1696	396	
2	Evanson, Ed.	(B)	1802	632-782	1057-1453	396	
3	Priestly, Joseph	(B)	1804	612-762	1281-1672	391	
4	Barnes, Albert	(B)	1805	622-772 (629-779)	1057-1453	391	
5	Chamberlin, Richard	(A)	1805	(150 years)	1282-1683	391	(+14)
6	Faber, G. S.	(B)	1806	612-762	1281-1672	391	
7	Johnstone, Bryce	(B)	1807	606-756	699-1090	391	(+15)
8	French, Lawrence	(B)	1810	612-762	1065/68-1453 (1299-1685)	391	(+15)
9	Buck, Charles	(B)	1811		1453-1844	391	
10	Cunninghame, William	(B)	1812	612-662	1281-1672 (1057-1448)	391	(or 296)
11	Kinne, Aaron	(A)	1814	612-762	1281-1672	391	(+15)
12	M'Leod, Alexander	(A)	1814	612-762	1281-1672	391	(+15)
13	Armstrong, Amzi	(A)	1815	612-762	1281-1672	391	(+15)
14	Brown, John	(B)	1815	610-780	1281-1672 (1302-1698)	391	
15	Frere, James H.	(B)	1815	612-762 (632-782)	1281-1697 (1063-1453)	391	
16	Holmes, James I.	(S)	1815	612-762	1281-1672	391	(+15)
17	Cornwallis, Mrs	(B)	1820	612-762	1281-1672	391	(+15)

No.	Expositor	Nationality	Date of Pub.	Fifth Trumpet	Sixth Trumpet	Period Length Years	Days
18	Gauntlett, (Henry)	(B)	1821	612-762	1281-1672	391	(+15)
19	Fry, John	(B)	1822	629-779 (632-762)	1453-1844	391	
20	Brown, J. A.	(B)	1823	(150 years)	1453-1844	391	
21	Cooper, Edward	(B)	1825	533-684 (1322-1798)	1301-1697	396	(or 391)
22	Park, J. R.	(B)	1826	612-762	1453-1844	391	
23	"Lajos"	(B)	1827	630-930 (390?)	1299-1690 (1326-1717)	391	
24	Cox, John	(B)			1453-1844	391	
25	Keyworth, Thomas	(B)	1828	612-762	1281-1672	391	(+15)
26	Addis, Alfred	(B)	1829	786-936			
27	Doolan, Pk.	(B)	1829		1453-1844	391	
28	Tudor, John	(B)	1829	622-762	391 yrs A fraction	391	
29	Anonymous	(B)	1829	632-782	1062-1453	391	
30	Dales, William	(B)	1830	620-779 (632-782)	1281-1672 (1062-1453)	391	(+15)
31	Shirley, William	(A)	1831		1452-1843	391	(+15)
			1832	1298-1448	1448-1839	395	(+15)
			1839	1299-1449	1449-1840	391	(+15)
32	Keith, Alexander	(A)	1832	622-772	1057-1453	396	(+193)
33	Smith, Ethan	(A)	1833		1453-1818	360	
34	Habershon Matthew	(B)	1834	612-762	1453-1844	391	(+15)
35	Bickersteth, Edward	(B)	1836	637-786	1453-1843/44 (1093-1453)	391	
36	Bogie, B. D.	(B)	1836	612-762	1300-1696	396	
37	Jenks, William	(A)	1838	612-762	1281-1672	391	(+15)
38	**Litch, Josiah**	**(A)**	**1838**	**1299-1449**	**1449-1840 (Aug.)**	**391**	**(+15)**
39	Wall	(A)	1840		1453-1849	396	
40	Whitaker & Thurstoe	(A)	1840		1453-1844	391	
41	Campbell, David	(A)	1840	612-762	1281-1692	391	(+15)
42	Crandall, A. I.	(A)	1841	636-766	1281-1672	391	
43	Fitch, Charles	(A)	1842	1299-1449	1449-1840	391	
44	Birks, T. R.	(B)	1843	632-682		391	
45	Stone, B. W.	(B)	1843	(1299-1449)	1449-1840	391	(+15)
46	Southard, Nath.	(A)	1843	1299-1449	1449-1840	391	(+15)
47	Anon. (Hypomb?)	(B)	1844		1281-1672(Aug.)	391	
48	Galusha, Elon	(A)	1844	1299-1449	1449-1840	391	(+15)
49	Elliott, E. B.	(B)	1844	612-762	1057-1453	396	(+130)
50	Claussen, Louis	(F)	1844		1453-1844	391	
51	Guinness, H. G	(B)	1844	622-762	1300-1699	396	
52	Junkin, George	(A)	1844	612-762	1281-1672	391	(+15)
53	Scott, James	(S)	1844		1453-1844	391	
54	Fysh, Frederick	(A)	1845	612-762 (607-757)	1301-1697 (1453-1849)	396	(+3 mos.)
55	Scott, Samuel	(A)	1848	622-822 (?)	1059-1453	398	
56	Thom, Adam	(B)	1848	606-756	1062-1453	391	
57	Wickes, Thomas	(A)	1851	612-762	1281-1672	391	(+15)
58	Jenour, Alfred	(F)	1852	632-786	1062-1453	391	(+15)
59	Bliss, Sylvester	(A)	1853	622-762	1453-1844	391	(+15)
60	Jones, Joseph	(B)	1853	Saracens	Turkish Invasion	391	(+15)
61	Williams, Thomas	(B)	1853	612-762	1281-1672	391	(+15)
62	Hore, J. B	(A)	1854	622-772	1057-1453 (1302-1698?)	396	(+15)
63	Cumming, John	(A)	1855	612-762	1057-1453	396	
64	Slight, Benjamin	(Can.)	1855	629-779	1057-1453	396	
65	Lyon, J. C.	(A)	1859	612-762	1057-1453	395	(+1861)
66	Butler, J. G.	(B)	1860	841-904	1057-1453	396	
67	Thomas, John	(A)	1861	632-782	1062-1453	391	(+30)
68	Boyce, P. E.	(A)	1864		1250-1641	391	(+30)
69	Smith, Uriah	(A)	1865	1299-1449	1449-1840	391	(+15)
70	Gardner, J. P	(A)	1867	Saracens	Turkish Invasion	391	(+15)
71	Hunt, E. M.	(A)	1870	612-762	1057-1453	396	
72	Steele, David	(A)	1870	612-762	1281-1672	391	
73	Pond, Enoch	(A)	1871	629-729	1062-1453	391	
74	De Puy, James	(A)	1873	728/30-879	1291-1682	391	
75	Simons, E. D	(A)	1875	612-762	1057-1453 (1062-1453)	391	(+15)
76	Orr, John	(A)	1876	606	Mohammedanism	396	
77	Johnson, B. W	(A)	1881	632-782	1057-1453	396	(+3 mos.)
78	Kimball, I. F.	(A)	1897		1449-1840	391	(+15)
79	Moore, T. W.	(A)	1897	Mohammedanism	1070/71-1453 (1085-1478/79)	391	
80	Tanner, Joseph	(B)	1898	612-762	1062-1453	396	(15 or 30)

VI. Twentieth Century

1	Hood, J. W.	(A)	1900	612-762	1281-1672	391	(+15)
2	Smith, U. G.	(A)	1908	Saracens	1281-1672	391	(+15)
3	Williams, H. C.	(A)	1917	612-672 (632-782)	1057-1453	396	
4	Briggs, H. C.	(A)	1923	612-762	1057-1453	391	
5	Rand, H. B.	(A)	1932		1453-1844	391	(+15)
6	Stewart, Basil	(B)	1934	612-762	1281-1672	391	

Total number of expositors, 124

Appendix E

WAS MUHAMMAD THE "PARACLETOS" OF JOHN 14?

Muslims insist that the Quranic verse found in 61:6 proves that Jesus predicted that Muhammad would come as a prophet after Him.

> And remember, Jesus, the son of Mary, said: 'O Children of Israel! I am the apostle of God (sent) to you, confirming the Law (which came) before me, and giving glad tidings of an apostle to come after me, whose name shall be Ahmad.

Muslim commentators claim that Ahmad is a variant for the name Muhammad. Therefore, they assert that the Quran states that the Bible records a saying of Jesus that foretells the appearance of the prophet Muhammad.

They allege that this is a reference to John 14:16, 26 where Jesus states that a "comforter" (Greek—*paracletos*) would come after Him. In Syriac *paracletos* can be translated as *munahhemana*. Such early Muslims as Ibn Ishaq believed that this was the equivalent to "Muhammad," therefore, establishing that the Bible and Quran agreed that John 14 was referring to the coming of Muhammad. This, obviously, contradicts the belief that most Christians hold (including Adventists) that the *paracletos* was referring to the Holy Spirit and its outpouring at Pentecost and to the end of the world. So was Muhammad the *paracletos* of John 14?

First, there is no conclusive evidence that "Muhammad" and "Ahmad" are the same names. Even Islamic scholars acknowledge that this is not a sure correlation. Up until the time of Muhammad, many boys were named Muhammad, but very few were named Ahmad. This trend continued for over a century after Muhammad.[226]

It is also not a sure correlation to say that the Syriac term *munahhemana* and "Muhammad" are equivalents. *Munahhemana* actually means "life-giver" but the

Was Muhammad the "Paracletos" of John 14? 313

Palestinian lectionary renders this term "comforter" when commenting on John 14—and this is the source that the early Muslim commentators used. However, the Syriac Bible actually follows the Greek *paracletos* (Syriac—*paraqleto'*).

Muslims have often asserted that Christian translators confused *paracletos* with *periklutos*, which means "celebrated," thus being an equivalent to *ahmad*, which means "praised."[227] It is a very big assumption to think that the *munahhemana* that the Syriac lectionary translates as "comforter" is a correct translation of *paracletos* and that Christian translators were confused between *periklutos* and *paracletos*.

Some Christians have assumed that Muslims inserted this passage into the Quran at a later date to back their claims for Muhammad when they discuss this with Christians. However, there is no evidence for these claims.

Probably the best explanation that explains both the Bible and the Quran is that the word *ahmad* was not used in Sura 61 as a proper name, but as an adjective. This was the belief that most Muslims held in the first century after Muhammad.[228] According to this explanation, the Quran would be stating that Jesus proclaimed that one would come after Him who was "praised" (*ahmad*). This would have been fulfilled by the Holy Spirit who was coming to glorify Jesus (John 16:24) and not Muhammad. This is the only translation that can be consistent with both the Quran and the Bible.

Endnotes

Foreword
1. Parrinder, *Jesus in the Qur'an*, p. 14.

Chapter 1
2. White, *Ellen G. White: The Early Years*, p. 77.
3. Goldstein, *Graffiti in the Holy of Holies*, pp. 172, 173.
4. White, "Greatness in Humility," *The Signs of the Times*.
5. Gilchrist, *Muhammad: the Prophet of Islam,* http://1ref.us/87. (As quoted in General Conference Adventist Muslim Relations Seminar Syllabus.)
6. White, *Gospel Workers*, p. 298.

Chapter 2
7. Nichol, ed., *Seventh-day Adventist Bible Commentary,* vol. 1, p. 317.
8. Ibid., p. 320.
9. Ibid., p. 317.
10. Neufeld, ed., *Seventh-day Adventist Bible Dictionary*, p. 513.
11. White, *Patriarchs and Prophets*, p. 174.
12. Nichol, ed., *Seventh-day Adventist Bible Commentary,* vol. 1, p. 514.
13. Bolotnikov, *Так Написано: Библейский Семинар о Торе (It is Written: A Bible Seminar on the Torah)*, DVD video presentation.
14. White, *The Desire of Ages,* p. 60.

Chapter 3

15. Nichol, ed., *Seventh-day Adventist Bible Commentary,* vol. 7, p. 777.

16. Esposito, ed., *The Oxford History of Islam*, p. 305.

Chapter 4

17. Fredericksen, "Christianity," Encyclopaedia Britannica, http://1ref.us/88.

18. Ibid.

19. "Monarchianism," Encyclopaedia Britannica, http://1ref.us/89.

20. Parrinder, *Jesus in the Qur'an*, p. 134; see also Gwatkin, *Selections from Early Christian Writers*, p. 129.

21. Fredericksen, "Christianity," Encyclopaedia Britannica, http://1ref.us/88.

22. Kelly, "Nestorius," Encyclopaedia Britannica, http://1ref.us/8b.

23. Ibid.

24. Aasi, *Muslim Understanding of Other Religions,* p. 121.

25. "Monophysite," Encyclopaedia Britannica, http://1ref.us/8c.

26. Fredericksen, "Christianity," Encyclopaedia Britannica, http://1ref.us/88.

27. Aasi, *Muslim Understanding of Other Religions*, p. 121.

28. Parrinder, *Jesus in the Qur'an*, p. 135.

29. Oster, *Islam Reconsidered*, p. 23. (Reference from William James Durant, *The Age of Faith: A history of medieval civilization-Christian, Islamic, and Judaic-from Constantine to Dante, C.E. 325–1300* [New York: Simon Schuster, 1950])

30. Oster, *Islam Reconsidered*, p. 24

31. Hyde, *Paganism to Christianity in the Roman Empire,* p. 54; quoted in Oster, *Islam Reconsidered*, p. 24.

32. Oster, *Islam Reconsidered*, p. 24.

33. Ibid., p. 25; see original quote in Payne, *The Holy Sword*, p. 4.

34. Tonstad, "Defining Moments in Christian-Muslim History—A Summary," Adventist Muslim Relations.

35. Swartley, ed., *Encountering the World of Islam,* p. 10.

36. Ibid.

37. Ibid., p. 37.

38. Tonstad, "Defining Moments in Christian-Muslim History—A Summary," Adventist Muslim Relations.

39. Ibid., italics supplied; quoted in Propcopius, *The Secret History*, p. 106.

40. Esposito, ed., *The Oxford History of Islam*, p. 306.

41. Ibid.

42. Oster, *Islam Reconsidered*, p. 26; quoted in Augustine, *Reply to Faustus the Manichaean*, XX. 4, trans. BPBF, 1st series.

Chapter 5

43. Ayoub, *Islam: Faith and History*, p. 14.

44. Nasr, "Muhammad," Encyclopædia Britannica, http://1ref.us/8d.

45. Ibid.

46. Ibid.

47. Gilchrist, *Muhammad and the Religion of Islam*, p. 93.

48. Margoliouth, *Mohammed and the Rise of Islam*, p. 143.

49. Spencer, *The Truth About Muhammad: Founder of the World's Most Intolerant Religion*, p. 79.

50. Ibid.; see Ishaq, *The Life of Muhammad*, pp. 165, 166.

51. Nasr, "Muhammad," Encyclopædia Britannica, http://1ref.us/8d.

52. Lings, *Muhammad: His Life Based on the Earliest Sources*, p. 139.

Chapter 6

53. Nasr, "Qur'an," Encyclopædia Britannica, http://1ref.us/b0.

54. Ibid.

Chapter 7

55. Akhmedov, *Иисус в Коране: Хронологический Обзор и Анализ* (Jesus in the Quran: a Chronological Review and Analysis). 's

56. Ali, *The Holy Qur'an: Text, Translation and Commentary*, p. 'an'an1714.

57. Akhmedov, *Иисус в Коране: Хронологический Обзор и Анализ*, p. 28.

58. Ibid., p. 29.

59. Ibid.

60. Ibid., p. 30.

61. Ibid., p. 31 (see Incilde ve Quranda Mesih. Baki: Yeni heyat, p. 8).

62. Ibid.

63. Ali, *The Holy Qur'an: Text, Translation and Commentary*, p. 772.

64. Akhmedov, *Иисус в Коране: Хронологический Обзор и Анализ*, p. 32.

65. Parrinder, *Jesus in the Qur'an*, p. 23.

66. Ali, *The Holy Qur'an: Text, Translation and Commentary,* p. 1337.

67. Akhmedov, *Иисус в Коране: Хронологический Обзор и Анализ,* p. 37.

68. Ibid., p. 40.

69. Ibid., p. 42 (as quoted in "Quran—Selim").

70. Ibid., p. 43

71. Ibid., p. 44.

72. Ibid.

73. Parrinder, *Jesus in the Qur'an,* p. 134 (quote from Ishaq, *The Life of Muhammad,* p. 271f)

74. Ibid., p. 133.

75. Akhmedov, *Иисус в Коране: Хронологический Обзор и Анализ,* p. 54.

76. Ayoub, *A Muslim View of Christianity,* p. 118.

77. Dysinger, "Son of God: a Word Study in Both the Quran and the New Testament," Adventist Muslim Relations Center.

78. Parrinder, *Jesus in the Qur'an,* p. 128.

79. Dysinger, "Son of God: a Word Study in Both the Quran and the New Testament."

80. Parrinder, *Jesus in the Qur'an,* p. 128.

81. Ibid., p. 66 (see Encyclopedia of Islam, "Art. Ka'ba"; K.A.C. Creswell, *A Short Account of Early Muslim Architecture,* 1958, 2)

82. Parrinder, *Jesus in the Qur'an,* p. 16.

Chapter 8

83. Ayoub, *Islam: Faith and History,* p. 74.

84. Ibid., p. 76.

85. Ibid., p. 77.

86. Ibid., p. 79.

87. Ibid., p. 81.

88. Ibid., p. 82.

89. Ibid., p. 83.

90. Ibid., p. 85.

91. "Umayyad Dynasty," Encyclopædia Britannica, http://1ref.us/b1.

92. Oster, *Islam Reconsidered,* p. 38.

93. Ibid.

94. Ibid.
95. Elide, ed., *Encyclopedia of Religion*, vol. 7, p. 305.
96. Aasi, *Muslim Understanding of Other Religions*, p. 26.
97. Swartley, ed., *Encountering the World of Islam*, p. 30; as quoted in Scher, ed., *Histoire Nestorienne (Chronicle of Seert)*, in PO t. 13, fasc. 4, no. 65, p. 581f.
98. Aasi, *Muslim Understanding of Other Religions*, p. 26; as quoted in Watt, *Islamic Political Thought*, p. 51.
99. Brown, *The World in Late Antiquity, AD 150–750*, p. 193.
100. Tonstad, "Defining Moments in Christian-Muslim History—A Summary," Adventist Muslim Relations.
101. Gilbert, ed., *The Illustrated Atlas of Jewish Civilization: 4,000 Years of Jewish History*, p. 66, 127.
102. Swartley, ed., *Encountering the World of Islam*, p. 45; as quoted in Briffault, *Rational Evolution: The Making of Humanity*, p. 138
103. Swartley, ed., *Encountering the World of Islam*, p. 63.
104. Ibid., p. 64.
105. Ibid., p. 65.
106. Ibid., p. 74.
107. Oster, *Islam Reconsidered*, p. 66.
108. Oster, *Islam Reconsidered*, p. 64; as quoted in Guillaume and Arnold, eds., *The Legacy of Islam*, p. ix.
109. Aasi, *Muslim Understanding of Other Religions*, p. xii.
110. Pulcini, *Exegesis as Polemical Discourse: Ibn Hazm on Jewish and Christian Scriptures*, p. 14.
111. Ibid., p. 29.
112. Ibid., p. 2.
113. Ibid., p. 8.
114. Aasi, Muslim Understanding of Other Religions, p. 202.
115. Pulcini, *Exegesis as Polemical Discourse: Ibn Hazm on Jewish and Christian Scriptures*, p. 195.
116. Ibid., pp. 190, 191.
117. Fiegenbaum, "Ibn Hazm," Encyclopaedia Britannica, http://1ref.us/b2.
118. Parrinder, *Jesus in the Qur'an*, p. 70.

Chapter 9

119. Finkel, *Osman's Dream: The History of the Ottoman Empire's*, p. 2.
120. Nichol, ed., *Seventh-day Adventist Bible Commentary*, vol. 7, pp. 795, 796.
121. Finkel, *Osman's Dream: The History of the Ottoman Empire*, p. 2.
122. Maxwell, *God Cares: The Message of Revelation for You and Your Family*, vol. 2, p. 255.
123. Esposito, ed., *The Oxford History of Islam*, p. 323.
124. Yapp, "Ottoman Empire," Encyclopaedia Britannica, http://1ref.us/b3.
125. Nelson, *Understanding the Mysteries of Daniel and Revelation*, p. 240.
126. Brown, *A New Introduction to Islam*, p. 240.
127. Finkel, *Osman's Dream: the History of the Ottoman Empire*, p. 142.
128. Ibid., p. 67.
129. Ibid., p. 19.

Chapter 10

130. Spencer, *The Truth About Muhammad: Founder of the World's Most Intolerant Religion*, p. 25.
131. Swartley, ed., *Encountering the World of Islam*, p. 39; see original quote in Goldhizer, *Mohammedanishe Suidien*, vol. 2, p. 19.
132. Gilchrist, *Muhammad and the Religion of Islam*, p. 239.
133. Johnson, *A History of the American People*, p. 342.
134. Parrinder, *Jesus in the Qur'an*, p. 39.
135. Ali, *The Holy Qur'an: Text, Translation and Commentary*, p.'an 1048.
136. Dimashqi, *Book of the End: Great Trials and Tribulations*, p. 67.
137. Ibid., p. 71.
138. Ibid.
139. Gilchrist, *Muhammad and the Religion of Islam* p. 28.
140. Ali, *The Holy Qur'an: Text, Translation and Commentary*, p. 75.
141. Spencer, *The Truth About Muhammad: Founder of the World's Most Intolerant Religion*, p. 115.
142. Ibid., p. 121.
143. Ibid., p. 129.
144. Ibid., p. 135.
145. Ishaq, *The Life of Muhammad*, p. 437.
146. Gilchrist, *Muhammad and the Religion of Islam* p. 43.

147. Spencer, *The Truth About Muhammad: Founder of the World's Most Intolerant Religion*, p. 175.
148. Nichol, ed., *Seventh-day Adventist Bible Commentary*, vol. 1, p. 1037.
149. Ali, *The Holy Qur'an: Text, Translation and Commentary*, p. 670.
150. Ibid, p. 179.
151. Ibid.
152. Ibid, p. 184.
153. Ibid, p. 1,510.
154. Ibid., p. 88.
155. Spencer, p. 170 (see "Vines calls founder of Islam a 'demon-possessed pedophile," *Biblical Recorder*, June 14, 2002).
156. Ibid., p. 171.
157. Ibid., p. 175 (see al-Tabari, *The History of al-Tabari, Volume VIII, The Victory of Islam*, p. 2).
158. Ibid. (see Sahih Bukhari, vol.1, book 6, no. 304).
159. Nichol, ed., *Seventh-day Adventist Bible Commentary*. vol. 1, p. 1037.
160. Ibid.
161. Neufeld, ed. *Seventh-day Adventist Bible Dictionary*, p. 1031.
162. Nichol, ed., *Seventh-day Adventist Bible Commentary*, vol. 5, p. 830.
163. Ibid., p. 831.
164. Tisdall, *The Original Sources of the Quran*, p. 148.
165. Ali, *The Holy Qur'an: Text, Translation and Commentary*, p. 727.
166. Parrinder, *Jesus in the Qur'an*, p. 78 (see Evangelis apocryphes, ii, p. I)
167. Chandler, *Pilgrims of Christ on the Muslim Road*, p. 16.
168. Parrinder, *Jesus in the Qur'an*, p. 161.
169. Ali, *The Holy Qur'an: Text, Translation and Commentary*, p. 'an'an1073.
170. Ibid., p. 1345.
171. Dimashqi, *Book of the End: Great Trials and Tribulations*, p. 55.
172. Ibid.
173. Ibid., p. 148.
174. Spencer, *The Truth About Muhammad: Founder of the World's Most Intolerant Religion*, p. 183's.
175. Ibid.

176. Ibid.

177. Ibid. (see Sa'd, *Kitab at-Tabaqat al-Kabir*, vol. 1, p.,422).

178. Ibid., (see Sa'd, *Kitab at-Tabaqat al-Kabir*, vol. 1, p.,432).

179. Ibid., (see Sa'd, *Kitab at-Tabaqat al-Kabir*, vol. 1, p.,433).

180. Ibid., (see al-Bukhari, *Sahih al-Bukhari: The Translation of the Meanings*, vol. 9, book 87, no. 6911).

181. Ibid.

182. Gilchrist, *Muhammad and the Religion of Islam*, p. 54 (see original quote in Smith, *Mohammed and Mohammedanism*, p. 148).

183. Ibid., p. 55.

184. Ibid. (see Muir, *The Life of Mahomet*, p. 54).

185. Ibid.

186. Ibid., p. 56.

187. Ibid., p. 54.

Chapter 11

188. Cragg, *The Call of the Minaret*, p. 113.

189. Nichol, ed., *Seventh-day Adventist Bible Commentary*, vol. 7, p. 38.

190. Ibid., p. 25.

191. Ibid., p. 28.

192. Chandler, *Pilgrims of Christ on the Muslim Road*, p. 9.

193. Wagner, *Opening the Qur'an: introducing Islam's Holy Book*, p. 112 (see Ishaq, *The Life of Muhammad*, p. 97 for original quote).

194. White, "Ye Are My Witnesses," *The Home Missionary*.

195. White, *The Desire of Ages*, p. 33.

196. Wehr, *A Dictionary of Modern Written Arabic: Arabic-English*, p. 227

197. *Webster's Seventh New Collegiate Dictionary*, p. 777.

198. White, *Testimonies for the Church*, vol. 5, p. 700.

199. White, *Conflict and Courage*, p. 7.

200. White, *Patriarchs and Prophets*, pp. 627, 628.

201. Ibid., p. 632.

202. Ibid., p. 623.

203. White, *Christ's Object Lessons*, p. 290.

204. Swartley, ed., *Encountering the World of Islam*, p. 8.
205. Ellen White, "Words to Ministers," *Review and Herald*.
206. Gilchrist, *Muhammad and the Religion of Islam*, p. 76.
207. White, "Rejoice in the Lord Alway," *Youth's Instructor*.
208. White, *The Desire of Ages*, p. 493.
209. Oster, *Cosmic Perspective of God and Man*, p. 13.
210. White, *Education*, p. 173.
211. Wood, "God Has Provided a Historic Opportunity: Let's Join Him in What He is Doing," *Mission Frontiers*, p. 4.
212. Naja, "Welcoming Muslim Neighbors into the Kingdom of God in East Africa," *Mission Frontiers*, p. 10.
213. Ayoub, *The Quran and Its Interpreters*, p. 3.
214. Oster, *Islam Reconsidered*, p. 26 (see Toynsbee, *Civilization on Trial*, p. 76).
215. Ibid., p. 29.
216. Gilchrist, *Muhammad and the Religion of Islam*, p. 20.
217. Ibid. (see original quote in Muir, *Mahomet and Islam*, p. 109).
218. Tisdall, *The Original Sources of the Qur'an*, p. 272.
219. Ibid., p. 267.
220. Ibid., p. 271.
221. White, "The Great Rebellion; or, the Conflict Ended," *The Signs of the Times*.
222. Parrinder. *Jesus in the Qur'an*, p. 163 (as quoted in Ishaq, *The Life of Muhammad*, pp. 14ff, 179).
223. Ibid. (see Ishaq, *The Life of Muhammad*, p. 270).
224. Ibid., p. 165.
225. Ibid., p. 172.
226. Ibid., p. 99.
227. Ibid.
228. Ibid.

Bibliography

Aasi, Ghulam Haider. *Muslim Understanding of Other Religions*. New Delhi: Adam Publishers, 2007.

Akhmedov, Rustam. *Иисус в Коране: Хронологический Обзор и Анализ* (Jesus in the Quran: a Chronological Review and Analysis). Bachelor's dissertation. Zaokski Seventh-day Adventist Seminary, Zaokski, Russia, 2003.

al-Bukhari, Muhammad Ibn Ismaiel. *Sahih al-Bukhari: The Translation of the Meanings*. Vol. 9, book 87. Translated by Muhammad M. Khan. Houston: Darussalam, 1997.

al-Tabari, Abu Ja'far Muhammad bin Jarir. *The History of al-Tabari, Volume VIII, The Victory of Islam*. Translated by Michael Fishbein. New York: State University of New York Press, 1997.

Ali, Abdullah Yusuf, trans. *The Holy Qur'an: Text, Translation and Commentary*. Elmhurst, NY: Tahrike Tarsile Qur'an, Inc, 2001.

Ayoub, Mahmoud M. *A Muslim View of Christianity*. Maryknoll, NY: Orbis Books, 2007.

———. *Islam: Faith and History*. Oxford: Oneworld Publications, 2004.

———. *The Quran and Its Interpreters*. Albany, NY: State University of New York Press, 1984.

Bolotnikov, Alexander. *Так Написано: Библейский Семинар о Торе (It is Written: A Bible Seminar on the Torah)*. DVD video presentation. Tula, Russia: Voice of Hope, 2006.

Briffault, Robert. *Rational Evolution: The Making of Humanity*. New York: MacMillan, 1930.

Brown, Daniel. *A New Introduction to Islam*. Malden, MA: Wiley Blackwell Publishers, 2009.

Brown, Peter. *The World in Late Antiquity, AD 150–750.* London: Thames and Hudson, 1971.

Chandler, Paul-Gordon. *Pilgrims of Christ on the Muslim Road.* Lanham, MD: Rowman & Littlefield Publishers Inc., 2007.

Cragg, Kenneth. *The Call of the Minaret.* New York: Oxford University Press, 1956.

Dimashqi, Al-Hafiz Ibn Katheer. *Book of the End: Great Trials and Tribulations.* Riyadh, Saudi Arabia: Darussalam Publishers, 2006.

Dysinger, Edwin. "Son of God: a Word Study in Both the Quran and the New Testament." Loma Linda, CA: Adventist Muslim Relations Center, 2000.

Elide, Mircea, ed. *Encyclopedia of Religion.* Vol. 7. New York: MacMillan Publishing Company, 1987.

Esposito, John, ed. *The Oxford History of Islam.* Oxford, UK: Oxford University Printing Press, 1999.

Fiegenbaum, J. W. "Ibn Hazm." Encyclopaedia Britannica. http://1ref.us/b2 (accessed June 10, 2015).

Finkel, Caroline. *Osman's Dream: The History of the Ottoman Empire.* New York: Basic Books, 2005.

Fredericksen, Linwood. "Christianity." Encyclopaedia Britannica. http://1ref.us/88 (accessed April 27, 2015).

Gilbert, Martin, ed. *The Illustrated Atlas of Jewish Civilization: 4,000 Years of Jewish History.* New York: MacMillan, 1990.

Gilchrist, John. *Muhammad: the Prophet of Islam.* Answering Islam. http://1ref.us/87 (accessed April 27, 2015).

———. *Muhammad and the Religion of Islam.* Roodeport, South Africa: Roodeport Mission Press, 1986.

Goldhizer, I. *Mohammedanishe Suidien.* Vol. 2. Halle: Niemeyer, 1889.

Goldstein, Clifford. *Graffiti in the Holy of Holies.* Nampa, ID: Pacific Press Publishing Association, 2003.

Guillaume, Alfred and Sir Thomas Arnold, eds. *The Legacy of Islam.* Oxford: Clarendon Press, 1931.

Gwatkin, Henry Melvill. *Selections From Early Christian Writers: Illustrative of Church History to the Time of Constantine.* Macmillan & Co., Ltd., 1893.

Hyde, Walter Woodburn. *Paganism to Christianity in the Roman Empire.* Philadelphia, PA: University of Pennsylvania Press, 1946.

Ishaq, Ibn. *The Life of Muhammad: A Translation of Ishaq's Sirat Rasul Allah.* Translated by A. Guiallame. Karachi, Pakistan: Oxford University Press, 1982.

Johnson, Paul. *A History of the American People*. New York: Harper Collins, 1997.

Kelly, John N.D., Rev. "Nestorius." Encyclopaedia Britannica. http://1ref.us/8b (accessed May 18, 2015).

Lings, Martin. *Muhammad: His Life Based on the Earliest Sources*. Rochester, VT: Inner Traditions, 2006.

Margoliouth, David S. *Mohammed and the Rise of Islam*. London: Blackie and Son Limited, 1939.

Maxwell, Mervyn. *God Cares: The Message of Revelation for You and Your Family*. Vol. 2. Nampa, ID: Pacific Press Publishing Association, 1985.

"Monarchianism." Encyclopaedia Britannica. http://1ref.us/89 (accessed April 27, 2015).

"Monophysite." Encyclopaedia Britannica. http://1ref.us/8c (accessed May 18, 2015).

Muir, Sir William. *The Life of Mahomet*. London: The Religious Tract Society, 1895.

———.*Mahomet and Islam*. London: The Religious Tract Society, 1895.

Naja, Ben. "Welcoming Muslim Neighbors into the Kingdom of God in East Africa." *Mission Frontiers*, July/August 2013. US Center for World Mission.

Nasr, Seyyed Hossein. "Muhammad." Encyclopaedia Britannica. http://1ref.us/8d (accessed May 18, 2015).

———. "Qur'an." Encyclopaedia Britannica. http://1ref.us/b0 (accessed June 9, 2015).

Nelson, Loren M.K. *Understanding the Mysteries of Daniel and Revelation*. Lansing, MI: Self published, 2010.

Neufeld, Don F., ed. *Seventh-day Adventist Bible Dictionary*. Washington, DC: Review and Herald Publishing Association, 1960.

Nichol, Francis D., ed. *Seventh-day Adventist Bible Commentary*. Vol. 1. Washington, DC: Review and Herald Publishing Association, 1953.

———. *Seventh-day Adventist Bible Commentary*. Vol. 5. Washington, DC: Review and Herald Publishing Association, 1956.

———. *Seventh-day Adventist Bible Commentary*. Vol. 7. Washington, DC: Review and Herald Publishing Association, 1957.

Oster, Kenneth. *Cosmic Perspective of God and Man*. Colfax, CA: self-published, 1992.

———. *Islam Reconsidered*. Smithtown, NY: Exposition Press, Inc., 1979.

Parrinder, Geoffrey. *Jesus in the Qur'an*. Oxford, UK: Oneworld Publications, 1965.

Payne, Robert. *The Holy Sword*. New York, NY: Harper and Row, 1959.

Propcopius. *The Secret History*. Translation G. A. Williamson. London: Penguin Books, 1966.

Pulcini, Theodore. *Exegesis as Polemical Discourse: Ibn Hazm on Jewish and Christian Scriptures*. Atlanta: Scholars Press, 1998.

Sa'd, Ibn. *Kitab at-Tabaqat al-Kabir*. Vol. 1. Translated by S. Moinul Haq and H K. Ghazanfar. New Delhi: Kitab Bhavan, n.d.

Scher, Addai, ed. *Histoire Nestorienne (Chronicle of Seert)*. Vol. 1. Piscataway, NJ: Gorgias Press, 1918.

Smith, R. Bosworth. *Mohammed and Mohammedanism*. London: Smith, Elder and Co., 1876.

Spencer, Robert. *The Truth About Muhammad: Founder of the World's Most Intolerant Religion*. Washington, DC: Regnery Publishing, 2006.

Swartley, Keith, ed. *Encountering the World of Islam*. Waynesboro, GA: Authentic Media, 2005.

Tisdall, W. St. Clair. *The Original Sources of the Quran*. London: Society for Promoting Christian Knowledge, 1905.

Tonstad, Sigve. "Defining Moments in Christian-Muslim History—A Summary." Adventist Muslim Relations Director. Seminar: Oslo, Norway, 2000.

Toynsbee, Arnold. *Civilization on Trial*. New York: Oxford University Press, 1948.

"Umayyad Dynasty." Encyclopædia Britannica. http://1ref.us/b1 (accessed June 10, 2015).

Wagner, Walter. *Opening the Qur'an: introducing Islam's Holy Book*. Notre Dame, IN: University of Notre Dame Press, 2008.

Watt, William Montgomery. *Islamic Political Thought*. London: Cambridge University Press, 1968.

Webster's Seventh New Collegiate Dictionary. Springfield, MA: G & C. Merriam Company, 1967.

Wehr, Hans. *A Dictionary of Modern Written Arabic: Arabic-English*. J. Milton Cowan, ed. Beirut: Librarie Du Liban, 1980.

White, Arthur. *Ellen G. White: The Early Years*. Washington, DC: Review and Herald Publishing Association, 1985.

White, Ellen G. *Christ's Object Lessons*. Review and Herald Publishing Association, 1900.

———. *Conflict and Courage*. Washington, DC: Review and Herald Publishing Association, 1970.

———. *The Desire of Ages*. Mountain View, CA: Pacific Press Publishing Association, 1898.

———. *Education*. Mountain View, CA: Pacific Press Publishing Association, 1903.

———. *Gospel Workers*. Washington, DC: Review and Herald Publishing Association, 1915.

———. "The Great Rebellion; or, the Conflict Ended." *The Signs of the Times*, September 16, 1880.

———. "Greatness in Humility." *The Signs of the Times*, July 9, 1896.

———. *Patriarchs and Prophets*. Washington, DC: Review and Herald Publishing Association, 1890.

———. "Rejoice in the Lord Alway." *The Youth's Instructor*, January 10, 1901.

———. *Testimonies for the Church*. Vol. 5. Mountain View, CA: Pacific Press Publishing Association, 1889.

———. *Testimonies for the Church*. Vol. 9. Mountain View, CA: Pacific Press Publishing Association, 1909

———. "Words to Ministers." *Review and Herald,* April 20, 1897.

———. "Ye Are My Witnesses." *The Home Missionary,* September 1, 1892.

Wood, Rick. "God Has Provided a Historic Opportunity: Let's Join Him in What He is Doing." *Mission Frontiers,* July/August 2013. US Center for World Mission.

Yapp, Malcolm Edward. "Ottoman Empire." Encyclopaedia Brittannica. http://1ref.us/b3 (accessed March 10, 2015).

We invite you to view the complete
selection of titles we publish at:

www.TEACHServices.com

*Scan with your mobile
device to go directly
to our website.*

Please write or email us your praises, reactions, or
thoughts about this or any other book we publish at:

P.O. Box 954
Ringgold, GA 30736

info@TEACHServices.com

TEACH Services, Inc., titles may be purchased
in bulk for educational, business, fund-raising,
or sales promotional use.
For information, please e-mail:

BulkSales@TEACHServices.com

Finally, if you are interested in seeing
your own book in print, please contact us at

publishing@TEACHServices.com

We would be happy to review your manuscript for free.

www.ingramcontent.com/pod-product-compliance
Lightning Source LLC
Chambersburg PA
CBHW071619170426
43195CB00038B/1450